Seventh Edition

Keys to Community College Success

Carol Carter

Sarah Lyman Kravits

PEARSON

Boston   Columbus   Indianapolis   New York   San Francisco   Upper Saddle River
Amsterdam   Cape Town   Dubai   London   Madrid   Milan   Munich   Paris   Montréal   Toronto
Delhi   Mexico City   São Paulo   Sydney   Hong Kong   Seoul   Singapore   Taipei   Tokyo

Editor-in-Chief: Jodi McPherson
Acquisitions Editor: Katie Mahan
Editorial Assistant: Erin Carreiro
Senior Development Editor: Shannon Steed
Senior Managing Editor: Karen Wernholm
Senior Author Support/Technology Specialist: Joe Vetere
Executive Marketing Manager: Amy Judd
Senior Procurement Specialist: Roy Pickering
Image Manager: Rachel Youdelman
Text Design: John Wincek
Production Coordination and Illustration: Electronic Publishing Services Inc.
Composition and Illustration: Aptara, Inc.
Associate Director of Design, USHE EMSS/HSS/EDU: Andrea Nix
EMSS Program Design Lead: Heather Scott
Cover Design: Tamara Newman
Cover Image: Pearson Education, Inc.

Photo Credits: p. iii (bottom): Sarah Lyman Kravits; p. iii (top): Carol Carter; p. xix: Alex Slobodkin/E+/Getty Images; p. xx (left): Pearson Education, Inc.; p. xx (right): Pearson Education, Inc.; p. xxx: Honzakrej/Fotolia; p. xxxiv: Risdon Photography; p. 2: Reprinted with permission from the California Wellness Foundation; p. 3: Zack Moore; p. 4: Sarah Lyman Kravits; p. 4: Sarah Lyman Kravits; p. 10: Orange Line Media/Shutterstock; p. 11: Kelpfish/Fotolia; p. 16: LifeBound, LLC; p. 20: Risdon Photography; p. 26: Lifebound, LLC; p. 27: Lifebound, LLC; p. 32: LifeBound, LLC; p. 34: Ming-Lun Wu; p. 35: Sarah Lyman Kravits; p. 37: LifeBound, LLC; p. 43: Kevin Eaves/Fotolia; p. 46: Lifebound, LLC; p. 55: Sarah Lyman Kravits; p. 56: Joyce Bishop; p. 56: Reflektastudios/Fotolia; p. 57: Joyce Bishop; p. 63: Pixland/Thinkstock; p. 73: Sade Gantt; p. 78: Joyce Bishop; p. 81: Rusya M./Fotolia; p. 83: Juniart/Fotolia; p. 88: Apops/Fotolia; p. 88: Fotofermer/Fotolia; p. 88: Gertrudda/Fotolia; p. 88: Helder Almeida/Fotolia; p. 88: Ivan Floriani/Fotolia; p. 88: Jacek Chabraszewski/Fotolia; p. 88: Michael Shake/Fotolia; p. 88: RusGri/Fotolia; p. 88: Swapan/Fotolia; p. 90: LifeBound, LLC. Photo credits continue on p. 346.

Credits and acknowledgments for material borrowed from other sources and reproduced, with permission, in this textbook appear on the appropriate page within text or on p. 346, which constitutes an extension of the copyright page.

Many of the designations by manufacturers and sellers to distinguish their products are claimed as trademarks. Where those designations appear in this book, and the publisher was aware of a trademark claim, the designations have been printed in initial caps or all caps.

Library of Congress Cataloging-in-Publication Data

Carter, Carol.
   Keys to community college success / Carol J. Carter, Sarah Lyman Kravits.—7th edition
      pages cm.
   ISBN 978-0-321-91853-6
   1. Community college students—United States—Handbooks, manuals, etc.   2. College student orientation—United States—Handbooks, manuals, etc.   3. Community college students—United States—Life skills guides.   I. Kravits, Sarah Lyman.   II. Title.
   LB2343.32.C3684 2014
   378.1'543—dc23   2013030233

1 2 3 4 5 6 7 8 9 10—RRD-ROA—17 16 15 14 13

ISBN 10: 0-321-91853-3
ISBN 13: 978-0-321-91853-6

Carol Carter has spent her entire career in the business world, where she has a track record of success in corporate America, entrepreneurship, and non-profit. Her student success work is driven by firsthand knowledge of what employers expect and demand from today's graduates. As President of LifeBound, an academic and career coaching company, she drives the company's goal to help middle school and high school students become competitive in today's world, and she teaches study, interpersonal, and career skills to students as well as training and certifying adults in academic coaching skills. Carol speaks on educational topics nationally and internationally and is an expert blogger for the Huffington Post under "Impact," "College," and "Business." Carol is a co-author on many books for Pearson including the *Keys to Success* series as well as *Keys to Business Communication* and the *Career Tool Kit*. She has also published a series of books for K-12 students through LifeBound, including *Dollars and Sense: How To Be Smart About Money* and *Majoring In the Rest of Your Life: Career Secrets for College Students*.

Sarah Kravits teaches student success at Montclair State University and has been researching and writing about student success for over 15 years. As a parent of three children (ages 14, 12, and 8), a collaborator, a co-author, and an instructor, she lives the strategies for success she writes about, striving daily for goal achievement, productive teamwork, and integrity. Sarah is a co-author on the *Keys to Success* series, including *Keys to College Success, Keys to Community College Success, Keys to College Success Compact, Keys to Effective Learning, Keys to Online Learning*, and *Keys to Success Quick*. Sarah presents workshops and trainings on student success topics such as critical thinking, risk and reward, and time management at schools all over the country. Having attended the University of Virginia as a Jefferson Scholar, she continues to manifest the Jefferson Scholars Program goals of leadership, scholarship, and citizenship with her efforts to empower college students to succeed in school and in all aspects of their lives.

BRIEF CONTENTS

CONTENTS

CHAPTER 4   Critical, Creative, and Practical Thinking   **78**

Solving Problems and Making Decisions

CHAPTER 8 **Test Taking   190**

Showing What You Know

CHAPTER 9   **Diversity and Communication**   **220**
Making Relationships Work

CHAPTER 10   Wellness and Stress Management   244
Staying Healthy in Mind and Body

CHAPTER 11   Managing Money   272
Living below Your Means

CHAPTER 12 Careers and More **298**
Building a Successful Future

YOU AND YOUR STUDENTS HAVE UNIQUE NEEDS
Keys books have changed to fulfill them

Keys recognizes how student and instructor needs have evolved, and have made the change from editions that catered to all institutions to specific programs (four year, two year, and one credit hour and/or those with blended and online students). In learning environments, it is important to get relevant information—at the time you need it. Now you can select course materials from *Keys* that reinforce your institution's culture (four year, two year, or one credit hour and/or blended and online) and speak directly to your specific needs.

CHOICE IS
yours

Keys to Success unlocks every student's potential to succeed in college, career, and life by challenging them to realize, "It's not just what you know . . . it's what you know **how** to do."

Keys sets the standard for connecting academic success to success beyond school, showing students how to apply strategies within college, career, and life. *Keys* retains its' tried-and-true emphasis on thinking skills and problem solving, re-imagined with two goals in mind: One, a **risk and reward** framework that reflects the demands today's students face, and two, a focus on student experience specific to **institution** with a more extensive research base. The material helps students take ownership, develop academic and transferable skills, and show the results of commitment and action so they are well equipped with the concentration, commitment, focus, and persistence necessary to succeed.

Choose the version of *Keys* that aligns best with your institution and student population, all while getting the hallmark features and content you've come to expect.

Four Year—*Keys to College Success 8e*. Written for students attending four year programs, it addresses today's university and college students.

Two Year—*Keys to Community College Success 7e*. Written for students attending two year programs, it addresses students in community, technical, and career colleges.

One credit or Blended and Online—*Keys to Success Compact 1e*. Written for one credit hour student success courses and/or those with blended and online students, it addresses the needs and challenges of students as digital learners. It aligns with learning outcomes from both the MyStudentSuccessLab (http://www.mystudentsuccesslab.com), and Student Success CourseConnect online course (http://www.pearsonlearningsolutions.com/courseconnect). Designed for use as a stand alone text or a print companion with one of these technologies for blended, online, or one credit hour student success courses.

NEW TO THIS
edition

Personalized Learning with MyStudentSuccessLab NEW! MyStudentSuccessLab (www.mystudentsuccesslab.com) is a Learning Outcomes based technology that promotes student engagement through:

- Full Course Pre- and Post-Diagnostic test based on Bloom's Taxonomy linked to key learning objectives in each topic.
- Each individual topic in the Learning Path offers a Pre- and Post-Test dedicated to that topic, an Overview of objectives to build vocabulary and repetition, access to Video interviews to learn about key issues 'by students, for students', Practice exercises to improve class prep and learning, and Graded Activities to build critical thinking skills and develop problem-solving abilities.

- Student Resources include Finish Strong 247 YouTube videos, Calculators, and Professionalism/Research & Writing/Student Success tools.
- Three Student Inventories are also available to increase self-awareness, and include *Golden Personality* (similar to Myers Briggs, gives insights on personal style), *ACES (Academic Competence Evaluation Scales)* (identifies at-risk), and *Thinking Styles* (shows how they make decisions).

College Connection to Career and Life Goals Infused with **risk and reward**.

- **NEW! Risk and Reward Theme.** To be rewarded with goal achievement in the fast-paced information age, students must take calculated, productive risks. The benefit of risks small (putting in the work your courses require) and large (aiming for a degree in a tough major, working toward a challenging career) is learning transferable skill building, persistence, and confidence. (Ex. — In every chapter.)
- **NEW! Inspiring, motivating case studies focused on risk and reward.** Students derive motivation from reading about how others have taken risks, gotten through struggles, overcome challenges, and earned rewards. Each chapter begins with a case study focusing on a personal challenge and details the risk taken to face and surmount it. The closing section at the end of each chapter finishes the story and shows the reward earned at that time and the rewards that the person has subsequently gained from continued risk and effort. This section also relates the story to the reader's life and challenges them to think expansively about how to make personal improvements related to the chapter. (Ex.—Beginning and end of each chapter, i.e., opening two-page chapter spread.)

Thinking Skills coverage

- **NEW! Brain-based learning and metacognition.** Cites research on building intelligence, the science of learning, the changes in the brain that happen when you remember, the cost of switch-tasking, brain development in adolescence and early adulthood, and more. This information builds student metacognition. (Ex.—Throughout the book as applicable, i.e., Chapter 1 (introduction), Chapter 4 (thinking), Chapter 7 (memory).)
- **REVISED! Successful Intelligence Framework.** Builds a comprehensive set of analytical, creative, practical thinking skills to empower students to strengthen their command of the problem solving process and take practical action. (Ex.—Introduced in Chapter 1; expounded upon in thinking chapter (Chapter 4); in-chapter exercises (**Get Analytical, Get Creative, Get Practical**).)
- **REVISED! In-chapter exercises focused on analytical, creative, and practical thinking, and financial literacy.** These exercises give readers a chance to apply a chapter idea or skill to their personal needs and situations in a particular type of thinking. (Ex.—In each chapter, i.e., Chapter 2.)
  - *Get Analytical* builds analytical thinking skill
  - *Get Creative* builds creative thinking skill
  - *Get Practical* builds practical thinking skill
  - The **NEW** exercise *Get $mart* builds financial literacy
- **REVISED! End-of-chapter exercises, each with a distinctive practical goal.** Re-titled and revised, targeted to develop a particular skill to have readers perform a chapter-related task that has specific personal value. (Ex.—End of chapter, i.e., Chapter 5.)
  - *Know It* builds critical thinking skill
  - *Write It* builds emotional intelligence and practical writing skill
  - *Work It* builds career readiness

Updated with a Focus on the Two Year Program experience

- **NEW! Tailored to the Two-year student.** Throughout the text, detail-level adjustments made in language, concepts, and topics to reflect the needs and concerns of the two-year college student.
- **REVISED! Case studies.** Each chapter opens with a real-life story of a college student and closes with a current update on that person. Case studies are relevant to two-year students and show how calculated risks lead to academic and career rewards. (Ex.—In each chapter, i.e., Chapter 11.)
- **REVISED! Student profiles.** Students share real-life application of chapter-related skills and how this leads to success in today's workplace. (Ex.—In each chapter, i.e., Chapter 5.)

- **REVISED! Expanded topics relevant to today's two-year student experience.** Topics new to this edition include learned optimism (Chapter 1), the distractions of technology (Chapter 2), multi-tasking vs. switch-tasking (Chapter 2), the brain science of thinking (Chapter 4), anxiety disorders (Chapter 9), staying safe on campus (Chapter 9), final exams (Chapter 8), and informational interviews (Chapter 12).

- **NEW! Citations of groundbreaking work on motivation as well as current research on a variety of topics.** Citations add to credibility of author voice as they support ideas with research, provide the "why" behind the "what to do", and make the book relevant to today's students. They also reflect the substance of these topics to readers who may enter the course thinking it is "lightweight". (Ex.—Throughout the book, i.e., Citations of work by Robert Sternberg, Carol Dweck, and Martin Seligman in Chapter 1.)

- **REVISED! "Status Check" self-assessment.** Readers gain more learning from a chapter if they start with an overview of the material; however, few students deliberately skim for that overview. This self-assessment provides a low-stakes way to grasp the scope of the chapter and think about where growth is needed. (Ex.—Beginning of each chapter, following the case study, i.e., Chapter 7.)

- **REVISED! Alignment of Learning Objectives.** Learning objectives, appearing at the beginning of each chapter, are restructured to align more closely to media and activities within MyStudentSuccessLab. (Ex.—Beginning of every chapter).

One last note: Many of our best suggestions come from you. Please contact your Pearson representative with questions or requests for resources or materials. Send suggestions for ways to improve *Keys to Community College Success* to Carol Carter at caroljcarter@lifebound.com or Sarah Kravits at kravitss@mail.montclair.edu. We look forward to hearing from you!

INSTRUCTOR
resources

Online Instructor's Manual This manual provides a framework of ideas and suggestions for activities, journal writing, thought-provoking situations, and online implementation including MyStudentSuccessLab recommendations.

Online PowerPoint Presentation A comprehensive set of PowerPoint slides that can be used by instructors for class presentations and also by students for lecture preview or review. The PowerPoint presentation includes summary slides with overview information for each chapter. These slides help students understand and review concepts within each chapter.

ACKNOWLEDGMENTS

The efforts of many have combined to make this 7th edition, Keys to Community College Success, more than the sum of its parts. We earnestly thank:

Seventh Edition Reviewers

Sheryl Bone, Kaplan University

Lyn Brown, Lamar Institute of Technology

Deidre Ann deLaughter, Gainesville State College

Kimberly Susan Forcier, University of Texas at San Antonio

Deb Holst, Metropolitan Community College

Janice Johnson, Missouri State—West Plains

Saundra Kay King, Ivy Tech Community College

Dr. John Paul Kowalczyk, University of Minnesota Duluth

Richard Marshall, Palm Beach State College

Carol Martinson, Polk State College

Donna Musselman, Santa Fe College

Jeffrey R. Pomeroy, Southwest Texas Junior College

Marie E. Provencio, California State University, Fresno

Mary Kay Scott-Garcia, Santa Fe College

Mary B. Silva, Modesto Junior College

Leigh Smith, Lamar Institute of Technology

Julie Stein, California State University, Easy Bay

Courtlann Thomas, Polk State College

Margaret Shannon Williamson, Dillard University

Jennifer Woltjen, Broome Community College

Reviewers for Previous Editions

Mary Adams, Northern Kentucky University

Peg Adams, Northern Kentucky University

Raishell Adams, Palm Beach Community College—Palm Beach Gardens

Veronica Allen, Texas Southern University

Fred Amador, Phoenix College

Angela A. Anderson, Texas Southern University

Robert Anderson, The College of New Jersey

Manual Aroz, Arizona State University

Dirk Baron, California State University—Bakersfield

Glenda Belote, Florida International University

Todd Benatovich, University of Texas at Arlington

John Bennett, Jr., University of Connecticut

Lynn Berkow, University of Alaska

Susan Bierster, Palm Beach Community College—Lake Worth

Ann Bingham-Newman, California State University—LA

Mary Bixby, University of Missouri—Columbia

Shawn Bixler, The University of Akron

Barbara Blandford, Education Enhancement Center at Lawrenceville, NJ

Jerry Bouchie, St. Cloud State University

D'Yonne Browder, Texas Southern University

Julia Brown, South Plains College

Mary Carstens, Wayne State College

Mona Casady, SW Missouri State University

Frederick Charles, Indiana University

Kobitta Chopra, Broward Community College

Christy Cheney, Valencia Community College—East Campus

Leslie Chilton, Arizona State University

Carrie Cokely, Curry College

Jim Coleman, Baltimore City Community College

Sara Connolly, Florida State University

Kara Craig, University of Southern Mississippi

Jacqueline Crossen-Sills, Massasoit Community College

Janet Cutshall, Sussex County Community College

Donna Dahlgren, Indiana University Southeast

Carolyn Darin, California State University—Northridge

Deryl Davis-Fulmer, Milwaukee Area Technical College

Valerie DeAngelis, Miami-Dade Community College

Joyce Annette Deaton, Jackson State Community College

Rita Delude, NH Community Technical College

Marianne Edwards, Georgia College and State University

Judy Elsley, Weber State University in Utah

Ray Emett, Salt Lake Community College

Jacqueline Fleming, Texas Southern University

Ann French, New Mexico State University

Patsy Frenchman, Santa Fe Community College

Rodolfo Frias, Santiago Canyon College

Ralph Gallo, Texas Southern University

Jean Gammon, Chattanooga State Technical Community College

Skye Gentile, California State University, Hayward

Bob Gibson, University of Nebraska—Omaha

Lewis Grey, Middle Tennessese State University

Jennifer Guyer-Wood, Minnesota State University

Sue Halter, Delgado Community College

Suzy Hampton, University of Montana

Karen Hardin, Mesa Community College

Patricia Hart, California State University, Fresno

Maureen Hurley, University of Missouri—Kansas City

Karen Iversen, Heald Colleges

Valerie Jefferson, Rock Valley College

Gary G. John, Richland College

Cynthia Johnson, Palm Beach Community College—Lake Worth

Elvira Johnson, Central Piedmont Community College
S. Renee Jones, Florida Community College at Jacksonville—North Campus
Georgia Kariotis, Oakton Community College
Laura Kauffman, Indian River Community College
Kathryn K. Kelly, St. Cloud State University
Cathy Keyler, Palm Beach Community College—Palm Beach Gardens
Quentin Kidd, Christopher Newport University
Nancy Kosmicke, Mesa State College
Patsy Krech, University of Memphis
Dana Kuehn, Florida Community College at Jacksonville—Deerwood Center
Noreen Lace, California State University—Northridge
Charlene Latimer, Daytona Beach Community College—Deland
Paul Lede, Texas Southern University
Lanita Legan, Texas State University
Linda Lemkau, North Idaho College
Kristina Leonard, Daytona Beach Community College—Flagler/Palm Coast
Christine A. Lottman, University of Cincinnati
Frank T. Lyman, Jr., University of Maryland
Judith Lynch, Kansas State University
Patricia A. Malinowski, Finger Lakes Community College
Marvin Marshak, University of Minnesota
Kathy Masters, Arkansas State University
Howard Masuda, California State University— Los Angeles
Antoinette McConnell, Northeastern Illinois University
Natalie McLellan, Holmes Community College
Caron Mellblom-Nishioka, California State University—Dominguez Hills
Jenny Middleton, Seminole Community College
Barnette Miller Moore, Indian River Community College
Gladys Montalvo, Palm Beach Community College
Rebecca Munro, Gonzaga University
Nanci C. Nielsen, University of New Mexico—Valencia Campus
Kimberly O'Connor, Community College of Baltimore City
Sue Palmer, Brevard Community College
Alan Pappas, Santa Fe Community College
Bobbie Parker, Alabama State University
Carolyn Patterson, Texas State Technical College— West Texas
Curtis Peters, Indiana University Southeast
Tom Peterson, Grand View University
Virginia Phares, DeVry of Atlanta
Brenda Prinzavalli, Beloit College
Margaret Quinn, University of Memphis
Corliss A. Rabb, Texas Southern University
Terry Rafter-Carles, Valencia Community College— Orlando

Jacqueline Robinson, Milwaukee Area Technical College
Eleanor Rosenfield, Rochester Institute of Technology
Robert Roth, California State University—Fullerton
Manuel Salgado, Elgin Community College
Jack E. Sallie Jr., Montgomery College
Rebecca Samberg, Housatonic Community College
Karyn L. Schulz, Community College of Baltimore County—Dundalk
Pamela Shaw, Broward Community County—South Campus
Tia Short, Boise State University
Jacqueline Simon, Education Enhancement Center at Lawrenceville, NJ
Carolyn Smith, University of Southern Indiana
Cheryl Spector, California State University—Northridge
Julie Stein, California State University
Rose Stewart-Fram, McLennan Community College
Joan Stottlemyer, Carroll College
Jill R. Strand, University of Minnesota—Duluth
Tracy Stuck, Lake Sumter Community College— Leesburg Campus
Toni M. Stroud, Texas Southern University
Karla Thompson, New Mexico State University
Cheri Tillman, Valdosta State University
Ione Turpin, Broward Community College
Thomas Tyson, SUNY Stony Brook
Joy Vaughan-Brown, Broward Community College
Arturo Vazquez, Elgin Community College
Eve Walden, Valencia Community College
Marsha Walden, Valdosta State University
Susannah Waldrop, University of South Carolina, Upstate
Rose Wassman, DeAnza College
Debbie Warfield, Seminole Community College
Ronald Weisberger, Bristol Community College
Jill Wilks, Southern Utah University
Angela Williams, The Citadel
Don Williams, Grand Valley State University
William Wilson, St. Cloud State University
Kim Winford, Blinn College
Tania Wittgenfeld, Rock Valley College
Michelle G. Wolf, Florida Southern College

■ Robert J. Sternberg, for his groundbreaking work on successful intelligence and for his gracious permission to use and adapt that work for this text.

■ Those who generously contributed personal stories, exhibiting courage in being open and honest about their life experiences: Kelly Addington and Becca Tieder, OneStudent.org; Joyce Bishop, Golden West College; Charlotte Buckley, Hinds Community College; Jay Dobyns, Jay Dobyns Group, LLC; Louise Gaile Edrozo; Jad El-Adaimi, California Polytechnic State University; Cindy Estrada, Goodman Networks; Dr. J. Raider Estrada, University of Chicago Medical Center; Norton Ewart, Hewlett-Packard; Sade Gantt,

Montclair State University; Aneela Gonzales, Golden West College; Andrew Hillman, Queens College; Kevin Ix, Bergen Community College; Tomohito Kondo, De Anza Community College; Joe Martin, RealWorld University; Sarah Martinez, Metropolitan State University of Denver; Gary Montrose, Montrose Healthcare Strategies; Zack Moore, University of Rhode Island; Stephen Oh, Chubb Group of Insurance Companies; Torian Richardson, Torianite Inc.; Jacob Rudolph, Northeastern University; Andrew Willard, Colorado State University; Ming-Lun Wu, National Chengchi University, Taipei, Taiwan; and Alexis Zendejas, Brigham Young University.

- Our Editor-in-Chief Jodi McPherson, for her commitment to the *Keys to Success* series and her vision of the relevance of risk and reward.

- Our Acquisitions Editor Katie Mahan, Senior Development Editor Shannon Steed, and Editorial Assistant Erin Carreiro for their dedication, creative ideas, and constant effort in moving us all toward the goal.

- Our production team for their patience, flexibility, and attention to detail, especially Image Manager Rachel Youdelman, Designer John Wincek, Designer Heather Scott, and Diana Neatrour and the team at Electronic Publishing Services Inc.

- Our marketing gurus for their continued support, especially Amy Judd, Executive Marketing Manager; Julie Hildebrand and the other national account managers who support career schools and alternative education on behalf of Pearson; and sales directors and content specialists.

- Charlotte Morrissey for her guidance, wisdom, and insight regarding college students, and for her ongoing and dedicated efforts on behalf of the *Keys* series.

- Greg Tobin, President of Higher Education English, Math, and Student Success, and Tim Bozik, CEO of U.S. Higher Education, for their support of the *Keys* series.

- The Pearson representatives and the management team led by Eric Severson, Executive Vice President, Higher Education Sales.

- The staff at LifeBound for their hard work and dedication: Maureen Breeze, Brittany Havey, Jim Hoops, Angelica Jestrovich, Kyle Kilroy, Michelle Stout, Noel Wilson, Jimmy Young.

- The students who helped us develop our ideas and improve the effectiveness of our materials: Thuyanh Astbury, University of Denver; Jacklynn Blanchard, University of Colorado Boulder; Liv Shehawk Bryan, Arapahoe Community College; Brandy Castner, Metropolitan State University of Denver; Mark Davis, Colorado State University; Grainne Griffiths, Tufts University; Jenna Jacobs, University of Minnesota; Jordan Jones, Metropolitan State University of Denver; Nicoll Laikola, Metropolitan State University of Denver; Jonathon Lasich, University of Colorado Denver; Natasha Malchow, Metropolitan State University of Denver; Sarah Martinez, Metropolitan State University of Denver; Dylan Mey, CEC with Denver Public Schools; Maddie Mey, Wheat Ridge High School; Claire Petras, University of Colorado Denver; Alivia Porpora, Regis University; Woody Roseland, Metropolitan State University of Denver; Trevor Scannell, Miami University Hamilton; Danny Starr, Fort Lewis University; Danielle Thomas, Central Michigan University; Michael Tyrrell-Ead, Golden High School; Jacob Voegele, Gonzaga University; Jeanette Young, School of Mines.

- Don Cameron for his thoughtful and persistent work in gathering, editing, and finalizing chapter opener case studies.

- Photographers Erin Neely and Michael Santiago for authentically representing the student perspective through their original contributions to the photo program.

- Dede DeLaughter, Manny Larenas, and Cheri Tillman for their input and sage advice.

- Our families and friends, who have encouraged us and put up with our commitments.

- Judy Block, who contributed research and writing to this book.

- Special thanks to Joyce Bishop, who created the learning preference assessments, contributed to the success of this book over the past fifteen years, and continues to support college students with her wisdom and insights.

Finally, for their ideas, opinions, and stories, we would like to thank all of the students and instructors with whom we work. Sarah would like to thank her students at Montclair State University who have granted her the privilege of sharing part of their journey through college, as well as the insightful instructors and advisors affiliated with the Center for Advising and Student Transitions. Carol would like to thank the people who have gone through her coaching trainings and who continue to strive to improve students' ability to succeed, including Barbara Gadis, Jennifer Gomez-Mejia, Vanessa Harris, Lynn Montrose, Lindsay Morlock, Lynn Troyka, Melissa Vito, and Kathy York. To all of our readers: We appreciate that, through reading this book, you give us the opportunity to learn and discover with you—in your classroom, in your home, on the bus, and wherever else learning takes place.

BREAKTHROUGH
To better results

Give your students
what they need to succeed.

As an instructor, you want to help your students succeed in college. As a mentor, you want to make sure students reach their professional objectives. We share these goals, and we're committed to partnering with educators to ensure that each individual student succeeds— in college and beyond.

Simply put, Pearson creates technologies, content, and services that help students break through to better results. When a goal as important as education is at stake, no obstacle should be allowed to stand in the way.

The following pages detail some of our products and services designed to help your students succeed. These include:

- Pearson Course Redesign

- MyFoundationsLab for Student Success

- MyStudentSuccessLab

- CourseConnect™

- Custom Services

- Resources for Students

- Professional Development for Instructors

PEARSON

Pearson Course Redesign
Collect, measure, and interpret data to support efficacy.

Rethink the way you deliver instruction.

Pearson has successfully partnered with colleges and universities engaged in course redesign for over 10 years through workshops, Faculty Advisor programs, and online conferences. Here's how to get started!

- Visit our course redesign site at **www.pearsoncourseredesign.com** for information on getting started, a list of Pearson-sponsored course redesign events, and recordings of past course redesign events.

- Request to connect with a Faculty Advisor, a fellow instructor who is an expert in course redesign, by visiting **www.mystudentsuccesslab.com/community**.

- Join our Course Redesign Community at **www.community.pearson.com/courseredesign** and connect with colleagues around the country who are participating in course redesign projects.

Don't forget to measure the results of your course redesign!

Examples of data you may want to collect include:

- Improvement of homework grades, test averages, and pass rates over past semesters

- Correlation between time spent in an online product and final average in the course

- Success rate in the next level of the course

- Retention rate (i.e., percentage of students who drop, fail, or withdraw)

Need support for data collection and interpretation?

Ask your local Pearson representative how to connect with a member of Pearson's Efficacy Team.

MyFoundationsLab®

Built on the success of MyMathLab, MyReadingLab, and MyWritingLab, **MyFoundationsLab** is a comprehensive online mastery-based resource for assessing and remediating college- and career-readiness skills in mathematics, reading, and writing. The system offers a rich environment of pre-built and customized assessments, personalized learning plans, and highly interactive activities that enable students to master skills at their own pace. Ideal for learners of various levels and ages, including those in placement test prep or transitional programs, MyFoundationsLab facilitates the skill development students need in order to be successful in college-level courses and careers.

New! MyFoundationsLab for Student Success

In response to market demand for more "non-cognitive" skills, Pearson now offers **MyFoundationsLab for Student Success**, which combines rich mathematics, reading, and writing content with the 19+ MyStudentSuccessLab modules that support ongoing personal and professional development. To see a complete list of content, visit **www.mystudentsuccesslab.com/mfl**.

If you're affiliated with boot camp programs, student orientation, a testing center, or simply interested in a self-paced, pre-course solution that helps students better prepare for college-level work in basic skills, contact your Pearson representative for more information.

"Students like learning at their own pace; they can go as fast or as slow as they need. MyFoundationsLab facilitates this structure; it's more driven by mastery learning, not by what the teacher says a student should be doing."

—Jennifer McLearen, Instructor,
Piedmont Virginia Community College

Data from January 2007 through June 2008 offers solid evidence of the success of MyFoundationsLab:

91% of students who retested in reading improved at least one course level

70% of students who retested in writing improved at least one course level

43% of students who retested in math improved at least one course level

MyStudentSuccessLab

Help students start strong and finish stronger.

MyStudentSuccessLab™

MyStudentSuccessLab helps students acquire the skills they need for ongoing personal and professional development. It is a learning-outcomes-based technology that helps students advance their knowledge and build critical skills for success. MyStudentSuccessLab's peer-led video interviews, interactive practice exercises, and activities foster the acquisition of academic, life, and professionalism skills.

Students have access to:

- Pre- and Post-Full Course Diagnostic Assessments linked to key learning objectives

- Pre- and Post-Tests dedicated to individual topics in the Learning Path

- An overview of objectives to build vocabulary and repetition

- Videos on key issues that are "by students, for students," conveniently organized by topic

- Practice exercises to improve class prep and learning

- Graded activities to build critical-thinking and problem-solving skills

- Student resources, including Finish Strong 24/7 YouTube videos, professionalism tools, research aids, writing help, and GPA, savings, budgeting, and retirement calculators

- Student Inventories designed to increase self-awareness, including Golden Personality and Thinking Styles

Students utilizing MyStudentSuccessLab may purchase Pearson texts in a number of cost-saving formats—including eTexts, loose-leaf Books à la Carte editions, and more. Contact your Pearson representative for more information.

Topics and features include:

- College Transition
- Communication
- Critical Thinking
- Financial Literacy
- Goal Setting
- Information Literacy
- Interviewing
- Job Search Strategies
- Learning Preferences
- Listening and Taking Notes in Class
- Majors/Careers and Resumes
- Memory and Studying
- Problem Solving
- Reading and Annotating
- Self-Management Skills at Work
- Stress Management
- Teamwork
- Test Taking
- Time Management
- Workplace Communication
- Workplace Etiquette

Assessment

Beyond the Pre- and Post-Full Course Diagnostic Assessments and Pre- and Post-Tests within each module, additional learning-outcome-based tests can be created using a secure testing engine, and may be printed or delivered online. These tests can be customized to accommodate specific teaching needs by editing individual questions or entire tests.

Reporting

Measurement matters—and is ongoing in nature. MyStudentSuccessLab lets you determine what data you need, set up your course accordingly, and collect data via reports. The high quality and volume of test questions allows for data comparison and measurement.

MyLabsPlus service is a teaching and learning environment that offers enhanced reporting features and analysis. With powerful administrative tools and dedicated support, MyLabsPlus offers an advanced suite of management resources for MyStudentSuccessLab.

Content and Functionality Training

Organized by topic, the **Instructor Implementation Guide** provides grading rubrics, suggestions for video use, and more to save time on course prep. Our **User Guide** and "How do I…" **YouTube videos** indicate how to use MyStudentSuccessLab, and show scenarios from getting started to utilizing the Gradebook.

Peer Support

The **Student Success Community** site is a place for you to connect with other educators to exchange ideas and advice on courses, content, and MyStudentSuccessLab. The site is filled with timely articles, discussions, video posts, and more. Join, share, and be inspired!
www.mystudentsuccesscommunity.com

The **Faculty Advisor Network** is Pearson's peer-to-peer mentoring program in which experienced MyStudentSuccessLab users share their best practices and expertise. Our Faculty Advisors are experienced in one-on-one phone and email coaching, webinars, presentations, and live training sessions. Contact your Pearson representative to connect with a Faculty Advisor or learn more about the Faculty Advisor Network.

Integration and Compliance

You can integrate our digital solutions with your learning management system in a variety of ways. For more information, or if documentation is needed for ADA compliance, contact your local Pearson representative.

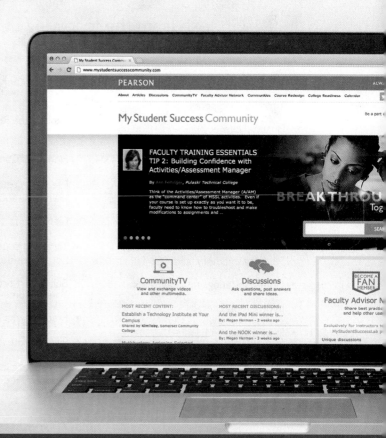

CourseConnect™
Trust that your online course is the best in its class.

Designed by subject matter experts and credentialed instructional designers, **CourseConnect** offers award-winning customizable online courses that help students build skills for ongoing personal and professional development.

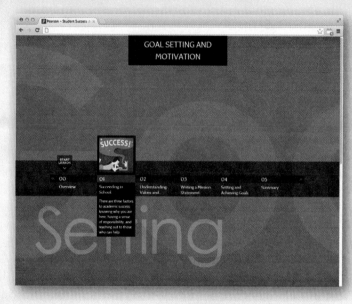

CourseConnect uses topic-based, interactive modules that follow a consistent learning path–from introduction, to presentation, to activity, to review. Its built-in tools–including user-specific pacing charts, personalized study guides, and interactive exercises– provide a student-centric learning experience that minimizes distractions and helps students stay on track and complete the course successfully. Features such as relevant video, audio, and activities, personalized (or editable) syllabi, discussion forum topics and questions, assignments, and quizzes are all easily accessible. CourseConnect is available in a variety of learning management systems and accommodates various term lengths as well as self-paced study. And, our compact textbook editions align to CourseConnect course outcomes.

Choose from the following three course outlines ("Lesson Plans")

Student Success

- Goal Setting, Values, and Motivation
- Time Management
- Financial Literacy
- Creative Thinking, Critical Thinking, and Problem Solving
- Learning Preferences
- Listening and Note-Taking in Class
- Reading and Annotating
- Studying, Memory, and Test-Taking
- Communicating and Teamwork
- Information Literacy
- Staying Balanced: Stress Management
- Career Exploration

Career Success

- Planning Your Career Search
- Knowing Yourself: Explore the Right Career Path
- Knowing the Market: Find Your Career Match
- Preparing Yourself: Gain Skills and Experience Now
- Networking
- Targeting Your Search: Locate Positions, Ready Yourself
- Building a Portfolio: Your Resume and Beyond
- Preparing for Your Interview
- Giving a Great Interview
- Negotiating Job Offers, Ensuring Future Success

Professional Success

- Introducing Professionalism
- Workplace Goal Setting
- Workplace Ethics and Your Career
- Workplace Time Management
- Interpersonal Skills at Work
- Workplace Conflict Management
- Workplace Communications: Email and Presentations
- Effective Workplace Meetings
- Workplace Teams
- Customer Focus and You
- Understanding Human Resources
- Managing Career Growth and Change

Custom Services

Personalize instruction to best facilitate learning.

As the industry leader in custom publishing, we are committed to meeting your instructional needs by offering flexible and creative choices for course materials that will maximize learning and student engagement.

Pearson Custom Library

Using our online book-building system, create a custom book by selecting content from our course-specific collections that consist of chapters from Pearson Student Success and Career Development titles and carefully selected, copyright-cleared, third-party content and pedagogy. www.pearsoncustomlibrary.com

Custom Publications

In partnership with your Custom Field Editor, modify, adapt, and combine existing Pearson books by choosing content from across the curriculum and organizing it around your learning outcomes. As an alternative, you can work with your Editor to develop your original material and create a textbook that meets your course goals.

Custom Technology Solutions

Work with Pearson's trained professionals, in a truly consultative process, to create engaging learning solutions. From interactive learning tools, to eTexts, to custom websites and portals, we'll help you simplify your life as an instructor.

Online Education

Pearson offers online course content for online classes and hybrid courses. This online content can also be used to enhance traditional classroom courses. Our award-winning CourseConnect includes a fully developed syllabus, media-rich lecture presentations, audio lectures, a wide variety of assessments, discussion board questions, and a strong instructor resource package.

For more information on custom Student Success services, please visit www.pearsonlearningsolutions.com or call 800-777-6872.

Resources for Students

Help students save and succeed throughout their college experience.

Books à la Carte Editions

The Books à la Carte (a.k.a. "Student Value" or "Loose Leaf") edition is a three-hole-punched, full-color version of the premium text that's available at 35% less than the traditional bound textbook. Students using MyStudentSuccessLab as part of their course materials can purchase a Books à la Carte edition at a special discount from within the MyLab course where "Click here to order" is denoted.

CourseSmart eTexbooks

CourseSmart eTextbooks offer a convenient, affordable alternative to printed texts. Students can save up to 50% off the price of a traditional text, and receive helpful search, note-taking, and printing tools.

Programs and Services

As the world's leading learning company, Pearson has pledged to help students succeed in college and reach their educational and career aspirations. We're so dedicated to this goal that we've created a unique set of programs and services that we call **Pearson Students**. Through this program, we offer undergraduate students opportunities to learn from, and interact with, each other and Pearson professionals through social media platforms, internships, part-time jobs, leadership endeavors, events, and awards. To learn more about our Pearson Students programs and meet our Pearson Students, visit **www.pearsonstudents.com**.

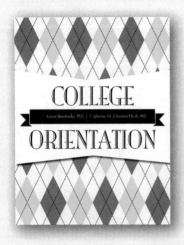

Orientation to College

In Bendersky's *College Orientation,* students learn how to adapt to college life and stay on track towards a degree—all while learning behaviors that promote achievement after graduation. This reference tool is written from an insider's point of view and has a distinct focus on promoting appropriate college conduct. It covers topics that help students navigate college while learning how to apply this knowledge in the workplace.

Help with Online Classes

Barrett's *Power Up: A Practical Student's Guide to Online Learning*, 2/e serves as a textbook for students of all backgrounds who are new to online learning, and as a reference for instructors who are also novices in the area or who need insight into the perspective of such students.

Effective Communication with Professors

In Ellen Bremen's *Say This, NOT That to Your Professor*, an award-winning, tenured communication professor takes students "inside the faculty mind," and guides them to manage their classroom experience with confidence. This book aims to facilitate improved relationships with professors, better grades, and an amazing college experience.

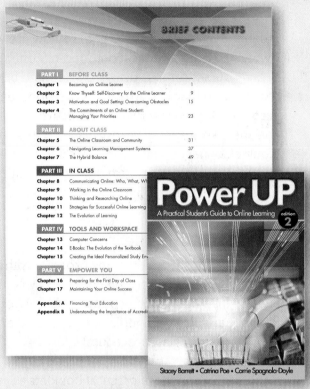

Power UP
A Practical Student's Guide to Online Learning
edition 2

Stacey Barrett • Catrina Poe • Carrie Spagnola-Doyle

Expert Advice

Our consumer-flavored *IDentity* series booklets are written by national subject-matter experts, such as personal finance specialist, author, and TV personality, Farnoosh Torabi. The authors of this series offer strategies and activities on topics such as careers, college success, financial literacy, financial responsibility, and more.

Quick Tips for Success

Our *Success Tips* series provides one-page "quick tips" on six topics essential to college or career success. The *Success Tips* series includes MyStudentSuccessLab, Time Management, Resources All Around You, Now You're Thinking, Maintaining Your Financial Sanity, and Building Your Professional Image. The *Success Tips for Professionalism* series includes Create Your Personal Brand, Civility Paves the Way Toward Success, Succeeding in Your Diverse World, Building Your Professional Image, Get Things Done with Virtual Teams, and Get Ready for Workplace Success.

Professional Development for Instructors
Augment your teaching with engaging resources.

Foster Ownership

Student dynamics have changed, so how are you helping students take ownership of their education? Megan Stone's *Ownership* series offers online courses for instructors, and printed booklets for students, on four key areas of professional development: accountability, critical thinking, effective planning, and study strategies. The instructor courses, in our CourseConnect online format, include teaching methods, activities, coaching tips, assessments, animations, and video. Online courses and printed booklets are available together or separately.

Promote Active Learning

Infuse student success into any program with our *Engaging Activities* series. Written and compiled by National Student Success Institute (NSSI®) co-founders Amy Baldwin, Steve Piscitelli, and Robert Sherfield, the material provides educators strategies, procedural information, and activities they can use with students immediately. Amy, Steve, and Robb developed these practical booklets as indispensable, hands-on resources for educators who want to empower teachers, professional development coordinators, coaches, and administrators to actively engage their classes.

Address Diverse Populations

Support various student populations that require specific strategies to succeed. Choose from an array of booklets that align with the needs of adult learners, digital learners, first-generation learners, international learners, English language learners, student athletes, and more.

Create Consistency

Instructional resources lend a common foundation for support. We offer **online Instructor's Manuals** that provide a framework of ideas and suggestions for online and in-class activities and journal writing assignments. We also offer comprehensive **online PowerPoint presentations** that can be used by instructors for class presentations, and by students to preview lecture material and review concepts within each chapter.

Helpful Information and Advice As You Begin

Quick Start to College contains information designed to help you feel more in control as you start your journey toward the achievement of a college education. Start by learning what your college expects of you—and what you have a right to expect in return as a consumer of education. Continue on to explore the people and resources that can help you while you are enrolled. As you read, consult your college handbook and/or website to learn about the specific resources, policies, and procedures of your college.

WHAT YOUR COLLEGE *expects of you*

If you clarify what it means to be a college student right at the start, you will minimize surprises that may be obstacles later on. What is expected of you may be different from anything you encountered in high school or in other educational settings. Since expectations differ from college to college, use the material that follows as general guidelines.

Follow Procedures and Fulfill Requirements

Understanding and following college procedures will smooth your path to success.

Registration

Registration most likely takes place through your school's computer network or via an automated phone system, although occasionally a school will still hold an in-person registration in a large venue such as an athletic facility or student union. Scan the college catalog and web site and consider these factors as you make your selections:

- Core/general requirements for graduation
- Your major or minor or courses in departments you are considering
- Electives that sound interesting, even if they are out of your field

Once you choose courses, but before you register, create a schedule that shows daily class times to see if the schedule will work out. Meet with your advisor for comments and approval. Some schools put a "hold" on your registration that is only lifted after you see your advisor.

Graduation and Curriculum Requirements

Every college has degree requirements stated in the catalog and website. Make sure you understand those that apply to you. Among the requirements you may encounter are:

- Number of credits needed to graduate, including credits in major and minor fields
- Curriculum requirements, including specific course requirements
- Departmental major requirements

School Procedures

Your college has rules and regulations, found in the college handbook and on the website, for all students to follow. Among the most common procedures are:

Adding or dropping a class.   This should be done within the first few days of the term if you find that a course is not right for you or that there are better choices. The sooner you make adjustments, the easier it will be to catch up with any new courses you add. Withdrawals after a predetermined date, other than those approved for special cases, receive a failing grade.

Taking an incomplete. If you can't finish your work due to circumstances beyond your control—an illness or injury, for example, or a death in the family—many colleges allow you to take a grade of Incomplete. The school will require approval from your instructor and you will have to make up the work later, usually by a predetermined date.

Transferring schools. Research the degree requirements of other schools and submit transfer applications. If you are a student at a community college and intend to transfer to a four-year school, take the courses required for admission to that school. In addition, be sure all your credits are transferable, which means they will be counted toward your degree at the four-year school.

Understand Your School's Grading System

GRADE POINT AVERAGE (GPA)
A measure of academic achievement computed by dividing the total number of grade points received by the total number of credits or hours of course work taken.

When you receive grades, remember that they reflect your work, not your self-worth. Most schools use grading systems with numerical grades or equivalent letter grades (see Key QS.1). Generally, the highest course grade is an A, or 4.0, and the lowest is an F, or 0.0.

In every course, you earn a certain number of college credits, called *hours*. For example, Accounting 101 may be worth three hours. These numbers generally refer to the number of hours the course meets per week. When you multiply each numerical course grade by the number of hours the course is worth, take the average of all these numbers, and divide by the total number of credit hours you are taking, you obtain your **grade point average,** or GPA.

Learn the minimum GPA needed to remain in good standing and to be accepted and continue in your major. Key QS.2 shows you how to calculate your GPA. You can also use web resources such as www.back2college.com/gpa.htm to calculate your GPA electronically.

Make The Most Of Your School's Computer System

A large part of college communication and work involves the computer. In a given day you might access a syllabus online, e-mail a student, use the Internet to tap into a library database, write a draft of an assignment on a computer, and send a paper draft to an instructor electronically. Most dorm rooms are wired for computers, and an increasing number of campuses have wireless networks. Some schools are even moving to a "paperless" system where all student notifications are sent via e-mail, requiring every student to activate an e-mail account and check it regularly. Here are some suggestions for using your computer effectively:

- *Get started right away.* Register for an email account and connect to the college network. In addition, register your cell phone number with the school so you can get emergency alerts.
- *Use the system.* Communicate with instructors and fellow students using e-mail. Browse the college website. Search databases at the college library.
- *Save and protect your work.* Save electronic work periodically onto a hard drive, CD, flash drive, or location in the cloud. Use antivirus software if your system needs it.
- *Stay on task.* During study time, try to limit Internet surfing, instant messaging, visiting MySpace and Facebook, and playing computer games.

One of the most important directives for college students communicating via computer is to follow guidelines when contacting instructors via email. When you submit assignments,

KEY QS.1 Understand letter grades and equivalent numerical grades per semester hour.

Letter grade	A	A–	B+	B	B–	C+	C	C–	D+	D	F
Numerical grade	4.0	3.7	3.3	3.0	2.7	2.3	2.0	1.7	1.3	1.0	0.0

COURSE	SEMESTER HOURS	GRADE	POINTS EARNED FOR THIS COURSE
Chemistry I	4	C (2.0 points)	4 credits × 2.0 points = 8
Freshman Writing	3	B+ (3.3 points)	3 credits × 3.3 points = 9.9
Spanish I	3	B− (2.7 points)	3 credits × 2.7 points = 8.1
Introduction to Statistics	3	C+ (2.3 points)	3 credits × 2.3 points = 6.9
Social Justice	2	A− (3.7 points)	2 credits × 3.7 points = 7.4
Total semester hours **Total grade points for semester**	**15**		**40.3**

GPA for semester (total grade points divided by semester hours): 40.3 divided by 15 = 2.69
Letter equivalent grade: C+/B−

take exams, or ask questions electronically, rules of etiquette promote civility and respect. Try these suggestions the next time you email an instructor:

- *Use your school account.* Instructors are likely to delete unfamiliar emails from their overloaded email inboxes. "Helen_Miller@yourschool.edu" will get read, but "disastergirl@yahoo.com" may not.
- *Don't ask for information you can find on your own or bother your instructor with minor problems.* Flooding your instructor with unnecessary emails may work against you when you really need help.
- *Write a clear subject line.* State exactly what the email is about.
- *Address the instructor by name and use his or her title.* "Hello Professor Smith" or "Hi Dr. Reynolds" is better than "Hey."
- *Be clear and comprehensive.* First, state your question or problem and what you want to achieve. For example, "In my essay, I believe I covered the key points. I would like to meet to discuss your critique." Next, if necessary, support your position, using bullet points if you have a number of support statements. Finally, end by thanking the instructor and typing your full name.
- *Avoid abbreviations and acronyms.* Write as though you were crafting a business letter, not a social email to a friend.
- *Use complete sentences, correct punctuation, and capitalization.* Be sure to reread your email before sending, so that you have a chance to correct any mistakes.
- *Give the instructor time to respond.* Don't expect a reply within two hours. If you hear nothing after a couple of days, send a follow-up note that contains the full text of your first message. A note that simply says "Did you get my last email?" won't be helpful if for any reason your instructor didn't receive or read the first one.

Read and Use Your Syllabi

You will receive a syllabus for each of your courses, either online or in person at the first class meeting (or both). Each syllabus is a super-resource for that course, providing information including:

SYLLABUS
A comprehensive outline of course topics and assignments.

- Focus and goals of the course
- Required and optional reading, with a schedule of when that reading is covered
- Dates of quizzes and exams and due dates for assignments
- The instructor's grading system and components of your final grade
- Your instructor's policy regarding latecomers and missed class meetings
- How and when to connect with your instructor in person, by phone, or online
- Important college-wide policies such as the academic integrity policy

You might consider each syllabus as a "contract" between you and your instructor, outlining what your instructor expects of you (readings, assignments, class participation) as well as what you can expect from your instructor (availability, schedule of topics, clarification of grading system).

Put this super-resource to use by reading syllabi thoroughly and referring to them throughout the term. When you have a question, look for an answer in your syllabus first before you contact your instructor. Marking up your syllabus will remind you of responsibilities, as will "backdating"—noting in your written or electronic planner the interim goals to achieve by particular dates in order to complete assignments. For example, if you have a 15-page paper due on October 12, you would enter dates in September and October for goals such as choosing a, first draft, and final draft.

Key QS.3 shows a portion of an actual syllabus with important items noted.

Get Involved

Extracurricular activities give you a chance to meet people who share your interests and to develop teamwork and leadership skills as well as other skills that may be important in your career. In addition, being connected to friends and a supportive network of people is one of the main reasons people stay in school.

Some new college students take on too many activities, and others, faced with a combination of responsibilities that can include commuting and jobs, don't get involved at all. Find a balance that enriches your experience without overwhelming you. You can always add or reduce activities later. Consider this: Studies have shown that students who join organizations tend to persist in their educational goals more than those who don't branch out.[1]

CONNECT WITH PEOPLE
and resources

During your first weeks of school, as you navigate through what may seem like a maze of classes and business offices, it is important to know that instructors, administrators, advisors, and a range of support staff are available to help. Groups and organizations also provide support and opportunities to broaden your experience. Tap into the following resources at your school.

Instructors and Teaching Assistants

The people who teach your courses—instructors and teaching assistants—are your most available human resources at college. You see them from one to five times per week and interact with them more directly than with any other authority on campus. They see your work and, if your class size is small, they hear your ideas and consequently may get to know you quite well. Instructors are potential resources and necessary allies in your education.

What kind of help might you seek from an instructor or teaching assistant?

- Clarification on material presented in class
- Help on homework
- Information about how to prepare for a test
- Consultation on a paper you are working on
- Details about why you received a particular grade on a test or assignment
- Advice about the department, courses and majoring, or related career areas

When you want to speak personally with an instructor for longer than a minute or two, choose your time carefully. Before or after class is usually not the best time for anything more than a quick question. When you need your instructor's full attention, there are three ways to get it: make an appointment during office hours, send an email, or leave a voicemail message.

Office hours. Instructors keep regular office hours. Generally, these appear on your syllabus and are posted on instructors' office doors and on instructors' or departmental web pages.

ENG 122 Spring 2007

How to connect with the instructor

Instructor:	Jennifer Gessner
Office Hours:	Tue & Thur 12:30–1:30 (or by appointment) in DC 305
Phone:	303-555-2222
E-mail:	jg@abc.xyz

Books and materials to get ASAP

Required Texts: *Good Reasons with Contemporary Arguments,* Faigley and Selzer
A Writer's Reference, 5th ed., Diana Hacker

Required Materials:

- a notebook with lots of paper
- a folder for keeping everything from this class
- an active imagination and critical thinking

Course Description: This course focuses on argumentative writing and the researched paper. Students will practice the rhetorical art of argumentation and will gain experience in finding and incorporating researched materials into an extended paper.

Course coverage, expectations, responsibilities

Writer's Notebook: All students will keep, and bring to class, a notebook with blank paper. Throughout the semester, you will be given writing assignments to complete in this book. You must bring to class and be prepared to share any notebook assignment. Notebook assignments will be collected frequently, though sometimes randomly, and graded only for their completeness, not for spelling, etc.

Grading:

How grades are determined for this course

- Major Writing Assignments worth 100 points each.
- Final Research Project worth 300 points.
- Additional exercises and assignments range from 10 to 50 points each.
- Class participation: Based on the degree to which you complete the homework and present this in a thoughtful, meaningful manner in class.
- Attendance: Attendance is taken daily and students may miss up to three days of class without penalty, but will lose 5 points for each day missed thereafter.
- Late work: All work will lose 10% of earned points per class day late. No work will be accepted after five class days or the last class meeting.

Final Grade: The average of the total points possible (points earned divided by the total possible points). 100–90% = A; 89–80% = B; 79–70% = C (any grade below 70% is not passing for this class).

Reflects school's academic integrity policy

Academic Integrity: Students must credit any material used in their papers that is not their own (including direct quotes, paraphrases, figures, etc.). Failure to do so constitutes plagiarism, which is illegal, unethical, <u>always recognizable</u>, and a guaranteed way to fail a paper. The definition of plagiarism is "to steal and use (the writings or ideas of another) as one's own."

Topic of that day's class meeting

Week 4
2/1   <u>The Concise Opinion.</u>
                HW: Complete paper #1 Rough Draft (5–7 pages double-spaced)

Notice of due date for paper draft

                How Professionals Argue
                HW: <u>Read Jenkins Essay (p 501 of *Good Reasons) and* Rafferty
                Essay (p 525)</u>; compare argumentative style, assess and explain
                efficacy of arguments.

Notice of reading assignments to complete

Notice of quiz

Week 5
2/15   Developing an Argument
                Essay Quiz on Jenkins and Rafferty Essays
                HW: Chap 5 of *Good Reasons;* based on components of a definition of
                argument, write a brief explanation of how your argument might fit into
                this type.

Notice of final due date for paper

2/17   Library Workday: Meet in Room 292
                PAPER #1 DUE

Source: Jennifer Gessner, Community College of Denver.

Always make an appointment for a conference. Face-to-face conferences are ideal for working through ideas and problems (for example, deciding on a term paper topic) or asking for advice (for example, looking for guidance on choosing courses in the department).

Email. Use email to clarify assignments and assignment deadlines, to ask questions about lectures or readings, and to clarify what will be covered on a test. Using the emailing guidelines presented earlier will increase the likelihood of receiving a positive response. Instructors' email addresses are generally posted on the first day of class and may also appear in your handbook or syllabus.

Voicemail. If something comes up at the last minute, you can leave a message in your instructor's voice mailbox. Make your message short, but specific ("This is Rick Jones from your ten o'clock Intro to Psychology class. I'm supposed to present my project today, but have a fever of 102 degrees"). Avoid calling instructors at home unless they give specific permission to do so.

If you are taking a large lecture course, you may have a primary instructor plus a *teaching assistant* (TA) who meets with a small group of students on a regular basis and grades your papers and exams. You may want to approach your TA with course-related questions and problems before approaching the instructor. Because TAs deal with fewer students, they may have more time to devote to specific issues.

Academic Advisors

In most colleges, every student is assigned an advisor who is the student's personal liaison with the college. (At some schools, students receive help at an advising center.) Your advisor will help you choose courses every term, plan your overall academic program, and understand college regulations, including graduation requirements. He or she will point out possible consequences of your decisions ("If you put off taking biology now, you're facing two lab courses next term"), help you shape your educational goals, and monitor your academic progress.

While you are responsible for fully understanding graduation requirements—including credit requirements—and choosing the courses you need, your advisor is there to help you with these critical decisions. You will most likely be required to meet with your advisor once each term; however, you can schedule additional meetings if and when you need them.

Mentors

MENTOR
A trusted counselor or guide who takes a special interest in helping you reach your goals.

You may find a mentor during college who can give you a private audience for questions and problems, advice tailored to your needs, support, guidance, and trust. In return, you owe it to a mentor to respectfully take advice into consideration. A mentor might be your advisor, an instructor in your major or minor field, or a resident assistant (RA). Some schools have faculty or peer mentoring programs to match students with people who can help them.

Tutors and Academic Centers

Tutors can give you valuable and detailed help on specific academic subjects. Most campuses have private tutoring available, and many schools offer free peer tutoring. If you feel you could benefit from the kind of one-on-one work a tutor can give, ask your instructor or your academic advisor to recommend a tutor. If your school has one or more academic centers, you may be able to find a tutor there. *Academic centers*, including reading, writing, math, and study-skills centers, offer consultations and tutoring to help students improve skills at all levels.

Administrators

Every college needs an administrative staff to operate smoothly and efficiently. One of the most important administrative offices for students is the Office of the Dean of Student Affairs, which, in many colleges, is the center for student services. Staff members there can answer your questions or direct you to others who can help. You will also encounter administrative offices involved with tuition payments, financial aid, and registration.

- The *bursar's office* (also called the office of finance or accounting office) issues bills for tuition and room and board and collects payments from students and financial aid sources.
- The *financial aid office* helps students apply for financial aid and understand the eligibility requirements of different federal, state, and private programs (see coverage of money management for more details on financial aid).
- The *registrar's office* handles course registration, sends grade reports, and compiles your official *transcript* (a comprehensive record of your courses and grades). Graduate school admissions offices require a copy of your transcript, as do many prospective employers.

Student-Centered Services

A host of services helps students succeed in college and deal with problems that arise. Here are some you may find.

Academic computer center. Most schools have computer facilities that are open daily, usually staffed by technicians who can assist you. Many facilities also offer training workshops.

Student housing or commuter affairs office. Residential colleges provide on-campus housing for undergraduate students. The housing office handles room and room-mate placement and deals with special needs (for example, an allergic student's need for a room air conditioner) and problems. Schools with commuting students may have transportation and parking programs.

Health services. Health services generally include sick care, prescriptions, routine diagnostic tests, vaccinations, and first aid. All clinics are affiliated with nearby hospitals for emergency care. In addition, psychological counseling is sometimes offered through health services or at a separate facility. Many colleges require proof of health insurance at the time of registration.

Career services. This office helps students find part-time and full-time jobs, as well as summer jobs and internships. Career offices have reference files on careers and employers; they also help students learn to write résumés and cover letters and search job sites on the Internet; and they hold career fairs and provide space for employers to interview students on campus.

Services for disabled students. For students with documented disabilities, federal law requires that assistance be provided in the form of accommodations ranging from interpreters for the hearing impaired to ramps for students in wheelchairs. If you have a disability, visit this office to learn what is offered, and remember that this office is your advocate if you encounter problems.

Veterans' affairs. The Office of Veterans' Affairs provides veterans with services including academic and personal counseling and current benefit status, which may affect tuition waivers.

Resources for Minority Students

The term *minority* includes students of color; gay, lesbian, and bisexual students; and students from underrepresented cultures or religious backgrounds. Along with activities that appeal to the general student population, most colleges have organizations and services that support minority groups, including specialized student associations, cultural centers, arts groups with a minority focus, minority fraternities and sororities, and political-action groups.

Many minority students seek a balance, getting involved with members of their group as well as with the college mainstream. For example, a student may join the Latino Students Association as well as clubs for all students, such as the campus newspaper or an athletic team.

You are beginning the journey of your college education and lifelong learning. The work you do in this course will help you achieve your goals in your studies, your personal life, and your career. Psychologist Robert J. Sternberg, the originator of the successful intelligence concept discussed in this text, said that those who achieve success "create their own opportunities rather than let their opportunities be limited by the circumstances in which they happen to find themselves."[2] Let this book and this course help you create new and fulfilling opportunities on your path to success.

CHAPTER

In college and beyond, your willingness to take targeted, productive risks will move you toward your desired reward – the achievement of the goals that spell "success" to you.

The Rewards of College

TAKING RISKS THAT MOVE YOU TOWARD SUCCESS

What Would You Risk? *Dr. J. Raider Estrada*

THINK ABOUT THIS SITUATION AS YOU READ, AND CONSIDER WHAT ACTION YOU WOULD TAKE. THIS CHAPTER JUMP-STARTS YOUR ENTRY INTO THE COLLEGE EXPERIENCE, WITH INFORMATION ON HOW TO MAKE THE TRANSITION AND GATHER THE INGREDIENTS FOR SUCCESS.

J. Raider Estrada's childhood in Los Angeles was defined by challenges. His parents separated when he was 10, and his neighborhood was dominated by gang culture. He grew close to an older boy named Rudy who belonged to one of the local gangs. One day as he and Rudy walked down the street, members of a rival gang drove up, jumped out of the car, and fatally stabbed Rudy on the spot. Raider, age 12 at the time, could only hold his best friend and watch him die.

This experience unleashed rage in Raider that he was unable to control. He joined the gang to which Rudy had belonged and participated in gang violence. He was repeatedly arrested for assault and battery. He went through several stints in juvenile hall and on probation, and he eventually lived in a group home for over a year. However, none of these interventions kept him from continuing to act violently on behalf of the gang.

When his stepmother discovered his gun and called the police, she disrupted Raider's plan to avenge the deaths of several fellow gang members. After two weeks of hiding out, he risked going to the police on his own volition. This time the intervention was different. He went to a program called Rite of Passage in the heart of the Nevada desert, where he found encouragement and motivation. A devoted teacher who worked with Raider sparked his desire to learn, which led to his earning a high school diploma, and a counselor helped him apply to college. He was admitted to Lassen College and started classes two days after leaving Rite of Passage. Now a new challenge loomed: How could Raider, as a former gang member with a history of failure and violence, earn the reward of a successful college career?

To be continued . . .

IN THIS TEXT, YOU WILL MEET PEOPLE LIKE RAIDER WHO HAVE TAKEN RISKS THAT HAVE HELPED THEM ACHIEVE IMPORTANT GOALS. WHETHER YOU HAVE SOMETHING IN COMMON WITH THESE PEOPLE OR NOT, THEY WILL EXPAND YOUR PERSPECTIVE AND INSPIRE YOU TO MOVE AHEAD ON YOUR OWN PATH. YOU'LL LEARN MORE ABOUT RAIDER, AND THE REWARD RESULTING FROM HIS ACTIONS, WITHIN THE CHAPTER.

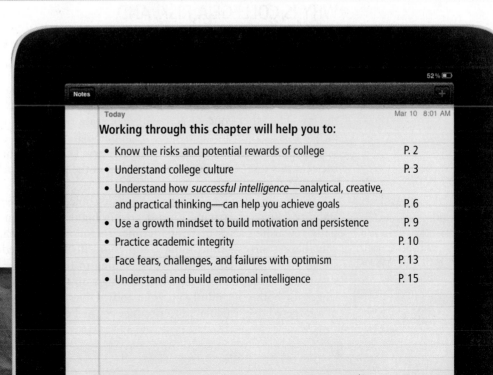

Notes

52%

Today   Mar 10 8:01 AM

Working through this chapter will help you to:

- Know the risks and potential rewards of college — P. 2
- Understand college culture — P. 3
- Understand how *successful intelligence*—analytical, creative, and practical thinking—can help you achieve goals — P. 6
- Use a growth mindset to build motivation and persistence — P. 9
- Practice academic integrity — P. 10
- Face fears, challenges, and failures with optimism — P. 13
- Understand and build emotional intelligence — P. 15

status CHECK

How Ready Are You to Risk Effort for the Rewards of College?

For each statement, fill in the number that best describes how often it applies to you.

1 = never   2 = seldom   3 = sometimes   4 = often   5 = always

1. I feel ready to handle college-level work. ① ② ③ ④ ⑤

2. I can identify how college culture differs from high school and workplace culture. ① ② ③ ④ ⑤

3. I am aware of what it takes to succeed in today's technology-driven, ever-changing workplace. ① ② ③ ④ ⑤

4. I believe my intelligence can increase as a result of my efforts. ① ② ③ ④ ⑤

5. I often combine critical, creative, and practical thinking to reach a goal. ① ② ③ ④ ⑤

6. I am willing to believe that effort and focus are more essential to success than ability or talent. ① ② ③ ④ ⑤

7. I can explain the reward of acting with academic integrity in college. ① ② ③ ④ ⑤

8. I am able to accurately perceive my own emotions, as well as those of others. ① ② ③ ④ ⑤

9. I relate well to others and can work effectively in a team. ① ② ③ ④ ⑤

10. I know that I will need to learn throughout my life to succeed in the workplace. ① ② ③ ④ ⑤

Each of the topics in these statements is covered in this chapter. Note those statements for which you filled in a 3 or lower. Skim the chapter to see where those topics appear, and pay special attention to them as you read, learn, and apply new strategies.

REMEMBER: NO MATTER HOW PREPARED YOU ARE TO SUCCEED IN COLLEGE, YOU CAN IMPROVE WITH EFFORT AND PRACTICE.

WHY IS COLLEGE A RISK, AND
what reward does it offer?

Think about the word *risk*. What, specifically, comes to mind? There are two different ways to think about risk. One involves risky behavior—impulsive decisions made with little or no forethought—such as substance abuse, unsafe sex, or breaking the law. The other concept is one of deliberate risk calculated to bring reward. Examples of this kind of productive risk include buying shares of stock in a new company or serving in the combat division of the military. This is the concept of risk that will take focus in this text—the one that will give you the power to achieve the rewards that are meaningful to you.

College is often seen as a risk-free, safe choice that increases your chances of career stability. However, striving for a degree in higher education is one of the most potentially rewarding risks of your lifetime. To follow this path, you will risk your most valuable resources—time, money, and yourself. You will dedicate time to learning and self-improvement. You, and anyone helping to finance your education, will commit a significant amount of money. You will sign up for years of responsibilities and challenges for both your mind and your body. Obtaining your degree is a perfect example of a targeted risk, calculated to produce reward down the line.

MyStudentSuccessLab
(www.mystudentsuccesslab.com) is an online solution designed to help you "Start Strong, Finish Stronger" by building skills for ongoing personal and professional development.

Well then, why take calculated risks? Why not save your money, time, and effort? Because only with productive risk-taking (not risky behavior) come the rewards essential to your success. Skills, intelligence, motivation, employment, growth, and advancement can be yours, but only as a result of hard work, dedication, and focus.

This text and your course are part of an experience this term that will:

- Show you the value of deliberate risk-taking in your day-to-day life
- Allow you to discover more about how you learn and what rewards you seek
- Build academic skills as well as transferable life skills
- Help you set and risk pursuing your most important goals
- Increase your ability to relate effectively to others and work in teams

When a high jumper or pole vaulter gets over a bar of a certain height, someone raises the bar so that the athlete can work toward a new goal. The college experience will "raise the bar" for you with tougher instructors, demanding coursework, and fellow students whose sights are set high. You, too, can risk raising the bar, aiming for the potential rewards of jumping over it. There is potential for improvement in every life—think about how or what *you* want to improve. You don't have to have experienced brutality as a gang member, as Raider did, to want to make changes for the better.

Begin your transition to college by looking at the present—the culture of college, what you can expect, and what college expects of you. Then, consider the future—what a college education means for you in the workplace and in life.

The Culture of College

Knowing what to expect in college will help you to transition more successfully. You are likely to experience most or all of the following aspects of college culture (your student handbook will contain details specific to your school). As you read, keep in mind that the reward you earn from college depends on the risk you take.

Independent learning. College offers the reward of freedom and independence in exchange for the risk of functioning without much guidance. This culture requires strong self-management skills. Instructors expect you to do the following—and more—on your own:

- Use syllabi to create and follow a schedule for the term (see Quick Start to College)
- Navigate course materials electronically if your school uses an learning management system (LMS) such as Blackboard
- Get to class on time with the materials you need
- Complete text and other reading with little to no in-class review of the reading
- Set up and attend study group meetings
- Turn in projects and coursework on time and be prepared for exams
- Seek help when you need it

Fast pace and increased workload. The pace of each course is typically twice as fast as high school courses and requires more papers, homework, reading, and projects. This demanding pace may energize and motivate you, especially if you did not feel inspired by high school assignments. However, it demands more effort and study time. For each hour spent in class, plan two to three hours of study and work time outside of class.

3

Understanding how to use research and communication technology is as important for day-to-day college activities as it is for the workplace.

Challenging work. Although challenging, college-level work can reward you with enormous opportunities to learn and grow. College texts often have more words per page, higher-level terminology, and more abstract ideas compared to high school texts. In addition, college often involves complex assignments, challenging research papers, group projects, lab work, and tests.

More out-of-class time to manage. The freedom of your schedule requires strong time management skills. On days when your classes end early, start late, or don't meet at all, you will need to use open blocks of time effectively as you juggle responsibilities, including perhaps a job and family.

Diverse culture. Typically, you will encounter different ideas and diverse people in college. Your fellow students may differ from you in age, life experience, ethnicity, political mindset, family obligations, values, student status (part or full time, commuter or resident), and more.

Higher-level thinking. You'll need to risk moving beyond recall. Instead of just summarizing and taking the ideas of others at face value, you will interpret, evaluate, generate new ideas, and apply what you know to new situations (more on thinking skills later in this chapter).

You are not alone as you adjust. Look for support resources such as instructors, academic advisors, mentors, other students or tutors; technology such as the Internet, library search engines, and electronic planning aids; and your text for this course. Seek help from campus officials. And, to give meaning to your efforts in college, consider how your efforts will serve you in your career.

College Prepares You for the Modern Workplace

Because the skills and strategies that bring success in college are so similar to those that bring success at work, this course can lay a foundation for career exploration and workplace skill development. You will need to distinguish yourself in a global marketplace, in which North American workers often compete with workers from other countries. Thomas Friedman, author of *The World Is Flat,* explains how the digital revolution has transformed the working environment:

> It is now possible for more people than ever to collaborate and compete in real time with more other people on more different kinds of work from more different corners of the planet and on a more equal footing than in any previous time in the history of the world—using computers, e-mail, networks, teleconferencing, and dynamic new software.[1]

These developments, combined with an enormous increase in knowledge work such as Internet technology, mean that you may compete for jobs with highly trained and motivated people around the globe. The workplace, too, has raised the bar, and you need to take greater risks to vault over it.

What can help you achieve career goals in this "flat" world?

College degree. Statistics show that getting a degree increases your chances of finding and keeping a highly skilled, well-paying job. College graduates earn, on average, around $20,000 more per year than those with a high school diploma (see Key 1.1). Furthermore, the unemployment rate for college graduates is less than half that of high school graduates (see Key 1.2).

DIGITAL REVOLUTION
The change in how people communicate, brought on by developments in computer systems.

KNOWLEDGE WORK
Work that is primarily concerned with information rather than manual labor.

KEY 1.1 More education is likely to mean more income.

Median annual income of persons with income 25 years old and over, by gender and highest level of education, 2009

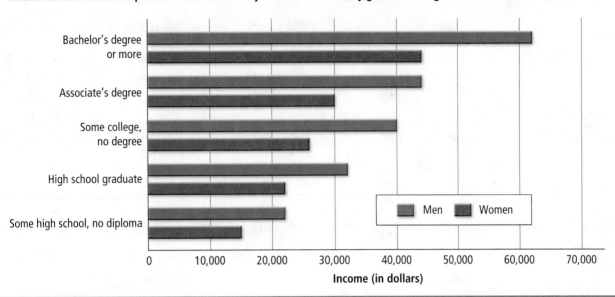

Source: U.S. Census Bureau. "Income, Poverty, and Health Insurance Coverage in the United States, 2009." *Current Population Reports,* Series P60–238, September 2010.

KEY 1.2 More education is likely to mean more consistent employment.

Unemployment rates of persons 25 years old and over, by highest level of education, 2009

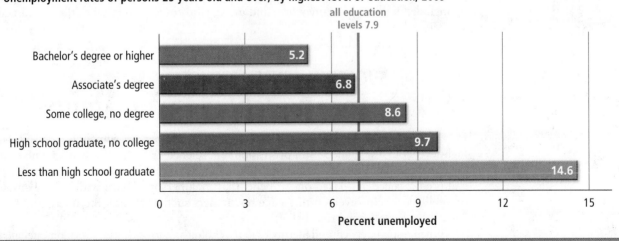

Source: U.S. Department of Labor, Bureau of Labor Statistics, Office of Employment and Unemployment Statistics. "Current Population Survey." May 2010.

21st century skills. Taking a careful look at what the current workplace demands of workers and what it rewards, education and business leaders founded an organization called the Partnership for 21st Century Skills. Together these leaders developed a "Framework for 21st Century Learning" shown in Key 1.3, delineating the categories of knowledge and skills that successful workers need to acquire.

KEY 1.3 The Framework for 21st Century Learning shows what you need to succeed.

CORE SUBJECTS AND 21ST CENTURY THEMES	LEARNING AND INNOVATION SKILLS
• Global Awareness • Financial, Economic, Business, and Entrepreneurial Literacy • Civic Literacy—Community Service • Health Literacy	• Creativity and Innovation • Critical Thinking and Problem Solving • Communication and Collaboration
INFORMATION, MEDIA, AND TECHNOLOGY SKILLS	**LIFE AND CAREER SKILLS**
• Information Literacy • Media Literacy • ICT (Information, Communications, and Technology) Literacy	• Flexibility and Adaptability • Initiative and Self-Direction • Social and Cross-Cultural Skills • Productivity and Accountability • Leadership and Responsibility

Source: Adapted from Partnership for 21st Century Skills Framework, www.p21.org/index.php?option=com_content&task=view&id=254&Itemid=120.

Looking at this framework, you will see that success in today's workplace requires more than just job-specific skills. Author Daniel Pink argues that the ability to create, interact interpersonally, generate ideas, and lead diverse teams—skills, all demanding risk-taking, found in the Framework for 21st Century Learning—will be more and more important in the modern workplace. Often, interpersonal and creative skills can be developed through in-class collaboration and teamwork, as well as volunteer work, internships, and jobs.[2]

As you read the content and do the exercises in *Keys to Success*, you will grow in every area of the Framework for 21st Century Skills. In fact, the three thinking skills that you will build throughout this course—analytical, creative, and practical thinking—are all included within the framework, and are critical to delivering what the world needs workers to do.

HOW CAN SUCCESSFUL INTELLIGENCE *help you achieve your goals?*

How do you define *intelligence*? Is an intelligent person someone who excels in high-level courses? A successful professional in science or law? Or a person who scores well on standardized tests? Using an IQ (intelligence quotient) test to gauge intelligence and predict success is based on the belief that each person is born with a fixed amount of intelligence. However, cutting-edge researchers such as Robert Sternberg and Carol Dweck have challenged that belief.[3]

When test anxiety caused Sternberg (a psychologist known for his work on intelligence and creativity) to score poorly on IQ and other standardized tests during elementary school, he delivered what was expected of him—very little. However, his fourth-grade teacher turned his life around when she expected more. Sternberg has conducted extensive research showing that traditional intelligence measurements lock people into poor performance and often do not reflect their potential.[4]

Researching how children cope with failure, Stanford psychologist Carol Dweck gave elementary school students a set of puzzles that grew increasingly difficult. To her surprise, certain students welcomed failure as an opportunity. "They knew that human qualities, such as intellectual skills, could be cultivated through effort. . . . Not only weren't they discouraged by failure, they didn't even think they were failing. They thought they were learning."[5] Dweck's research since then has focused on the idea that mindset sets the stage for intellectual growth.

Sternberg's, Dweck's, and others' research suggests that intelligence is *not* fixed; people have the capacity to increase intelligence. In other words, the risk of effort and focus can produce the reward of greater brain power. Studies in neuroscience show that a learning brain can develop throughout life. Recent research shows that when you learn, your brain and nerve cells (neurons) form new connections (synapses) among one another by growing new branches (dendrites).[6] These increased connections then enable the brain to do and learn more.

The Three Thinking Skills

How can you take productive risks that move you toward your important goals in college, work, and life? According to Sternberg, it takes three types of thinking: analytical (critical), creative, and practical. Together, he calls them *successful intelligence*,[7] a concept that he illustrates with a story of a book-smart boy and a street-smart boy running from a bear in the forest. While the book-smart boy is figuring out the exact amount of time they have before being attacked, the street-smart boy puts on his running shoes and dashes off, having realized that he only needed to outrun the first boy in order to survive. [8]

This story shows that successful goal achievement and problem solving requires more than book smarts. When confronted with a problem, using *only* analytical thinking put the first boy at a disadvantage. On the other hand, the second boy *analyzed* the situation, *created* options, and took practical *action*. He took the wisest risk and earned his reward: living to tell the tale.

How Thinking Skills Move You toward Your Goals

Sternberg explains that although those who score well on tests display strong recall and analytical skills, they are not necessarily able to put their knowledge to work.[9] No matter how high you score on a library science test, for example, as a librarian you will also need to devise useful keyword searches (creative thinking) and communicate with patrons (practical thinking). Of course, having only practical "street smarts" isn't enough either. Neither boy in the bear story, if rushed to the hospital with injuries sustained in a showdown with the bear, would want to be treated by medical personnel lacking in analytical skills.

What does each of the three thinking skills contribute to goal achievement?

- Commonly known as *critical thinking*, analytical thinking starts with engaging with information through asking questions and then involves analyzing and evaluating information, often to work through a problem or decision. It often involves comparing, contrasting, and cause-and-effect thinking.
- Creative thinking involves generating new and different ideas and approaches to solving problems, and, often, viewing the world in ways that disregard convention. It can involve imagining and considering different perspectives. Creative thinking also means taking information that you already know and thinking about it in a new way.
- Practical thinking refers to putting what you've learned into action to solve a problem or make a decision. Practical thinking often means learning from experience and emotional intelligence (explained later in the chapter), enabling you to work effectively with others and to accomplish goals despite obstacles.

Together, these abilities move you toward a goal, as Sternberg explains:

> Analytical thinking is required to solve problems and to judge the quality of ideas. Creative intelligence is required to formulate good problems and ideas in the first place. Practical intelligence is needed to use the ideas and their analysis in an effective way in one's everyday life.[10]

get analytical

DEFINE YOUR "COLLEGE SELF"

Complete the following on paper or in digital format.

When you understand who you are as a student, you will be more able to seek out the support that will propel you toward your goals. Using the following questions as a starting point, analyze and describe your "college self." Write and save your description to revisit later in the course.

- What is your student status—traditional or returning, full or part time, resident or commuter?
- How long are you planning to be at your current college? Have you transferred in, or is it likely that you will transfer in the future?
- What goals or rewards do you aim to achieve by going to college?
- What family and work obligations do you have?
- What is your culture, ethnicity, gender, age, lifestyle?
- What are your biggest fears right now, and how do they affect your willingness to take risks?
- What challenges (physical or learning disabilities, emotional issues, language struggles) do you face?
- Has your family gone to college for generations, or are you a first-generation student?
- What do you like to study, and why does it interest you?

The following example illustrates how this works.

The goal-achieving thinking skills of Raider Estrada.

- He *analyzed* his situation when hiding out from the police, and determined that he would experience more reward from the risk of turning himself in.
- He *created* a vision of himself as a high school graduate and a college student.
- He took *practical action* to get help from teachers and counselors and risked time and effort to earn his high school diploma and apply for college.

Why is developing successful intelligence so important to your success?

1. *It improves understanding and achievement, increasing your value in school and on the job.* People with critical, creative, and practical thinking skills are in demand because they can apply what they know to new situations, be innovative, and accomplish their goals.

2. *It boosts your motivation.* Because it helps you understand how learning propels you toward goals and gives you ways to move toward those goals, it increases your willingness to risk.

3. *It shows you where you can grow.* Students who have trouble with analytical skills can see the role that creative and practical thinking play. Students who test well but have trouble innovating or taking action can improve creative and practical skills.

get $mart

ORGANIZE YOUR FINANCES

Avoid discovering that stack of bills, statements, and receipts at midterm time. Set yourself up to stay aware and in control of your day-to-day financial activities:

1. Find a place to store financial paperwork—perhaps a file drawer or filing box—and set up folders for each category (bank statements, tuition/financial aid, paid bills, and so on).

2. If you want to pay some or all of your bills online, set up online payments with those accounts. If you can choose due dates, cluster your due dates together at the same time of the month so you can pay bills all at once.

3. Make sure that you are set up to stay on top of tuition payments and financial aid responsibilities. Note payment or financial aid filing deadlines in your planner, phone calendar, or online calendar. Consider setting smartphone reminders and alarms.

Although thinking skills provide tools with which you can achieve college and life goals, you need motivation to put them to work and gain rewards from your efforts. Explore a mindset that will motivate you to vault over that bar (and perhaps set a higher one).

> MOTIVATION
> A goal-directed force that moves a person to action.

HOW CAN A "GROWTH MINDSET"
motivate you to persist?

Different people have different forces or *motivators*—grades, love of a subject, the drive to earn a degree—that encourage them to keep pushing ahead. Motivators can change with time and situations. Your motivation can have either an external or internal *locus of control*, meaning that you are motivated by external factors (your parents, circumstances, luck, grades or instructors' feedback, and so on) or internal factors (values and attitudes).

Internal motivation may have a greater influence on success, because although you cannot control what happens around you, you *can* control your attitude, or *mindset*. Based on years of research, Carol Dweck has determined that the perception that talent and intelligence can develop with effort—what she calls a *growth mindset*—promotes success. "This view creates a love of learning and resilience that is essential for great accomplishment," reports Dweck.[11] By contrast, people with a *fixed mindset* believe that they have a set level of talent and intelligence, and they tend to work and risk less. "In one world [that of the fixed mindset], effort is a bad thing. It . . . means you're not smart or talented. If you were, you wouldn't need effort. In the other world [growth mindset], effort is what *makes* you smart or talented."[12]

For example, two students do poorly on an anatomy midterm. One blames the time of day of the test and says she is horrible in science, while the other feels that it was a challenging test and she didn't put in enough study time. The first student couldn't change the material or class time, of course, and didn't see the point of changing her approach to the material (no risk or extra effort). As you may expect, she did poorly on the final. The second student put in more study time after the midterm

(risk and increased effort) and improved her grade on the final as a result. This student knows that the risk of focused effort brings valuable reward.

You don't have to be born with a growth mindset; you can build one. "You have a choice," says Dweck. "Mindsets are just beliefs. They're powerful beliefs, but they're just something in your mind, and you can change your mind."[13] Actions that may help you change your mind include being responsible, practicing academic integrity, and facing adversity with optimism.

Build Self-Esteem with Responsible Actions

You may think that you need to have strong self-esteem to take action toward your goals. In fact, the reverse is true. Taking responsible action builds strong self-esteem because it gives you something to be proud of. Your actions change your thinking. Basketball coach Rick Pitino explains: "If you have established a great work ethic and have begun the discipline that is inherent with that, you will automatically begin to feel better about yourself."[14]

A growth mindset helps you build self-esteem because it encourages you to put forth effort. If you know you can earn the reward of accomplishing something, you will be more likely to risk trying. A research study of employees taking a course in computer training supports this idea. Half of the employees were told their success depended on innate ability, and these people lost confidence by the end of the course. By contrast, the other half were told that their skills could be developed through practice, and they reported a good deal *more* confidence after they had completed the same course and made, in many cases, the same mistakes.[15]

Even simple responsible actions can build the foundation for powerful self-esteem. What actions will you take to build your confidence? Consider using Key 1.4 as a starting point for ideas. Taking daily responsible actions such as these will help you to succeed in any course. Your efforts will enable you to grow no matter what your starting point.

SELF-ESTEEM
Belief in one's value as a person that builds as you achieve your goals.

Practice Academic Integrity

Each action you take in college has an effect that shapes your immediate experience and perhaps your life. Although academic integrity may seem to consist of two basic rules—don't cheat on tests and don't use copied, unattributed material in papers and projects—it encompasses far more. Having academic integrity means taking action based on *ethics* (your sense of what is right to do) and a value of hard work. The International Center for Academic Integrity (ICAI) defines academic integrity as a commitment to five fundamental values:[16]

ACADEMIC INTEGRITY
Following a code of moral values in all aspects of academic life, such as classes, assignments, tests, papers, projects, and relationships with students and faculty.

- *Honesty.* Honesty defines the pursuit of knowledge and implies a search for truth in your classwork, papers, and lab reports, and your teamwork with other students.
- *Trust.* Trust means being true to your word. Mutual trust—between instructor and student, as well as among students—makes the exchange of ideas possible.
- *Fairness.* Instructors must create a fair academic environment where students are judged against clear standards and in which procedures are well defined.
- *Respect.* In a respectful academic environment, both students and instructors accept and honor a wide range of opinions, even if the opinions are contrary to core beliefs.
- *Responsibility.* You are responsible for making choices that will provide you with the best education—choices that reflect fairness and honesty.

KEY 1.4 Success often depends on the basics.

Moving towards graduation...

Seek help when needed

Study for exams

Complete assignments on schedule

Listen attentively, take notes, and participate in discussions

Attend class on time and with a positive attitude

Notice that students are not the only ones who need to act with integrity. Bill Taylor, emeritus professor of political science at Oakton Community College in Des Plaines, Illinois, wrote a letter to his students explaining that academic integrity makes requirements of both students and instructors, and that these requirements are in five distinct areas, as detailed in Key 1.5.[17]

The role of electronic materials

With a few clicks of a mouse, any amount of digitized text can be instantly copied and pasted into a document that a student is creating for an assignment. Furthermore, the availability of electronic information has led many students to believe that it has no author and is free to use without citation.[18] As a result of these technological developments, plagiarism has become more prevalent in recent years.

> **PLAGIARISM**
> Using another writer's words, content, unique approach, or illustrations without crediting the author.

In this environment, it's easy to plagiarize without even knowing it, for example by copying something from a website that doesn't list an author and forgetting to go back and determine the source of the material. However, the fact that technology makes plagiarism quick and easy does not make it acceptable. To avoid plagiarism, use this one general directive: Do not submit as your own any words you did not write or any image you did not create. Resources must be properly cited and either quoted (if used word-for-word) or paraphrased. The effort and attention that following this rule requires are no more than what true learning demands.

Note that even as technology facilitates plagiarism, it presents tools to detect it. Sites like Turnitin.com allow instructors to check student work for plagiarism, and WriteCheck helps students do the same with their own work before submitting it.

Violations, regulations, and consequences

Violations of academic integrity include turning in previously submitted work, using unauthorized devices during an exam, providing unethical aid to another

KEY 1.5 Academic integrity involves both students and instructors.

AREAS OF ACTION	ACADEMIC INTEGRITY REQUIRES THAT STUDENTS . . .	ACADEMIC INTEGRITY REQUIRES THAT INSTRUCTORS . . .
Preparation for class	• Read assigned materials before class • Come up with questions • Be prepared to contribute	• Know the material they are teaching • Plan a class that is worth students' time
In class	• Treat instructors and other students with respect • Arrive and leave on time • Participate in discussions • Ask questions and pay attention	• Treat students with respect • Arrive and leave on time • Use class time well
With regard to exams	• Be as prepared as possible • Not use cheat sheets • Not copy or get help from another student • Not give help to another student	• Prepare students effectively • Create a fair exam • Be available to help students prepare • Grade fairly
With regard to written assignments	• Take the time you need to do good work • Hand in work that is entirely your own, not copied from another person's work or from work you've done in another course • Cite sources for ideas, facts, and excerpts completely and according to guidelines	• Clearly explain assignments • Create assignments that relate effectively to coursework • Evaluate carefully and grade fairly
With regard to your final grade	• Do your best on all aspects that are incorporated in your final grade • Consult the instructor if you feel your grade is unfair	• Weigh all aspects involved in the grade, as defined in the syllabus • Grade fairly

Source: William M. Taylor, Oakton Community College, Des Plaines, IL, "Academic Integrity: A Letter to My Students" (http://www.academicintegrity.org/educational_resources/pdf/LetterToMyStudentsRev2010.pdf).

student, and downloading passages or whole papers from the Internet. Consequences of violations vary from school to school and include academic integrity seminars, grade reduction or course failure, suspension, or expulsion. Many schools have legal systems that investigate and try accused students in a court-like atmosphere, with decisions made by honor council members (often a mix of students and faculty members).

When you enrolled, you agreed to abide by your school's code of honor or academic integrity policy. Find it in your student handbook, on the school website, or in your syllabus, and read it thoroughly so you know exactly what it asks of you. Measure the consequences of violating the policy against the risk of working hard to complete your degree with integrity. Which reward would you choose?

How academic integrity benefits you now and in the future

It may seem that a slip here and there is no big deal. However, as Professor Taylor states in his letter, "Personal integrity is . . . a quality of character we need to nurture, and this requires practice in both meanings of that word (as in practice the piano and practice a profession). We can only be a person of integrity if we practice it every day."[19] Finally, know that a growth mindset can help. Because academic integrity comes naturally to students who aim to grow and see struggle and failure as opportunities to learn, maintaining a growth mindset promotes academic integrity and makes its rewards more obvious (see Key 1.6).

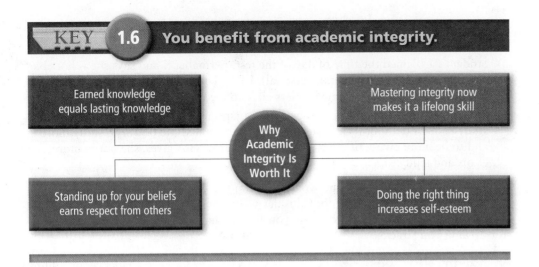

KEY · 1.6 · **You benefit from academic integrity.**

- Earned knowledge equals lasting knowledge
- Mastering integrity now makes it a lifelong skill

Why Academic Integrity Is Worth It

- Standing up for your beliefs earns respect from others
- Doing the right thing increases self-esteem

Face Fears, Challenges, and Failures with Optimism

Every single person experiences adversity in the form of fears, challenges, and failures. Dr. Martin Seligman, a psychologist who has spent most of his career studying how and why some people persist and cope with bad things successfully while others give up and give in, has determined that optimism greatly improves one's chances for life success. He presents what he calls *learned optimism* as a skill that can be learned and used by anyone, no matter how optimistic or pessimistic a person may be naturally.[20]

Your explanatory style

Through extensive research, Dr. Seligman has determined that *explanatory style*—how you explain and think about adversity—predicts how well you are able to cope with it, learn from it, and move on. Furthermore, an optimistic explanatory style has been proven to contribute to better physical health, less depression, and more personal and professional success. Key 1.7 describes the optimistic and pessimistic sides to the three aspects of how people explain adversity.

Explanatory style and the growth mindset

Using an optimistic explanatory style goes hand-in-hand with maintaining a growth mindset in the face of adversity. When you believe that you can learn and improve, you are more able to see a problem as temporary, specific, and not personal, and to manage it and move on.

KEY · 1.7 · **Adversity can be explained optimistically or pessimistically.**

ASPECTS OF EXPLANATORY STYLE	OPTIMISTIC PERSPECTIVE	PESSIMISTIC PERSPECTIVE
Permanence: how long the adversity will last	*Temporary*: "It's not forever; it is tough but it will pass."	*Permanent*: "It will always be like this for me."
Pervasiveness: how far ranging the effect of the adversity is	*Specific*: "This situation is bad but there are good things going on in other areas of my life."	*General*: "Every part of my life is like this. Everything is a catastrophe."
Personalization: what is to blame for the adversity	*External*: "There are some specific causes for this failure that I can examine."	*Personal*: "This is all my fault. I'm a failure."

How can you put an optimistic explanatory style to work for you? For an example, look again at those two anatomy students.

- Student #1 blamed the time of day of the test (permanent) and says she is horrible at science (permanent, general, personal). Faced with problems that she feels she can never change, she became helpless and stopped trying.
- Student #2 thought it was a challenging test (specific, not personal) and she didn't study enough (temporary). Understanding that she had the power to study more and to be more aware of the type of tests this instructor gives, she put in more effort and study time.

The second student has done what an optimistic explanatory style and a growth mindset give you the power to do: Consider what you can do better, take action, and learn from the experience. Here's how you follow that lead the next time something stops you in your tracks.

Analyze the situation realistically. Look carefully at the fear, challenge, or failure and what has caused it. For example, imagine that you forgot about a U.S. history paper. If your first thought is that your memory is useless, get yourself off that pessimistic path to helplessness by looking at some facts. First, you had a chemistry test on the day that the paper was due, and you spent most of that week studying for it. Second, you have not checked your calendar consistently over the week. Third, chemistry is required for the associate's degree you are considering.

Come up with potential actions. You can request an appointment with the instructor to discuss the paper. You can set alarms in your planner and check due dates more regularly. Realizing that chemistry is a priority for you, you can accept that it's okay to put it first when time is short.

Take action and cope with consequences. Meet with your history instructor to discuss the situation, accepting that there may be consequences for handing in your paper late. Commit to better monitoring of your planner, perhaps setting dates for individual tasks related to assignments and trying to complete papers a day or two before they are due so you have time for last-minute corrections.

Failure approached with a growth mindset can spark motivation, showing you what you can do better and driving you to improve. Keep in mind that increased effort in the face of failure is a hallmark of successful people. Thomas Edison, one of the most prolific inventors in the history of the United States, and his employees tried over 3,000 different materials before finding the material they originally used as a filament in the electric bulb. His ability to see each "failure" as a step closer to the right answer enabled him to persist.

talk risk and reward . . .

Risk asking tough questions to be rewarded with new insights. Use the following questions to inspire discussion with classmates, either in person or online.

- Describe a dream you have that you feel is out of reach. Why does it feel impossible? Why do you still dream it? How might a growth mindset help you achieve it?

- How do you tend to respond to a challenge? Do you risk dealing with it, run away, ignore it? What tends to result from your action (or inaction)?

CONSIDER THE CASE: If you knew Raider Estrada in his teen years when he was a member of the gang, would you have thought that he had any hope of going to college? Moving in a new direction, for him, resulted from his stepmother's risk-taking. Who believes in you, and what do they risk for you? What do they think you can achieve?

get creative

CONSIDER HOW TO CONNECT

Complete the following on paper or in digital format.

Making early connections with people and groups in your school can benefit you later on. List and describe your ideas about how you would like to spend whatever time you have available outside of your obligations (class time, work, family). Try one or more of the following questions as a starting point:

- If you had no fear of risk, for what horizon-broadening experience would you sign up?

- When you were in elementary school, what were your favorite activities? Which ones might translate into current interests and pursuits?

- What kinds of organizations, activities, groups, experiences, or people make you think "Wow, I want to do that"?

- Think about the people that you feel bring out the best in you. What do you like to do with them? With what kinds of activities are they involved?

Although adversity can raise all kinds of emotional reactions, people who can manage those emotions are more likely to learn from the experience. They also demonstrate the last of this chapter's ingredients in the recipe for success—emotional intelligence.

WHY DO YOU NEED
emotional intelligence?

Success in a diverse world depends on relationships, and effective relationships demand emotional intelligence. Psychologists John Mayer, Peter Salovey, and David Caruso define *emotional intelligence* (EI) as the ability to understand "one's own and others' emotions and the ability to use this information as a guide to thinking and behavior."[21] An emotionally intelligent person uses an understanding of emotions to make choices about how to think and how to act.

Modern neuroscience holds that thought and emotion function together in the brain and depend on one another. One particular research project showed that brain-injured patients who cannot perceive their own feelings experience severe difficulty in thinking, highlighting the importance of emotion.[22] "Emotions influence both what we think about and how we think," says Caruso. "We cannot check our emotions at the door because emotions and thought are linked – they cannot, and should not, be separated."[23]

Emotions also connect you to other people. Research has demonstrated that the brain and nervous system have cells called mirror neurons. When a friend of yours is happy, sad, or fearful, you may experience similar feelings out of concern or friendship. An MRI brain scan would show that the same area of your friend's brain that lit up during this emotional experience lit up in your brain as well.[24]

MIRROR NEURONS
Specialized brain cells that fire both when a person performs an action and when that person watches someone else perform an action.

15

How Emotional Intelligence Promotes Success

Two short stories illustrate the power of emotional intelligence.

1. Two applicants are competing for a job at your office. The first has every skill the job requires, but doesn't respond well to cues when you interview him. He answers questions indirectly and keeps going back to what he wants to say. The second isn't as skilled, but you feel during the interview as though you are talking with a friend. He listens carefully, picks up on emotional cues, and communicates a strong willingness to learn on the job. Whom would you hire?

2. Two students are part of your group for a project. One always gets her share of the job done but has no patience for anyone who misses a deadline. She is quick to criticize group members. The other is sometimes prepared, sometimes not, but responds thoughtfully to what is going on with the group. She makes up for it when she hasn't gotten everything done, and when she is on top of her tasks she helps others. Whom would you work with again?

To be clear: Skills are crucial. However, emotional intelligence in communication and relationships is a necessary component of success along with job-specific skills. Research using an assessment measuring emotional intelligence (MSCEIT) shows how strongly it predicts work and life success:[25]

- Emotionally intelligent people are more competent in social situations.
- Managers in the workplace with high emotional intelligence have more productive working relationships.
- Employees scoring high in emotional intelligence were more likely to receive positive ratings and raises.

The bottom line is that more emotional intelligence means stronger relationships and more goal achievement.

Emotional intelligence helps you build positive and productive relationships in and out of college.

The Abilities of Emotional Intelligence

Emotional intelligence is a set of skills, or abilities, that can be described as *reasoning with emotion* (an idea illustrating how thought and emotion work together). Key 1.8 shows how you move through these skills when you reason with emotion.

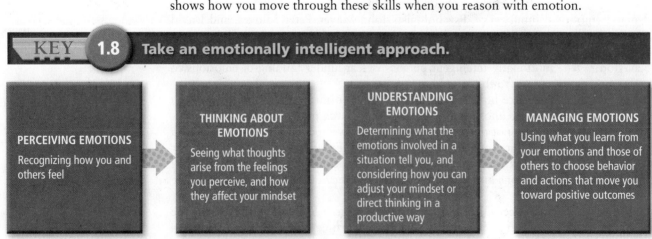

KEY 1.8 Take an emotionally intelligent approach.

PERCEIVING EMOTIONS
Recognizing how you and others feel

THINKING ABOUT EMOTIONS
Seeing what thoughts arise from the feelings you perceive, and how they affect your mindset

UNDERSTANDING EMOTIONS
Determining what the emotions involved in a situation tell you, and considering how you can adjust your mindset or direct thinking in a productive way

MANAGING EMOTIONS
Using what you learn from your emotions and those of others to choose behavior and actions that move you toward positive outcomes

Source: Adapted from Mayer, John D., Peter Salovey, and David R. Caruso, "Emotional Intelligence: New Ability or Eclectic Traits?" *American Psychologist,* vol. 63, no. 6, pp. 505–507. September 2008. Reprinted by Permission of the American Psychological Association.

get practical

USE EMOTIONAL INTELLIGENCE TO GET INVOLVED

Complete the following on paper or in digital format.

First, look in your student handbook at the resources and organizations your school offers. These may include some or all of the following:

Academic centers (reading, writing, etc.)
Academic organizations
Adult education center
Arts clubs (music, drama, dance, etc.)
Fraternities/Sororities
Groups for students with disabilities
International student groups
Minority student groups

On-campus work opportunities
Religious organizations
School publications
School TV/radio stations
Sports clubs
Student associations
Student government
Volunteer groups

As you read the list, take note of how different organizations or activities make you feel. What interests you right away? What makes you turn the page? What scares you? What thoughts do your feelings raise—for example, why do you think you like or fear a particular activity? Is a positive outcome possible from trying something that scares you at first?

Thinking about this emotional intelligence feedback as well as your self-analysis from other exercises, risk trying some new experiences. List three offices or organizations you plan to explore this term. Then, using school publications or online resources, find and record the following information for each:

- Location

- Hours, or times of meetings

- What it offers

- Phone number, web site, or e-mail

Finally, when you have made contact, note what happened and whether you are considering getting involved.

As you encounter references to emotional intelligence in this course and elsewhere, think of it as *thinking skills applied to relationships.* Putting emotional intelligence to work means taking in and analyzing how you and others feel, seeing the ideas those feelings create, and taking action in response—all with the purpose of achieving a goal.

HOW WILL YOUR WORK NOW PREPARE *you for life success?*

This text is designed to help you build what you need for success in school and beyond, including thinking skills, attitudes, and emotional abilities that you can use to reach your goals. Topics will broaden your understanding, and exercises will have you put it into action in personal and productive ways. Self-assessments and journal questions will encourage reflection. Your thinking skills will grow and will transfer to any task or situation in your life.

One of the most essential skills you will build is *learning for life*. The signs in Key 1.9 point to the need to be a lifelong learner, continuing to build knowledge and skills as your career and life demand. Your work in this course will help you fulfill that need.

Finally, you will strengthen your ability and willingness to take calculated risks large and small. You will find threaded throughout this text the concept of targeted, productive risk leading to a desired reward. In everything you approach in life, a reward waits in exchange for your risk. Here are just a few examples of how to take action, earn rewards, and build your risk-taking habit while in college:

- Risk looking confused by asking a question in class or in an online class forum, for the reward of greater understanding.
- Risk the time it takes to match or exceed your abilities on a project, for the reward of increased knowledge and skill (and perhaps an excellent grade).
- Risk the awkwardness of reaching out to an instructor, for the reward of a relationship that can deepen your academic experience and perhaps provide career guidance.

KEY 1.9 A changing world means learning is for life.

If you stop learning, your knowledge base will be inadequate to keep up with the changes in your career, thus affecting your marketability.

The Internet and technology will shape communications and improve knowledge and productivity during the next 20 years—and will require continual learning.

Knowledge in nearly every field is doubling every two to three years.

Technology is changing how you live and work.

The global economy is moving from a product and service base to a knowledge and talent base.

Workers are changing jobs and careers more frequently.

In the United States and abroad, jobs are being created that ask workers to think critically to come up with solutions.

Every time you decide to start a new career, you need new knowledge and skills.

student PROFILE

Zack Moore
UNIVERSITY OF RHODE ISLAND, KINGSTON

About me:

I major in communications, have added a business minor, and play wide receiver on the URI (University of Rhode Island) football team. Although I have some great mentors in several fields, I am not sure what my career choice will be. I hope to play football for as long as possible, but when I am done on the field, I might like to become a motivational speaker, open a warehouse-style gym, or help my grandfather run Horseless Carriage Carriers, his automobile transportation business.

What I focus on:

Ever since I was a toddler, my parents encouraged me to interact with as many people as possible. My life experiences have brought me in contact with people of many backgrounds, ages, races, and beliefs. I've developed an ability to carry on a conversation with practically anyone about practically anything. I like to think that I make as great an impact on people I meet as they often do on me.

Two years into my college career, I find it interesting to look back at how far I have come since arriving at summer football camp before my freshman year. Not only have I learned a lot in the classroom, but daily interactions with classmates, professors, teammates, coaches, roommates, and others in the college community have shaped me in ways that I would never have anticipated.

To me, college is a place where I am exploring who I am, gaining a better understanding of what makes others tick, and figuring out who I will be when I enter the professional world.

What will help me in the workplace:

While I don't know exactly what I will do with my life, I believe that the communication, social, and emotional skills I am developing each day will help me succeed in whatever career I choose.

- Risk the work required to prepare for a test rather than cheating, for the reward of learning you can use in higher-level courses or in the workplace—as well as the habit of integrity, which is essential for life success.
- Risk saying no to a substance or activity for the reward of greater health, even if it costs you a friend or an affiliation.

Imagine that you are sitting in class with your *growth mindset*, ready to risk and learn. You are prepared to use analytical and creative skills to examine knowledge and come up with new ideas. You are motivated to use your practical skills to move toward your goals. Your emotional intelligence has prepared you to adjust to and work with all kinds of people. The bar has been raised: Risk using *Keys to Success* to fly over it and find out just how much reward waits for you.

revisit RISK AND REWARD

What happened to Raider? All too aware of the consequences of falling back into anger, Raider risked working hard and challenged himself to sit in the front row in every class. "All the students were smarter than I was," he says, "but I worked a lot harder than they did." His work rewarded him with two years of straight As. Raider completed his undergraduate degree at Pepperdine, keeping the hard work going despite failing chemistry more than once. He then earned a medical degree from Georgetown University Medical School and completed his internship and residency at the University of Chicago Medicine.

Now married, a father, and a fellow in cardiology, he plans to continue taking productive risks by focusing his medical practice on disadvantaged communities similar to where he grew up. He also speaks out—both in person and in a public service announcement made by the California Wellness Foundation's Violence Prevention Initiative—about the public health issue of violence, hoping to save children and families from its brutal consequences.

What does this mean for you? Everyone has challenges to either face with risk-taking or avoid. These roadblocks can serve as opportunities to find out what you are capable of. Name a challenge—or challenges—that you face now. Consider what might happen if you avoid this challenge. On the other hand, consider what growth and rewards wait for you if you risk facing it with hard work. As you think the situation through, be specific about what that hard work looks like.

What risk may bring reward beyond your world? Part of Raider's mission as a successful professional is to reach out to families and young people who need him as a role model. Although you might not think of yourself as a role model, the fact that you are here beginning college says that you have something to offer. Think outside yourself and consider who looks up to you—a younger family member, a friend still in high school, someone in your neighborhood, someone you know from an online group. Consciously act as a role model to that person. You may be surprised at how your actions can provide rewards for others.

RISK ACTION

FOR COLLEGE, CAREER, AND LIFE REWARDS

Complete the following on paper or in digital format.

KNOW IT *Think Critically*

Activate Yourself

Robert Sternberg found that people who reach their goals successfully have 20 particular characteristics in common that motivate them to persist.[26] Each of the "I" statements in the list below identifies one of the characteristics.

Build basic skills. Use this self-assessment to see how well you think you can get motivated *right now*.

1	2	3	4	5
Not at All Like Me	Somewhat Unlike Me	Not Sure	Somewhat Like Me	Definitely Like Me

Please circle the number that best represents your answer:

1. I motivate myself well.   1 2 3 4 5

2. I can control my impulses.   1 2 3 4 5

3. I know when to persevere and when to change gears.   1 2 3 4 5

4. I make the most of what I do well.   1 2 3 4 5

5. I can successfully translate my ideas into action.   1 2 3 4 5

6. I can focus effectively on my goal.   1 2 3 4 5

7. I complete tasks and have good follow-through.   1 2 3 4 5

8. I initiate action—I move people and projects ahead.   1 2 3 4 5

9. I have the courage to risk failure.   1 2 3 4 5

10. I avoid procrastination.   1 2 3 4 5

11. I accept responsibility when I make a mistake.   1 2 3 4 5

12. I don't waste time feeling sorry for myself.   1 2 3 4 5

13. I independently take responsibility for tasks.   1 2 3 4 5

14. I work hard to overcome personal difficulties.   1 2 3 4 5

15. I create an environment that helps me concentrate on my goals.   1 2 3 4 5

16. I don't take on too much work or too little.   1 2 3 4 5

17. I can delay gratification to receive the benefits.   1 2 3 4 5

18. I can see both the big picture and the details in a situation.   1 2 3 4 5

19. I am able to maintain confidence in myself.   1 2 3 4 5

20. I can balance analytical, creative, and practical thinking skills.   1 2 3 4 5

Take it to the next level. Choose three characteristics you most want to develop throughout the term. Circle or highlight them on the self-assessment. Then, pretend to be an instructor recommending you for a job. On a separate sheet of paper or digital file, write a short email about the ways in which you display strength in those three characteristics. Set a goal to deserve those compliments in the future.

Move toward mastery. Select one of your three chosen characteristics. Then do the following:

1. Find material in your text that will help you develop this characteristic. If you wish to procrastinate less, for example, look for information on time management.
2. Skim the section you find and note a concept or strategy that catches your attention. Copy it onto paper or into an electronic file. Briefly describe how you plan to use it.
3. Take action in the next week based on your plan. You are on the road to growth.

In your course, you may have the opportunity to revisit this self-assessment and get more specific about actions you have taken, and plan to take, to promote personal growth.

WRITE IT *Communicate*

Emotional intelligence journal: How you are feeling now. First, describe what you are feeling right now about college. What do those feelings tell you about how ready you are for the experience? Generate ideas for actions that will help you be as prepared as possible to benefit from the experience of college. (For example, if shyness prevents you from feeling ready to meet new people on campus, one action might be to join an organization or study group that will help you get to know people more easily.)

Real-life writing: Skills you have now. No matter what professional goals you ultimately pursue, the skills that the 21st century workplace demands will be useful in any career area. Look back at Key 1.3 to remind yourself of the four skill areas, and the individual skills within each category, defined as essential for 21st century success. Identify three skills you have already built and can demonstrate. For each skill, write a short paragraph that contains the following elements:

- A description of your abilities in this skill area
- Specific examples, from school or work, demonstrating these abilities
- Jobs or coursework in which you have built this skill

   Keep this information on hand for when you build a resume—or, if you already have a resume, use it to update your information and add detail that will keep your resume current.

WORK IT *Build Your Brand*

Assess Your Successful Intelligence

A "brand" is an image or concept that people connect with a product or service. A key factor in your ability to succeed in the modern workplace is your ability to "build your brand." Identify the qualities and skills that best define you, and emphasize them in how you market yourself. Seeing yourself as a product can help you work to package that product in the best possible way.

   Compiling a portfolio of personal documents can help you build your brand as you work toward career exploration and planning goals. This is one of several that you may create throughout the term. Type your work and save the documents electronically in one file folder. Use loose paper for assignments that ask you to draw or make collages, and make copies of assignments that ask you to write in the text. For safekeeping, scan and save loose or text pages to include in your portfolio file.

21st Century Learning Building Blocks

- **Initiative and self-direction**
- **Critical thinking and problem solving**

   As you begin this course, use this exercise to get a big-picture look at how you perceive yourself as an analytical, creative, and practical thinker. For the statements in each of the three self-assessments, circle the number that best describes how often it applies to you.

Assess Your Analytical Thinking Skills

For each statement, circle the number that feels right to you, from 1 for "not at all true for me" to 5 for "very true for me."

1. I recognize and define problems effectively. 1 2 3 4 5

2. I see myself as a thinker and as analytical and studious. 1 2 3 4 5

3. When working on a problem in a group setting, I like to break down the problem into its components and evaluate them. 1 2 3 4 5

4. I need to see convincing evidence before accepting information as fact. 1 2 3 4 5

5. I weigh the pros and cons of plans and ideas before taking action. 1 2 3 4 5

6. I tend to make connections among bits of information by categorizing them. 1 2 3 4 5

7. Impulsive, spontaneous decision-making worries me. 1 2 3 4 5

8. I like to analyze causes and effects when making a decision. 1 2 3 4 5

9. I monitor my progress toward goals. 1 2 3 4 5

10. Once I reach a goal, I evaluate the process to see how effective it was. 1 2 3 4 5

Total your answers here: _____

Assess Your Creative Thinking Skills

For each statement, circle the number that feels right to you, from 1 for "not at all true for me" to 5 for "very true for me."

1. I tend to question rules and regulations. 1 2 3 4 5

2. I see myself as unique, full of ideas, and innovative. 1 2 3 4 5

3. When working on a problem in a group setting, I generate a lot of ideas. 1 2 3 4 5

4. I am energized when I have a brand-new experience. 1 2 3 4 5

5. If you say something is too risky, I'm ready to give it a shot. 1 2 3 4 5

6. I often wonder if there is a different way to do or see something. 1 2 3 4 5

7. Too much routine in my work or schedule drains my energy. 1 2 3 4 5

8. I tend to see connections among ideas that others do not. 1 2 3 4 5

9. I feel comfortable allowing myself to make mistakes as I test out ideas. 1 2 3 4 5

10. I'm willing to champion an idea even when others disagree with me. 1 2 3 4 5

Total your answers here: _____

Assess Your Practical Thinking Skills

For each statement, circle the number that feels right to you, from 1 for "not at all true for me" to 5 for "very true for me."

1. I can find a way around any obstacle. 1 2 3 4 5

2. I see myself as a doer and the go-to person; I make things happen. 1 2 3 4 5

3. When working on a problem in a group setting, I like to figure out who will do what and when it should be done. 1 2 3 4 5

4. I apply what I learn from experience to improve my response to similar situations.

1 2 3 4 5

5. I finish what I start and don't leave loose ends hanging.

1 2 3 4 5

6. I note my emotions about academic and social situations and use what they tell me to move toward a goal.

1 2 3 4 5

7. I can sense how people feel and use that knowledge to interact with others effectively.

1 2 3 4 5

8. I manage my time effectively.

1 2 3 4 5

9. I adjust to the teaching styles of my instructors and the communication styles of my peers.

1 2 3 4 5

10. When involved in a problem-solving process, I can shift gears as needed.

1 2 3 4 5

Total your answers here: _____

With your scores in hand, use the Wheel of Successful Intelligence to look of all the skills at once. In each of the three areas of the wheel, draw a curved line approximately at the level of the number of your score and fill in the wedge below that line. What does the wheel show about the balance you perceive in your three thinking skills? If it were a real wheel, would it roll?

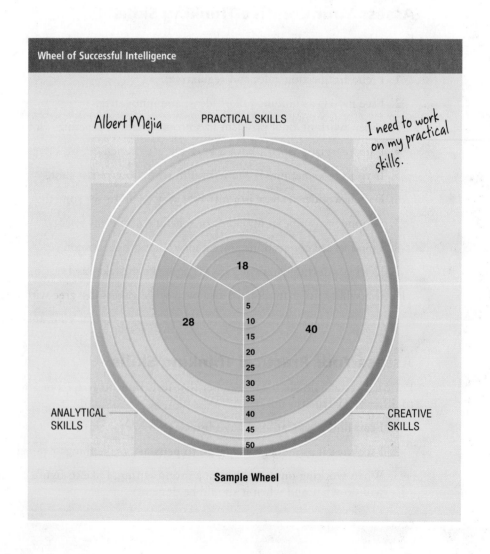

Sample Wheel

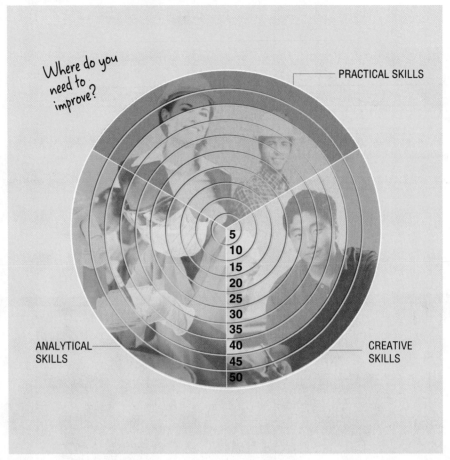

Where do you need to improve?

PRACTICAL SKILLS

ANALYTICAL SKILLS

CREATIVE SKILLS

5
10
15
20
25
30
35
40
45
50

Source: Based on "The Wheel of Life" model developed by the Coaches Training Institute. © Co-Active Space 2000.

Based on the appearance of the wheel, in which skill do you most need to build strength? Keep this goal in mind as you proceed through the term.

2

Values are the foundation of effective goal setting and time management. You are most motivated to achieve goals and accomplish tasks that reflect what is most important to you.

Values, Goals, and Time

MANAGING YOURSELF

What Would You Risk? *Sarah Martinez*

THINK ABOUT THIS SITUATION AS YOU READ, AND CONSIDER WHAT ACTION YOU WOULD TAKE. THIS CHAPTER TAKES A CLOSER LOOK AT YOUR PERSONAL VALUES, THE GOALS YOU SET REFLECTING THOSE VALUES, AND HOW YOU MANAGE YOUR TIME TO ACHIEVE THOSE IMPORTANT GOALS.

When Sarah Martinez was five years old, she began complaining of frequent headaches. Her mother, a nurse, had been noticing how Sarah's left eye looked strange and droopy. She took her daughter to a pediatrician, and after several tests and CT scans the doctors found that Sarah had a rare and malignant tumor called a rhabdomyosarcoma behind her left eye.

This discovery immediately catapulted Sarah and her family into the tumultuous world of cancer treatment. Sarah endured several surgeries, multiple rounds of chemotherapy, and radiation to the left side of her head. During the year over which treatment took place, Sarah spent over 100 days in the hospital. It was a difficult time for Sarah and her family. Luckily, the treatment did the job; Sarah was declared cancer-free. She did have to contend with side effects, including hearing loss and stunted growth from radiation damage. She needed growth hormone shots for five years and now wears a hearing aid in her left ear.

In remission from the cancer, Sarah moved back into a more habitual rhythm of life through the rest of her childhood. As a high school student she was involved in theater and excelled in academics. Things changed, however, during her first year of college at Metro State University. After getting through the first semester she found that living on her own was lonely in a way that she had never experienced. She began to sense that the cancer had left her with more than just physical damage to contend with. Feeling depressed and burnt out, she stopped going to class and lost focus on her studies. She knew something had to change, but wasn't sure what kind of risk would help – or whether she could motivate herself to take a risk at all.

To be continued . . .

STAYING MOTIVATED AND CONNECTED IS AN ESSENTIAL GOAL FOR EVERY STUDENT TRANSITIONING TO COLLEGE. YOU'LL LEARN MORE ABOUT SARAH, AND THE REWARD RESULTING FROM HER ACTIONS, WITHIN THE CHAPTER.

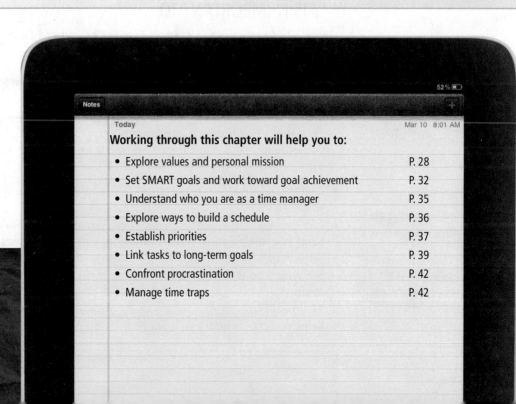

Working through this chapter will help you to:

status CHECK

How Developed Are Your Self-Management Skills?

For each statement, fill in the number that feels right to you, from 1 for "not at all true for me" to 5 for "very true for me."

1. I am aware of my values and beliefs.   ① ② ③ ④ ⑤

2. I have a system for reminding myself of what my goals are.   ① ② ③ ④ ⑤

3. I find ways to motivate myself when I am working toward a goal.   ① ② ③ ④ ⑤

4. When I set a long-term goal, I break it down into a series of short-term goals.   ① ② ③ ④ ⑤

5. I am aware of my time-related needs and preferences.   ① ② ③ ④ ⑤

6. I understand what my time traps are and have ways to avoid them.   ① ② ③ ④ ⑤

7. I know how to use the SMART system to plan achievable goals.   ① ② ③ ④ ⑤

8. I record tasks, events, and responsibilities in a planner and refer to it regularly.   ① ② ③ ④ ⑤

9. When I procrastinate, I know how to get back on track.   ① ② ③ ④ ⑤

10. I understand how minimizing "switch-tasking" can help reduce stress.   ① ② ③ ④ ⑤

Each of the topics in these statements is covered in this chapter. Note those statements where you filled in a 3 or lower. Skim the chapter to see where those topics appear, and pay special attention to them as you read, learn, and apply new strategies.

REMEMBER: NO MATTER HOW EFFECTIVELY YOU SET GOALS AND MANAGE TIME, YOU CAN IMPROVE WITH EFFORT AND PRACTICE.

WHY IS IT IMPORTANT TO
know what you value?

VALUES
principles or qualitites that you consider important.

You make life choices—what to do, what to believe, what to buy, how to act—based on your personal **values**. The choice to pursue a degree, for example, may reflect how you value the personal and professional growth that come from a college education. If you like to be on time for classes, you may value punctuality. If you pay bills regularly and on time, you may value financial stability.

Values help you achieve important goals and use time wisely, because they allow you to:

- *Understand what you want out of life.* Your most meaningful goals reflect what you value most.
- *Choose how to use your valuable time.* When your day-to-day activities align with what you think is most important to do, you gain greater fulfillment from them.
- *Build "rules for life."* Your values form the foundation of your decisions and behavior. You will repeatedly return to them for guidance, especially in unfamiliar territory.
- *Find people who inspire you.* Spending time with people who share similar values helps you clarify how you want to live and provides support for your goals.

MyStudentSuccessLab
(www.mystudentsuccesslab.com) is an online solution designed to help you "Start Strong, Finish Stronger" by building skills for ongoing personal and professional development.

get analytical

EXPLORE YOUR VALUES

Rate each of the values in the list on a scale from 1 to 5, 1 being least important to you and 5 being most important. Write each rating next to the corresponding value.

Knowing yourself	Being liked by others	Reading
Self-improvement	Taking risks	Time to yourself
Improving physical/mental health	Time for fun/relaxation	Lifelong learning
Leadership and teamwork skills	Staying fit through exercise	Competing and winning
Pursuing an education	Spiritual/religious life	Making a lot of money
Good relationships with family	Community involvement	Creative/artistic pursuits
Helping others	Keeping up with the news	Getting a good job
Being organized	Financial stability	Other _____

Complete the following on a sheet of paper or digital file.

1. Write your top three values.

2. Choose one top value that is a factor in an educational choice you have made. Explain the choice and how the value was involved. Example: A student who values financial stability chooses to take a personal finance course.

3. Name an area of study that you think would help you live according to this value.

How Values Develop and Change

Your value system is complex, built piece by piece over time. It comes from many sources—family, friends, culture, media, school, work, neighborhood, religious beliefs, and world events. These powerful external influences can so effectively instill your values that you don't even think about *why* you believe what you believe. However, you have a *choice* whether to adopt any value. Taking advantage of the power to choose requires evaluating values by asking questions like the following:

- Where did the value come from?
- Is this value something from my family or culture that I have accepted without question, or have I truly made it my own?
- What other different values could I consider?
- What might happen as a result of adopting this value?
- Have I made a personal commitment to this choice? Have I told others about it?
- Do my life goals and day-to-day actions reflect this value?

Values often shift over time. For example, Sarah's ordeal changed and reordered her family's values. Life changes make it even more crucial to think about what's truly important to you.

How Values Affect Your Life Experience

Because what you value often determines the choices you make, your values also shape your life experiences. For example, the fact that you value education may have led you to college. The reward of this productive risk is help in building skills and persistence, choosing a major and career direction, finding meaningful friends and activities, and achieving learning goals.

Here's another example: Today's college campuses have increasingly diverse student bodies. This diversity is also seen in the workplace. If you value human differences, going to college is an important step on the way to working successfully with people of various cultures, stages of life, and value systems.

Values become goals when you've transformed your beliefs into something tangible and long lasting. Not every value becomes a goal, but every goal stems from your values.

HOW DO YOU SET
and achieve goals?

GOAL
An end toward which you direct your efforts.

When you set a **goal**, you focus on what you want to achieve and then create a path to get you there. Setting goals involves defining what you are aiming for in both long-term and short-term time frames. *Long-term goals* are broader objectives you want to achieve over a long period of time, perhaps a year or more. *Short-term goals* are smaller steps that move you toward a long-term goal, making it manageable and achievable, piece by piece (see Key 2.1).

Establish Your Personal Mission

Before you get involved setting specific goals, get clear about your *personal mission* in life. This helps you anchor your values and goals to a "big picture" view of what you want out of life. Think of a personal mission as your longest-term goal, within which all other long-term and short-term goals should fit.

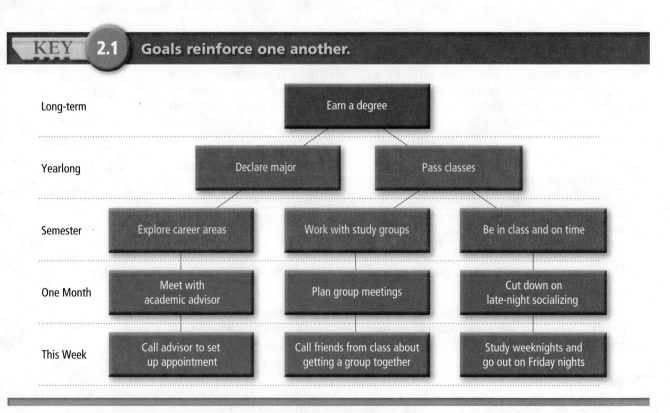

KEY 2.1 **Goals reinforce one another.**

Long-term		Earn a degree	
Yearlong	Declare major		Pass classes
Semester	Explore career areas	Work with study groups	Be in class and on time
One Month	Meet with academic advisor	Plan group meetings	Cut down on late-night socializing
This Week	Call advisor to set up appointment	Call friends from class about getting a group together	Study weeknights and go out on Friday nights

Your personal mission can be spelled out in a mission statement. Dr. Stephen Covey, author of *The Seven Habits of Highly Effective People*, defines a *mission statement* as a philosophy outlining what you want to be (character), the rewards you aim for (contributions and achievements), and the principles by which you live (your values).[1] For example, here is a mission statement written by Carol Carter, one of the authors of *Keys to Success*:

> My mission is to use my talents and abilities to help people of all ages, stages, backgrounds, and economic levels achieve their human potential through fully developing their minds and their talents. I aim to create opportunities for others through work, service, and family. I also aim to balance work with people in my life, understanding that my family and friends are a priority above all else.

How can you start formulating a mission statement? Try using Covey's three aspects of personal mission as a guide. Think through the following:

- *Character.* What aspects of character do you think are most valuable? When you consider the people you admire most, which of their qualities stand out?
- *Contributions and achievements.* What do you want to accomplish in your life? Where do you want to make a difference? What are you willing to risk to make it happen?
- *Values.* How do your values inform your life goals? What in your mission could help you live according to what you value most highly?

What you want out of life changes as you do, so make sure your personal mission remains flexible and open to revision. Think of your mission as a road map for your personal journey. It can give meaning to your daily activities, promote responsibility, and encourage you to take risks that lead you toward the long-term rewards you've laid out. You will have a chance to craft a personal mission at the end of this chapter.

Set Long-Term Goals

What do you want your life to look like in 5 or 10 years? What degree do you want to earn, what job do you want, where do you want to live? How do you want to live your values and activate your personal mission? Answers to questions like these help identify long-term goals.

Long-term goals are goals that sit out on the horizon, at least six months to a year away. They're goals that you can imagine and maybe even visualize, but they're too far away for you to touch. These are goals that outline the rewards you want in a way that reflects who you are and what you value. The more you know about yourself, the better able you are to set and work toward meaningful long-term goals.

Defining long-term goals in terms of the risks needed to achieve them—in other words, the steps that will take you toward them—makes them more reachable. For example, suppose your long-term goal is to become a family doctor and build a business in which you create opportunities to expose young people in your community to the medical field. Now suppose you are in your first year at a community college. You might prepare to move toward this reward with these one-year, long-term goals:

- Find and investigate medical practices in the area that could serve as a model for your business.
- Choose a major or certificate that builds toward a medical degree, and make sure the credits will transfer to a bachelor's degree program.

Achieving academic goals requires focus. It helps to find a place to work that has the materials and technology you need and offers minimal distractions.

To determine your long-term goals, think about the values that anchor your personal mission. For example, if you are someone who values health and fitness, a possible long-term goal might involve working for an organic food company or training as a physical therapist. The stronger the link between your values and your long-term goals, the more motivated and successful you are likely to be in achieving them.

Set Short-Term Goals

Short-term goals narrow your focus and encourage progress toward long-term goals. They can last for as long as several months or as little as an hour. For example, if you have a long-term goal of getting a nursing degree, you might set these short-term goals for the next six months:

- I will learn the names, locations, and functions of every human bone and muscle.
- I will work with a study group to understand the muscular-skeletal system.

You can break down these goals into even smaller parts, such as the following one-month goals:

- I will work with on-screen tutorials of the muscular-skeletal system until I understand and memorize the material.
- I will spend three hours a week with my study partners.

Short-term goals can extend for a week, a day, or even a couple of hours. To support your goal of regularly meeting with your study partners, you might set the following short-term goals:

- *By the end of today.* Text or email my study partners to ask them when they can meet.
- *One week from now.* Schedule each of our weekly meetings for this month.
- *Two weeks from now.* Hold our first meeting.
- *Three weeks from now.* Type and distribute notes; have second meeting.

These short-term goals might not seem risky to you. However, any action that requires energy and subjects your work to scrutiny is a risk. The smallest ways in which you "put yourself out there" can lead, step by step, to the greatest rewards.

Set Up a SMART Goal-Achievement Plan

Use the SMART system to make rewarding goals concrete and increase your chances of achieving them. SMART is an acronym for a five-part system that makes your goals **S**pecific, **M**easurable, **A**chievable, **R**ealistic, and attached to a **T**ime frame.

- *Specific.* Make your goal concrete by using as many details as possible. Focus on behaviors and events that are under your control and map out specific steps that will get you there.
- *Measurable.* Define your goal in a measurable way, and set up a progress evaluation system such as keeping a journal, setting an alarm on your phone or computer, or reporting to a friend.

GOAL: To decide on a major.

SMART GOAL CHARACTERISTICS	HOW TO ENGAGE EACH CHARACTERISTIC	EXAMPLE
Specific	Describe exactly how you will achieve your goal.	I will read the list of available majors, meet with my academic advisor, talk with instructors, and choose a major by the deadline.
Measurable	Find ways to measure your progress over time.	I will set alarms on my smartphone to remind me of when I should have accomplished each step. I will ask my mom to check in to make sure I'm getting somewhere.
Achievable	Set a goal that your abilities and drive can handle.	I'm driven to declare a major because I want to earn my degree, graduate, and gain work-ready skills.
Realistic	Define a goal that is workable given the resources (time and money) and other circumstances.	Because I'm starting early and already know how the process works, I should have time to think through this carefully.
Time frame	Set up a time frame for achieving you goal and identify the steps for working toward it.	I have a year until the deadline. I will read the catalog in the next month; I will meet with my advisor by the end of the term; I will talk with instructors at the beginning of next term; and I will declare a major by the end of next term.

- *Achievable.* Determine whether the goal aligns with your interests and values. Then, reflect on whether you have the skills or resources needed. If you're missing something, plan out how to get it.

- *Realistic.* Make sure your risks are reasonable and calculated. Create deadlines that will help you stay on track without making you feel rushed. Avoid the struggle of a timeline that is too short.

- *Time frame linked.* All goals need a time frame so you have something to work toward. If a goal is "a dream with a deadline," then without the deadline, your goal is only a dream.

> **MAJOR OR CONCENTRATION**
> An academic subject area chosen as a field of specialization, requiring a specific course of study.

Key 2.2 illustrates how to apply SMART goal-setting to an important goal that nearly every college student needs to achieve: declaring a **major** or **concentration** (for the sake of simplicity, the term "major" will appear in this text).

Setting goals is only the start. The real risk is in working toward them, and the real reward is in reaching them. Follow these steps, noting where your SMART system actions fit in.

- *Step 1: Define an achievable, realistic goal.* What do you want? Write out a clear description.

- *Step 2: Define an action plan.* How will you get there? Brainstorm different paths. Choose one; then map out its steps. Break a long-term goal into short-term subgoals.

- *Step 3: Link your goal to a time frame.* When do you want to accomplish your goal? Define a realistic time frame. Create specific deadlines for each step on the path.

- *Step 4: Identify resources and support.* What and who will keep you on track? Use helpful web sites or apps. Find people who will push you in a supportive way.

- *Step 5: Be accountable.* How will you assess your progress? Create a system to measure how you move toward your goal, keeping your time frame in mind.

Values, Goals, and Time

33

get creative

FIND WAYS TO GET UNSTUCK

In the center bubble of this visual organizer, write a problem you frequently encounter. It could be scheduling homework around extracurricular activities, finding time to hang out with friends around studying, coming up with interesting career paths, or simply figuring out the theme of a literary work.

Now use the organizer to come up with possible solutions. Begin filling in the surrounding bubbles with as many solutions as you can think of. Open your mind to risk-taking and keep writing until you've filled in every bubble with a possible solution. Read through them all.

Do any of them stick out to you? Circle the one that seems to have the most potential to reward you.

Guess what? You just got yourself unstuck. Consider using this creative and productive method to solve any problem you may encounter.

■ *Step 6: Prepare to get unstuck.* What will you do if you hit a roadblock? Anticipate problems and define strategies for handling them. Reach out to people who can help you. Remind yourself of the benefits of your goal.

- *Step 7: Take action.* How will you persist? Follow the steps in your plan until you achieve your goal.
- *Step 8: Celebrate!* How will you recognize your accomplishments? Appreciate your hard work with something you enjoy—a movie night, an outing with friends, something you've been wanting to buy, maybe even a long nap.

As you work toward your most important goals, consider how well you are using your time. No matter how well you define the steps to your goals, you need to set those steps within a time frame to achieve them.

WHO ARE YOU AS A
time manager?

Everyone has 24 hours in a day, and 7 to 8 of those hours involve sleeping (or should, if you want to remain healthy and alert enough to achieve your goals). You can't manage how time passes, but you *can* manage how you use it.

The first step in time management is to investigate your personal relationship with time. The more you're aware of your own time-related behaviors, the better you can create a schedule that maximizes your strengths, minimizes your weaknesses, and reduces stress. Determine who you are as a time manager by exploring your preferences and assessing your needs.

Identify Your Preferences

People have unique body rhythms and habits that affect how they deal with time. Some people have lots of energy late at night. Others do their best work early in the day. Some people are chronically late, while others get everything done with time to spare. The following steps will help you create a personal time "profile":

- *Identify your energy patterns.* At what time of day does your energy tend to peak? When do you tend to have the least energy?
- *Notice your on-time percentage.* Do you tend to be early, on time, or late? If you are early or late, by how many minutes are you normally off schedule? Do you set your clocks five or ten minutes early to trick yourself into being on time?
- *Look at your stamina.* Do you focus more effectively if you have a long block of time in which to work? Or do you need regular breaks in order to perform effectively?
- *Evaluate the effects of your preferences.* Which of your time-related preferences are likely to have a positive impact on your success at school? Which are likely to cause problems? Which can you make adjustments for, and which will just require you to cope?
- *Establish an ideal schedule.* Describe an ideal schedule that illustrates your preferences. For example, a student studies better during the day and prefers a long block of time. His ideal schedule may read: "Classes bunched together on Mondays, Wednesdays, and Fridays. Tuesdays and Thursdays free for studying and research. Study primarily during daytime hours."

get $mart

FINANCIAL VALUES

Complete the following on paper or in digital format.

Imagine yourself in five years . . .

1. What kind of work do you hope to be doing?

2. How much money do you hope to earn each year doing that work?

3. What type of major purchase might you make at that time? For ideas about this, consider your interests, needs, skills, and concerns.

4. How much might it cost (total cost or down payment)?

5. How much money would you have to save each month to have the money to make that major purchase at the end of five years? Monthly savings = total cost ÷ (5 years ×12 months per year)

6. Name two actions you can take to try to save that amount on a monthly basis.

Assess Your Needs

Of course, very few people are able to perfectly align their schedules to their profile and preferences. Everyone has needs that may or may not fit his or her ideal schedule. Needs include:

- Certain courses, for core requirements or for your major
- Work hours, if you have a job
- Family responsibilities, if you care for children, parents, or others

The goal is to consider your needs and your ideal schedule together, and come up with the best possible option—one that fulfills your needs but also takes your preferences into account. Consider what might happen to the student in the ideal schedule example. Looking to schedule next term's classes on Monday, Wednesday, and Friday, he finds that one class he has to take meets only on Tuesday and Thursday. He has a choice of 11 A.M. and 4 P.M., though, so he chooses 4 P.M., because that will give him a bigger block of time to study and do research during the day prior to the class.

Finally, remember that you will have more control over some things than others. For example, a student who functions best late at night may not have much luck finding courses that meet after 10 P.M. (unless she attends one of several colleges that have begun to schedule late-night classes to handle an overload of students).

HOW CAN YOU
schedule and prioritize?

With your preferences and needs in mind, you are ready for the central time management strategy—creating and following a schedule. An effective schedule can help you gain control of your life in two ways: It provides segments of time for goal-related tasks, and it reminds you of tasks, events, due dates, responsibilities, and deadlines.

Choose a Planner

Your first step is to find a planner that will help you achieve the control that a schedule can provide. Time-management expert Paul Timm says, "rule number one in a thoughtful planning process is: use some form of a planner where you can write things down."[2]

Choose a planner that works for how you live. There are two major types:

- A book or notebook, showing either a day or a week at a glance, where you note your commitments. Some planners contain sections for monthly and yearly goals.
- An electronic planner or smartphone, such as an iPhone or iPod Touch, a BlackBerry, or an Android device. Basic functions allow you to schedule days and weeks, note due dates, make to-do lists, perform mathematical calculations, and create and store an address book. Because most smartphone calendars have companion programs on computers, you can usually back up your schedule on a computer and view it there. You might also consider online calendars, such as Google calendar, which can communicate with your phone or other device.

Balance means getting your work done as well as finding time to have some fun with friends.

Although electronic planners are handy, powerful, and capable of all kinds of functioning, they are not cheap, the software can fail, and their batteries can die. Analyze your preferences and finances and choose the best tool for you. A blank notebook, used consistently, may work as well as a top-of-the-line smartphone.

Establish Priorities

Prioritizing helps you focus the bulk of your energy and time on your most important tasks. Since many top-priority items (classes, work) occur at designated times, prioritizing helps you lock in these activities and schedule less urgent tasks around them.

Whether it's a task or a goal you're scheduling, here are some basic ways to assign priorities. Think about what results your risks might bring, and what may result from taking *no* risks.

- *Priority 1*. These are crucial, high-reward items that you must do, usually at a specific time. They may include attending class, working at a job, picking up a child from day care, and paying bills.
- *Priority 2*. These are important items that have some flexibility in scheduling. Examples include study time and exercising.
- *Priority 3*. These are less important items that offer low-key rewards. Examples include calling a friend or downloading songs onto your iPod.

You should also prioritize long-term and short-term goals. Consider keeping high priority long-term goals visible alongside your daily schedule, so you can make sure your day-to-day activities move you ahead toward those goals. For instance, arriving at school a half hour early so you can meet with an advisor can be a step toward a long-term goal of deciding on a major.

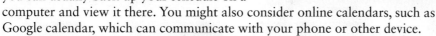

PRIORITIZE
To arrange or deal with in order of importance.

Build a Schedule

Scheduling and goal setting work hand in hand to get you where you want to go. The most clearly defined goal won't be achieved without being put into a time frame, and the most organized schedule won't accomplish much unless it is filled with tasks

Monday, March 14		
Time	Tasks	Priority
6:00 A.M.		
7:00		
8:00	Up at 8am — finish homework	
9:00		
10:00	Business Administration	
11:00	Renew driver's license @ DMV	
12:00 P.M.		
1:00	Lunch	
2:00	Writing Seminar (peer editing to...	
3:00	↓	
4:00	check on Ms.Schwartz's office h...	
5:00	5:30 work out	
6:00	↳ 6:30	
7:00	Dinner	
8:00	Read two chapters for	
9:00	Business Admin.	
10:00		
11:00		
12:00		

Monday, March 28				
8		Call: Mike Blair		1
9	BIO 212	Financial Aid Office		2
10				3
11	CHEM 203	EMS 262	*Paramedic	4
12			role-play*	5
Evening	6pm yoga class			

Tuesday, March 29				
8	Finish reading assignment!	Work @ library		1
9				2
10	ENG 112		(study for quiz)	3
11	↓			4
12				5
Evening			until 7pm	

Wednesday, March 30			
8		Meet w/advisor	1
9	BIO 212		2
10		EMS 262	3
11	CHEM 203 *Quiz		4
12		Pick up photos	5
Evening	6pm Dinner w/study group		

related to important goals. Key 2.3 shows parts of both a daily schedule and a weekly schedule.

Be detailed and methodical about building your schedule. Follow these steps:

1. *Enter Priority 1 items in your planner first.* This means class times and days for the term, including labs and other required commitments; work hours; and essential personal responsibilities such as health-related appointments or childcare.

2. *Enter key dates from your course syllabi.* When you get your syllabi for the term, enter all test and quiz dates, due dates for assignments, presentation dates for projects, holidays, and breaks in your planner right away. This will give you a big picture view of responsibilities and help you prepare for crunch times. For example, if you see that you have three tests and a presentation all in one week later in the term, you might rearrange your schedule during the preceding week to create extra study time.

3. *Enter dates of events and commitments.* Put commitments in your schedule where you can see and plan for them. Include club and organizational meetings, events you need to attend for class or for other purposes, and personal commitments such as medical appointments, family events, work obligations, or important social events.

4. *Schedule Priority 2 items around existing items.* Once you have the essentials set, put in study time, workouts, study group meetings, and other important but flexible items. Schedule class prep time—reading and studying, writing, and working on assignments and projects—in the planner as you would any other activity. As a rule, schedule at least two hours of preparation for every hour of class—that is, if you take 12 credits, you'll spend 24 hours or more a week on course-related activities in and out of class.

5. *Include Priority 3 items where possible.* Schedule these items, such as social time or doing errands, around the items already locked in.

When you are scheduling and evaluating the potential rewards of various tasks, be careful not to equate "reward" with "fun." They are not necessarily one and the same. For example, you might consider spending an hour on Instagram a lot more fun than studying for a test for that same hour. However, the reward for working toward a good test grade may ultimately be more desirable to you than whatever you would gain from posting and liking photos.

Link Tasks to Long-Term Goals

Linking day-to-day events in your planner to your values and long-term goals gives meaning to your efforts and keeps you motivated. For example, planning study time for an economics test will mean more to you if you link that time to your goal of being accepted into business school and your value of meaningful employment. If you were a student with a goal of entering business school, you might link these action steps for the next year to your goal:

- *This year.* Maintain my class standing while completing enough courses to meet curriculum requirements for business school.
- *This term.* Complete my economics class with a B average or higher.
- *This month.* Set up economics study group schedule to coincide with quizzes and tests.
- *This week.* Meet with study group; go over material for Friday's test.
- *Today.* Go over Chapter 3 in economics text.

You can then arrange a schedule that moves you in the direction of your goal, scheduling activities that support your short-term goal of doing well on your economics test and entering them in your planner. Your long-term goal of going to business school provides motivation to do well.

Another important way to link short-term tasks to a long-term goal is to schedule milestones toward major papers and assignments. If you know you have a huge project or research paper due at the end of the term, brainstorm a list of steps toward that goal—for example, research goals, different drafts, peer review—and set them up in your calendar.

Before each week begins, remind yourself of your long-term goals and what you can accomplish over the next seven days to move you closer to those goals. Every once in a while, take a hard look at your schedule to see if you are spending enough time on what you really value.

Make To-Do Lists

When you have a cluster of tasks to accomplish, you may find it useful to create a to-do list and check off the items as you complete them. A to-do list can be helpful during exam week, in anticipation of an especially busy day, for a long-term or complicated assignment, or when keyed to a special event. Some people keep a separate to-do list focused on low-priority tasks.

Use a code to prioritize the items on your list so that you address the most important items first. Some people just list items in priority order and number them. Some use letters (A, B, C) and some use different-colored pens. Others use electronic planners, choosing different highlighting or font colors. Each time you complete a task, check it off your to-do list or delete it from your electronic scheduler. This physical action can enhance the feeling of confidence that comes from getting something done.

Manage Your Schedule

The most detailed schedule won't do you any good unless you actively manage it. Here are some strategies that can help:

- *Plan regularly.* Set aside a time each day to plan your schedule (right before bed, with your morning coffee, on your commute to or from school, or whatever time and situation works best for you). Check your schedule at regular intervals throughout the day or week.
- *Use monthly and yearly calendars at home.* A standard monthly or yearly wall calendar is a great place to keep track of your major commitments. A wall calendar gives you the "big picture" overview you need. Key 2.4 shows a monthly calendar.
- *Get ahead if you can.* If you can take the small risk of getting a task done ahead of time, get it done, and see how you appreciate the reward of avoiding pressure later. Focus on your growth mindset, reminding yourself that achievement requires persistent effort.

 **KEY 2.4** **Keep track of your time with a monthly calendar.**

MARCH

SUNDAY	MONDAY	TUESDAY	WEDNESDAY	THURSDAY	FRIDAY	SATURDAY
	1 WORK	2 Turn in English paper topic	3 Dentist 2 pm	4 WORK	5	6
7 Frank's birthday	8 Psych Test 9 am WORK	9	10 6:30 pm Meeting @ Acad Ctr	11 WORK	12	13 Dinner @ Ryan's
14	15 English paper due WORK	16 Western Civ paper	17	18 Library 6 pm WORK	19 Western Civ makeup class	20
21	22	23 2 pm meeting, psych group WORK	24 Start running: 2 miles	25 WORK	26 Run 2 miles	27
28 Run 3 miles	29 WORK	30 Western Civ paper due	31 Run 2 miles			

Risk asking tough questions to be rewarded with new insights. Use the following questions to inspire discussion with classmates, either in person or online.

- What time management issues do you see others face? How do they handle them? What happens when they take risks—or don't?

- When you come up against a roadblock to an important goal, how do you react—with risk-taking or retreat? What is the result? If you want to change how you "get unstuck," what adjustments would you make?

CONSIDER THE CASE: Sarah found herself in a situation where she sensed she needed to take action, but didn't know what or how. Have you ever been in a similar place, feeling paralyzed by a problem and unable to figure out the first step? If you had a friend in this type of situation, how would you motivate him or her?

- *Schedule downtime.* It's easy to get so caught up in completing tasks that you forget to relax and breathe. Even a half-hour of down time a day will refresh you and improve your productivity when you get back on task.
- *Schedule sleep.* Sleep-deprived bodies and minds have a hard time functioning, and research reports that one-quarter of all college students are chronically sleep-deprived.[3] Figure out how much sleep you need and do your best to get it. With adequate rest, your mind is better able to function, which has a direct positive impact on your schoolwork.

One last overarching strategy: *Be flexible.* Sudden changes can upset your plans. Although you cannot control all the events that occur, you can control how you respond to them.

For changes that occur frequently, such as a job that tends to run into overtime, set up a backup plan (or two) ahead of time. For sudden changes, such as car breakdowns, or serious changes, such as failing a course or a major health issue like the one Sarah experienced, use problem-solving skills to help you through (your course this term may include more detailed information about problem solving). Your ability to evaluate situations, come up with creative options, and put practical plans to work will help you manage changes.

Resources at your college can help you deal with change, as well as with any scheduling or time-management problem. Your academic advisor, counselor, dean, financial aid advisor, and instructors can provide ideas and assistance.

Time Management Is Stress Management

If you are feeling more stress in your everyday life as a student, you are not alone. Stress levels among college students have increased dramatically.[4] Stress factors for college students include being in a new environment, increased workload, difficult decisions, and juggling school, work, and personal responsibilities.

Dealing with the stress of college life is one of your biggest challenges. But here's some good news: Every time-management strategy you are reading about in this chapter contributes to your ability to cope with stress. Remember that stress refers to how you *react* to pressure. When you create and follow a schedule that gets you places on time and helps you take care of tasks and responsibilities, you reduce pressure. With less pressure comes less stress.

> STRESS
> *Physical or mental strain or tension produced in reaction to pressure.*

HOW CAN YOU
handle time traps?

Everyone experiences *time traps*—situations and activities that eat up time you could spend in a more productive way. With thought and focus, you can address and conquer time traps. Note that this doesn't mean *never* doing things like chatting with friends on Facebook or watching Funny or Die videos; it means making conscious decisions about when and how long you do certain activities so that they don't derail your most important goals. It also means thinking ahead about risks—both the risk of being unproductive, as well as the risk of prioritizing work over your social life—and what rewards may or may not come from them.

Some time traps are a part of daily life—unavoidable, but able to be managed and addressed. Key 2.5 lists the ones students encounter most often and offers ideas for how to take control of them. Other time traps are linked to choices that people make. It can be risky to put out the high level of attention and focus that your work may demand, but the reward is an education that can help you fulfill your life's most significant goals. Make your most productive choices by confronting procrastination, setting effective limits, and minimizing multitasking.

Confront Procrastination

PROCRASTINATION
The act of putting off a task until another time.

It's human, and common for busy students, to leave difficult or undesirable tasks until later. However, if taken to the extreme, procrastination can develop into a habit that causes serious problems. For example, procrastinators who don't get things done in the

---

KEY 2.5 Take control of time wasters.

1. **Commute:** Although we cannot always control it, the time spent commuting from one place to another is staggering.
   Take Control: Use your time on a bus or train to do homework, study, read assignments, or work on your monthly budget.

2. **Fatigue:** Being tired can lead to low-quality work that you have to redo. Fatigue can also make you feel ready to quit altogether.
   Take Control: Determine a stop time for yourself. When your stop time comes, put down the book, turn off the computer and *go to bed*. During the day, when you can, take naps to recharge your battery.

3. **Confusion:** When you don't fully understand an assignment or problem, you may spend unintended amounts of time trying to figure it out.
   Take Control: The number one way to fight this is to *ask questions*. As the saying goes, ask early and ask often. Students who seek help show they want to learn.

4. **Preference and schedule mismatches:** When your schedule goes against who you are as a time manager, you can waste a lot of time trying to stay focused. For example, a night person who is consistently late to morning classes will spend extra time getting caught up on material he missed.
   Take Control: You aren't likely to get a perfect match, but take your preferences into account as much as you can when scheduling classes, work, and study time.

workplace may prevent others from doing their work, sabotage a project, or even lose a promotion or a job because of it.

If procrastination can cause such major issues, why do it? One reason people procrastinate is to avoid the truth about what they can achieve. "As long as you procrastinate, you never have to confront the real limits of your ability, whatever those limits are,"[5] say procrastination experts Jane B. Burka and Lenora Yuen, authors of *Procrastination: Why You Do It and What to Do About It*. A fixed mindset is another factor, because it naturally leads to procrastination. A person with a fixed mindset thinks, "I can't do it, so what's the point of trying?"

Here are some strategies that can help you avoid procrastination and its negative effects.

- *Analyze the effects.* What reward will remain out of reach if you continue to put off a task? Chances are you will benefit more in the long term by facing the task head-on.
- *Set reasonable goals.* Because unreasonable goals can immobilize, take manageable risks. If you concentrate on achieving one small step at a time, the task becomes less burdensome.
- *Get started whether you "feel like it" or not.* Break the paralysis of doing nothing by doing something—anything. Most people, once they start, find it easier to continue.
- *Ask for help.* Once you identify what's holding you up, find someone to help you face the task. Another person may come up with an innovative method to get you moving again.
- *Don't expect perfection.* People learn by approaching mistakes with a growth mindset. Richard Sheridan, President of Menlo Innovations, fosters a culture of exploration by telling his employees to "make mistakes faster."[6]
- *Acknowledge progress.* When you accomplish a task, celebrate with whatever feels like fun to you.

Set Effective Limits

Many people find it challenging to resist the pull of relaxing and fun activities such as video games, YouTube surfing, and socializing virtually or in person. However, the fun stuff can run away with your time, preventing you from taking care of responsibilities and ultimately causing serious problems. Because technology is so much a part of modern life, it can seem risky to limit your exposure to it. However, controlling when and for how long you interface with technology will earn you the reward of its benefits minus the suffering from its drawbacks.

There is a saying that goes, "The river needs banks to flow." Within those banks—the reasonable limits that you set on activities that tend to eat up time—you can be the thriving, healthy river, flowing toward the goals that are most important to you. Without the banks, and without the limits, you (the river) can spill out all over, losing the power to head in any single direction.

How can you set limits that will empower you and provide balance? Consider the following:

- *Know what distracts you.* Be honest with yourself about what draws your attention and drains your time—chatting or texting on your cell phone, watching reality TV, visiting Facebook, managing your Twitter account, and so on.
- *Set boundaries.* Determine when, and for how long, you can perform these activities without jeopardizing your studies. Then schedule them with built-in boundaries: "I will spend

get practical

CONQUER YOUR TIME TRAPS

Complete the following on paper or in digital format.

Think of two common time traps that you encounter. For each, come up with two ways to manage it effectively. Here's an example:

Time Trap: Texting

Response 1: Tell friend: "I'll call you in an hour. I need to finish this paper."

Response 2: Decide I will respond to my text messages after I've read two chapters.

1. Your turn: For each time trap of yours, name it and describe two possible responses.

2. Next, for each of the two time traps you identified, name which of the two responses will most help you to take control of the situation and why.

3. Finally, what did this exercise teach you about your personal time traps? Do you find yourself needing to be stricter with your time? Why, and how?

10 minutes on Facebook for every 50 minutes of studying." "I will choose one TV show per day." Stick to your limits—use a cellphone alarm if you need it. You can even set up innovative browser plug-ins to block certain time-wasting sites for specific periods of time. Check out LeechBlock (for Firefox) or StayFocused (for Google Chrome).

- *Think before you commit.* Whatever you are asked to do—whether work-related, family-related, in connection with a school organization, or another activity—don't say "yes" right away. Consider how the commitment will affect your schedule now and in the near future. If you determine the reward isn't worth the risk, say "no" respecfully but firmly.

- *Be realistic about time commitments.* Many students who combine work and school find they have to trim one or the other. Overloaded students often fall behind and experience high stress levels. Determine what is reasonable for you; you may find that taking longer to graduate is a viable option if you need to work while in school. You may also decide that you can handle easing up on work hours in order to spend more time on schoolwork.

The Myth of Multitasking

Over the years, people have come to believe that multitasking is a crucial skill. However, recent research has shown that the human brain is biologically capable of doing only one thinking task at a time—at best, it can only switch rapidly

student PROFILE

Ming-Lun Wu

NATIONAL CHENGCHI UNIVERSITY, TAIPEI, TAIWAN
(GRADUATE) UNIVERSITY OF DENVER, COLORADO

About me:

I grew up in Taiwan. After completing high school and my undergraduate degree in Taiwan, I traveled to Boston, Massachusetts, for a summer ESL program and, later to Denver, Colorado, for graduate school. I'm currently attending the University of Denver and am working on my master's degree in marketing.

What I focus on:

Growing up in Taiwan, I had a dream of experiencing education in the United States. To me, American schools seemed more open-minded than the schools I attended in Taiwan. That dream became my goal and I quickly started to pay attention to any information related to studying abroad. When I received a chance to make that dream a reality, I jumped at it. However, even though I had my chance, I knew I needed to improve my English immensely if I wanted to succeed.

When I arrived in Boston for a study-abroad experience, I began looking for opportunities to work on my language skills. I joined a Toastmasters club and an English training club that focused on leadership skills and public speaking. In the summer, I went to a Boston-based language school. Besides improving my language skills, experiences like applying for my visa, finding a host family, and scheduling trips around Boston helped me gain independence and confidence in a strange place.

I had to test both my language skills and my independence to achieve my goal and succeed in the United States.

What will help me in the workplace:

Even though knowing the big picture is essential, understanding every baby step necessary to accomplish a vision is vital. And having the hands-on plan for moving toward that vision, little by little, is absolutely essential.

between tasks. When you think you are multitasking, you are really only "switch-tasking."[7]

This means that if you try to do two tasks at once, you can actually work on only one at a time. What you do is interrupt the first activity with the second and then switch back. The time it takes to switch from one thinking activity to another called *switching time*. For example, suppose you're talking to a member of your study group by phone, discussing a homework assignment. If you decide to read through your email while you are on the phone, you will be unable to listen to what's being said on the phone call.

According to two researchers, David Meyer and Dr. John Medina, switching time increases errors and the amount of time it takes to finish the tasks you are working on by an average of 50%. This means the more activities you juggle, the more your brain is interrupted, the more switching you do, the longer it takes to complete your activities, and the more mistakes you make.[8] The cost to the quality of your work may not be worth the juggling.

If you want to be successful at your work, consider the words of Tony Schwarz: "Difficult as it is to focus in the face of the endless distractions we all now face, it's far and away the most effective way to get work done."[9] Focusing on one task at a time will save you time, mistakes, and stress. The minor risks of managing yourself in the present will reward you with learning and accomplishment in the future— and don't worry, you will still find time to play.

revisit RISK AND REWARD

What happened to Sarah? Compelled to find a way out of her combination of depression and severe social anxiety, Sarah took the risk to reach out for help. She went to her college's counseling center and saw both a counselor and a psychologist, both in one-on-one settings. Through these conversations she realized that she had emotional damage from her cancer experience, feelings that had been covered up but were surfacing as a result of her transition to college. As she began to feel more comfortable sharing her thoughts, she joined an "interpersonal processing group" on campus – a therapy group focused on working through issues together.

Sarah's willingness to risk and to expose her vulnerability earned her the reward of greater self-knowledge, improvement with her issues, and a bonus: A career direction. "I realized that I wasn't so different from other people, and I want to help people like me with social anxiety or depression," she says. She had chosen English as a major but had not yet connected it with a career goal. Now she plans to continue her education with a master's degree in social work.

What does this mean for you? Sarah found trust and support in the group therapy experience. Initially intimidated, she took the risk and now has a community of people that she looks forward to seeing.

What group might you risk trying out at your school? It can be challenging to connect with others, and sometimes it takes a little push to get moving in a direction that could bring great reward. Set a SMART goal to find a group, whether therapeutic, social, or goal-oriented, this term. Write out your goal in terms of the SMART components and take action.

What risk may bring reward beyond your world? Sarah's idea that she could help others was cemented during a summer internship with LifeBound, a company that provides academic and career coaching to high school and college students. Observing coaching and being coached one-on-one by a student in a coaching class made her even more certain that helping people in a one-on-one environment was right for her. Set a goal to participate in an internship when you next have an opportunity. You may want to consult www.internships.com for a general overview of what's possible, and then narrow your search to local areas and specific careers. Whether you discover the perfect career area or find out an area that doesn't work out for you, you will have acquired essential information for your path toward fulfillment.

Complete the following on paper or in digital format; for the time management exercise, use the in-text grids.

KNOW IT *Think Critically*

Discover How You Spend Your Time

Build basic skills. Everyone has exactly 168 hours in a week. How do you spend your hours? Start by guessing or estimating the time you spend on three particular activities. How much time do you spend on each of these activities in a week?

Studying? _____ hours
Sleeping? _____ hours
Interacting with media and technology (computer, online services, cell phone, texting, video games, television) for non-academic purposes? _____ hours

To find out the real story, record how you actually spend your time for seven days. The Weekly Time Log chart has blocks showing half-hour increments. As you go through the week, write down what you do each hour, indicating when you start and when you stop. Include sleep and leisure time. Record your *actual* activities instead of the activities you think you *should* be doing. There are no wrong answers.

After a week, note how many hours you spent on each activity using the Weekly Summary chart. Round off the times to half-hours—if you spent 31 to 44 minutes on an activity, mark it as a half-hour; if you spent 45 to 59 minutes, mark it as one hour. Log the hours in the boxes in the chart using tally marks, with a full mark representing one hour and a half-size mark representing a half-hour. In the third column, total the hours for each activity. Finally, add the totals in that column to make sure your grand total is approximately 168 hours (if it isn't, go back and check your grid and calculations and fix any errors you find). Leave the Ideal Time in Hours column blank for now.

Take it to the next level. Look over your results, paying special attention to how your *estimated* hours for sleep, study, and technology activities compare to your *actual* logged activity hours for the week. Use a separate sheet of paper or electronic file to answer the following questions:

- What surprises you about how you spend your time?
- Do you spend the most time on the activities that represent your most important values—or not?
- Where do you waste the most time? What do you think that is costing you?
- On which activities do you think you should spend *more* time? On which should you spend *less* time?

Move toward mastery. Go back to the Weekly Summary chart and fill in the Ideal Time in Hours column with the number of hours you think would make the most sense. Consider the difference between your actual hours and you ideal hours. What changes are you willing to make to get closer to how you want to ideally spend your time? Write a short paragraph describing, in detail, two time-management changes you plan to make this term so you focus your time more effectively on your most important goals and values.

TIME	MONDAY activity	TUESDAY activity	WEDNESDAY activity	THURSDAY activity
6:00 A.M.				
6:30 A.M.				
7:00 A.M.				
7:30 A.M.				
8:00 A.M.				
8:30 A.M.				
9:00 A.M.				
9:30 A.M.				
10:00 A.M.				
10:30 A.M.				
11:00 A.M.				
11:30 A.M.				
12:00 P.M.				
12:30 P.M.				
1:00 P.M.				
1:30 P.M.				
2:00 P.M.				
2:30 P.M.				
3:00 P.M.				
3:30 P.M.				
4:00 P.M.				
4:30 P.M.				
5:00 P.M.				
5:30 P.M.				
6:00 P.M.				
6:30 P.M.				
7:00 P.M.				
7:30 P.M.				
8:00 P.M.				
8:30 P.M.				
9:00 P.M.				
9:30 P.M.				
10:00 P.M.				
10:30 P.M.				
11:00 P.M.				
11:30 P.M.				
12:00 A.M.				
12:30 A.M.				
1:00 A.M.				
1:30 A.M.				
2:00 A.M.				

CHAPTER 2

TIME	FRIDAY activity	SATURDAY activity	SUNDAY activity
6:00 A.M.			
6:30 A.M.			
7:00 A.M.			
7:30 A.M.			
8:00 A.M.			
8:30 A.M.			
9:00 A.M.			
9:30 A.M.			
10:00 A.M.			
10:30 A.M.			
11:00 A.M.			
11:30 A.M.			
12:00 P.M.			
12:30 P.M.			
1:00 P.M.			
1:30 P.M.			
2:00 P.M.			
2:30 P.M.			
3:00 P.M.			
3:30 P.M.			
4:00 P.M.			
4:30 P.M.			
5:00 P.M.			
5:30 P.M.			
6:00 P.M.			
6:30 P.M.			
7:00 P.M.			
7:30 P.M.			
8:00 P.M.			
8:30 P.M.			
9:00 P.M.			
9:30 P.M.			
10:00 P.M.			
10:30 P.M.			
11:00 P.M.			
11:30 P.M.			
12:00 A.M.			
12:30 A.M.			
1:00 A.M.			
1:30 A.M.			
2:00 A.M.			

Values, Goals, and Time

Weekly Summary

Activity	Time Tallied Over One-Week Period	Total Time in Hours	Ideal Time in Hours
Example: Class	~~IIII~~ ~~IIII~~ ~~IIII~~ II	16.5	
Class			
Work			
Studying			
Sleeping			
Eating			
Family time/child care			
Commuting/traveling			
Chores and personal business			
Friends and important relationships			
Telephone time			
Leisure/entertainment			
Spiritual life			
Other			

WRITE IT *Communicate*

Emotional intelligence journal: How you feel about your time management. Think and then write about how your most time-demanding activities make you feel. Paying attention to your feelings can be a key step toward making time management choices that are more in line with your values. What makes you happiest, most fulfilled, and most satisfied? What makes you the most anxious, frustrated, most drained? What do these feelings tell you about your day-to-day choices? Describe how you could adjust your mindset or make different choices to feel better about how you spend your time.

Real-life writing: Examine two areas of academic specialty. Use your course catalog to identify two academic areas that look interesting to you. Write a short report comparing and contrasting the majors or concentrations in these areas. Consider GPA requirements, number of courses, relevance to career areas, campus locations of departments, "feel" of the departments, other requirements, and discussions with students and instructors. Conclude your report with observations about how this comparison and evaluation process has refined your thinking.

WORK IT *Build Your Brand*

Explore Career Goals through Personal Mission

21st Century Learning Building Blocks

- Initiative and self-direction
- Creativity and innovation
- Productivity and accountability

No matter what employment goals you ultimately pursue, a successful career should be grounded in your personal mission in one or more ways.

First, write a draft of your personal mission. Refer to the section on page 30 to remind yourself of the elements of a personal mission statement. Use the following scenarios and questions to get you thinking about your mission.

1. You are at your retirement dinner. You have had an esteemed career in your chosen field. Your best friend stands up and talks about the five aspects of your character that have taken you to the top. What do you think they are?

2. You are preparing for a late-in-life job change. Updating your résumé, you need to list your contributions and achievements. What would you like them to be?

3. You have been told that you have one year to live. With family or close friends, you talk about the values that mean the most to you. Based on that discussion, how do you want to spend your time in this last year? What choices reflect what is most important to you?

After you have a personal mission statement to provide vision and motivation, take some time to think more specifically about your working life. Spend 15 minutes thinking about everything that you wish you could be, do, have, or experience in your career 10 years from now—skills you want to have, money you want to earn, benefits, things you want to experience, travel you want to do, anything you can think of. Depict your wishes by listing them, drawing them, cutting out images from magazines, or combining any of these ideas—whatever you like best.

Now, group your wishes in order of priority. Take three pieces of paper and label them: Priority 1, Priority 2, and Priority 3. Put each wish on the paper where it belongs, according to its priority (1 = high importance, 2 = medium importance, and 3 = low importance).

Look at the wishes on your priority lists. What do they tell you about what is most important to you? What fits into your personal mission and what doesn't? Identify those wishes that don't seem to have anything to do with your personal mission and cross them out. Circle or highlight three high-priority wishes that do mesh with your personal mission. For each wish, write down one action step you could take in the near future to make that wish come true.

You may want to look back at these materials at the end of the term to see what changes may have taken place in your priorities.

Values, Goals, and Time

3

The more you know about yourself, the more effectively you can analyze
courses, evaluate partners, and decide what, how, and where to study and work.
With the information you discover, you can take the risks that will prove most

Learning How You Learn

MAKING THE MOST OF YOUR ABILITIES

What Would You Risk? *Joyce Bishop, PhD*

THINK ABOUT THIS SITUATION AS YOU READ, AND CONSIDER WHAT ACTION YOU WOULD TAKE. THIS CHAPTER HELPS YOU ASSESS YOUR PREFERENCES FOR LEARNING AND INTERACTION, AND SHOWS YOU HOW TO USE THIS INFORMATION TO MAKE PRACTICAL DECISIONS ABOUT WORK AND STUDYING.

As a college student, Joyce Bishop was confused by her spotty record—she did well in some classes and felt totally lost in others, especially those that were lecture-based. She couldn't make sense of what she was hearing when she wasn't familiar with the information. If she read the material ahead of time, she could visualize pictures in her mind, look up words, and research concepts. This helped her understanding, but there wasn't often time to do it ahead of class.

In small classes, Joyce was distracted by the voices around her while she strained to hear the instructor. She would borrow classmates' notes in exchange for typing their term papers. The notes and typing helped her retain information better. When Joyce realized that science classes were somewhat less difficult for her, she majored in biology and managed to graduate.

Despite her challenges, Joyce later took the risk to pursue a master's in public health. Concerned about stress on her eyes, her eye doctor sent her to a center that usually tested small children for learning disabilities. The therapist who tested her determined that Joyce processed language on a fourth-grade level, a condition that has not changed during her adult life. Guessing that she had not made it past the tenth grade, the therapist was shocked to hear she was completing her master's degree.

Finally Joyce began to understand what was behind so many years of mediocre grades and an intense struggle to learn. She had always been willing to risk, but wondered if she had the ability to achieve the reward she sought.

To be continued . . .

YOU DON'T HAVE TO HAVE A LEARNING DISABILITY TO FACE LEARNING CHALLENGES. FOR JOYCE, PARTICIPATING IN ADVENTURE SPORTS, LIKE RIDING ATVs, IS A WAY TO GROW BY TAKING A RISK AND LEARNING FROM IT, AS SHE DID WHEN WORKING THROUGH HER LEARNING DISABILITY. YOU'LL LEARN MORE ABOUT JOYCE, AND THE REWARD RESULTING FROM HER ACTIONS, WITHIN THIS CHAPTER.

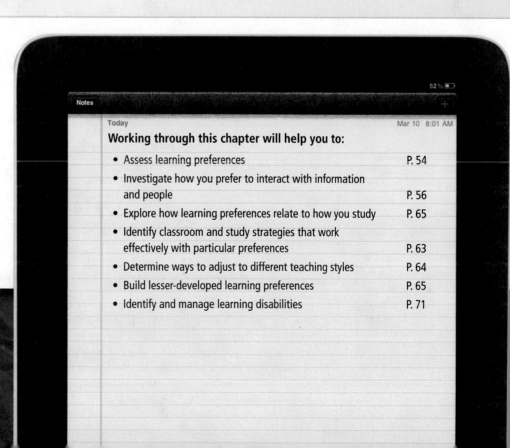

Working through this chapter will help you to:

status CHECK

How Aware Are You of How You Learn?

For each statement, fill in the number that best describes how often it applies to you.

1 = never   2 = seldom   3 = sometimes   4 = often   5 = always

1. I believe I can develop my skills and abilities through self-knowledge and hard work. ① ② ③ ④ ⑤

2. I have a pretty clear idea of my strengths and abilities. ① ② ③ ④ ⑤

3. I understand which subjects and situations make it more difficult for me to learn. ① ② ③ ④ ⑤

4. I try to maximize what I do well in the classroom and outside of it. ① ② ③ ④ ⑤

5. I recognize that being comfortable with the subject matter isn't necessarily enough to succeed in a particular course. ① ② ③ ④ ⑤

6. I assess an instructor's teaching style and figure out how to maximize my learning. ① ② ③ ④ ⑤

7. I choose study techniques that tap into how I learn best. ① ② ③ ④ ⑤

8. I try to use forms of technology that work well with the way I learn. ① ② ③ ④ ⑤

9. I've taken a skills or interests inventory to help find a major or career area that suits me. ① ② ③ ④ ⑤

10. I understand what a learning disability is and am aware of several different types of disabilities. ① ② ③ ④ ⑤

Each of the topics in these statements is covered in this chapter. Note those statements for which you filled in a 3 or lower. Skim the chapter to see where those topics appear, and pay special attention to them as you read, learn, and apply new strategies.

REMEMBER: NO MATTER HOW WELL KNOW YOURSELF AS A LEARNER, YOU CAN IMPROVE WITH EFFORT AND PRACTICE.

WHY EXPLORE

who you are as a learner?

Have you thought about how you learn? College is an ideal time to think about how you learn, think, and function in the world. "Thinking about thinking" is known as *metacognition* (something you are building with each Status Check). Building meta-cognition and self-knowledge can help you choose the risks that will most effectively lead you to rewards you value. The more you know about yourself, the more effectively you can analyze courses, study environments, evaluate partners, and decide what, how, and where to study.

LEARNING PREFERENCE A way in which a person most effectively receives and processes information.

Use Assessments to Learn About Yourself

Each person in the world is born with particular levels of ability and potential in differ-ent areas. As you grow, you develop learning preferences based on your abilities and potential. Learning preferences combine with effort and environment to create a "recipe" for what you can achieve. Part of this recipe is the way you perceive yourself, a perception that may come from many different sources. Maybe your mother thinks

MyStudentSuccessLab
(www.mystudentsuccesslab.com) is an online solution designed to help you "Start Strong, Finish Stronger" by building skills for ongoing personal and professional development.

you are "the funny one" or "the quiet one." A grade school teacher may have called you a "thinker" or "slacker," a "go-getter" or "shy." These labels—from yourself and others—influence your ability to set and achieve goals, and can prevent you from taking productive risks if you use them to define yourself too rigidly.

Accepting a label as truth can put you in a fixed mindset and limit your potential. Instead, realize that you are not simply stuck with a label. Brain studies show that humans of any age can build new neuropathways and thereby learn new ideas and skills. This means that intelligence can grow when you risk the work to keep learning.

Picture a bag of rubber bands of different sizes. Some are thick and some thin; some are long and some short—but all of them can stretch. A small rubber band, stretched out, can reach the length of a larger one that lies unstretched. In other words, with effort and focus, you can develop whatever raw material you start with, perhaps beyond the natural gifts of someone who makes no effort. Joyce's story illustrates how far effort can stretch a person's natural abilities.

Ask yourself: Who am I right now? Where would I like to be in five years? Assessments focused on how you prefer to learn and interact with others can help you answer some of these big questions. Whereas a test attempts to identify a level of performance, an assessment, according to professor and psychologist Howard Gardner, is "the obtaining of information about a person's skills and *potentials* . . . providing useful feedback to the person [emphasis added]."[1] Think of an assessment as an honest exploration that will produce interesting and helpful information.

The assessments in this chapter provide questions to get you thinking about your strengths and challenges. *Note:* Learning disabilities are specific, diagnosed issues that differ from the learning challenges that all students face. They are discussed at the end of the chapter.

As you search for answers, you are gathering important information about yourself. With this information, you will be able to define your rubber band and get ready to stretch it to its limit.

POTENTIALS
Abilities that may be developed.

Use Assessments to Make Choices and to Grow

There may be much about yourself, your surroundings, and your experiences that you cannot control. However, with self-knowledge, you do have control over how you respond to circumstances. For example, even though you cannot control the courses you are required to take or how your instructors teach, you can manage how you respond to those courses and instructors.

The two assessments in this chapter—Multiple Pathways to Learning and the Personality Spectrum—will give you greater insight into your strengths and weaknesses. The material following the assessments shows you how to maximize what you do well and compensate for challenging areas by making specific choices about what you do in class, during study time, and in the workplace. Understanding yourself and others as learners also helps you choose how to respond to people in a group situation. In a study group, classroom, or workplace, each person takes in material in a unique way. You can use what you know about others' learning preferences to improve communication and teamwork.

Remember: There are no "right" answers, no "best" scores. Completing a self-assessment is like wearing glasses to correct blurred vision. The glasses don't create new paths and possibilities, but they help you to see more clearly the ones in front of you at this moment. As you gain experience, build skills, and learn, your learning preferences are apt to change over time. If you take the assessments again in the future, your results may shift. Finally, to enjoy the reward of useful results, take the risk of answering questions honestly, reflecting who you *are* as opposed to who you *wish* you were.

WHAT TOOLS CAN HELP YOU ASSESS HOW YOU
learn and interact with others?

INTELLIGENCE
As defined by H. Gardner, an ability to solve problems or create products that are of value in a culture.[2]

A variety of tools exist to help you become more aware of different aspects of yourself. Some tools focus on learning preferences; some on areas of potential; and others on personality type. This chapter examines two assessments in depth. The first, Multiple Pathways to Learning, is a learning preferences assessment focusing on eight areas of potential, referred to as intelligences. It is based on Howard Gardner's Multiple Intelligences (MI) theory. The second, the Personality Spectrum, is a personality-type assessment based on the Myers-Briggs Type Indicator (MBTI). It helps you evaluate how you react to people and situations.

Following each assessment is information about the typical traits of each type of intelligence and each Personality Spectrum dimension. As you will see from your scores, you have abilities in all areas, though some are more developed than others.

Assess Your Multiple Intelligences with Pathways to Learning

In 1983, Howard Gardner changed the way people perceived intelligence and learning with his theory of Multiple Intelligences. Like Robert Sternberg, Gardner believed that the traditional view of intelligence, based on mathematical, logical, and verbal measurements that made up an intelligence quotient (IQ), did not reflect the true spectrum of human ability. Sternberg focused on the spectrum of actions that help people achieve important goals, but Gardner chose to examine the idea that humans possess a number of different areas of natural ability and potential that he called *multiple intelligences*.

The theory of Multiple Intelligences

Gardner's research identified eight unique types of intelligence or areas of ability. These included two areas traditionally associated with the term *intelligence*—verbal and logic skills—but expanded beyond them, to encompass a wide range of potentials of the human brain.[3] These intelligences almost never function in isolation. You will almost always use several at the same time for any significant role or task.[4]

As you look at Key 3.1, study the description of each intelligence and then examine the examples of people who have unusually high levels of ability in that area. Although few people have the verbal-linguistic intelligence of William Shakespeare or the interpersonal intelligence of Oprah Winfrey, everyone has some level of ability in every intelligence. Your goal is to identify what your levels are and to work your strongest intelligences to your advantage.

The way Gardner defines intelligence heightens the value of different abilities in different arenas. In Tibet, for example, mountain dwellers prize the bodily-kinesthetic ability of a Himalayan mountain guide. In Detroit, automakers appreciate the visual-spatial talents of a master car designer. Send the car designer up Mount Everest, or have the Sherpa design a car for Chrysler, and suddenly a person who is exceptionally intelligent in one area may falter in another.

Students drawn to the sciences may find that they have strengths in logical-mathematical or naturalistic thinking.

INTELLIGENCE	DESCRIPTION AND SKILLS	HIGH-ACHIEVING EXAMPLE
Verbal-Linguistic	Ability to communicate through language; listening, reading, writing, speaking	• Author J.K. Rowling • Orator and President Barack Obama
Logical-Mathematical	Ability to understand logical reasoning and problem solving; math, science, patterns, sequences	• Physicist Stephen Hawking • Mathematician Svetlana Jitomirskaya
Bodily-Kinesthetic	Ability to use the physical body skillfully and to take in knowledge through bodily sensation; coordination, working with hands	• Gymnast Nastia Liukin • Survivalist Bear Gryllis
Visual-Spatial	Ability to understand spatial relationships and to perceive and create images; visual art, graphic design, charts and maps	• Artist Walt Disney • Designer Stella McCartney
Interpersonal	Ability to relate to others, noticing their moods, motivations, and feelings; social activity, cooperative learning, teamwork	• Media personality Ellen Degeneres • Former Secretary of State Colin Powell
Intrapersonal	Ability to understand one's own behavior and feelings; self-awareness, independence, time spent alone	• Animal researcher Jane Goodall • Philosopher Friedrich Nietzche
Musical	Ability to comprehend and create meaningful sound; sensitivity to music and musical patterns	• Singer and musician Alicia Keys • Composer Andrew Lloyd Webber
Naturalist	Ability to identify, distinguish, categorize, and classify species or items, often incorporating high interest in elements of the natural environment	• Social activist Wangari Maathai • Bird cataloger John James Audubon

Your own eight intelligences

Gardner believes that all people possess all eight intelligences, but each person has developed some intelligences more fully than others. When you find a task or subject easy, you are probably using a more fully developed intelligence. When you have trouble, you may be using a less developed intelligence.[5]

Gardner also believes your levels of development in the eight intelligences can grow or recede throughout your life, depending on effort and experience. For example,

MULTIPLE PATHWAYS TO LEARNING

Each intelligence has a set of numbered statements. Consider each statement on its own. Then, on a scale from 1 (lowest) to 4 (highest), rate how closely it matches who you are right now and write that number on the line next to the statement. Finally, total each set of six questions. Enter your scores in the grid on page 59.

1. rarely   2. sometimes   3. usually   4. always

1. _____ I enjoy physical activities.

2. _____ I am uncomfortable sitting still.

3. _____ I prefer to learn through doing.

4. _____ When sitting I move my legs or hands.

5. _____ I enjoy working with my hands.

6. _____ I like to pace when I'm thinking or studying.

_____ **TOTAL for BODILY-KINESTHETIC**

1. _____ I enjoy telling stories.

2. _____ I like to write.

3. _____ I like to read.

4. _____ I express myself clearly.

5. _____ I am good at negotiating.

6. _____ I like to discuss topics that interest me.

_____ **TOTAL for VERBAL-LINGUISTIC**

1. _____ I use maps easily.

2. _____ I draw pictures/diagrams when explaining ideas.

3. _____ I can assemble items easily from diagrams.

4. _____ I enjoy drawing or photography.

5. _____ I do not like to read long paragraphs.

6. _____ I prefer a drawn map over written directions.

_____ **TOTAL for VISUAL-SPATIAL**

1. _____ I like math in school.

2. _____ I like science.

3. _____ I problem-solve well.

4. _____ I question how things work.

5. _____ I enjoy planning or designing something new.

6. _____ I am able to fix things.

_____ **TOTAL for LOGICAL–MATHEMATICAL**

1. _____ I listen to music.

2. _____ I move my fingers or feet when I hear music.

3. _____ I have good rhythm.

4. _____ I like to sing along with music.

5. _____ People have said I have musical talent.

6. _____ I like to express my ideas through music.

_____ **TOTAL for MUSICAL**

1. _____ I need quiet time to think.

2. _____ I think about issues before I want to talk.

3. _____ I am interested in self-improvement.

4. _____ I understand my thoughts and feelings.

5. _____ I know what I want out of life.

6. _____ I prefer to work on projects alone.

_____ **TOTAL for INTRAPERSONAL**

1. _____ I like doing a project with other people.

2. _____ People come to me to help settle conflicts.

3. _____ I like to spend time with friends.

4. _____ I am good at understanding people.

5. _____ I am good at making people feel comfortable.

6. _____ I enjoy helping others.

_____ **TOTAL for INTERPERSONAL**

1. _____ I like to think about how things, ideas, or people fit into categories.

2. _____ I enjoy studying plants, animals, or oceans.

3. _____ I tend to see how things relate to, or are distinct from, one another.

4. _____ I think about having a career in the natural sciences.

5. _____ As a child I often played with bugs and leaves.

6. _____ I like to investigate the natural world around me.

_____ **TOTAL for NATURALISTIC**

Source: Developed by Joyce Bishop, PhD, Golden West College, Huntington Beach, CA. Based on Howard Gardner, *Frames of Mind: The Theory of Multiple Intelligences*, New York: Harper Collins, 1993.

SCORING GRID FOR MULTIPLE PATHWAYS TO LEARNING

For each intelligence, shade the box in the row that corresponds with the range where your score falls. For example, if you scored 17 in bodily-kinesthetic intelligence, you would shade the middle box in that row; if you scored a 13 in visual-spatial, you would shade the last box in that row. When you have shaded one box for each row, you will see a "map" of your range of development at a glance.

A score of 20–24 indicates a high level of development in that particular type of intelligence, 14–19 a moderate level, and below 14 an underdeveloped intelligence.

	20–24 (HIGHLY DEVELOPED)	14–19 (MODERATELY DEVELOPED)	BELOW 14 (UNDERDEVELOPED)
Bodily-Kinesthetic			
Visual-Spatial			
Verbal-Linguistic			
Logical-Mathematical			
Musical			
Interpersonal			
Intrapersonal			
Naturalistic			

although you will not become a world-class pianist if you have limited musical ability, you can develop what you have with focus and work. Conversely, even a highly talented musician will lose ability without practice. This reflects how the brain grows with learning and becomes sluggish without it.

Note: A related self-assessment is the VAK or VARK questionnaire. VAK/VARK assesses learning preferences in three (or four) areas: visual, auditory, read/write (in VARK), and kinesthetic. This text focuses on the Multiple Intelligences (MI) assessment because it incorporates elements of VAK/VARK and expands upon them, giving you a comprehensive picture of your abilities. Keep in mind that auditory learning is part of two MI dimensions:

- Many auditory learners have strong verbal intelligence but prefer to hear words (in a lecture or discussion or on a recording) instead of reading them.
- Many auditory learners have strong musical intelligence and remember and retain information based on sounds and rhythms.

If you tend to absorb information better through listening, try study suggestions for these two intelligences. Some instructors convert their lectures into podcasts, which can be very helpful. For further information about VAK/VARK, go to www.vark-learn.com, or search online using the keywords "VAK assessment."

Complete the Multiple Pathways to Learning assessment and scoring grid to determine where you are right now in the eight intelligence areas. Then look at Key 3.2, immediately following the assessment, to identify specific skills associated with each area. Elsewhere in your text, you may find information about how to apply your learning styles knowledge to key success skills and to specific areas of study.

Assess Your Style of Interaction with the Personality Spectrum

Personality assessments help you understand how you respond to the world around you, including people, work, and school. They also can help guide you as you explore majors and careers.

The concept of dividing human beings into different "personality types" goes as far back as Aristotle and Hippocrates, two ancient Greek philosophers. In the early 20th

Verbal-Linguistic		• Remembering terms easily • Mastering a foreign language • Using writing or speech to convince someone to do or believe something
Musical-Rhythmic		• Sensing tonal qualities • Being sensitive to sounds and rhythms in music and in spoken language • Using an understanding of musical patterns to hear music
Logical-Mathematical		• Recognizing abstract patterns • Using facts to support an idea, and generating ideas based on evidence • Reasoning scientifically (formulating and testing a hypothesis)
Visual-Spatial		• Recognizing relationships between objects • Representing something graphically • Manipulating images
Bodily-Kinesthetic		• Strong mind–body connection • Controlling and coordinating body movement • Using the body to create products or express emotion
Intrapersonal		• Accessing your internal emotions • Understanding your own feelings and using them to guide your behavior • Understanding yourself in relation to others
Interpersonal		• Seeing things from others' perspectives • Noticing moods, intentions, and temperaments of others • Gauging the most effective way to work with individual group members
Naturalistic		• Ability to categorize something as a member of a group or species • Understanding of relationships among natural organisms • Deep comfort with, and respect for, the natural world

TYPOLOGY
A systematic classification or study of types.

century, psychologist and philosopher Carl Jung focused on personality **typology** based on these characteristics:[6]

- *An individual's preferred "world."* Jung said that extroverts tend to prefer the outside world of people and activities, while introverts tend to prefer the inner world of thoughts, feelings, and fantasies.
- *Different ways of dealing with the world, or "functions."* Jung defined four distinct interaction dimensions used to different degrees: sensing (learning through your senses), thinking (evaluating information rationally), intuiting (learning through an instinct that comes from many integrated sources of information), and feeling (evaluating information through emotional response).

Later, in the 1960s and 1970s, Katharine Briggs and her daughter Isabel Briggs Myers developed an assessment based on Jung's typology, called the Myers-Briggs Type Inventory, or MBTI (information is available online at www.myersbriggs.org). One of the most widely used personality inventories in the world, it consists of 16 possible personality types from the four dimensions. David Keirsey and Marilyn Bates later condensed the MBTI types into four temperaments, creating the Keirsey Sorter (found at www.keirsey.com).

When Joyce Bishop developed the Personality Spectrum assessment, she adapted and simplified the Keirsey Sorter and MBTI material into four personality types: Thinker, Organizer, Giver, and Adventurer. Like the assessments on which it is based, the Personality Spectrum helps you identify the kinds of interactions that are most and least comfortable for you.

Complete the Personality Spectrum assessment and then plot your results on the scoring diagram. As with multiple intelligences, these results may change over time as you experience new things, change, and continue to learn. Key 3.3 then shows the skills associated with each personality type.

Personality Spectrum Assessment

PERSONALITY SPECTRUM

STEP 1 Rank-order all four responses to each question from most like you (4) to least like you (1) so that for each question you use the numbers 1, 2, 3, and 4 one time each. Place numbers on the lines next to the responses.

4. most like me   3. more like me   2. less like me   1. least like me

1. I like instructors who
   a. _____ tell me exactly what is expected of me.
   b. _____ make learning active and exciting.
   c. _____ maintain a safe and supportive classroom.
   d. _____ challenge me to think at higher levels.

2. I learn best when the material is
   a. _____ well organized.
   b. _____ something I can do hands-on.
   c. _____ about understanding and improving the human condition.
   d. _____ intellectually challenging.

3. A high priority in my life is to
   a. _____ keep my commitments.
   b. _____ experience as much of life as possible.
   c. _____ make a difference in the lives of others.
   d. _____ understand how things work.

4. Other people think of me as
   a. _____ dependable and loyal.
   b. _____ dynamic and creative.
   c. _____ caring and honest.
   d. _____ intelligent and inventive.

5. When I experience stress I would most likely
   a. _____ do something to help me feel more in control of my life.
   b. _____ do something physical and daring.
   c. _____ talk with a friend.
   d. _____ go off by myself and think about my situation.

6. I would probably not be close friends with someone who is
   a. _____ irresponsible.
   b. _____ unwilling to try new things.
   c. _____ selfish and unkind to others.
   d. _____ an illogical thinker.

7. My vacations could be described as
   a. _____ traditional.
   b. _____ adventuresome.
   c. _____ pleasing to others.
   d. _____ a new learning experience.

8. One word that best describes me is
   a. _____ sensible.
   b. _____ spontaneous.
   c. _____ giving.
   d. _____ analytical.

STEP 2   Add up the total points for each letter.

TOTAL FOR   a. _____ Organizer   b. _____ Adventurer   c. _____ Giver   d. _____ Thinker

STEP 3   Plot these numbers on the brain diagram on page 62.

SCORING DIAGRAM FOR PERSONALITY SPECTRUM

Write your scores from page 61 in the four squares just outside the brain diagram—Thinker score at top left, Giver score at top right, Organizer score at bottom left, and Adventurer score at bottom right.

Each square has a line of numbers that go from the square to the center of the diagram. For each of your four scores, place a dot on the appropriate number in the line near that square. For example, if you scored 15 in the Giver spectrum, you would place a dot between the 14 and 16 in the upper right-hand line of numbers. If you scored a 26 in the Organizer spectrum, you would place a dot on the 26 in the lower left-hand line of numbers. Connect the four dots to create a shape.

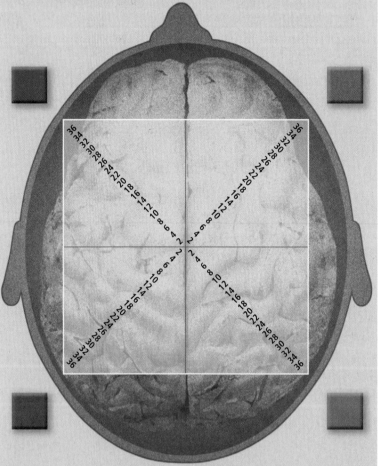

The more balanced the shape (closer to a square), the more equally developed the four spectrums of your personality. However, many people's shapes show one or two areas that are more developed than the others.

THINKER

Technical
Scientific
Mathematical
Dispassionate
Rational
Analytical
Logical
Problem Solving
Theoretical
Intellectual
Objective
Quantitative
Explicit
Realistic
Literal
Precise
Formal

ORGANIZER

Tactical
Planning
Detailed
Practical
Confident
Predictable
Controlled
Dependable
Systematic
Sequential
Structured
Administrative
Procedural
Organized
Conservative
Safekeeping
Disciplined

GIVER

Interpersonal
Emotional
Caring
Sociable
Giving
Spiritual
Musical
Romantic
Feeling
Peacemaker
Trusting
Adaptable
Passionate
Harmonious
Idealistic
Talkative
Honest

ADVENTURER

Active
Visual
Risking
Original
Artistic
Spatial
Skillful
Impulsive
Metaphoric
Experimental
Divergent
Fast-paced
Simultaneous
Competitive
Imaginative
Open-minded
Adventuresome

For the Personality Spectrum,
26–36 indicates a strong tendency in that dimension
14–25 indicates a moderate tendency
0–13 indicates a minimal tendency

Source for brain diagram: Understanding Psychology, 3rd ed., by Charles G. Morris, © 1996.
Reproduced by permission of Pearson Education, Inc./Prentice Hall, Inc.

KEY 3.3 Particular abilities and skills are associated with each Personality Spectrum dimension.

Thinker		• Solving problems
		• Developing models and systems
		• Analytical and abstract thinking
Organizer		• Responsibility, reliability
		• Neatness, organization, attention to detail
		• Comprehensive follow-through on tasks
Giver		• Successful, close relationships
		• Making a difference in the world
		• Negotiation, promoting peace
Adventurer		• Courageous and daring
		• Hands-on problem solving
		• Active and spontaneous style

Also based on Jung's work is the Golden Personality Assessment, which identifies sixteen personality types as does the MBTI. It is available to students using MyStudentSuccessLab, and can provide an interesting and detailed portrait of your traits.

HOW CAN YOU USE
your self-knowledge?

As you analyze learning preferences through completing the assessments, you develop a clearer picture of who you are and how you interact with others. Then, and most importantly, you figure out what to do with this heightened self-knowledge. Use your thinking skills to choose effective strategies for interacting in the classroom, managing study time, dealing with your workplace, and working with technology. These more targeted and personal efforts can help you earn the reward of deeper and more lasting learning.

Classroom Choices

Most students have to complete a set of "core curriculum" courses, as well as whatever courses their majors and certificates require. As you sign up for the sections that fit into your schedule, you may be asking, "How is it possible to make choices based on my learning preferences?"

The opportunity for choice lies in how you interact with your instructor and how you function in the classroom. It is impossible for instructors to tailor classroom presentations to 15, 40, or 300 unique learners. As a result, you may find yourself in sync

Broaden your experience of your courses, and your education, by interacting with instructors outside of class time.

TEACHING STYLE	WHAT TO EXPECT IN CLASS
Lecture, verbal focus	Instructor speaks to the class for the entire period, with little class interaction. Lesson is taught primarily through words, either spoken or written on the board, on PowerPoints in class or online, with handouts or text, or possibly through podcasts.
Lecture with group discussion	Instructor presents material but encourages class discussion.
Small groups	Instructor presents material and then breaks class into small groups for discussion or project work.
Visual focus	Instructor uses visual elements such as PowerPoint slides, diagrams, photographs, drawings, transparencies, in-class or "YouTube for Schools" videos, or movies.
Logical presentation	Instructor organizes material in a logical sequence, such as by steps, time, or importance.
Random presentation	Instructor tackles topics in no particular order, and may jump around a lot or digress.
Conceptual presentation	Instructor spends the majority of time on the big picture, focusing on abstract concepts and umbrella ideas.
Detailed presentation	Instructor spends the majority of time, after introducing ideas, on the details and facts that underlie them.
Hands-on presentation	Instructor uses demonstrations, experiments, props, and class activities to show key points.

with one teacher and mismatched with another. Sometimes, the way the class is structured can affect your success more than the subject matter; for example, a strong interpersonal learner who has trouble writing may do well in a composition course emphasizing group work.

Just as you have learning preferences, instructors have ways they are most comfortable teaching. After several class meetings, you should be able to assess each instructor's dominant teaching styles (see Key 3.4) and determine how those fit with your learning preferences. As with learning preferences, most instructors will demonstrate a combination of teaching styles.

Although styles vary and instructors may combine styles, the word-focused lecture is still most common. For this reason, the traditional college classroom generally works best for the verbal or logical learner or the Thinker and the Organizer. What can you do when your learning preferences don't match up with how your instructor teaches? Here are three suggestions:

- *Play to your strengths.* For example, if you're a kinesthetic learner, you might rewrite or type your lecture notes, make flash cards, or take walks while saying important terms and concepts out loud. Likewise, if you are a Giver with an instructor who delivers straight lectures, consider setting up a study group to go over details and fill in factual gaps.

- *Work to strengthen weaker areas.* As a visual learner reviews notes from a structured lecture, he could use logical-mathematical strategies such as outlining notes or thinking about cause-and-effect relationships within the material. An Organizer, studying for a test from notes delivered by an instructor with a random presentation, could organize her material using tables and timelines.

- *Ask your instructor for help.* Connect through email or during office hours. Communicating your struggle can feel like a risk, but building a relationship with an

Complete the following on paper or in digital format.

Considering what you know about yourself as a learner and about your instructors' teaching styles this term, decide which classroom situation is the most challenging for you. Use this exercise to think analytically, creatively, and practically about the situation.

1. Name the course and describe the instructor's style.

2. Analyze the problem that is making this class challenging.

3. Generate and write down three ideas about actions you can take to improve the situation.

4. Finally, choose one action and put it to practical use. Briefly note what happened. Was there any improvement as a result?

instructor or teaching assistant can be extremely rewarding. This is especially true in large lectures where you are anonymous unless you speak up. For example, a visual learner might ask the instructor to recommend figures or videos to study that illustrate the lecture.

The adjustments you make for your instructor's teaching style will build flexibility that you need for career and life success. Just as you can't hand pick your instructors, you will rarely, if ever, be able to choose your work colleagues. You will have to adjust to them, and help them adjust to you. Keep in mind, too, that research shows a benefit from learning in a variety of ways—kind of like cross-training for the brain. Knowing this, some instructors may challenge you to learn in ways that aren't comfortable for you.

A final point: Some students try to find out more about an instructor by asking students who have already taken the course or looking up comments online. Be cautious, as you may not be able to trust an anonymous poster. Even if you hear a review from a friend you trust, every student–instructor relationship is unique, and an instructor your friend loved may be a bad match for you. Prioritize the courses you need, and know that you can make the most of what your instructors offer, regardless of their teaching styles.

Study Choices

Start now to use what you learned about yourself to choose the best study techniques. If you tend to learn successfully from a linear, logical presentation, look for order (for example, a timeline of information organized by event dates) as you review notes. If you are strong in interpersonal intelligence, you could work with study groups whenever possible.

When faced with a task that challenges your weaknesses, use strategies that boost your ability. For example, if you are an Adventurer who does *not* respond well to linear information, try applying your strengths to the material by using a hands-on approach.

Or you could try developing your area of weakness by learning study skills that work well for Thinker-type learners.

When you study with others, you and the entire group will be more successful if you understand one another's learning preferences, as in the following examples.

- An Interpersonal learner could take the lead in teaching material to others.
- An Organizer could coordinate the group schedule.
- A Naturalistic learner might organize facts into categories that solidify concepts.

Look at Key 3.5 for study strategies that suit each intelligence and Key 3.6 for study strategies that suit each Personality Spectrum dimension. Because you have

KEY 3.5	Choose study techniques to maximize each intelligence.

Verbal-Linguistic		<ul><li>Read text; highlight selectively</li><li>Use a computer to retype and summarize notes</li><li>Outline chapters</li><li>Recite information or write scripts/debates</li></ul>
Musical-Rhythmic		<ul><li>Create rhythms out of words</li><li>Beat out rhythms with hand or stick while reciting concepts</li><li>Write songs/raps that help you learn concepts</li><li>Write out study material to fit into a wordless tune you have on a CD or MP3 player; chant or sing the material along with the tune as you listen</li></ul>
Logical-Mathematical		<ul><li>Organize material logically; if it suits the topic, use a spreadsheet program</li><li>Sequentially explain material to someone</li><li>Develop systems and find patterns</li><li>Analyze and evaluate information</li></ul>
Visual-Spatial		<ul><li>Develop graphic organizers for new material</li><li>Draw "think links" (mind maps)</li><li>Use a computer to develop charts and tables</li><li>Use color in your notes for organization</li></ul>
Bodily-Kinesthetic		<ul><li>Move while you learn; pace and recite</li><li>Rewrite or retype notes to engage "muscle memory"</li><li>Design and play games to learn material</li><li>Act out scripts of material</li></ul>
Intrapersonal		<ul><li>Reflect on personal meaning of information</li><li>Keep a journal</li><li>Study in quiet areas</li><li>Imagine essays or experiments before beginning</li></ul>
Interpersonal		<ul><li>Study in a group</li><li>As you study, discuss information over the phone or send instant messages</li><li>Teach someone else the material</li><li>Make time to discuss assignments and tests with your instructor</li></ul>
Naturalistic		<ul><li>Break down information into categories</li><li>Look for ways in which items fit or don't fit together</li><li>Look for relationships among ideas, events, facts</li><li>Study in a natural setting if it helps you focus</li></ul>

Thinker		• Convert material into logical charts, flow diagrams, and outlines • Reflect independently on new information • Learn through problem solving • Design new ways of approaching material or problems
Organizer		• Define tasks in concrete terms • Use a planner to schedule tasks and dates • Organize material by rewriting and summarizing class and/or text notes • Create, or look for, a well-structured study environment
Giver		• Study with others in person, on the phone, or using instant messages • Teach material to others • Seek out tasks, groups, and subjects that involve helping people • Connect with instructors, advisors, and tutors
Adventurer		• Look for environments/courses that encourage nontraditional approaches • Find hands-on ways to learn • Use or develop games or puzzles to help memorize terms • Fight boredom by asking to do something extra or perform a task in a more active way

some level of ability in each area and because you will sometimes need to boost your ability in a weaker area, you may find useful suggestions under any of the headings. Try different techniques. Pay attention to what works best for you. You may be surprised at what is useful, as Joyce was when she discovered how much typing helped her retain information.

Technology Choices

Technology is everywhere. People communicate using email, text messaging, and social networking sites; they read blogs, listen to podcasts, and use apps on their cell phones. Technology also plays a significant role in academic settings, where you may encounter:

- Instructors who communicate primarily via email
- Course websites and learning management systems where you can access syllabi and connect with resources and classmates
- Textbooks with associated websites through which you complete and email assignments
- Online research that takes you from website to website as you follow links
- Projects where students create media such as a YouTube video or social media campaign

Technology has profoundly affected how we get information and share it with others. According to the Pew Research Center, it "is producing a fundamentally new kind of learner, one that is self-directed, better equipped to capture information, more reliant on feedback from peers, [and] more inclined to collaborate."[7] These "new learners" are more likely to research online, share content through social media sites, and create media content.

For some students, technology tools such as search engines and GoogleDocs come easily, but others may struggle. Knowing your learning preferences can help you fit technology tools to your assignment and use online resources effectively. Are you strong in the logical-mathematical intelligence or Thinker dimension? Working with an online tutorial may be a good choice. Are you an interpersonal learner? Find a tech savvy classmate to help you get the hang of it. An Adventurer may try out the features of a text or course website randomly, according to what looks interesting, whereas an Organizer may click through features in their listed order.

If you're having trouble with a particular type of technology, find a teaching assistant, instructor, or skilled classmate to help you understand how to use it. Finally, remember that technology cannot make you learn—it can simply make information accessible to you. To achieve the reward of learning, evaluate different technologies carefully and use them in ways that are most productive for you.

Workplace Choices

Knowing how you learn and interact with others will help you work more effectively and take more targeted and productive career planning risks. How can an employee or job candidate benefit from self-awareness?

Better performance and teamwork. When you understand your strengths, you can find ways to use them on the job more readily, as well as determine how to compensate for tasks that take you out of your areas of strength. In addition, you will be better able to work with others. For example, a team leader might offer an intrapersonal team member the chance to take material home to think about before attending a meeting; an Adventurer might find ways to spearhead new projects, while delegating the detailed research to a Thinker on the team.

INTERNSHIP
A temporary work program that allows you to gain supervised, practical experience in a job and career area.

Better career planning. Exploring ways to use your strengths in school will help you make better choices about what internships, jobs, or careers will suit you. For most college students, majors and **internships** are more immediate steps on the road to a career. Internships can be extremely rewarding risks, giving you a chance to "try out" your major in a workplace setting. You might even discover you don't have an interest in a career in that area and need to switch majors.

Key 3.7 links majors and internships to the eight intelligences. This list is by no means complete; rather, it represents only a fraction of the available opportunities.

talk risk and reward . . .

Risk asking tough questions to be rewarded with new insights. Use the following questions to inspire discussion with classmates, either in person or online.

- When you have trouble doing something, what is your first reaction—to risk trying again, or to give up? Do you say "I need a different approach" or "I'm no good at this"?

- Do people perceive their own strengths accurately, or do you often see strengths in others that they don't believe they have?

CONSIDER THE CASE: Not knowing about Joyce Bishop's learning disability, what would you have assumed as an instructor of hers in college? Consider what an instructor might assume about you that is not accurate. What risk can you take to clear up that assumption?

MULTIPLE INTELLIGENCE	CONSIDER MAJORING IN	THINK ABOUT AN INTERNSHIP AT A
Bodily-Kinesthetic	• Massage or physical therapy • Kinesiology • Construction engineering • Sports medicine • Dance or theater	• Sports physician's office • Physical or massage therapy center • Construction company • Dance studio or theater company • Athletic club
Intrapersonal	• Psychology • Finance • Computer science • Biology • Philosophy	• Accounting firm • Biology lab • Pharmaceutical company • Publishing house • Computer or Internet company
Interpersonal	• Education • Public relations • Nursing • Business • Hotel/restaurant management	• Hotel or restaurant • Social service agency • Public relations firm • Human resources department • Charter school
Naturalistic	• Geology • Zoology • Atmospheric sciences • Agriculture • Environmental law	• Museum • National park • Environmental law firm • Zoo • Geological research firm
Musical	• Music • Music theory • Voice • Composition • Performing arts	• Performance hall • Radio station • Record label or recording studio • Children's music camp • Orchestra or opera company
Logical-Mathematical	• Math • Physics • Economics • Banking/finance • Computer science	• Law firm • Consulting firm • Bank • Information technology company • Research lab
Verbal-Linguistic	• Communications • Marketing • English/literature • Journalism • Foreign languages	• Newspaper or magazine • PR/marketing firm • Ad agency • Publishing house • Network TV affiliate
Visual-Spatial	• Architecture • Visual arts • Multimedia designs • Photography • Art history	• Photo or art studio • Multimedia design firm • Architecture firm • Interior design firm • Art gallery

Use what you see here to inspire thought and spur investigation. If something from this list or elsewhere interests you, consider looking for an opportunity to "shadow" someone (follow the individual for a day to see what he or she does) to see if you might want to commit to an internship or major.

Learning How You Learn

get $mart

YOUR FINANCIAL PREFERENCES

As your unique preferences affect how you learn, they also influence how you approach your finances. Based on your learning preferences, take a look at how you think about and interact with money. Circle your answers to the following questions:

1. How often do you use a credit card?
   a. Never
   b. Less than twice a month
   c. Less than twice a week
   d. Daily

2. When you see something you like at the store, what do you do?
   a. Go to other stores to compare prices
   b. Think about it for a day or two
   c. Ask your friends what they think
   d. Purchase it immediately

3. How many credit cards do you have?
   a. 0
   b. 1
   c. 2
   d. 3 or more

4. How much credit card debt do you incur each month (in other words, how much money do you spend on credit monthly)?
   a. $0
   b. $1 to $100
   c. $101 to $500
   d. More than $500

5. How much of your credit card balance do you typically pay off each month?
   a. 100%
   b. 50% to 99%
   c. 25% to 49%
   d. Less than 24%

Now add up the number of a, b, c, and d answers:

   a _____   b _____   c _____   d _____

- Thinkers and Organizers often have more a and b answers because they tend to be careful with money, thinking about the financial impact of their purchases, and planning for the future.

- Givers may also be careful with their money, but often end up helping others or giving gifts, which might give them more c answers.

- Adventurers are usually risk-takers, which means they may be willing to take on more debt. They are likely to have more d answers.

Although all students have areas of strength and weakness, some challenges are more significant and are diagnosed as learning disabilities. Focused assistance can help students with learning disabilities to manage their conditions and succeed in school.

HOW CAN YOU IDENTIFY AND MANAGE
learning disabilities?

Some learning disabilities cause reading problems, some produce difficulties in math, some cause issues that arise when working with others, and some make it difficult for students to process the language they hear. The following will help you understand learning disabilities as well as the tools people use to manage them.

Identifying a Learning Disability

The National Center for Learning Disabilities (NCLD) states that learning disabilities:[8]

- Are neurological disorders that interfere with one's ability to store, process, and produce information
- Do *not* including mental retardation, autism, behavioral disorders, impaired vision, hearing loss, or other physical disabilities
- Do *not* include attention deficit disorder and attention deficit hyperactivity disorder, although these problems may accompany learning disabilities[9]
- Often run in families and are lifelong conditions, although specific strategies can help people with learning disabilities manage and even overcome areas of challenge

How can you determine whether you should be evaluated for a learning disability? According to the NCLD, persistent problems in any of the following areas may indicate a problem:[10]

- Reading or reading comprehension
- Math calculations or understanding language and abstract concepts
- Social skills or interpreting social cues
- Following a schedule, being on time, meeting deadlines
- Reading or following maps
- Balancing a checkbook
- Following directions, especially on multi-step tasks
- Understanding spoken language
- Writing, sentence structure, spelling, and organizing written work

Details on specific learning disabilities appear in Key 3.8. For an evaluation, contact your school's learning center, disability office, or student health center for a referral to a licensed professional. A professional diagnosis is required for a person with learning disabilities to receive federally funded aid.

Managing a Learning Disability

If you are diagnosed with a learning disability, valuable information is available—information Joyce never know about until she entered graduate school. Maximize your ability to learn by learning about and managing your disability.

- *Find information about your disability.* Search the library and the Internet—try NCLD at www.ncld.org or LD Online at www.ldonline.org or call NCLD

DISABILITY OF CONDITION	WHAT ARE THE SIGNS?
Dyslexia and related reading disorders	Problems with reading (spelling, word sequencing, comprehension, reading out loud) and with translating written language into thought or thought into written language
Dyscalculia (developmental arithmetic disorders)	Difficulty recognizing numbers and symbols, memorizing facts, understanding abstract math concepts, applying math to life skills (time management, handling money), and performing mental math calculations
Developmental writing disorders	Difficulty composing sentences, organizing a writing assignment, or translating thoughts coherently to the page
Handwriting disorders (dysgraphia)	Distorted or incorrect language, inappropriately sized and spaced letters, wrong or misspelled words, difficulty putting thoughts on paper or grasping grammar, large gap between spoken language skills and written skills
Speech and language disorders	Problems with producing speech sounds, using spoken language to communicate, or understanding what others say
LD-related social issues	Problems recognizing facial or vocal cues from others, understanding how others are feeling, controlling verbal and physical impulsivity, and respecting others' personal space
LD-related organizational issues	Difficulty scheduling and organizing personal, academic, and work-related materials

Source: Information from the Language and Math section of the National Center for Learning Disabilities website. Accessed on December 24, 2011, from http://www.ncld.org/ld-basics/ld-explained

at 1–888–575–7373. If you have an individualized education program (IEP) (a document describing your disability and recommended strategies) read it and make sure you understand it.

- *Seek assistance from your school.* Speak with your advisor about getting a referral to the counselor who can arrange specific assistance for your classes. Accommodations mandated by law for students who are learning disabled include:
  - Extended time on tests
  - Note-taking assistance (for example, having another student take notes for you)
  - Assistive technology devices (MP3 players, tape recorders, laptop computers)
  - Modified assignments
  - Alternative assessments and test formats

  Other services that may be offered include tutoring, study skills assistance, and counseling.

- *Determine when and how to disclose your status.* When or if you tell people about your disability is up to you. You may disclose it prior to enrollment (if you need help with applying), at the time of enrollment or during a course (if you know or realize you will need accommodations for your coursework), after a diagnosis (if you are diagnosed during your course of study), or never (if you believe you can manage on your own).[11]

- *Be a dedicated student.* Be on time and attend class. Read assignments *before* class. Sit where you can focus. Review notes soon after class. Spend extra time on assignments. Ask for help.

student PROFILE

Sade Gantt
MONTCLAIR STATE UNIVERSITY, MONTCLAIR, NJ

About me:

I entered college right out of high school, but soon became pregnant. Shocked by the news and challenged by the experience of pregnancy and motherhood, I struggled with college for a year and a half, withdrawing frequently from classes or just not going. When my daughter was seven months old I decided that something needed to change. At a job fair I discovered the U.S. Army, and signed my contract soon after I met with recruiters. After a year's tour of duty I came home and returned to school, receiving my A.S. in Education and then pursuing my B.A. at MSU.

What I focus on:

I am a strong verbal-linguistic learner, and since I majored in English, I have plenty of books to read. While reading, I highlight words I don't understand as well as important quotes and sections. I use a different color highlighter for each subject so that I can manage my loose papers. The night before a class, I make sure I have all the questions for that segment of reading to be discussed. Then during class I make sure to answer those questions. This helps me prepare for the next section of reading as well as upcoming tests.

Being in the military also brought out the organizer in me, helping me to become more focused and disciplined in setting goals. I have a different folder for each subject and attached to the folder is the class syllabus – trust me, it really helps me make sure the work gets done when and how it is supposed to.

What will help me in the workplace:

Both school and the military have given me the discipline of being on time, staying alert, and paying attention. My experience has also taught me the importance of working toward a goal, which allows me to plan ahead of time so that I can still have time to play and enjoy life. The Army saying "Be all you can be" instilled in me a drive to succeed that will help me be there for my daughter, achieve my degree, and make a difference in the world we live in as an American soldier.

■ *Understand your learning preferences.* If you have a learning disability, some of your multiple intelligences may always remain underdeveloped, but you can use your strengths to compensate. For example, even though Joyce could not understand much of what she heard, she typed her notes and drew diagrams, making use of her visual-spatial, logical-mathematical, and bodily-kinetic abilities.

Finally, build a positive attitude. Focus on what you have achieved and on how far you have come. Rely on support from others, knowing it will give you the best possible chance to succeed.

revisit RISK AND REWARD

What happened to Joyce? Dr. Bishop now understands how her learning disability, *auditory processing disorder,* causes problems with understanding words she hears. Recognizing how her strengths in visual-spatial, logical-mathematical, and bodily-kinesthetic intelligence served her well in science studies, she chose study strategies for those strengths and over time earned the reward of her master's and Ph.D. degrees. Now a tenured psychology professor at Golden West College in California, Dr. Bishop won Teacher of the Year twice at her school. Always willing to take risks that serve her intention to learn throughout her life, she learned how to teach online courses and now trains other teachers in online teaching strategies. She continues to find reward from the hard work of managing her learning disability.

What does this mean for you? Getting perspective on strengths and weaknesses isn't just for those with diagnosed learning disabilities. Dr. Bishop got her wake-up call from an eye doctor and a therapist. Who can provide an outside perspective for you? First, make your own list of your three strongest and three weakest qualities. Then, find someone who knows you well enough to have an honest and constructive opinion about you. Set a time to meet in person, and take the risk to ask this person for his or impression of your strengths and your challenges. Compare what you learn with the items on your list. What matches up? What surprises you?

What risk may bring reward beyond your world? Broaden your knowledge of learning disabilities so you can avoid inaccurate assumptions about people and learn how to support them in reaching their potential. Go to www.ldonline.org and read the article entitled "LD Basics." Then search the keyword "adults" and browse the articles to focus more closely on how adults with learning disabilities navigate school, work, and life. Finally, think about an assumption you may have made about someone with whom you live, work, or go to school. Risk addressing your possibly false idea by approaching that person with an open mind from this point forward, looking for strengths as well as working reasonably with challenges. Developing a more perceptive and supportive perspective can bring the reward of increased productivity in this, or any, relationship.

Complete the following on paper or in digital format.

KNOW IT *Think Critically*

Link How You Learn to Coursework and Major

Apply what you know about yourself to some future academic planning.

Build basic skills. Summarize in a paragraph or two what you know about yourself as a learner. Focus on what you learned from the assessments.

Take it to the next level. Schedule a meeting with your academic advisor. Note the following:

- Name of advisor
- Office location/contact information
- Time/date of meeting

At the meeting, give the advisor an overview of your learning strengths and challenges based on the summary you wrote. Ask for advice about courses that might interest you and majors that might suit you. Take notes. As a result of your discussion, name two courses to consider in the next year.

Move toward mastery. Think about the courses you listed and other courses related to them. Toward what majors might each of them lead you? Based on those courses, name two majors to investigate. Then, create a separate to-do list of how you plan to explore one course offering and one major. Set a deadline for each task. If you are having trouble choosing a major because you are unsure of a career direction, see an advisor in the career center for guidance.

WRITE IT *Communicate*

Emotional intelligence journal: Your interactions with others. With your Personality Spectrum profile in mind, think about how you generally relate to people. Describe the type(s) of people with whom you tend to get along. How do you feel when you are around these people? Then, describe the types that tend to irk you. How do those people make you feel? Use your emotional intelligence to discuss what those feelings tell you. Consider how you can adjust your mindset or take action to create the best possible outcome when interacting with people with whom you just don't get along.

Real-life writing: Ask an instructor for support. Reach out to an instructor of a course that clashes with your learning preference in terms of material, teaching style, or how the classroom is run. Draft a respectful e-mail that introduces you, describes how you perceive yourself as a learner, and details your issue. Include any ideas you have about how the instructor might help you. Thank the instructor in advance. Finally, when you are done, make something happen: Send the email and follow through on any response you receive.

WORK IT *Build Your Brand*

Self-Portrait

21st Century Learning Building Blocks

- Creativity and innovation
- Initiative and self-direction

Because self-knowledge helps you to shape your future, a self-portrait is an important exploration tool as you consider possible careers as well as majors that may lead you to those careers.

KEY 3.9 This is one example of a self-portrait.

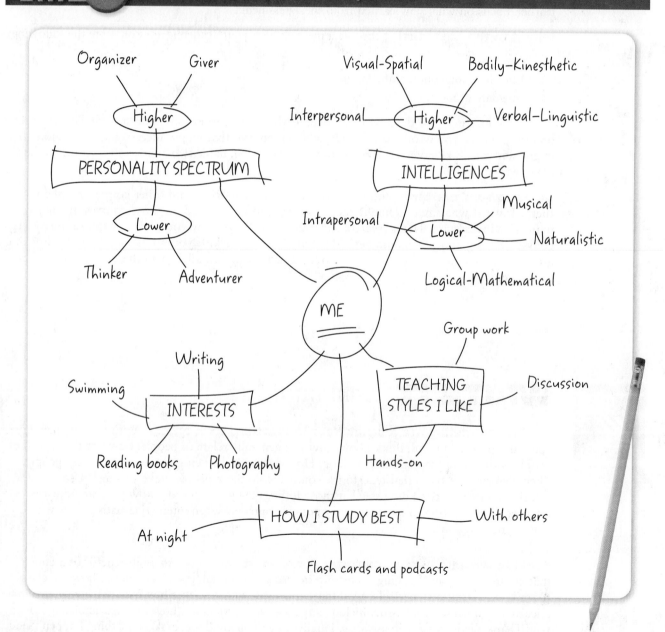

Use this exercise to synthesize what you've learned about yourself into one comprehensive portrait. Design it as a "think link" or mind map, using words and visual shapes to describe your: (1) dominant Multiple Intelligences, (2) Personality Spectrum dimensions, (3) values, (4) abilities and interests, (5) personal characteristics, and (6) anything else that you have discovered through self-exploration. Key 3.9 shows an example. You can create it freehand or use a graphics program.

A *think link* is a visual presentation of related ideas, similar to a map or web, that represents your thought process. Put your ideas inside geometric shapes (boxes or circles) and attach related ideas and facts to those shapes using lines (you may find additional information on note taking elsewhere in your text).

To get started, try using the style shown in Key 3.9. Put your main idea ("Me") in a shape in the center and then create a wheel of related ideas coming off that central shape. Spreading out from each of those related ideas (interests, values, and so forth), draw lines connecting the thoughts that go along with each idea. For example, you might connect singing, stock market, and history with the "interests" idea.

Let your design reflect who you are, just as what you write does. You may want to look back at it at the end of the term to see how your self-image has changed and grown.

4

When you need to solve a problem or make a decision, combining analytical, creative, and practical thinking skills gives you the greatest chance of achieving your goal.

Critical, Creative, and Practical Thinking

SOLVING PROBLEMS AND MAKING DECISIONS

What Would You Risk? *Joe Martin*

THINK ABOUT THIS SITUATION AS YOU READ, AND CONSIDER WHAT ACTION YOU WOULD TAKE. THIS CHAPTER BUILDS PROBLEM-SOLVING AND DECISION-MAKING SKILLS THAT WILL HELP YOU FACE CHALLENGES IN COLLEGE AND BEYOND.

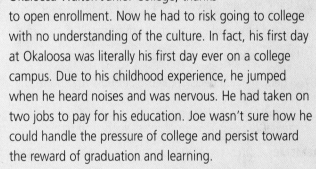

Joe Martin grew up in the housing projects of Miami, Florida, in an environment in which six of his friends died—either from drug involvement or murder—by the time he was in high school. No one in his family even considered going to college. Although he had friends and family members who were in prison or caught up in crime and drugs, his mother reminded him to never accept the situation. He knew things could be different, but he wasn't sure how.

Joe planned to join the military after high school. However, when he was a senior, he had a change of heart. Looking at his college-bound friends, he decided that if they could go to college, so could he. When he told the Navy recruiter he wanted to attend school, the man said he was not college material. With his low SAT scores, the recruiter said, "they won't let you drive by college, let alone get in."

This challenge made Joe determined to risk applying to colleges. Having barely passed high school and dogged by those low SAT scores, he got turned down by so many schools he lost count. Finally he was accepted at Okaloosa Walton Junior College, thanks to open enrollment. Now he had to risk going to college with no understanding of the culture. In fact, his first day at Okaloosa was literally his first day ever on a college campus. Due to his childhood experience, he jumped when he heard noises and was nervous. He had taken on two jobs to pay for his education. Joe wasn't sure how he could handle the pressure of college and persist toward the reward of graduation and learning.

To be continued . . .

JOE'S DETERMINATION TO MOVE BEYOND THE PAST HAS LED HIM TO BE A POWERFUL PROBLEM SOLVER. YOU'LL LEARN MORE ABOUT JOE, AND REVISIT HIS SITUATION, WITHIN THE CHAPTER.

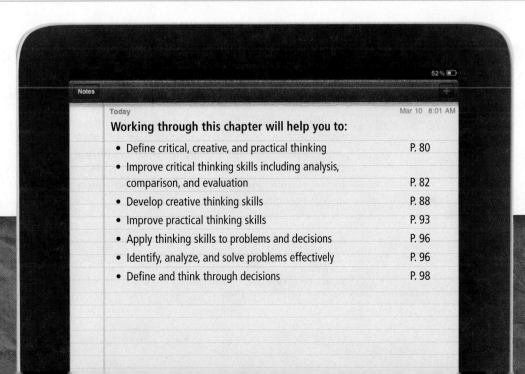

Today   Mar 10 8:01 AM

Working through this chapter will help you to:

statusCHECK

How Developed Are Your Thinking Skills?

For each statement, fill in the number that best describes how often it applies to you.

1 = never   2 = seldom   3 = sometimes   4 = often   5 = always

1. I discover information, make decisions, and solve problems by asking and answering questions. ① ② ③ ④ ⑤

2. I don't take everything I read or hear as fact—I question how useful, truthful, and logical it is before I decide whether I can use it. ① ② ③ ④ ⑤

3. I look for biased perspectives when I read or listen because I am aware of how they can lead me in the wrong direction. ① ② ③ ④ ⑤

4. Even if it seems like there is only one way to solve a problem, I brainstorm to think of other options. ① ② ③ ④ ⑤

5. I try not to let the idea that things have *always* been done a certain way stop me from trying different approaches. ① ② ③ ④ ⑤

6. When I work in a group, I try to manage my emotions and notice how I affect others. ① ② ③ ④ ⑤

7. I think about different solutions before I choose one and take action. ① ② ③ ④ ⑤

8. I spend time researching different possibilities before making a decision. ① ② ③ ④ ⑤

9. I avoid making decisions at the spur of the moment. ① ② ③ ④ ⑤

10. When I make a decision, I consider how my choice will affect others. ① ② ③ ④ ⑤

Each of the topics in these statements is covered in this chapter. Note those statements for which you filled in a 3 or lower. Skim the chapter to see where those topics appear, and pay special attention to them as you read, learn, and apply new strategies.

REMEMBER: NO MATTER HOW DEVELOPED YOUR THINKING SKILLS ARE, YOU CAN IMPROVE WITH EFFORT AND PRACTICE.

WHY IS IT IMPORTANT TO ASK
and answer questions?

What is thinking? According to experts, it is what happens when you ask questions and move toward the answers.[1] "To think through or rethink anything," says Dr. Richard Paul, director of research at the Center for Critical Thinking and Moral Critique, "one must ask questions that stimulate our thought. Questions define tasks, express problems and delineate issues . . . only students who have questions are really thinking and learning."[2] It's human to feel as though asking questions makes you look ignorant. However, the risk of questioning is what *combats* ignorance and earns you the reward of learning.

Effective Questioning

As you answer questions, you turn information into material that you can use to achieve goals. A *Wall Street Journal* article entitled "The Best Innovations Are Those That Come from Smart Questions" relays the story of a cell biology student, William Hunter, whose professor told him that "the difference between good science and great science is the quality of the questions posed." Now a physician, Dr. Hunter asks questions about new ways to use drugs. His risk-taking has helped his company reach the reward of developing a revolutionary product—a drug-coated mesh used to strengthen diseased blood vessels.[3] How can you question effectively?

Know why you question. To ask useful questions, you need to know *why* you are questioning. Define your purpose by asking: "What am I trying to accomplish, and why?" For example, if Joe's purpose for questioning his choice to go into the military was to find a different job, that would generate an entirely different set of questions than if he intended to determine his personal mission.

Question in different ways. Use questions to:

- Analyze ("How bad is my money situation?")
- Come up with creative ideas ("How can I earn more money?")
- Apply practical solutions ("Who do I talk to about getting a job on campus?")

Want to question. Knowing why you are questioning also helps you *want* to think. "Critical-thinking skills are different from critical thinking dispositions, or a willingness to deploy these skills," says cognitive psychologist D. Alan Bensley of Frostburg State University in Maryland. In other words, having the skills isn't enough—you also need the willingness to risk using them.[4] Having a clear understanding of your desired reward can motivate you to work to achieve it.

Your Primary Questioning Tool: The Prefrontal Cortex

One of the most significant research findings of the last decade is that your brain's prefrontal cortex, which controls your most complex thinking actions, undergoes its last and most comprehensive phase of development from around 18 to 25 years of age. During this phase, dendrites grow thicker, frequently used synapses become stronger, and nerve fibers become more heavily insulated, making "the entire brain a much faster and more sophisticated organ."[5] The prefrontal cortex controls executive function, which allows people to perceive possible future consequences of a choice, weigh pros and cons of different choices, and risk putting one to work, based on what seems to offer the greatest reward.

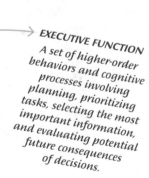

EXECUTIVE FUNCTION
A set of higher-order behaviors and cognitive processes involving planning, prioritizing tasks, selecting the most important information, and evaluating potential future consequences of decisions.

One key takeaway from this research is the fact that executive function is still under construction in the brains of people under the age of 25. Younger students who fall into this category might struggle to think through decisions and problems effectively, tend toward impulsive and physically risky actions, and make choices without anticipating pros and cons. However, the advantage is that college, offering both academic learning and new experiences, provides exactly the training ground for thinking that a brain 18 to 25 years old needs at that stage.[6]

All college students have entered a different phase of life; for younger students, this phase involves a new level of independence, and for older students who are already independent, it involves a need for increased focus on personal goals. If you can apply risk-taking tendencies to the actions you take on behalf of your education, you may be more receptive to relationships, information, and experiences that will change and develop your mind.[7] The richer networks you build among the neurons in your brain will increase your ability to think analytically, creatively, and practically in the service of solving problems and making decisions—your two most important and frequently used thinking processes.

As you read and work, keep in mind your sense of where your strengths and challenges lie in the three thinking skill areas. If you are using the MyStudentSuccessLab, you may also want to complete the My Thinking Styles inventory to get a view of your thinking skills in terms of the seven styles this inventory evaluates (insightful, open-minded, timely, analytical, inquisitive, systematic, and truth seeking).

When you need to solve a problem or make a decision, combining all three thinking skills gives you the greatest chance of achieving your goal.[8] This chapter will explore analytical, creative, and practical thinking each individually, ultimately showing how they work together to help you to solve problems and make decisions effectively. Asking questions opens the door to each thinking skill, and in each section you will find examples of the kinds of questions that drive that skill. Begin by exploring analytical thinking skills.

HOW CAN YOU IMPROVE YOUR
analytical thinking skills?

Analytical thinking is the process of gathering information, breaking it into parts, examining and evaluating those parts, and making connections for the purposes of gaining understanding, solving a problem, or making a decision.

Through the analytical process, you look for how pieces of information relate to one another, setting aside any pieces that are unclear, unrelated, unimportant, or biased. You may also form new questions that change your direction. Be open to them and to where they may lead you.

Gather Information

Information is the raw material for thinking, so to start the thinking process you must first gather your raw materials. This requires analyzing how much information you need, how much time you should spend gathering it, and whether it is relevant. Say, for instance, that you have to write a paper on one aspect of the media (TV, radio, Internet) and its influence on a particular group. Here's how analyzing can help you gather information for that paper:

- Reviewing the assignment terms, you note two important items: The paper should be approximately 10 pages and describe at least three significant points of influence.
- At the library and online, you find thousands of articles in this topic area. Analyzing your reaction to them and how many articles focus on certain aspects

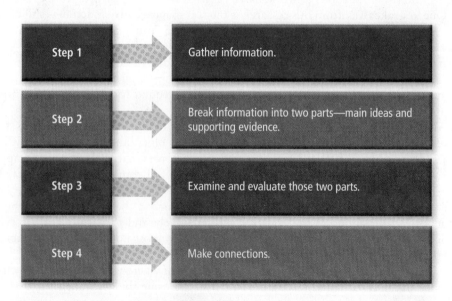

Step 1	Gather information.
Step 2	Break information into two parts—main ideas and supporting evidence.
Step 3	Examine and evaluate those two parts.
Step 4	Make connections.

of the topic, you decide to focus your paper on how the Internet influences young teens (ages 13–15).

- Examining the summaries of six comprehensive articles leads you to three in-depth sources.

In this way you achieve a sub-goal—a selection of useful materials—on the way to your larger goal of writing a well-crafted paper.

Break Information into Parts

The next step is to search for the two most relevant parts of the information: The main idea(s) (also called the argument or viewpoint) and the evidence that supports them (also called reasons or supporting details).

Separate the ideas. Identify each of the ideas conveyed in what you are reading. You can use lists or a mind map to visually separate ideas from one another. For instance, if you are reading about how teens aged 13 to 15 use the Internet, you could identify the goal of each method of access they use (websites, blogs, messaging through social networking).

Identify the evidence. For each main idea, identify the evidence that supports it. For example, if an article claims that young teens rely on app-based messaging three times more than on emails, note the facts, studies, or other evidence cited to support the truth of the claim.

Many types of work, such as the construction project these architects are discussing, involve analytical thinking.

ARGUMENT
A set of connected ideas, supported by examples, made by a writer to prove or disprove a point.

Examine and Evaluate

The third step is by far the most significant, and lies at the heart of analytical thinking. Now you examine the information to see if it is going to be useful for your purposes. Keep your mind open to all useful information, setting aside personal prejudices. A student who thinks that the death penalty is wrong, for example, may have a hard time analyzing arguments that defend it, or may focus his research on materials that support his perspective. Set aside personal prejudices when you analyze information. The extra time you risk with careful evaluation will reward you with the most accurate and useful information available.

Here are four different questions that will help you examine and evaluate effectively.

1. Do examples support ideas?

When you encounter an idea or claim, examine how it is supported with examples or *evidence*—facts, expert opinion, research findings, personal experience, and so on (see Key 4.1 for an illustration). How useful an idea is to your work may depend on whether, or how well, it is backed up with solid evidence or made concrete with examples. Be critical of the information you gather; don't take it at face value.

For example, a blog written by a 12-year-old may make statements about what kids do on the Internet. The word of one person, who may or may not be telling the truth, is not adequate support. However, a study of youth technology use by the Department of Commerce under the provisions of the Children's Internet Proctection Act may be more reliable.

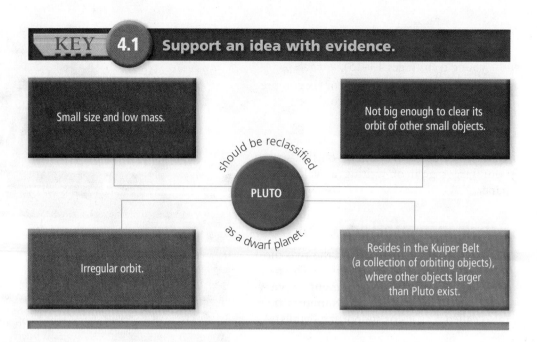

KEY 4.1 Support an idea with evidence.

Small size and low mass.

Not big enough to clear its orbit of other small objects.

should be reclassified

PLUTO

as a dwarf planet.

Irregular orbit.

Resides in the Kuiper Belt (a collection of orbiting objects), where other objects larger than Pluto exist.

2. Is the information factual and accurate, or is it opinion?

A *statement of fact* is information presented as objectively real and verifiable (e.g., "The Internet is a research tool"). In contrast, a *statement of opinion* is a belief, conclusion, or judgment that is inherently difficult, and sometimes impossible, to verify (e.g., "The Internet is always the best and most reliable research tool"). When you critically evaluate materials, one test of the evidence is whether it is fact or opinion. Key 4.2 defines important characteristics of fact and opinion.

KEY 4.2 Examine how fact and opinion differ.

FACTS INCLUDE STATEMENTS THAT . . .	OPINIONS INCLUDE STATEMENTS THAT . . .
. . . deal with actual people, places, objects, or events. Example: "In 2002, the European Union introduced the physical coins and banknotes of a new currency—the euro—that was designed to be used by its member nations."	**. . . show evaluation.** Any statement of value indicates an opinion. Words such as *bad, good, pointless,* and *beneficial* indicate value judgments. Example: "The use of the euro has been beneficial to all the states of the European Union."
. . . use concrete words or measurable statistics. Example: "The charity event raised $50,862."	**. . . use abstract words.** Complicated words like *misery* or *success* usually indicate a personal opinion. Example: "The charity event was a smashing success."
. . . describe current events in exact terms. Example: "Mr. Barrett's course has 378 students enrolled this semester."	**. . . predict future events.** Statements about future occurrences are often opinions. Example: "Mr. Barrett's course is going to set a new enrollment record this year."
. . . avoid emotional words and focus on the verifiable. Example: "Citing dissatisfaction with the instruction, seven out of the twenty-five students in that class withdrew in September."	**. . . use emotional words.** Emotions are unverifiable. Words such as *delightful* or *miserable* express an opinion. Example: "That class is a miserable experience."
. . . avoid absolutes. Example: "Some students need to have a job while in school."	**. . . use absolutes.** Absolute qualifiers, such as *all, none, never,* and *always,* often express an opinion. Example: "All students need to have a job while in school."

Source: Adapted from Ben E. Johnson, *Stirring Up Thinking.* New York: Houghton Mifflin, 1998, pp. 268–270.

get analytical

ANALYZE A STATEMENT

Complete the following on paper or in digital format.

Consider the statement below; then analyze it by answering the questions that follow.

> *"There's no point in pursuing a career area that you love
> if it isn't going to earn you a living."*

1. Is this statement fact or opinion? Why?
2. What examples can you think of that support or negate this statement?
3. What perspective(s) are guiding this statement?
4. What assumption(s) underlie the statement? What negative effects might result from accepting these assumptions and therefore agreeing with the statement?
5. As a result of your critical thinking, what is your evaluation of this statement?

3. Do causes and effects link logically?

Look at the reasons given for why something happened (causes) and the explanation of its consequences (effects, both positive and negative). For example, an article might detail what causes young teens to use the Internet after school, and the effects that this has on their family life. The cause-and-effect chain in the article should make sense to you.

An important caution: Analyze carefully to seek out key or "root" causes—the true and significant causes of a problem or situation. For example, many factors may be involved in why young teens spend large amounts of time on the Internet, including availability of service, previous experience, and education level of parents, but on careful examination one or two factors seem to be more significant than others.

4. Is the evidence biased?

Evidence with a bias is evidence that is slanted in a particular direction. Searching for a bias involves looking for hidden perspectives or assumptions that lie within the material.

A perspective can be broad (such as a generally optimistic or pessimistic view of life) or more focused (such as an attitude about whether students should commute or live on campus). Perspectives are associated with assumptions. For example, the perspective that people can maintain control over technology leads to assumptions such as "Parents can control children's exposure to the Internet." Having a particular experience with children and the Internet can build or reinforce a perspective.

Assumptions often hide within questions and statements, blocking you from considering information in different ways. Take this classic puzzler as an example: "Which came first, the chicken or the egg?" Thinking about this question, most people assume that the egg is a chicken egg. If you think past that assumption and come up with a new idea—such as, the egg is a dinosaur egg—then the obvious answer is that the egg came first. Key 4.3 offers examples of how perspectives and assumptions can affect what you read or hear through the media.

Examining perspectives and assumptions helps you judge whether material is *reliable*. The less bias you can identify, the more reliable the information.

BIAS
A preference or inclination, especially one that prevents even-handed judgment.

PERSPECTIVE
A characteristic way of thinking about people, situations, events, and ideas.

ASSUMPTION
A judgment, generalization, or bias influenced by experience and values.

get $mart

THINKING ANALYTICALLY ABOUT MONEY

Complete the following on paper or in digital format.

Analyzing potential purchases helps you decide whether the pros outweigh the cons. To practice, write down your thoughts on three potential purchases and their consequences. Use this format: "If I buy [fill in the blank] for [$ amount], I will be able to [whatever this purchase will allow you to do] but I won't [whatever sacrifice you will have to make because of the expenditure]."

Here is an example to get you started:

> If I buy <u>the latest iPhone</u> for <u>$299</u>, I will be able to <u>access the Internet, take videos, and store music and photos</u>, but I won't <u>have money for my sociology books, and I won't be able to buy coffee every morning</u>.

 **4.3** **Different articles may present different perspectives on the same topic.**

Topic: *How teens' grades are affected by Internet use*

STATEMENT BY A TEACHING ORGANIZATION	STATEMENT BY A PR AGENT FOR AN INTERNET SEARCH ENGINE	STATEMENT BY A PROFESSOR SPECIALIZING IN NEW MEDIA AND EDUCATION
"Too much Internet use equals failing grades and stolen papers."	"The Internet use allows students access to a plethora of information, which results in better grades."	"The effects of the Internet on young students are undeniable and impossible to overlook."

After the questions: What information is most useful to you?

You've examined your information, looking at its evidence, its validity, its perspective, and any underlying assumptions. Now, based on that examination, you evaluate whether an idea or piece of information is important or unimportant, relevant or not, strong or weak, and why. You then set aside what is not useful and use the rest to form an opinion, possible solution, or decision.

In preparing your paper on young teens and the Internet, for example, you've analyzed a selection of information and materials to see how they applied to the goal of your paper. You then selected what you believe will be most useful, in preparation for drafting.

Make Connections

The last part of analytical thinking is when, after you have broken information apart, you find new and logical ways to connect pieces together. This step is crucial for research papers and essays because it is where your original ideas are born, and it is also where your creative skills get involved (more on that in the next section). When you begin to write, you focus on your new ideas, supporting them effectively with information you've learned from your analysis. Here are some ways to make connections.

Compare and contrast. Look at how ideas are similar to, or different from, each other. You might explore how different young teen subgroups (boys vs. girls, for example) have different purposes for setting up pages on sites such as Facebook or creating Twitter handles.

Look for themes, patterns, and categories. Note connections that form as you look at how bits of information relate to one another. For example, you might see patterns of Internet use that link young teens from particular cultures or areas of the country together into categories.

Come to new information ready to hear and read new ideas, think about them, and make informed decisions about what you believe. The process will educate you, sharpen your thinking skills, and give you more information to work with as you encounter life's problems. See Key 4.4 for some questions you can ask to build and use analytical thinking skills.

Pursuing your goals, in school and in the workplace, requires not just analyzing information but also thinking creatively about how to use what you've learned from your analysis.

KEY 4.4 Ask questions like these to analyze.

To gather information — ask
- What kinds of information do I need to meet my goal?
- What information is available? Where and when can I get to it?
- Of the sources I found, which ones will best help me achieve my goal?

To analyze — ask
- What are the parts of this information?
- What is similar to this information? What is different?
- What are the reasons for this? Why did this happen?
- What ideas, themes, or conclusions emerge from this material?
- How would you categorize this information?

To see whether evidence or examples support an idea — ask
- Does the evidence make sense?
- How do the examples support the idea/claim?
- Are there examples that might disprove the idea/claim?

To distinguish fact from opinion — ask
- Do the words in this information signal fact or opinion?
- What is the source of this information? Is the source reliable?
- If this is an opinion, is it supported by facts?

To examine perspectives and assumptions — ask
- What perspectives might the author have, and what may be emphasized or deemphasized as a result?
- What assumptions might lie behind this statement or material?
- How could I prove—or disprove—an assumption?
- How might my perspective affect the way I see this material?

To evaluate — ask
- What information will support what I'm trying to prove or accomplish?
- Is this information true or false, and why?
- How important is this information?

Source: Adapted from www-ed.fnal.gov/trc/tutorial/taxonomy.html (Richard Paul, *Critical Thinking: How to Prepare Students for a Rapidly Changing World,* 1993) and from www.kcmetro.edu/longview/ctac/blooms.htm (Barbara Fowler, Longview Community College "Bloom's Taxonomy and Critical Thinking").

HOW CAN YOU IMPROVE YOUR
creative thinking skills?

Think of the word *creativity*, and of people whom you consider to be "creative." What comes to mind? Are you thinking of music, visual arts, design, and dance? Are Adele, Zac Posen, Natalie Portman, or Jay-Z in your thoughts? Because creativity is often equated with visual and performing arts, many people don't grasp what this section of your text will illustrate—the range of human experience that depends on creativity. Take a look at Key 4.5 for examples of what it means to be creative.

KEY 4.5   Creativity is everywhere.

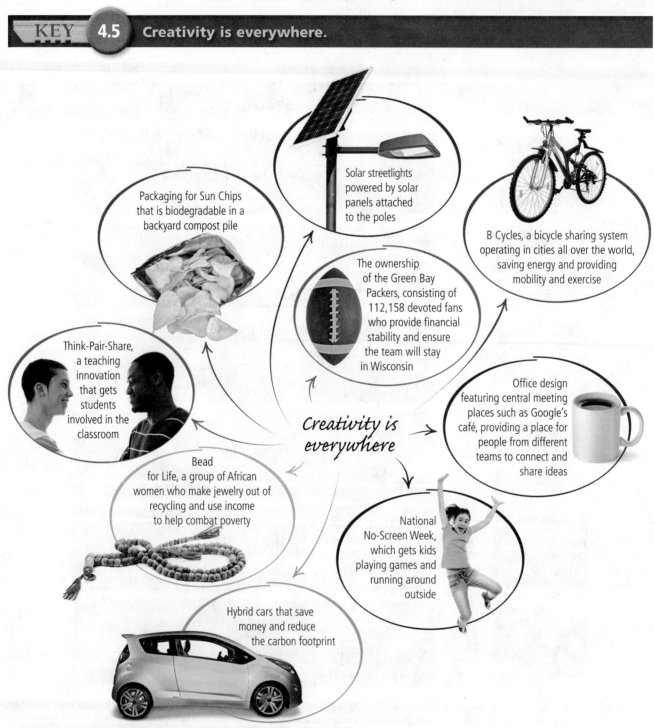

Packaging for Sun Chips that is biodegradable in a backyard compost pile

Solar streetlights powered by solar panels attached to the poles

B Cycles, a bicycle sharing system operating in cities all over the world, saving energy and providing mobility and exercise

The ownership of the Green Bay Packers, consisting of 112,158 devoted fans who provide financial stability and ensure the team will stay in Wisconsin

Think-Pair-Share, a teaching innovation that gets students involved in the classroom

Office design featuring central meeting places such as Google's café, providing a place for people from different teams to connect and share ideas

Creativity is everywhere

Bead for Life, a group of African women who make jewelry out of recycling and use income to help combat poverty

National No-Screen Week, which gets kids playing games and running around outside

Hybrid cars that save money and reduce the carbon footprint

There are many ways to define creativity. Here are a few to ponder:

- Combining existing elements in an innovative way to create a new purpose or result (using a weak adhesive to mark pages in a book, a 3M scientist created Post-it notes).
- Generating new ideas from looking at how things are related (noting what ladybugs eat inspired organic farmers to bring them in to consume crop-destroying aphids).[9]
- The ability to make unusual connections—to view information in quirky ways that bring about unique results (after examining how burrs stuck to his dog's fur after a walk in the woods, the inventor of Velcro imagined how a similar system of hooks and loops could make two pieces of fabric stick to each other).

To think creatively is to generate new ideas that promote useful change, whether the change consists of world-altering communication technology or a tooth brushing technique that more effectively prevents cavities. Prepare to power up your creative thinking ability by gathering the following five ingredients.

The Five Ingredients of Creativity

This recipe produces both the mindset and the inspiration that allow you to think creatively.

1. *Belief that you can develop creativity.*   Even though some people seem to have more or better ideas than others, creative thinking is a skill that can be developed. In an essay about the role of creativity in medicine, Jennifer Gibson, PharmD, notes, "Creativity is not restricted to great artists, but it can be fostered by training, encouragement, and practice. . . . Everyone has the power to be creative; while not everyone will paint a masterpiece or write a great novel, everyone can be curious, seek change and take risks."[10]

2. *Curiosity and exploration.*   Seeking out new information and experiences will broaden your knowledge, giving you more raw materials with which to build creative ideas.[11] Think about what sparks your curiosity, and make a point to know more about it—take a course in it, read a book about it, check out a website or some music. If you are curious about something you don't think you'd like, explore it anyway to see if you have misjudged your reaction.

3. *Time alone.*   Despite how American society values speed (so much so that we equate being "quick" with being smart)[12] and working in teams, research indicates that creativity demands time and independent thinking.[13] Think of the stereotypes of the writer alone in a cabin or a painter alone in an attic studio. Business offers examples as well, such as Apple CEO Steve Jobs's collaborator, Steve Wozniak. Mr. Wozniak worked alone for long hours over many months to develop the personal computer that Mr. Jobs marketed so ingeniously. Comparing inventors and engineers to artists in his memoir, Mr. Wozniak provides some advice that he says "might be hard to take. That advice is: Work alone."[14]

4. *Risk-taking and hard work.*   Although most people think of creativity as coming in lightning flashes of inspiration, it demands that you risk time, ideas, and enormous effort in the quest for reward. "All creative geniuses work passionately hard and produce incredible numbers of ideas, most of which are bad," reports creativity expert Michael Michalko, recounting, among other examples, the fact that Picasso created more than 20,000 pieces of art.[15] He also advocates regular practice, noting that "the more times you try to get ideas, the more active your brain becomes and the more creative you become."[16] Like any other consistent action, working on ideas builds new neural pathways in your brain.

5. *Acceptance of mistakes as part of the process.*   When you can risk messing up, you open yourself to ideas and promote productivity. Michalko repackages the idea of failure as a learning experience along the way to something better. "Whenever you try to do something and do not succeed," he says, "you do not fail. You have learned something that does not work."[17]

You have set the stage for creativity with this recipe. Next, explore actions that will help you build your creative thinking skill: braingaming, shifting your perspective, and taking risks.

Go Beyond Brainstorming

You've likely heard of *brainstorming*—letting your mind freely associate to come up with different ideas or answers to a question. This longstanding creative technique demands that you generate ideas without regard to usefulness, and evaluate their quality later. New research calls the value of brainstorming into question, showing that avoiding evaluating idea quality can result in fewer and less effective ideas. Researchers report that constructive criticism and dissent generate *more* ideas and promote the rethinking and refining that lead to an idea's most productive form.[18] "All these errant discussions add up," says Lehrer. "In fact, they may even be the most essential part of the creative process. . . . It is the human friction that makes the sparks."[19]

Teamwork is crucial in today's workplace, and the most productive teamwork will incorporate constructive dissent and questioning. Instead of brainstorming, think of it as *braingaming*—a term that incorporates the challenges and back-and-forth that can take groups to new heights of creativity.[20] Remember that you don't have to sacrifice civility to have a successful braingaming session. At Pixar, groups use a technique called "plussing," which refers to positive, productive criticism that includes way of improving on the idea being discussed.[21] Keep the "plus" in mind as you contribute and evaluate. Use the following strategies to get the most out of your braingaming.

Avoid looking for one right answer. Questions may have many "right answers"— answers that have degrees of usefulness. The more possibilities you generate, the better your chance of finding the best one. Thomas Edison is said to have tried over 2,000 filaments before he found the right one for the tungsten electric bulb.

Mix collaboration with private time. Group members can become inspired by, and make creative use of, one another's ideas.[22] However, creativity also requires time alone, and working in groups can have drawbacks, including team members letting others do all the work or mimicking others' ideas out of peer pressure.[23] Consider having members generate ideas on their own before bringing them to the group. Sharing ideas electronically is often extremely productive because group members can feel independent while taking in ideas from others at the same time.

Keep recording tools at the ready. Creative ideas can fly out of your mind as quickly as they enter. Get in the habit of recording ideas as you think of them. Keep a pen and paper by your bed, your smartphone in your pocket, a notepad in your car, or a recorder in your backpack so you can record creative thoughts before they fade.

Shift Your Perspective

If no one ever questioned established opinion, people would still think the sun revolved around the Earth. Here are some ways to change how you look at a situation or problem.

Challenge assumptions. Taking the risk of going against what people assume to be true can lead you down innovative paths. In the late 1960s, for example, most people assumed that school provided education and television provided entertainment. Jim Henson, a pioneer in children's television, asked, "Why can't we use TV to educate young children?" From that question, the characters of Sesame Street, and many other educational programs, were born. Another example

When you think through something with others in a group, the variety of ideas gives you a better chance of finding a workable solution to a problem.

is the company 2Kool and the clothing and workshops it produces, founded by graffiti artists Bimmer Torres and Ratha Sok who challenged the assumption that graffiti is simply defacement of property.

Try on another point of view. Ask others for their perspectives, read about new ways to approach situations, or risk going with the opposite of your first instinct.[24] Then use what you learn to inspire creativity. For a political science course, for example, you might craft a position paper for a senatorial candidate that goes against your position on that particular issue. For a fun example of how looking at something in a new way can unearth a totally different idea, look at the perception puzzles in Key 4.6.

Ask "what if" questions. Set up imaginary environments in which new ideas can grow, such as "What if I had unlimited money or time?" For example, the founders of Seeds of Peace, faced with long-term conflict in the Middle East, took the risk to ask: What if Israeli and Palestinian teens met at a summer camp in Maine to build mutual understanding and respect? Based on the ideas that came up, they created an organization that provides enormous reward to teenagers from the Middle East, helping them to develop leadership and communication skills.

Take Risks

Creative breakthroughs can come from targeted risk-taking.

Go against established ideas. The founders of Etsy.com went against the idea that the American consumer prefers cheap, conventional, mass-produced items. In 2005, they took the risk of creating an online company that allows artisans to offer one-of-a-kind, handmade products to the consumer, and were rewarded with a thriving site that has also created a community of artists and personally connects each artist to his or her customers.

Risk leaving your comfort zone. Rewards can come when you seek out new experiences and environments. Go somewhere you've never been. Play music you've never heard of. Seek out people who interest you but with whom you would not normally connect. Check out an international or independent film or documentary that is completely outside of your experience. Even small risks like these can create ideas that generate big changes.

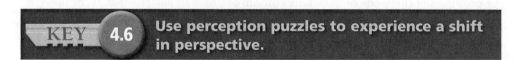

KEY 4.6 **Use perception puzzles to experience a shift in perspective.**

There are two possibilities for each image. What do you see?
(See page 105 for answers.)

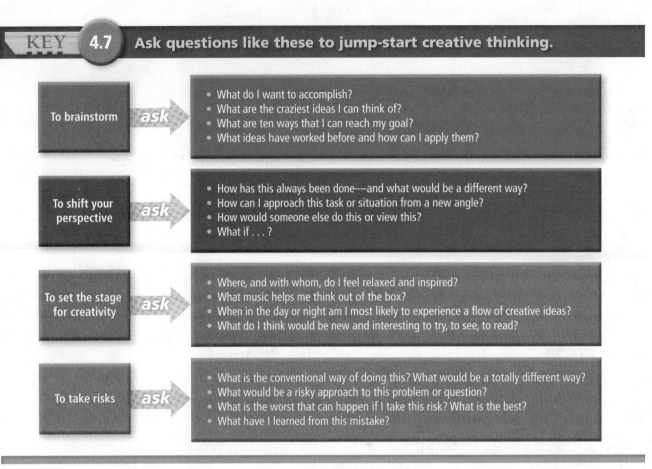

KEY 4.7 Ask questions like these to jump-start creative thinking.

To brainstorm *ask*
- What do I want to accomplish?
- What are the craziest ideas I can think of?
- What are ten ways that I can reach my goal?
- What ideas have worked before and how can I apply them?

To shift your perspective *ask*
- How has this always been done—and what would be a different way?
- How can I approach this task or situation from a new angle?
- How would someone else do this or view this?
- What if . . . ?

To set the stage for creativity *ask*
- Where, and with whom, do I feel relaxed and inspired?
- What music helps me think out of the box?
- When in the day or night am I most likely to experience a flow of creative ideas?
- What do I think would be new and interesting to try, to see, to read?

To take risks *ask*
- What is the conventional way of doing this? What would be a totally different way?
- What would be a risky approach to this problem or question?
- What is the worst that can happen if I take this risk? What is the best?
- What have I learned from this mistake?

Throughout your course you will explore real-life, day-to-day ways that creative thinking makes a difference: solving financial issues, deciding how to handle communication problems, creative ways to manage your time, and much more. Later in this chapter you will see the starring role that creativity plays in problem solving and decision making. Your efforts to be creative will enable you to grow and change over time, adding value to your relationships and to whatever you choose to do in your life.

As with analytical thinking, asking questions powers creative thinking. See Key 4.7 for examples of the kinds of questions you can ask to get your creative juices flowing.

Creativity connects analytical and practical thinking. When you generate ideas, solutions, or choices, you need to think analytically to evaluate their quality. Then, you need to think practically about how to make the best solution or choice happen.

talk risk and reward . . .

Risk asking tough questions to be rewarded with new insights. Use the following questions to inspire discussion with classmates, either in person or online.

- What problem(s) do you see others avoid? What happens as a result?
- What problem(s) do you avoid? What do you risk when avoiding these problems? What might result from the different risk you take to address them?

CONSIDER THE CASE: What problems do you think Joe may have experienced in his first term as a college student? If you had known him at school, what risks would you have advised him to take that may have helped him adjust to college life?

get creative

ACTIVATE YOUR CREATIVE POWERS

Complete the following on paper or in digital format.

Think about your creativity over the past month.

1. First, describe three creative acts you performed—one in the process of studying course material, one in your personal life, and one at work or in the classroom.
2. Now think of a problem or situation that is on your mind. Generate one new idea for how to deal with it.
3. Write down a second idea, but focus on the risk-taking aspect of creativity. What would be a risky way to handle the situation? How do you hope it would pay off?
4. Finally, sit with the question. Write down one more idea *only* after you have been away from this exercise for at least 24 hours.

Keep these ideas in mind. You may want to use one soon!

HOW CAN YOU IMPROVE YOUR
practical thinking skills?

You've analyzed a situation. You've come up with ideas. Now, with your practical skill, you make things happen.

Practical thinking—also called *common sense* or *street smarts*—refers to how you adapt to your environment (both people and circumstances), or shape or change your environment to adapt to you, to pursue important goals. Let's say your goal is to pass freshman composition. You learn most successfully through visual presentations. To achieve your goal, you can use the instructor's PowerPoints or other visual media to enhance your learning (adapt to your environment) or enroll in a heavily visual Internet course (change your environment to adapt to you)—or both.

Why Practical Thinking Is Important

Real-world problems and decisions require you to add understanding of experiences and social interactions to your analytical abilities. Your success in a sociology class, for example, may depend almost as much on getting along with your instructor as on your academic work. Similarly, the way you solve a personal money problem may have more impact on your life than how you work through a problem in an accounting course.

Keep in mind, too, that in the workplace you need to use practical skills to apply academic knowledge to problems and decisions. For example, while students working toward an associate's degree in elementary education may successfully quote child development facts on an exam, their career success depends on their ability to evaluate and address real children's needs in the classroom. Successfully solving real-world problems demands a practical approach.

Through Experience, You Build Emotional Intelligence

You gain much of your ability to think practically from personal experience, rather than from formal training.[25] What you learn from experience answers "how"

93

questions—how to talk, how to behave, how to proceed.[26] For example, after completing several papers for a course, you may learn what your instructor expects, or, after a few arguments with a friend or partner, you may learn how to manage "hot button" topics more effectively. See Key 4.8 for one example of how this can happen, shown in terms of "if–then" statements.

Emotional intelligence gives you steps you can take to promote success. For example, when Joe was told he wasn't college material, he was angry about it. With effort, his response involved these practical and emotionally intelligent actions:

- *Perceiving emotions:* After he heard the comment, recognizing his feelings of being hurt and insulted
- *Thinking about emotions:* Noting what perception arose from those feelings (at first, "I'm not good enough") and how it affected his mindset (at first, made him feel badly about himself)
- *Understanding emotions:* Determining that the emotions told him he was of little value, and considering how to adjust that mindset to increase self-worth and determination
- *Managing emotions:* Using what he learned, making a decision to prove the recruiter wrong and supporting that goal with actions such as applying to colleges

KEY 4.8 One way to map out what you learn from experience.

Goal: You want to talk to the soccer coach about your status on the team.

IF the team has had a good practice and IF you've played well during the scrimmage and IF the coach isn't rushing off somewhere, THEN grab a moment with him right after practice ends.

IF the team is having a tough time and IF you've been sidelined and IF the coach is in a rush and stressed, THEN drop in during his office hours tomorrow.

Through these actions, Joe's emotional intelligence made it more likely that he would achieve his goal of attending college and earning a degree.

If you know that social interactions are difficult for you, enlist someone to give you some informal coaching. As Dr. Norman Rosenthal reports in "10 Ways to Enhance Your Emotional Intelligence," you may not realize how much others can tell what you are feeling. "Ask someone who knows you (and whom you trust) how you are coming across," he recommends.[27] For example, ask a friend to role-play the meeting with your instructor (with the friend playing the instructor) and give you feedback on your words, tone, and body language. Or, bring a friend with you to the actual meeting and talk later about how things went.

Practical Thinking Means Action

Action is the logical result of practical thinking. Basic student success strategies that promote action—staying motivated, making the most of your strengths, managing time, seeking help from instructors and advisors, and believing in yourself—will keep you moving toward your goals.[28] Learning from mistakes and failure is an especially important part of practical thinking. As psychologist Barry Schwartz points out, "Wisdom comes from experience, and not just any experience. You need permission to be allowed to improvise, to try new things, occasionally to fail, and to learn from your failures."[29] When people resist making mistakes, they deny themselves chances to learn and develop their powers of reasoning.

The key to making practical knowledge work is to use what you discover, assuring that you will not have to learn the same lessons over and over again. As Sternberg says, "What matters most is not how much experience you have had but rather how much you have profited from it—in other words, how well you apply what you have learned."[30]

See Key 4.9 for some questions you can ask in order to apply practical thinking to your problems and decisions.

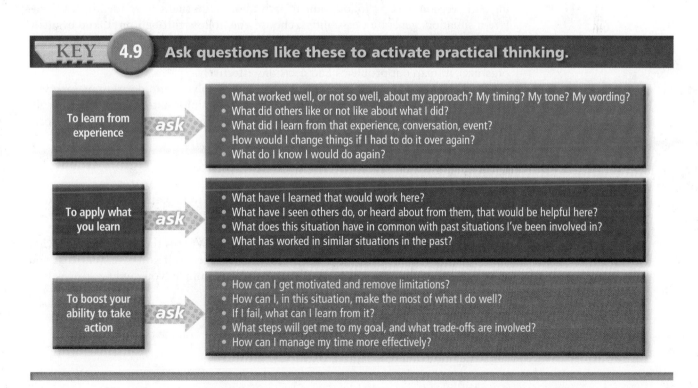

KEY 4.9 Ask questions like these to activate practical thinking.

To learn from experience — *ask*
- What worked well, or not so well, about my approach? My timing? My tone? My wording?
- What did others like or not like about what I did?
- What did I learn from that experience, conversation, event?
- How would I change things if I had to do it over again?
- What do I know I would do again?

To apply what you learn — *ask*
- What have I learned that would work here?
- What have I seen others do, or heard about from them, that would be helpful here?
- What does this situation have in common with past situations I've been involved in?
- What has worked in similar situations in the past?

To boost your ability to take action — *ask*
- How can I get motivated and remove limitations?
- How can I, in this situation, make the most of what I do well?
- If I fail, what can I learn from it?
- What steps will get me to my goal, and what trade-offs are involved?
- How can I manage my time more effectively?

get practical

TAKE A PRACTICAL APPROACH TO BUILDING SUCCESSFUL INTELLIGENCE

Complete the following on paper or in digital format.

Considering the three thinking skills, write the one in which you most need to build strength (look back at your Wheel of Successful Intelligence if you completed one in your text).

Then, name and describe two practical actions you can take that will improve your skills in that area. For example, someone who wants to be more creative could take a course focused on creativity; someone who wants to be more practical could work on paying attention to social cues; someone who wants to be more analytical could decide to analyze one newspaper article every week. Be as specific as you can about your plans, noting what you will do, when, and how.

CHAPTER 4

HOW CAN YOU SOLVE PROBLEMS AND
make decisions effectively?

Successful problem solvers and decision makers put their analytical, creative, and practical thinking skills together to solve problems and make decisions. Problem solving and decision making follow similar paths, both requiring you to identify and analyze a situation, generate possibilities, choose one, follow through on it, and evaluate its success. Key 4.10 gives an overview of the paths, indicating how you think at each step. Later in the chapter, Keys 4.12 and 4.13 show how to use this path, and a visual organizer, to map out problems and decisions effectively.

Understanding the differences between problem solving and decision making will help you know how to proceed. See Key 4.11 for more information. Whereas all problem solving involves decision making, only some decision making requires you to solve a problem.

Solve a Problem

Use these strategies as you move through the problem-solving process outlined in Key 4.10.

Use probing questions to define problems. Ask: What is the problem? And what is *causing* the problem? Engage your emotional intelligence. If you determine that you are not motivated to do your work for a class, for example, you could ask questions like these:

- Do my feelings stem from how I interact with my instructor or classmates?
- Is the subject matter difficult? Uninteresting? Is the volume of work too much?

Chances are that how you answer one or more of these questions may help you define the problem—and ultimately solve it.

KEY 4.10 Solve problems and make decisions using successful intelligence.

PROBLEM SOLVING	THINKING SKILL	DECISION MAKING
Define the problem—recognize that something needs to change, identify what's happening, look for true causes.	STEP 1 DEFINE	**Define the decision**—identify your goal (your need) and then construct a decision that will help you get it.
Analyze the problem—gather information, break it down into pieces, verify facts, look at perspectives and assumptions, evaluate information.	STEP 2 ANALYZE	**Examine needs and motives**—consider the layers of needs carefully, and be honest about what you really want.
Generate possible solutions—use creative strategies to think of ways you could address the causes of this problem.	STEP 3 CREATE	**Name and/or generate different options**—use creative questions to come up with choices that would fulfill your needs.
Evaluate solutions—look carefully at potential pros and cons of each, and choose what seems best.	STEP 4 ANALYZE (EVALUATE)	**Evaluate options**—look carefully at potential pros and cons of each, and choose what seems best.
Put the solution to work—persevere, focus on results, and believe in yourself as you go for your goal.	STEP 5 TAKE PRACTICAL ACTION	**Act on your decision**—go down the path and use practical strategies to stay on target.
Evaluate how well the solution worked—look at the effects of what you did.	STEP 6 ANALYZE (REEVALUATE)	**Evaluate the success of your decision**—look at whether it accomplished what you had hoped.
In the future, apply what you've learned—use this solution, or a better one, when a similar situation comes up again.	STEP 7 TAKE PRACTICAL ACTION	**In the future, apply what you've learned**—make this choice, or a better one, when a similar decision comes up again.

KEY 4.11 Examine how problems and decisions differ.

SITUATION	YOU HAVE A PROBLEM IF . . .	YOU NEED TO MAKE A DECISION IF . . .
PLANNING SUMMER ACTIVITIES	Your low GPA means you need to attend summer school—and you've already accepted a summer job.	You've been accepted into two summer abroad internship programs.
DECLARING A MAJOR	It's time to declare, but you don't have all the prerequisites for the major you want.	There are three majors that appeal to you and you qualify for them all.
HANDLING COMMUNICA-TIONS WITH INSTRUCTORS	You are having trouble following the lecture style of a particular instructor.	Your psychology survey course has seven sections taught by different instructors; you have to choose one.

Analyze carefully. Gather information that will help you examine the problem. Consider how the problem is similar to, or different from, other problems. Clarify facts. Note your own perspective, and look for others. Make sure your assumptions are not getting in the way.

Generate possible solutions based on causes, not effects. Addressing a cause provides a lasting solution, whereas "putting a Band-Aid on" an effect cannot. Say, for example, that your shoulder hurts when you type. Getting a massage is a helpful but temporary solution, because the pain returns whenever you go back to work. Changing your keyboard height is a better idea and a lasting solution to the problem, because it eliminates the cause of your pain.

Consider how possible solutions affect you and others. Which risk rewards you most? Which takes other people's needs into consideration? Is it possible to maximize reward for all involved?

Evaluate your solution and act on it in the future. Once you choose a solution and put it into action, ask yourself: What worked that you would do again? What didn't work that you would avoid or change in the future?

What happens if you don't work through a problem comprehensively? Take, for example, a student having an issue with an instructor. He may get into an argument with the instructor, stop showing up to class, or do halfhearted work on assignments. All of these choices have negative consequences. Now look at how the student might work through this problem using analytical, creative, and practical thinking skills. Key 4.12 shows how his effort can pay off.

Make a Decision

As you use the steps in Key 4.10 to make a decision, remember these strategies.

Look at the given options—then try to think of more. Some decisions have a given set of options. For example, your school may offer AA, AS, AGS, and certificate programs. However, within the program you choose, you may be able to work with an advisor to come up with creative options for majoring. Consider similar situations you've been in or heard about, what decisions were made, and what resulted from those decisions.

Think about how your decision affects others. What you choose might have an impact on friends, family, and others around you.

Gather perspectives. Talk with others who made similar decisions. If you listen carefully, you may hear ideas you never thought about. Consider choices with different levels of risk.

Look at the long-term effects. As with problem solving, it's key to examine what happened after you put the decision into action. For important decisions, do a short-term evaluation and another evaluation after a period of time. Consider whether your decision sent you in the right direction or whether you should rethink your choice.

What happens when you make important decisions too quickly? Consider a student trying to decide whether to transfer schools. If she makes her decision based on a reason that ultimately is not the most important one for her (for example, a boyfriend or close friends go to the other school), she may regret her choice later.

Now look at how this student might make an effective decision. Key 4.13 shows how she worked through the analytical, creative, and practical parts of the process.

Keep Your Balance

No one has equal strengths in analytical, creative, and practical thinking. Successfully intelligent thinkers are able to analyze their abilities, come up with creative ideas about how to maximize their strengths and build their weaknesses, and put them to use with practical action. Staying as balanced as possible requires that you

- Use what you've learned in this chapter and the rest of the text to maximize your analytical, creative, and practical abilities.
- Reflect on what you do well, and focus on strengthening weaker skills.

KEY 4.12 Work through a problem: An issue with an instructor.

Critical, Creative, and Practical Thinking

DEFINE PROBLEM HERE:	ANALYZE THE PROBLEM
I don't like my Sociology instructor	We have different styles and personality types—I am not comfortable working in groups and being vocal. I'm not interested in being there, and my grades are suffering from my lack of motivation.

Use boxes below to list possible solutions:

POTENTIAL POSITIVE EFFECTS	SOLUTION #1	POTENTIAL NEGATIVE EFFECTS
List for each solution: Don't have to deal with that instructor	Drop the course	*List for each solution:* Grade gets entered on my transcript
Less stress		I'll have to take the course eventually; it's required for my major
Getting credit for the course	SOLUTION #2	Stress every time I'm there
Feeling like I've honored a commitment	Put up with it until the end of the semester	Lowered motivation Probably not such a good final grade
A chance to express myself	SOLUTION #3	Have to face instructor one-on-one
Could get good advice An opportunity to ask direct questions of the instructor	Schedule meetings with advisor and instructor	Might just make things worse

Now choose the solution you think is best—circle it and make it happen.

ACTUAL POSITIVE EFFECTS	PRACTICAL ACTION	ACTUAL NEGATIVE EFFECTS
List for chosen solution: Got some helpful advice from advisor Talking in person with the instructor actually promoted a fairly honest discussion I won't have to take the course again	I scheduled and attended meetings with both advisor and instructor and opted to stick with the course.	*List for chosen solution:* Still have to put up with some group work I still don't know how much learning I'll retain from this course

FINAL EVALUATION: Was it a good or bad solution?

The solution has improved things. I'll finish the course, and I got the chance to fulfill some class responsibilities on my own or with one partner. I feel more understood and more willing to put my time into the course.

KEY 4.13 Make a decision about whether to transfer schools.

DEFINE PROBLEM HERE:	EXAMINE NEEDS AND MOTIVES
Whether or not to transfer schools	My father has changed jobs and can no longer afford my tuition. My goal is to become a physical therapist, so I need a school with a full physical therapy program. My family needs to cut costs. I need to transfer credits.

Use boxes below to list possible solutions:

POTENTIAL POSITIVE EFFECTS	SOLUTION #1	POTENTIAL NEGATIVE EFFECTS
List for each solution: No need to adjust to a new place or new people Ability to continue course work as planned	Continue at the current college	*List for each solution:* Need to finance most of my tuition and costs on my own Difficult to find time for a job Might not qualify for aid
Some coursework available that would apply toward physical therapy degree Reasonable tuition Parents have a friend who works in advising there	SOLUTION #2 Transfer to less expensive school	No personal contacts there that I know of Will have to investigate whether credits will transfer No full physical therapy program
Opportunity to earn tuition money Could live at home Status should be intact	SOLUTION #3 Stop out for a year	Could forget so much that it's hard to go back Could lose motivation A year might turn into more

Now choose the solution you think is best—circle it and make it happen.

ACTUAL POSITIVE EFFECTS	PRACTICAL ACTION	ACTUAL NEGATIVE EFFECTS
List for chosen solution: Money saved Opportunity to spend time on studies rather than on working to earn tuition money Availability of classes I need	Go to less expensive school for two years; then transfer to a school that offers complete physical therapy coursework in connection with a B.A.	*List for chosen solution:* Less contact with friends Will need to transfer again at some point Additional time and effort required to map out new academic plan

FINAL EVALUATION: Was it a good or bad solution?
I'm satisfied with the decision. It can be hard adjusting to a new place and making new friends, but with fewer social distractions I'm getting more work done. And the reduced cost suits my needs perfectly right now.

student PROFILE

Jacob Rudolph
NORTHEASTERN UNIVERSITY, BOSTON, MASSACHUSETTS

About me:

I am a freshman currently pursuing a degree in music business. I am also an advocate for LGBT teens for the Human Rights Campaign. As a high school senior, I publicly came out as LGBT in front of over 300 classmates at a school awards ceremony, and plan to continue working on behalf of the LGBT community during college and throughout my life.

What I focus on:

To me, every decision deserves consideration proportional to its magnitude. The biggest decision I have made was when I publicly came out of the closet. Realizing the situation's importance, I took three days to draft up a list of pros and cons regarding the ramifications of coming out in the manner in which I wanted. I listed all of my fears as well as the outcomes for which I could only have hoped. Still left with much uncertainty about the situation, I showed the list to a teacher who pointed out that all of my "cons" were hypothetical, while most of my "pros" were definite. This helped me realize that anytime we fear something, it is because we are forced to reconcile the unknown.

Working efficiently is a constant struggle for me. After coming out of the closet, however, I can honestly say that I have become more productive than ever. When I took action to face my problems head-on, a major source of stress and concern in my life transformed into something wonderful and healthy.

What will help me in the workplace:

My experience has given me confidence that I am my own person, and certainty that nothing should be allowed to restrain all of the potential we have cooped up inside of us. This attitude will help me excel in any job or career that lies ahead, as will my ability to understand the reality of a problem, identify outcomes, and take action. Productivity is the name of the game, and problem-solvers produce.

- Combine all three thinking skills to accomplish your goals, knowing when and how to apply your analytical, creative, and practical abilities.
- Believe in your skills as a thinker.

"Successfully intelligent people," says Sternberg, "defy negative expectations, even when these expectations arise from low scores on IQ or similar tests. They do not let other people's assessments stop them from achieving their goals. They find their path and then pursue it, realizing that there will be obstacles along the way and that surmounting these obstacles is part of the challenge."[31] Let the obstacles come, as they will for everyone, in all aspects of life. You can take the risk to face them, and earn the reward of overcoming them, with the power of your successfully intelligent thinking.

revisit RISK AND REWARD

What happened to Joe? The stress of what Joe had left behind motivated him to move ahead. Driven to succeed, Joe prioritized his work—and earned the reward of a 4.0 in his first term. The pressure of maintaining that success presented a different sort of challenge, to which he responded by taking two distinct risks: Putting an enormous amount of time and effort into the rest of his experience, and refusing to drink and do drugs. He socialized "strategically," making friends in groups that he joined so that he could have fun and accomplish something at the same time. He finished community college, transferred to the University of West Florida, and graduated at the top of his class with a bachelor's degree.

After college, a motivational speaker helped him realize he could make a living by communicating ideas to students growing up in poverty. Now, having earned master's and doctoral degrees and spoken to more than a quarter of a million people about student success through courses, speeches, books, and recorded programs, he can reach students all over the globe through his website, Real World University. As a professor and educational consultant, he takes risks every day for the reward of helping students make the most of their gifts and talents.

What does this mean for you? Joe worked hard to move away from environments, people, and situations that he thought would not allow him to achieve the rewards he valued. Think about an environment, person, or situation that presents a problem for you and prevents you from living the way you want to live. Think through the problem. Assess its causes, determine the reward you aim for, and come up with potential risks you could take that might move you in that direction. Evaluate the pros and cons of each solution. You may not choose one right away, but commit to taking action on this problem soon.

What risk may bring reward beyond your world? One person making positive changes sets an example for others, and can have an effect that stretches through many different networks of people. Joe Martin's website (www.rwuniversity.com) is his way of putting his positive changes out there for others to consider. Risk making a change that your friends will notice—a change in how you spend your time, study, stay well, or anything else that can improve your day-to-day life. If anyone questions your choice, let that person know what you are doing and what reward you seek. Maybe you will inspire others to think, and even to follow your lead.

Complete the following on paper or in digital format.

KNOW IT *Think Critically*

Make an Important Decision

Build basic skills. List the steps of the decision-making process.

Take it to the next level. Think about how you would put the decision-making process to work on something that matters to you. Write an important long-term goal that you have, and define the decision that will help you fulfill it. Example: "My goal is to become a nurse. My decision: What to specialize in."

Move toward mastery. Use the empty flowchart (Key 4.14) to apply the decision-making process to your goal. Follow the steps below.

- *Examine needs and concerns.* What are your needs, and how do your values come into play? What is most needed in the health market, and how can you fulfill that need? What roadblocks might be involved? List what you come up with in the "Analyze the problem/decision" section. For example, the prospective nurse might list needs like: "I need to feel that I'm helping people. I intend to help with the shortage of perinatal or geriatric nurses. I need to make a good living."

- *Generate options.* Ask questions to imagine what's possible. Where might you work? What might be the schedule and pace? Who might work with you? What would you see, smell, and hear on your job? What would you do every day? Make a separate list of all of the options you know of. The prospective nurse, for example, might list perinatal surgery, neonatal intensive care unit, geriatric nursing in a hospital or in a retirement community, etc.

- *Evaluate options.* Think about how well your options will fulfill your needs. Select three options to analyze. Write potential positive and negative effects (pros and cons) of each.

- *Imagine acting on your decision.* Choose one practical course of action, based on your thinking so far, that you might follow. List the specific steps you would take. For example, the prospective nurse might list actions that help him determine what type of nursing suits him best, such as interning, summer jobs, academic goals, and talking to working nurses. If you eventually act on this choice, you can fill in actual positive and negative effects in the flowchart, as well as a final evaluation.

An additional practical action is to go where the job is and talk to people. The prospective nurse might go to a hospital, a clinic, and a health center at a retirement community. Get a feel for what the job is like day-to-day so that can be part of your decision.

KEY 4.14 Work through a decision or problem using this flowchart.

DEFINE PROBLEM/DECISION: | **ANALYZE PROBLEM/DECISION**

Use center boxes to list possible options:

POTENTIAL POSITIVE EFFECTS	**OPTION #1**	**POTENTIAL NEGATIVE EFFECTS**
List for each:		*List for each:*

OPTION #2

OPTION #3

Now choose the one you think is best—circle it and make it happen.

ACTUAL POSITIVE EFFECTS	**PRACTICAL ACTION**	**ACTUAL NEGATIVE EFFECTS**
List for chosen option:		*List for chosen option:*

FINAL EVALUATION: Did your action, overall, have a positive or negative result?

Source: Based on heuristic created by Frank T. Lyman Jr. and George Eley, 1985.

WRITE IT *Communicate*

Emotional intelligence journal: Make a wiser choice. Think about a decision you made that you wish you had handled differently. Describe the decision and what feelings resulted from it. Then, describe what you would do if you could approach the decision again, thinking about what mindset and actions might produce more positive feelings and a better outcome.

Real-life writing: Address a problem. Think about a problem you have right now—difficulty with a course, a scheduling nightmare, conflict with a classmate. Write a letter—to an advisor, instructor, friend, or someone else—asking for support. Be specific about what you need and how the person can help. Assess the effect that the letter may have, and if you decide that it may help, have someone you trust review it for you and then send it via mail or email.

WORK IT *Build Your Brand*

Generate Ideas for Internships

21st Century Learning Building Blocks

- Financial, economic, business, and entrepreneurial literacy
- Leadership and responsibility
- Communication and collaboration

Pursuing internships is a practical way to get experience, learn what you like and don't like, and make valuable connections. Even if you intern in a career area that you don't ultimately pursue, you build skills that are useful in any career. The creative thinking skills you've built will help you generate ideas for where you might intern at some point during your college career.

First, use personal contacts to gather information about career fields. Generate the names of two people whom you want to interview about their fields or professions. Note the following for each:

- Name and contact information
- Field
- Why you want to interview him or her

Then talk to the people you have listed, and take notes.

Next, look up each of these fields in the Occupational Outlook Handbook published by the U.S. Department of Labor (available at the library or online). To get a better idea of whether you would want to intern in these fields, read OOH categories for each such as Nature of the Work, Training, Working Conditions, Advancement, Job Outlook, Earnings, and so on. Take notes and compare the fields based on what you've learned.

Finally, consult someone in your school's career office about local companies that offer internships. Note specific information about internship job descriptions, timing (during the term, summer), and whether there is any pay involved.

Analyze what you have learned from your reading, your interviews, and the career office information. Based on your analysis, name what field or fields in which you would like to intern and why. Then, describe what practical action you plan to take to secure an internship within the next two years.

Answers to perception puzzles on p. 91

First puzzle: A duck or a rabbit
Second puzzle: Lines or a letter

You live in an information age. Your future demands that you be able to read, understand, and critically evaluate information on a daily basis in school, on the job, and in life.

Reading and Information Literacy

LEARNING FROM PRINT AND ONLINE MATERIALS

What Would You Risk? *Gary Montrose*

THINK ABOUT THIS SITUATION AS YOU READ, AND CONSIDER WHAT ACTION YOU WOULD TAKE. THIS CHAPTER FOCUSES ON HOW TO UNDERSTAND WHAT YOU READ AND RESEARCH, ANALYZE IT CRITICALLY, DECIDE WHAT IS IMPORTANT, AND USE WHAT IS RELEVANT.

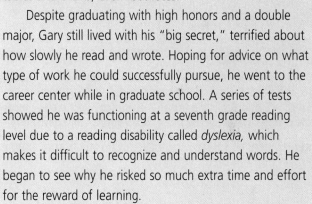

Gary Montrose had no idea why he struggled with reading in grade school, and neither did his family or teachers. He was the first to sit down during spelling bees and the last to turn in exams, even though his risk-taking rewarded him with the title of student body president at Palmdale High School. His guidance counselor told him he "wasn't college material" and should consider going straight into a job putting rivets into airplanes at the local Lockheed assembly plant.

Determined to persevere, Gary risked enrolling at Antelope Valley College in Palmdale, California. After two years of hard work, he was able to transfer to the University of California at Berkeley, but the confusing struggle remained, damaging his self-confidence and forcing him to develop survival strategies. For example, he avoided courses with in-class timed exams—an absolute terror for him—and looked for ones featuring papers he could write on his own time. He also risked giving up 90% of a normal college student's social life to spend endless hours reading. Knowing he was unlikely to complete any reading assignment, he "unpacked" his textbooks by studying the table of contents, chapter headings, titles of tables and charts, even footnotes.

Despite graduating with high honors and a double major, Gary still lived with his "big secret," terrified about how slowly he read and wrote. Hoping for advice on what type of work he could successfully pursue, he went to the career center while in graduate school. A series of tests showed he was functioning at a seventh grade reading level due to a reading disability called *dyslexia*, which makes it difficult to recognize and understand words. He began to see why he risked so much extra time and effort for the reward of learning.

To be continued . . .

GARY'S ABILITY TO MOVE OUT OF HIS COMFORT ZONE AND FIND WAYS TO OVERCOME HIS DYSLEXIA TURNED LEARNING INTO AN ADVENTURE THAT HE CONTINUES AS A WORLDWIDE TRAVELER. YOU'LL LEARN MORE ABOUT GARY, AND THE REWARD RESULTING FROM HIS ACTIONS, WITHIN THE CHAPTER.

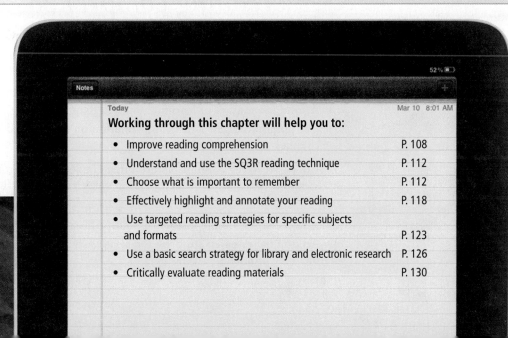

52%

Notes

Today   Mar 10 8:01 AM

Working through this chapter will help you to:

status CHECK

How Developed Are Your Reading and Information Literacy Skills?

For each statement, fill in the number that best describes how often it applies to you.

1 = never   2 = seldom   3 = sometimes   4 = often   5 = always

1. To improve my comprehension, I make choices about when and how I read. ① ② ③ ④ ⑤

2. Before reading a textbook, I look for content and organization clues by skimming and scanning front matter, chapter elements, and back matter. ① ② ③ ④ ⑤

3. I develop questions to guide me before I begin to read. ① ② ③ ④ ⑤

4. I recite what I've learned using techniques such as working with a study partner, taking notes, and using flash cards. ① ② ③ ④ ⑤

5. I turn materials into study tools by taking notes and highlighting key information. ① ② ③ ④ ⑤

6. I have an effective process for reading on-screen assignments and articles. ① ② ③ ④ ⑤

7. I prioritize my reading assignments to focus on what is most important. ① ② ③ ④ ⑤

8. When I get a research or writing assignment, I go first to general references for an overview. ① ② ③ ④ ⑤

9. I don't just rely on the Internet for research; I also consult library materials. ① ② ③ ④ ⑤

10. I evaluate every Internet source for signs of bias, validity, credibility, and reliability. ① ② ③ ④ ⑤

Each of the topics in these statements is covered in this chapter. Note those statements for which you filled in a 3 or lower. Skim the chapter to see where those topics appear, and pay special attention to them as you read, learn, and apply new strategies.

REMEMBER: NO MATTER HOW DEVELOPED YOUR READING AND INFORMATION LITERACY SKILLS ARE, YOU CAN IMPROVE THEM WITH EFFORT AND PRACTICE.

WHAT SETS YOU UP FOR

reading comprehension?

Reading comprehension is the gateway to success in school and beyond. Why? Because if you can read and *understand* something, you can learn it and *use* it. In exchange for your risk of effort and commitment, you can earn the following rewards:

- A broad and deep range of knowledge
- A solid foundation of learning that will help you perform in advanced courses
- The ability to digest and use information on the job and to stay up-to-date on changes

College reading assignments are often challenging, requiring more focus and new strategies on your part. During any given week you may have a variety of assignments, such as:

- A text chapter on the history of South African apartheid (world history)
- An original research study on the relationship between sleep deprivation and memory problems (psychology)

MyStudentSuccessLab

(www.mystudentsuccesslab.com) is an online solution designed to help you "Start Strong, Finish Stronger" by building skills for ongoing personal and professional development.

- The first three chapters in John Steinbeck's classic novel, *The Grapes of Wrath* (American literature)
- A technical manual on the design of computer anti-virus programs (software design)

To face reading challenges like these, use specific techniques. Here's how to prepare for making the most of your reading, even before you open a book or log onto a computer.

Define Your Reading Purpose

The first step in improving your reading comprehension is to ask yourself *why* you are reading particular material. With a clear purpose or reward in mind, you can decide how much time and effort to risk. Key 5.1 shows four common reading purposes. Depending on what your instructor expects, you may have as many as three reading purposes for one assignment, such as understanding, critical evaluation, and practical application.

Use the class syllabus to help define your purpose for each assignment. For example, if your syllabus shows that inflation is the topic of your next economics class lecture, read the assigned chapter with that focus in mind: mastering the definition of inflation, evaluating historical economic events that caused inflation, and so on. In addition, remain open to the possibility that any reading assignment with purpose 1, 2, or 3 may also bring you enjoyment (purpose 4).

Take an Active and Positive Approach

Instructors expect you to complete most reading assignments on your own. How can you approach difficult reading material actively and positively?

- *Start with a questioning attitude.* Before reading, ask questions, such as "How can I connect the reading to what I

Looking at your schedule, you may find useful segments of time in between classes. Try using this time for reading assignments.

 **KEY 5.1** Establish why you are reading a given piece of material.

WHAT'S MY PURPOSE?	EXPLANATION
1. To understand	Read to comprehend concepts and details, and to explain them in your own words. Concepts provide a framework for details and details help explain or support general concepts.
2. To evaluate analytically	Read with an open mind as you examine causes and effects, evaluate ideas, and ask questions that test arguments and assumptions. Develop a level of understanding beyond basic information recall (see pages 82–87 for more on this topic).
3. For practical application	Read to find information to help reach a specific goal. For instance, when you read a lab manual for chemistry, your goal is to successfully perform the lab experiment.
4. For pleasure	Read for entertainment, such as reading *Sports Illustrated* magazine or a science fiction, mystery, or romance novel.

already know?" Look at chapter headings and question what the material might mean and why it is being presented in this way.

- *Look for order.* Use SQ3R and critical reading strategies (explained later in the chapter) to discover patterns, logic, and relationships. Text cues—how the material is organized, outlines, bolded terms, and more—help you anticipate what's coming next.

- *Have an open mind.* Be careful not to prejudge assignments as impossible, boring, or a waste of time before you even begin.

- *Plan for multiple readings.* Don't expect to master challenging material on the first pass. Get an overview of key concepts and basic organization during your first reading. Use later readings to build understanding, relate information to what you already know, and apply information. Recall how Gary had to read assignments several times to succeed.

- *Get help.* If material is tough to understand, consult resources including instructors, study-group partners, tutors, related texts, and websites. Build a library of texts in your major and minor areas of study and refer to them whenever necessary.

Choose the Right Setting

Where, when, and with whom you study has a significant effect on your success.

- *Locations.* Choose settings that distract you least—at home, at a library, outdoors, in an empty classroom, whatever works. Your schedule may limit your choices. For example, if you can only study when libraries are closed, you will probably have to work at home; if you commute, mass transit may be a good study spot. Evaluate how effectively you focus. If you spent too much time being distracted at a particular location, try somewhere different.

- *Times.* Pay attention to your natural rhythms, and try to read when you tend to be most alert and focused. For example, night owls tend to be productive when everyone else is sleeping, but morning people may have a hard time reading late at night.

Learn to Concentrate

Even well-written college textbooks may require a lot of focus, especially when you encounter complex concepts and new terms. That kind of focus is also often necessary when assignments are from primary sources rather than from secondary sources. When you focus your attention on one thing and one thing alone, you are engaged in the act of *concentration*. The following are active learning methods for remaining focused as you study. Many involve tapping into your emotional and social intelligence.

PRIMARY SOURCES
Original documents, including academic journal articles and scientific studies.

SECONDARY SOURCES
Other writers' interpretations of primary source documents.

- *Deal with internal distractions.* When worries come up, such as to-do list items for other projects, write them down and deal with them later. Sometimes you may want to take a break to deal with what's bothering you. For example, if you are hungry, get a snack; if you lose focus, an exercise break may energize you and help you concentrate.

- *Take control of technology.* Web surfing, emailing, texting, or instant messaging can distract you. Plus, forcing your brain to switch back and forth between tasks can increase work time and errors. Instead, save technology for breaks or after you finish your work.

- *Structure your work session.* Set realistic goals and a specific plan for dividing your time. Tell yourself, "I'm going to read 30 pages and then go online for 30 minutes."

- *Manage family obligations.* Set up activities or childcare if you have kids. Tell your family what your education means to them and to you. Help them understand the importance of uninterrupted study time.

- *Have a break planned.* Think of something you would look forward to doing during your break. You deserve it!

The strongest motivation to concentrate comes from within. When you see the connection between what you study and your short- and long-term goals, you will be better able to focus, to remember, to learn, and to apply what you have learned.

Expand Your Vocabulary

As reading materials become more complex, your vocabulary influences how much and how easily you understand. The more you read, the more words you are exposed to, and the greater your word comprehension becomes. When reading a textbook, the first "dictionary" to search is the end-of-book glossary explaining technical words and concepts (if applicable). The definitions there are usually limited to the meanings used in the text. Standard dictionaries provide broader information such as word origin, pronunciation, part of speech, synonyms, antonyms, and multiple meanings. Buy a standard dictionary and use websites like www.dictionary.com. The suggestions in Key 5.2 will help you make the most of your dictionary.

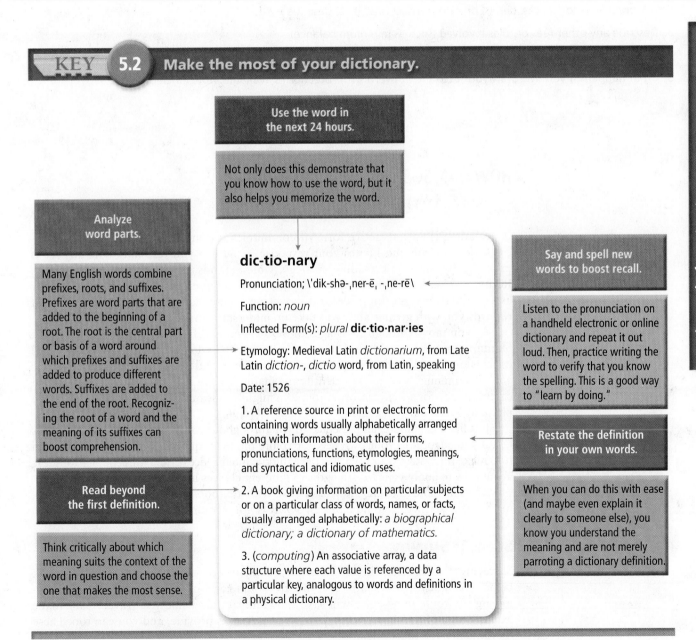

KEY 5.2 Make the most of your dictionary.

Use the word in the next 24 hours.

Not only does this demonstrate that you know how to use the word, but it also helps you memorize the word.

Analyze word parts.

Many English words combine prefixes, roots, and suffixes. Prefixes are word parts that are added to the beginning of a root. The root is the central part or basis of a word around which prefixes and suffixes are added to produce different words. Suffixes are added to the end of the root. Recognizing the root of a word and the meaning of its suffixes can boost comprehension.

Read beyond the first definition.

Think critically about which meaning suits the context of the word in question and choose the one that makes the most sense.

dic·tio·nary

Pronunciation; \'dik-shə-,ner-ē, -,ne-rē\

Function: *noun*

Inflected Form(s): *plural* **dic·tio·nar·ies**

Etymology: Medieval Latin *dictionarium*, from Late Latin *diction-*, *dictio* word, from Latin, speaking

Date: 1526

1. A reference source in print or electronic form containing words usually alphabetically arranged along with information about their forms, pronunciations, functions, etymologies, meanings, and syntactical and idiomatic uses.

2. A book giving information on particular subjects or on a particular class of words, names, or facts, usually arranged alphabetically: *a biographical dictionary; a dictionary of mathematics.*

3. (*computing*) An associative array, a data structure where each value is referenced by a particular key, analogous to words and definitions in a physical dictionary.

Say and spell new words to boost recall.

Listen to the pronunciation on a handheld electronic or online dictionary and repeat it out loud. Then, practice writing the word to verify that you know the spelling. This is a good way to "learn by doing."

Restate the definition in your own words.

When you can do this with ease (and maybe even explain it clearly to someone else), you know you understand the meaning and are not merely parroting a dictionary definition.

get $mart

READ THE FINE PRINT

Complete the following on paper or in digital format.

Use your reading skills to make sure you understand your bank's policies about the account you use most (checking or savings). Look up your type of account on your bank's website, and read the rules. Then answer the following questions.

1. Can you make withdrawals and deposits online, without a fee?

2. Can you make withdrawals and deposits in the bank, without a fee?

3. Can your transfer money electronically between accounts?

4. Is there a monthly fee? _____ If so, how much is it?

5. Is there a limit for checks, debits, or ATM transactions? If so, describe it.

6. Describe any other fees or rules involved (such as minimum balance).

7. What happens if a check you write bounces? What if someone else's check bounces?

8. What happens if you overdraw your account? If overdraft protection is available, how much does it cost?

HOW CAN SQ3R IMPROVE *your reading?*

Reading is an interactive form of communication in which an author communicates ideas to you and invites your response. How can you respond? One answer is provided by the SQ3R reading strategy, which stands for Survey, Question, Read, Recite, and Review.[1] This technique requires that you interact with reading material by asking questions, marking ideas, discovering connections, and more. In return, it rewards you with greater ability to take in, understand, and remember what you read.

As you move through the stages of SQ3R, you will first skim and scan your text. Skimming refers to rapidly reading chapter elements such as section introductions and conclusions, boldfaced or italicized terms, pictures and charts, and summaries. The goal of skimming is to quickly identify the main ideas. In contrast, scanning involves a careful search for specific information. You might use scanning during the SQ3R review phase to locate particular facts.

Just like many strategies presented to you throughout your college career, SQ3R works best if you adapt it to your own needs. Explore the techniques, evaluate what works, and then make the system your own. See the Multiple Intelligences grid in this chapter for ideas about how to apply your MI strengths to different choices in the SQ3R process.

Keep in mind that SQ3R works best with textbook-based courses like science, math, social sciences, and humanities. SQ3R is *not* recommended for literature courses.

SKIMMING
Rapid, superficial reading of material to determine central ideas and main elements.

SCANNING
Reading material in an investigative way to search for specific information.

Step 1: Survey

Surveying, the first stage in SQ3R, is the process of previewing, or pre-reading a book before you study it. Compare surveying to looking at a map before a road trip; determining the route in advance will save time and trouble while you travel. Gary made extensive use of the survey tools that most textbooks provide, and you can too. These tools include the following:

multiple intelligence strategies

Name an upcoming reading assignment (material, course, date due): _____.
In the right-hand column, record specific ideas for how MI strategies can help you complete it.

INTELLIGENCE	USE MI STRATEGIES TO BECOME A BETTER READER	IDENTIFY MI READING STRATEGIES THAT CAN HELP YOU IMPROVE COMPREHENSION
Verbal-Linguistic	• Use the steps in SQ3R, focusing especially on writing Q-stage questions, summaries, and so on. • Make marginal text notes as you read.	
Logical-Mathematical	• Logically connect what you are reading with what you already know. Consider similarities, differences, and cause-and-effect relationships. • Draw charts showing relationships and analyze trends.	
Bodily-Kinesthetic	• Use text highlighting to take a hands-on approach to reading. • Take a hands-on approach to learning experiments by trying to re-create them yourself.	
Visual-Spatial	• Make charts, diagrams, or think links illustrating difficult ideas you encounter as you read. • Take note of photos, tables, and other visual aids in the text.	
Interpersonal	• Discuss reading material and clarify concepts in a study group. • Talk to people who know about the topic you are studying.	
Intrapersonal	• Apply concepts to your own life; think about how you would manage. • Try to understand your personal strengths and weaknesses to lead a study group on the reading material.	
Musical	• Recite text concepts to rhythms or write a song to depict them. • Explore relevant musical links to the material.	
Naturalistic	• Tap into your ability to notice similarities and differences in objects and concepts by organizing reading materials into relevant groupings.	

Reading and Information Literacy

Front matter. Skim the table of contents for the chapter titles, main topics in each chapter and the order in which they will be covered, as well as special features. Then skim the preface, which is a personal note from the author telling you what the book will cover and its point of view. For example, the preface for the American history text, *Out of Many*, states that it highlights "the experiences of diverse communities of Americans in the unfolding story of our country."[2] This tells you that cultural diversity is a central theme.

Chapter elements. Text chapters generally use different devices to structure their information and highlight content.

- Chapter titles establish the topic and often the author's perspective.
- Chapter introductions or outlines generally list objectives or key topics.
- Level headings (first, second, third), including those in question form, break down material into bite-size chunks.
- Margin materials can include definitions, quotes, questions, and exercises.
- Tables, charts, photographs, and captions illustrate important concepts visually.
- Sidebars or boxed features are connected to text themes and introduce extra tidbits of information that supplement the text.
- Different styles or arrangements of *type* (**boldface**, *italics*, underlining, larger fonts, • bullet points, boxed text) can flag vocabulary or important ideas.
- End-of-chapter summaries review chapter content and main ideas.
- Review questions and exercises help you understand and apply content in creative and practical ways.

Back matter. Some texts include a glossary that defines text terms, an index to help you locate topics, and a bibliography that lists additional readings.

Key 5.3 shows a typical page from the college textbook *Psychology: An Introduction,* by Charles G. Morris and Albert A. Maisto. As you examine it, how many chapter elements do you recognize? How do these elements help you grasp the subject even before reading it?

Step 2: Question

The next step in SQ3R is to ask questions about your assignment. Questioning leads you to discover knowledge, rewarding you with a greater investment in the material and improved ability to remember it. Here's the process.

Ask yourself what you know

Before you begin reading, think about, and summarize in writing if you can, what you already know about the topic. This prepares you to apply what you already know to new material. Building on current knowledge helps you learn faster. It is especially important in your major, where the concepts you learn in introductory courses prepare you for higher-level courses.

Write questions linked to chapter headings

Next, examine the chapter headings and, on a separate page or in the text margins, write questions about them. When you encounter an assignment without headings, divide the material into logical sections and develop questions based on what you think is the main idea of each section. There are no "correct" questions. Given the same headings, two students could create two different sets of questions. The goal of questioning is to guide your reading so you learn more from it.

186 Chapter 5 • Learning

Classical (or Pavlovian) conditioning The type of learning in which a response naturally elicited by one stimulus comes to be elicited by a different, formerly neutral stimulus.

Unconditioned stimulus (US) A stimulus that invariably causes an organism to respond in a specific way.

Unconditioned response (UR) A response that takes place in an organism whenever an unconditioned stimulus occurs.

Conditioned stimulus (CS) An originally neutral stimulus that is paired with an unconditioned stimulus and eventually produces the desired response in an organism when presented alone.

Conditioned response (CR) After conditioning, the response an organism produces when only a conditioned stimulus is presented.

you are experiencing insight. When you imitate the steps of professional dancers you saw last night on television, you are demonstrating observational learning. Like conditioning, cognitive learning is one of our survival strategies. Through cognitive processes, we learn which events are safe and which are dangerous without having to experience those events directly. Cognitive learning also gives us access to the wisdom of people who lived hundreds of years ago, and it will give people living hundreds of years from now some insight into our experiences and way of life.

Our discussion begins with *classical conditioning*. This simple kind of learning serves as a convenient starting point for examining what learning is and how it can be observed.

Classical Conditioning

How did Pavlov's discovery of classical conditioning help to shed light on learning?

Ivan Pavlov (1849–1936), a Russian physiologist who was studying digestive processes, discovered classical conditioning almost by accident. Because animals salivate when food is placed in their mouths, Pavlov inserted tubes into the salivary glands of dogs to measure how much saliva they produced when they were given food. He noticed, however, that the dogs salivated before the food was in their mouths: The mere sight of food made them drool. In fact, they even drooled at the sound of the experimenter's footsteps. This aroused Pavlov's curiosity. What was making the dogs salivate even before they had the food in their mouths? How had they learned to salivate in response to the sound of the experimenter's approach?

To answer these questions, Pavlov set out to teach the dogs to salivate when food was not present. He devised an experiment in which he sounded a bell just before the food was brought into the room. A ringing bell does not usually make a dog's mouth water but, after hearing the bell many times just before getting fed, Pavlov's dogs began to salivate as soon as the bell rang. It was as if they had learned that the bell signaled the appearance of food, and their mouths watered on cue even if no food followed. The dogs had been conditioned to salivate in response to a new stimulus—the bell—that would not normally have prompted that response (Pavlov, 1927). Figure 5–1, shows one of Pavlov's procedures in which the bell has been replaced by a touch to the dog's leg just before food is given.

Elements of Classical Conditioning

Generally speaking, **classical (or Pavlovian) conditioning** involves pairing an *involuntary* response (for example, salivation) that is usually evoked by one stimulus with a different, formerly neutral stimulus (such as a bell or a touch on the leg). Pavlov's experiment illustrates the four basic elements of classical conditioning. The first is an **unconditioned stimulus (US)**, such as food, which invariably prompts a certain reaction—salivation, in this case. That reaction—the **unconditioned response (UR)**—is the second element and always results from the unconditioned stimulus: Whenever the dog is given food (US), its mouth waters (UR). The third element is the neutral stimulus—the ringing bell—which is called the **conditioned stimulus (CS).** At first, the conditioned stimulus is said to be "neutral" with respect to the desired response (salivation), because dogs do not salivate at the sound of a bell unless they have been conditioned to react in this way by repeatedly presenting the CS and US together. Frequent pairing of the CS and US produces the fourth element in the classical conditioning process: the **conditioned response (CR).** The conditioned response is the behavior that the animal has learned in response to the conditioned stimulus. Usually, the unconditioned response and the conditioned

Reading and Information Literacy

get analytical

SURVEY A TEXT

Complete the following on paper or in digital format.

Practice will improve your surveying skills. Start now with this text or another you are currently using.

1. Skim the front matter, including the table of contents and preface. What does this material tell you about the theme? About the book's approach and point of view?

2. Are there unexpected topics listed in the table of contents? Are there topics you expected to see that are missing?

3. Now look at a typical chapter. List the devices that organize the structure and content of the material. (Refer to "Step 1: Survey," for a list of chapter elements.)

4. After skimming the chapter, what do you know about the material? What elements helped you skim quickly?

5. Finally, skim the back matter. What elements can you identify?

6. How do you plan to use each of the elements you identified in your text survey when you begin studying?

Key 5.4 shows how questioning works. The column on the left contains primary and secondary headings from a section of *Out of Many*. The column on the right rephrases these headings in question form.

Use Bloom's Taxonomy to formulate questions

Asking different types of questions provides different types of understanding and involves different levels of analytical thinking. To help you understand and use different types of questions, consider the system that educational psychologist Benjamin Bloom developed, based on the idea that deeper learning occurs when the effort to

KEY 5.4 Create questions from headings.

HEADINGS	QUESTIONS
The Meaning of Freedom	What did freedom mean for both slaves and citizens in the United States?
Moving About	Where did African Americans go after they were freed from slavery?
The African American Family	How did freedom change the structure of the African American family?
African American Churches and Schools	What effect did freedom have on the formation of African American churches and schools?
Land and Labor After Slavery	How was land farmed and maintained after slaves were freed?
The Origins of African American Politics	How did the end of slavery bring about the beginning of African American political life?

understand is more rigorous.[3] Although some questions require simple recall to answer, said Bloom, others require higher thinking levels.

Key 5.5 shows the six levels of learning identified by Bloom: knowledge, understanding, application, analysis, synthesis, and evaluation. Beneath the illustration of the levels, the table explains what each level is (column 1), lists common verbs associated with each level (column 2), and provides an example question for that level of learning (column 3). When you read, use these verbs to create specific questions that will help you learn. For instance, if you were to continue creating questions based on the headings from *Out of Many* discussed in Key 5.4, the questions would change based on the level specified by Bloom's Taxonomy and look like those in column 3.

KEY 5.5 Use Bloom's Taxonomy to formulate questions at different levels.

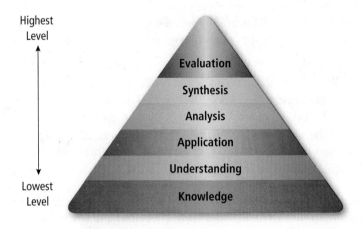

The table below explains each level in the taxonomy illustration, provides common verbs to help you recognize each level, and provides a sample question you might ask at that level. The questions are based on the headings from *Out of Many*.

LEVEL OF LEARNING	COMMON VERBS THAT INDICATE THE LEVEL	SAMPLE QUESTIONS DEMONSTRATING THE LEVEL OF LEARNING
Knowledge. Memorize words and ideas.	average, define, duplicate, label, list, memorize, name, order, recognize, relate, recall, repeat, reproduce, state	*List* three main characters of the early African American political scene.
Understanding. Explain ideas in your own words.	classify, describe, discuss, explain, express, identify, indicate, locate, recognize, report, restate, review, select, translate	*Explain* the struggles faced by African American politicians.
Application. Apply what you learn.	apply, choose, demonstrate, dramatize, employ, illustrate, interpret, operate, practice, schedule, sketch, solve, use, write	*Interpret* the impact of slavery on the early African American politicians.
Analysis. Analyze information and look at similarities and differences.	analyze, appraise, calculate, categorize, compare, contrast, criticize, differentiate, discriminate, distinguish, examine, experiment, question, test	*Compare and contrast* the Caucasian political environment of the time with that of the emerging African American politicians.
Synthesis. Put together information "from scratch."	arrange, assemble, collect, compose, construct, create, design, develop, formulate, manage, organize, plan, prepare, propose, set up, write	*Arrange* the major events of the era as they corresponded with the emerging political movement.
Evaluation. Examine different ideas and make decisions about their merit.	appraise, argue, assess, attach, choose, compare, defend, estimate, evaluate, judge, predict, rate, score, select, support, value	*Rate* the effectiveness of the first African American political campaign and note any changes since.

Step 3: Read

Your text survey and questions give you a starting point for reading, the first R in SQ3R. Remembering what you read requires an active approach.

- *Focus on the key points of your survey.* Pay attention to information in the headings, boldface type, chapter objectives, the summary, and other emphasized text.
- *Focus on Q-stage questions.* Read the material with the purpose of answering each question. Write or highlight ideas and examples that relate to your questions.
- *Create text tabs.* Place plastic index tabs or adhesive notes at the start of different chapters so you can flip back and forth with ease.

Annotate your text

You are now ready to dig into the text, ask more questions, and identify what's important. Here are two ways to identify important information.

Mark up your text. If the book is yours, write notes in the margins or on separate paper, circle main ideas, or underline supporting details. If you are reading an e-book, use the "insert comments" feature. These cues will boost memory and help you study for exams. Here are some tips for annotating—taking notes in the margins of your textbook pages:

- Use pencil so you can erase comments or questions that are answered later.
- Write your Q-questions in the margins next to text headings.
- Mark critical sections with marginal notations such as "def." for definition, "e.g." for a helpful example, "concept" for an important concept, and so on.
- Write notes at the bottom of the page connecting the text to what you learned in class or in research. You can also attach adhesive notes with your comments.
- Circle the topic sentence in a paragraph to focus on the most important information.

TOPIC SENTENCE
A statement describing the main idea of a paragraph.

Highlight your text. The goal of *highlighting* is to call out important concepts and information so that they get your attention. Use these tips to make highlighting work for you:

- *Develop a system and stick to it.* Decide if you will use different colors to highlight different elements, bracket long passages, or underline. When working with e-books, use the highlighting function to color over important text.
- *Consider using a regular pencil or pen instead of a highlighter pen.* The copy will be cleaner and look less like a coloring book than a textbook.
- *Mark text carefully if you are using a rented book or a book to be re-sold.* Use pencil and erase your marks at the end of the course. Write on sticky notes. Make copies of important chapters or sections and mark up the pages. If renting, check with the rental service to see what it permits.
- *Read an entire paragraph before you begin to highlight, and don't start until you have a sense of what is important.* Only then put pencil or highlighter to paper as you pick out the main idea, key terms, and crucial supporting details and examples.
- *Avoid overmarking.* Underlining or highlighting everything makes it impossible to tell what's important. If you decide that a whole passage is important to call out, try marking it with brackets.
- *Know that highlighting is just the beginning of learning the material.* To learn the information you've highlighted, interact with it through surveying, questioning, reciting, and review.

Key 5.6 shows a page from an introduction to business textbook that describes the concepts of target marketing and market segmentation. The page illustrates how to underline and take marginal notes. Then, the Get Practical example gives you a chance to do some more reading and practice marking up the text.

Chapter 10: Understanding Marketing Processes and Consumer Behavior   **297**

How does target marketing and market segmentation help companies sell product?

■ TARGET MARKETING AND MARKET SEGMENTATION

Marketers have long known that products cannot be all things to all people. Buyers have different tastes, goals, lifestyles, and so on. The emergence of the marketing concept and the recognition of consumer needs and wants led marketers to think in terms of **target markets**—groups of people with similar wants and needs. Selecting target markets is usually the first step in the marketing strategy.

Target marketing requires **market segmentation**—dividing a market into categories of customer types or "segments." Once they have identified segments, companies may adopt a variety of strategies. Some firms market products to more than one segment. General Motors *(www.gm.com)*, for example, offers compact cars, vans, trucks, luxury cars, and sports cars with various features and at various price levels. GM's strategy is to provide an automobile for nearly every segment of the market.

In contrast, some businesses offer a narrower range of products, each aimed toward a specific segment. Note that segmentation is a strategy for analyzing consumers, not products. The process of fixing, adapting, and communicating the nature of the product itself is called *product positioning*.

How do companies identify market segments?

Identifying Market Segments

By definition, members of a market segment must share some common traits that affect their purchasing decisions. In identifying segments, researchers look at several different influences on consumer behavior. Three of the most important are *geographic, demographic,* and *psychographic variables*.

What effect does geography have on segmentation strategies?

Geographic Variables Many buying decisions are affected by the places people call home. The heavy rainfall in Washington State, for instance, means that people there buy more umbrellas than people in the Sun Belt. Urban residents don't need agricultural equipment, and sailboats sell better along the coasts than on the Great Plains. **Geographic variables** are the geographical units, from countries to neighborhoods, that may be considered in a segmentation strategy.

These patterns affect decisions about marketing mixes for a huge range of products. For example, consider a plan to market down-filled parkas in rural Minnesota. Demand will be high and price competition intense. Local newspaper ads may be

Handwritten margin notes:

Definitions ↓

target market Group of people that has similar wants and needs and that can be expected to show interest in the same products

← *GM eg*

market segmentation Process of dividing a market into categories of customer types

GM makes cars for diff. market segments

Buying decisions influenced by where people live

geographic variables Geographical units that may be considered in developing a segmentation strategy

— good eg — selling parkas in Minnesota

Thought Geographical variables change with the seasons

Source: Ronald J. Ebert and Ricky W. Griffin, *Business Essentials,* 5th ed., © 2005. Printed and electronically reproduced by permission of Pearson Education, Inc., Upper Saddle River, NJ.

Reading and Information Literacy

get practical

MARK UP A PAGE TO LEARN A PAGE

Below, the text material in Key 5.6 continues. Read it and mark it up, highlighting concepts and taking marginal notes. Compare your efforts to those of your classmates to see how each of you approached the task and what you can learn from each other's methods.

---

effective, and the best retail location may be one that is easily reached from several small towns.

Although the marketability of some products is geographically sensitive, others enjoy nearly universal acceptance. Coke, for example, gets more than 70 percent of its sales from international markets. It is the market leader in Great Britain, China, Germany, Japan, Brazil, and Spain. Pepsi's international sales are about 15 percent of Coke's. In fact, Coke's chief competitor in most countries is some local soft drink, not Pepsi, which earns 78 percent of its income at home.

demographic variables
Characteristics of populations that may be considered in developing a segmentation strategy

Demographic Variables Demographic variables describe populations by identifying such traits as age, income, gender, ethnic background, marital status, race, religion, and social class. For example, several general consumption characteristics can be attributed to certain age groups (18–25, 26–35, 36–45, and so on). A marketer can, thus, divide markets into age groups. Table 10.1 lists some possible demographic breakdowns. Depending on the marketer's purpose, a segment can be a single classification (*aged* 20–34) or a combination of categories (*aged* 20–34, *married with children, earning* $25,000–$34,999). Foreign competitors, for example, are gaining market share in U.S. auto sales by appealing to young buyers (under age 30) with limited incomes (under $30,000). Whereas companies such as Hyundai (*www.hyundai.net*), Kia (*www.kia.com*), and Daewoo (*www.daewoos.com*) are winning entry-level customers with high quality and generous warranties, Volkswagen (*www.vw.com*) targets under-35 buyers with its entertainment-styled VW Jetta.[4]

psychographic variables
Consumer characteristics, such as lifestyles, opinions, interests, and attitudes, that may be considered in developing a segmentation strategy

Psychographic Variables Markets can also be segmented according to such **psychographic variables** as lifestyles, interests, and attitudes. Take, for example, Burberry (*www.burberry.com*), whose raincoats have been a symbol of British tradition since 1856. Burberry has repositioned itself as a global luxury brand, like Gucci (*www.gucci.com*) and Louis Vuitton (*www.vuitton.com*). The strategy, which recently resulted in a 31-percent sales increase, calls for attracting a different type of customer—the top-of-the-line, fashion-conscious individual—who shops at such stores as Neiman Marcus and Bergdorf Goodman.[5]

Psychographics are particularly important to marketers because, unlike demographics and geographics, they can be changed by marketing efforts. For example, Polish companies have overcome consumer resistance by promoting the safety and desirability of using credit rather than depending solely on cash. One product of changing attitudes is a booming economy and the emergence of a robust middle class.

TABLE 10.1
Demographic Variables

Age	Under 5, 5–11, 12–19, 20–34, 35–49, 50–64, 65+
Education	Grade school or less, some high school, graduated high school, some college, college degree, advanced degree
Family life cycle	Young single, young married without children, young married with children, older married with children under 18, older married without children under 18, older single, other
Family size	1, 2–3, 4–5, 6+
Income	Under $9,000, $9,000–$14,999, $15,000–$24,999, $25,000–$34,999, $35,000–$45,000, over $45,000
Nationality	African, American, Asian, British, Eastern European, French, German, Irish, Italian, Latin American, Middle Eastern, Scandinavian
Race	Native American, Asian, Black, White
Religion	Buddhist, Catholic, Hindu, Jewish, Muslim, Protestant
Sex	Male, female

talk risk and reward . . .

Risk asking tough questions to be rewarded with new insights. Use the following questions to inspire discussion with classmates, either in person or online.

- How can reading be a risk, and what reward would it bring? What risk do you take if you do *not* read?

- What steps do you take to ensure that you understand what you have read? Have those strategies worked for you so far? Why or why not?

CONSIDER THE CASE: What step (or steps) from SQ3R were most helpful to Gary in dealing with his particular challenge? What step or steps do you think will be most helpful to *you*?

Yes, annotating your textbook carries the risk that you will not be able to sell it back. However, students who interact with material stand to gain greater depth of learning than those who don't. If you aim to learn, the reward of annotating your text is worth the financial risk.

Step 4: Recite

Once you finish reading a section of text, recite answers to the questions you raised in the Q stage—say them aloud, silently speak them to yourself, "teach" them to someone, or write them in note form. The action of speaking or writing anchors material in your brain. This is the second R in SQ3R. Repeat the question-read-recite cycle until you complete the chapter you are reading.

Writing is often the most effective way to learn new material. Write responses to your Q-stage questions and use your own words to explain new concepts. Save your writing as a study tool for review. Writing gives you immediate feedback. When your writing agrees with the material you are studying, you know the information. When it doesn't, you still need work.

Keep your learning preferences in mind when you explore different strategies. For example, an intrapersonal learner may prefer writing, while an interpersonal learner may choose to recite answers aloud to a classmate. A logical-mathematical learner may benefit from organizing material into detailed outlines or charts, while a musical learner might want to chant information aloud to a rhythm.

When do you stop to recite? Waiting until the end of a chapter is too late, but stopping at the end of one paragraph is too soon. The best plan is to recite at the end of each text section, right before a new heading. Repeat the question-read-recite cycle until you complete the chapter. If you fumble for thoughts, reread the section until you are on solid ground.

Step 5: Review

Reviewing is the third R in SQ3R. When you review early and often in the days and weeks after you read, you will better memorize, understand, and learn material. *Reviewing is your key to learning*. Reviewing the same material over several short sessions will also help you identify knowledge gaps. It's natural to forget material between study sessions, especially if it's complex. When you come back after a break, you can focus on where you need the most help.

get creative

USE SQ3R TO MAKE A CONNECTION

Complete the following on paper or in digital format.

For this exercise, partner with someone in your class. Before you meet, each of you will write a mini-autobiography, approximately three paragraphs in length, answering the following questions:

- Where are you from?

- How would you describe your family?

- How has your family influenced the student you are today?

- What are three things you would like someone to know about you?

Check your work for spelling, punctuation, and clarity, and title the biography. Then meet with your partner and switch papers. Read each other's biography using SQ3R:

1. *Survey:* Scan your partner's paper for any words that stand out or phrases that seem important. Circle or highlight anything you notice right away.

2. *Question:* Thinking about what you learned from your survey, write questions in the margins. Your questions should reflect what you expect to learn.

3. *Read:* Read through the biography. Make notes in the margins when you find answers to your Q-stage questions. Use your pen to circle or underline main ideas.

4. *Recite:* Discuss what you learned from the paper with your partner. How accurate was your comprehension of the biography? Were there any areas that were not clear or that you misunderstood? If so, what might help in those cases?

5. *Review:* Write a summary of the biography of your partner. If there is time, recite the summary aloud in front of the class. Introduce your partner to the class as if he or she had just joined, focusing on the most interesting and unique information.

Finally, discuss the impact of using SQ3R with your partner. How did it impact your comprehension of their biography? What might you try differently next time?

Examine the following reviewing techniques. Try them all, and use the ones that work best for you. Try using more than one strategy when you study. Switching among several different strategies tends to strengthen learning and memory.

- Reread your notes, then summarize them from memory.

- Review and summarize in writing the text sections you highlighted or bracketed.

- Rewrite key points and main concepts in your own words. Create written examples that will help solidify the content in your mind.

- Answer the end-of-chapter review, discussion, and application questions.

- Reread the preface, headings, tables, and summary.

- Recite important concepts to yourself (although you may risk looking silly, this technique's high effectiveness may be a worthwhile reward).

- Record information and play it back.

CHAPTER 5

- Listen to MP3 audio recordings of your text and other reading materials on your iPod.
- Make hard-copy or electronic flash cards with a word or concept on one side and a definition, examples, or other related information on the other. Test yourself daily.
- Quiz yourself, using the questions you raised in the Q-stage.
- Discuss the concepts with a classmate or in a study group. Answer one another's Q-stage questions.
- Ask your instructor for help with difficult material.

Refreshing your knowledge is easier and faster than learning it the first time. Make a weekly review schedule and stick to it. A combination of short daily reviews in the morning, between classes, or in the evening is far more effective than an all-night cramming session before a test.

WHAT WILL HELP WITH SPECIFIC
subjects and formats?

If your college has general education requirements, you may have to take a wide variety of courses to graduate. Knowing how to approach reading materials in different academic areas will make learning easier.

Math and Science

Math and science courses relate closely to one another, since almost all science courses require basic math knowledge. Mathematical and scientific strategies help you develop thinking and problem-solving skills. In a world transformed by new discoveries and technologies, a strong math and science background prepares you for tomorrow's jobs. It also helps you create monthly budgets, choose auto insurance, understand illnesses, and more.

Math and science textbooks move *sequentially*. That is, your understanding of later material depends on how well you learned material in earlier chapters because the topics build upon one another. Try the following strategies to get the most from your textbooks, and get extra help right away when you are confused.

Interact with math material actively through writing. Math textbooks are made up of problems and solutions. As you read, highlight important information and take notes of examples. Work out any missing problem steps on your pad or in the book. Draw sketches to help visualize the material. Try not to move on until you understand example problems and how they relate to the central ideas. Write questions for your instructor or fellow students.

Pay attention to formulas. Math and science texts are filled with formulas. Try to learn the ideas behind each formula so that if you forget one, you can re-create it (this is called "deriving" a formula). Always do the practice problems, using the formulas to make sure your understanding sticks.

Use memory strategies to learn science. Science textbooks are packed with field-specific vocabulary (for example, an environmental science text may refer to the *greenhouse effect*). Use mnemonic devices, test yourself with flash cards, and rehearse aloud or silently.

Consider solving all sample problems. Risk a little extra work for the reward of greater comprehension. The more problems you do, the more solid your understanding will be.

GENERAL EDUCATION REQUIREMENTS
Courses in a variety of academic fields, including the humanities, social sciences, math, and science, that are required for graduation.

FORMULAS
General facts, rules, or principles usually expressed in mathematical symbols.

Social Sciences and Humanities

Courses in the social sciences and humanities prepare you to be a well-rounded person, able and ready to fulfill responsibilities to yourself, your family, and a free democracy. They also prepare you for 21st century jobs by focusing on critical thinking skills, civic and historic knowledge, and ethical reasoning. As you study these disciplines, look for themes with critical thinking as the foundation for your work. Build knowledge by using what you know to learn new material.

Themes

The National Council for the Social Studies (www.socialstudies.org) organized the study of the social sciences and humanities into ten themes:[4]

- Culture
- Time, continuity, and change
- People, places, and environment
- Individual development and identity
- Individuals, groups, and institutions
- Power, authority, and governance
- Production, distribution, and consumption
- Science, technology, and society
- Global connections
- Ideals and practices of citizenship

Look for these themes as you read, even if they are not spelled out. For example, as you read a chapter in a political science text on presidential politics, you might think of the history of presidential elections or how the Internet is changing electoral politics.

Think critically

Courses in the social sciences ask hard questions about ethics, human rights and freedoms, and personal and community responsibility, looking at these topics over time across cultures. Critical thinking helps you ask questions about what you read, think of material in terms of problems and solutions, look for evidence for arguments, consider possible bias of the writers, and examine big-picture statements for cause-and-effect logic.

Literature

Even if you're not an English major, you will probably take one or more literature courses. Books you read for these courses let you experience other times and cultures, build your understanding of how others react to the problems of daily life, and provide insight into your own thinking. Literature courses ask you to look at different literary elements to find meaning on various levels. As you read, use critical-reading skills to consider:

- *Character.* How do characters reveal who they are? How are the main characters similar or different? How do a character's actions change the course of the story?
- *Plot.* How would you evaluate the power of the story? Did it hold your interest?
- *Setting.* How does the setting relate to the actions of the major and minor characters?
- *Point of view.* How are the author's views expressed through the characters' actions?
- *Style.* How would you describe the writing style?

- *Imagery.* How does the author use imagery as part of the theme?
- *Theme.* What is the goal of the work? What is it trying to communicate?

Visual Aids

Many textbooks on many subjects use visual aids—tables, charts, drawings, maps, and photographs, for example—to show, clarify, or summarize information. Pay attention to these visuals as you read; they often contain important information not found elsewhere. Visual learners may expecially benefit from information delivered in a format other than text.

Certain types of visual aids, such as word and data tables, as well as charts and graphs, are designed to compare information and statistics that show the following information:

- *Trends over time.* For example, the number of computers with Internet connections per household in 2010 as compared to the number in 2002.
- *Relative rankings.* For example, the sizes of the advertising budgets of four major companies.
- *Distributions.* For example, student performance on standardized tests by geographic area.
- *Cycles.* For example, the regular upward and downward movement of the nation's economy as defined by periods of prosperity and recession.

Key 5.7 demonstrates the appearance of common types of charts: pie, bar, and line.

Online Materials

Almost any student's success in college depends on being able to effectively read both printed and on-screen materials. For some "digital natives" who grew up with technology and the Internet, screen reading comes naturally and may even be preferable. Others may prefer to read printed materials they can hold in their hands and write on. Either way, you are likely to have to read some material online.

Students have more choices than ever before about how they access reading materials. Digital tools for reading include desktop or laptop computers, touch screen smartphones, and tablets such as the iPad. Many, although not all, reading materials are available in formats and applications that can be used on these devices. Although college students are more likely to use digital devices for research and studying than for reading, a recent survey of students who own digital devices indicated that over 60% had used them to read an electronic textbook at least once, and almost half did so regularly.[5]

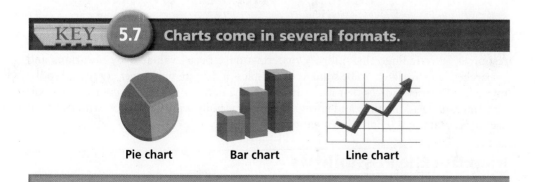

KEY 5.7 **Charts come in several formats.**

Pie chart   Bar chart   Line chart

Screen readers tend to notice heads and subheads, bullet points, and visuals, scanning material for the important points instead of staying focused through long paragraphs or articles.[6] They may also develop what Web researcher Jakob Nielsen calls *F-pattern reading*—reading across the line at the beginning of a document, then reading less and less of the full width of the line as you move down the page, and only seeing the left-hand text by the time you reach the bottom of the document.[7]

Nielsen suggests making the most of screen reading using a step-by-step process, which includes aspects of SQ3R:

1. *Skim through the article.* See whether it contains important ideas.
2. *Before reading in depth, save the article on your computer or device.* This gives you the ability to print the article if you prefer to highlight and add notes on hard copy.
3. *Survey the article.* Read the title, subtitle, headings, figures, charts, and tables.
4. *Come up with questions to guide your reading.* Ask yourself what general and specific information you want to learn from the article.
5. *Read the article in depth.* You have already judged that the material is important, so take it much slower than you would normally.
6. *Highlight and take notes.* Use the program's highlighter and comment functions.
7. *Print out articles you would rather study on hard copy.* Make sure printouts include any electronic highlighting and comments you've created.
8. *Review your notes.* Combine them with your class and text notes.

Finally, remember that "it is not so much about the tool and what it can do, but more about the purpose for using the tool," says educator Mary Beth Hertz.[8] Every choice, from the latest iPad to a book and a pencil, has pros and cons. Evaluate on a case-by-case basis and see what works best for you, especially if you are a "digital native" who gravitates toward technology.

Much, although not all, research can be done using online databases. Get to know the databases and other resources your school makes available to students.

HOW CAN YOU BE AN INFORMATION LITERATE
reader and researcher?

When it comes to research, most students' first instinct is to power up the computer and start jumping around on Google. However, there are a myriad of research resources at your fingertips. Library materials have been evaluated by librarians and researchers and are likely to be solid and credible—a definite time-saver compared to the myriad of Internet sources that may turn out to be nothing more than conjecture, opinion, and rants. Risking time and effort to search carefully will reward you with the most useful, accurate, and reliable information.

Map Out the Possibilities

To select the most useful information for your research, get an overview of what is available. Sign up for a library orientation session. Familiarize yourself with the library

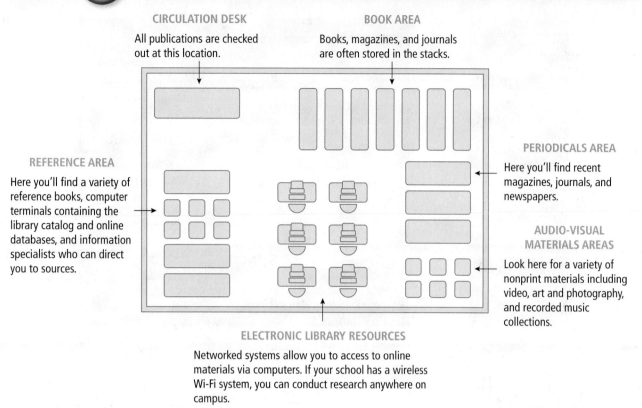

CIRCULATION DESK

All publications are checked out at this location.

BOOK AREA

Books, magazines, and journals are often stored in the stacks.

REFERENCE AREA

Here you'll find a variety of reference books, computer terminals containing the library catalog and online databases, and information specialists who can direct you to sources.

PERIODICALS AREA

Here you'll find recent magazines, journals, and newspapers.

AUDIO-VISUAL MATERIALS AREAS

Look here for a variety of nonprint materials including video, art and photography, and recorded music collections.

ELECTRONIC LIBRARY RESOURCES

Networked systems allow you to access to online materials via computers. If your school has a wireless Wi-Fi system, you can conduct research anywhere on campus.

resources as shown in Key 5.8. Furthermore, get to know a librarian who can assist you in locating unfamiliar or hard-to-find sources, navigating catalogs and databases, uncovering research shortcuts, and dealing with unpredictable equipment. At most schools, you can query a librarian by email or text. Know what you want to accomplish before asking a question.

Conduct an Information Search

To avoid being overwhelmed, use a practical, step-by-step search method. Key 5.9 shows how to start wide and then narrow your search for a closer look at specific sources.

When using virtual or online catalogues, you will need to adjust your research methods. Searching library databases requires a *keyword search*—an exploration that uses a topic-related, natural-language word or phrase as a starting point to locate other information. To narrow your search and reduce the number of *hits* (results returned by your search), add more keywords to your search criteria. For example, instead of searching through the broad category "art," focus on "French art" or, more specifically, "nineteenth-century French art." Key 5.10 shows how to use the keyword system to narrow your search with what is called *Boolean logic*.

Be a Critical Internet Searcher

Unlike your college library collection or databases, Internet resources are not always evaluated by anyone who vouches for their quality. As a result, your research depends

KEY 5.9 Use a step-by-step search method.

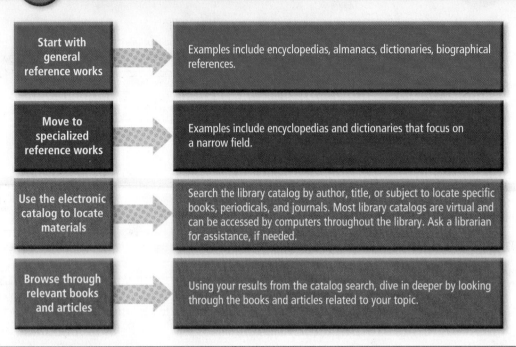

Start with general reference works	Examples include encyclopedias, almanacs, dictionaries, biographical references.
Move to specialized reference works	Examples include encyclopedias and dictionaries that focus on a narrow field.
Use the electronic catalog to locate materials	Search the library catalog by author, title, or subject to locate specific books, periodicals, and journals. Most library catalogs are virtual and can be accessed by computers throughout the library. Ask a librarian for assistance, if needed.
Browse through relevant books and articles	Using your results from the catalog search, dive in deeper by looking through the books and articles related to your topic.

KEY 5.10 Perform an effective keyword search with Boolean logic.

IF YOU ARE SEARCHING FOR ...	DO THIS	EXAMPLE
A word	Type the word normally.	Aid
A phrase	Type the phrase in its normal word order (use regular word spacing) or surround the phrase with quotation marks ("x"). Quotation marks ensure the search engine finds the words together in the same phrase, rather than the individual words on the same page.	financial aid, "financial aid"
Two or more keywords without regard to order	Type the words in any order, surrounding the words with quotation marks. Use *and* to separate the words.	"financial aid" and "scholarships"
Topic A *and* topic B	Type the words in any order, surrounding the words with quotation marks. Use *and* to separate the words. The search engine will list a result only if it contains BOTH topics A and B.	"financial aid" and "scholarships"
Topic A *or* topic B	Type the words in any order, surrounding the words with quotation marks. Use *or* to separate the words. The search engine will list a result if it contains EITHER A or B.	"financial aid" or "scholarships"
Topic A *but not* topic B	Type topic A first within quotation marks, and then topic B within quotation marks. Use *not* to separate the words. The search engine will list a result if it contains only Topic A and does not contain Topic B.	"financial aid" not "scholarships"

on critical thinking to sort out the valid, credible materials from the invalid, not-so-credible ones.

Start with search engines

Among the most popular and effective search engines are Google (www.google.com) and Yahoo! (www.yahoo.com). Search engines aimed at academic audiences include the Librarian's Index to the Internet (www.lii.org) and INFOMINE (www.infomine.com). At these academic directories, someone has screened the sites and listed only those sources that are reputable and regularly updated.

In addition, your school may include access to certain nonpublic academic search engines in the cost of your tuition. Sites like LexusNexus, InfoTrac, GaleGroup, and OneFile are known for their credibility in the academic world, as well as their vast amounts of information. Risk going beyond Google for the reward of accessing extensive banks of information and resources. Check with your school's library to see how to access these sites.

Use a search strategy

The World Wide Web has been called "the world's greatest library, with all its books on the floor." With no librarian in sight, you need to master a practical Internet search strategy.

1. *Use natural language phrases or keywords to identify what you are looking for.* University of Michigan professor Eliot Soloway recommends first phrasing your search in the form of a question. Then he advises identifying the important words in the question, as well as related words. This will give you a collection of terms to use in different combinations as you search (see example below).[9]

   Initial question: What vaccines are given to children before age 5?
   Important words: vaccines, children, before age 5
   Related words: polio, shot, pediatrics
   Final search criteria (important + related words): vaccines children "before age 5" "polio shot" pediatrics

   Note: Some of the terms in the final search critera above are enclosed in quotes and others are not. By putting terms in quotes, you tell the search engine that the words *must* appear next to one another, rather than at different locations on the same web page.

2. *Use a search engine to isolate valuable sites.* Enter your questions, phrases, and keywords in various combinations to generate lists of hits. Vary word order to see what you can generate. If you get too many hits, try using more specific keywords.

3. *Evaluate the list of results.* The first links in the list of search results are not always the most relevant. Often, the top hits belong to individuals or companies that have paid money to have their sites show up first. Scan through the list of results, reading the short synopsis that accompanies each. You may need to look further down the list of hits, and maybe even go to the second or third page of results, to find what you need.

4. *Skim sites to evaluate what seems most useful.* Once you identify a potentially useful link, go to the site and evaluate it. Does the site seem relevant and reputable? What is its purpose? For example, a blog is apt to focus on opinion; a

company's site is likely to promote its products; an article in a scholarly journal may focus on research findings.

5. *Save, or bookmark, the sites you want to focus on.* Make sure you can access them again. You may want to copy URLs and paste them into a separate document. Consider printing Internet materials that you know you will need to reference over and over again.

6. *When you think you are done, start over.* Choose another search engine and search again. Different systems access different sites.

The limitations of Internet-only research make it smart to combine Internet and library research. Search engines cannot find everything for several reasons:

- Not all sources are in digital format.
- The Internet prioritizes current information and may not find older information.
- Some digital sources may not be part of your library's subscription offerings.
- Internet searches require electricity or battery power and an online connection.

Use the Internet as a starting point to get an idea of the various documents you may want to locate in the library and read in print. When you find a blog or website that provides only a short extract of important information and then references the rest, find that original article or book and read the information in its entirety. Often, risking the time and effort that extra searching takes will reward you with more accurate, in-depth, and useful information.

Your need to be an effective researcher doesn't stop at graduation, especially in a workplace dominated by information and media. The skills you develop as you research school projects will serve you well in any kind of job that requires use of the Internet and other resources to find and evaluate information.

HOW CAN YOU RESPOND CRITICALLY
to what you read?

Question everything you read—books, articles, online documents, and even textbooks (which are supposed to be as accurate as possible). Think of the critical reading process as an archaeological dig. First, you excavate a site and uncover the artifacts. Then you sort what you've found, make connections among items, and judge their importance. This process of questioning, analysis, and evaluation rewards you with the ability to focus on the most important materials.

Reading for different purposes engages different parts of critical reading. When you read to learn and retain information or to master a skill, you focus on important information (analyzing and evaluating how the ideas are structured, how they connect, and what is most crucial to remember). When you read to search for truth, you ask questions to evaluate arguments (analyzing and evaluating the author's point of view as well as the credibility, accuracy, reliability, and relevancy of the material).

Focus on Important Information

Before determining how to respond to something you've read, ask yourself what is important and what you need to remember. According to Adam Robinson, cofounder of The Princeton Review, "The only way you can effectively absorb the relevant information is to ignore the irrelevant information."[10] The following questions should help you determine what is relevant (if you answer "yes," it's probably relevant):

- Does it contain headings, charts, tables, and captions; key terms and definitions; or an introduction or summary? (For a textbook, check mid-chapter or end-of-chapter exercises.)
- Does it offer definitions, crucial concepts, examples, an explanation of a variety or type, critical relationships, or comparisons?
- Does it spark questions and reactions as you read?
- Does it surprise or confuse you?
- Does it mirror what your instructor emphasizes in class or in assignments?

When trying to figure out what to study and what to skim, ask yourself whether your instructor would expect you to know the material. If you are unsure and the topic is not on your syllabus, email your instructor and ask for clarification.

Ask Questions to Evaluate Arguments

An *argument* refers to a persuasive case—a set of connected ideas supported by examples—that a writer makes to prove or disprove a point. Many scholarly books and articles, in print form or on the Internet, are organized around particular arguments. However, other online articles, websites, and blogs offer *claims* instead—arguments that appear to be factual but don't have adequate evidence to support them. Critical readers evaluate arguments and claims to determine whether they are accurate and logical. When quality evidence combines with sound logic, the argument is solid. Just because you read it online or in print does not mean it's true.

It's easy to accept or reject an argument according to whether it fits with your point of view. If you risk asking questions, however, you can determine the argument's validity and gain the reward of greater depth of understanding, regardless of your opinion. Evaluating an argument involves several factors:

EVIDENCE
Facts, statistics, and other materials that are presented in support of an argument.

- The quality of the evidence (facts, statistics, and other materials supporting an argument)
- Whether the evidence fits the idea concept
- The logical connections

Approach every argument with healthy skepticism. Have an open mind to assess whether you are convinced or still have serious questions. Key 5.11 shows you how to do this.

KEY 5.11 Ask questions like these to evaluate arguments.

EVALUATE THE VALIDITY OF THE EVIDENCE	DETERMINE WHETHER THE EVIDENCE SUPPORTS THE CONCEPT
Is the source reliable and free of bias?	Is there enough evidence?
Who wrote this and with that intent?	Do examples and ideas logically connect?
What assumptions underlie this material?	Is the evidence convincing?
Is this argument based on opinion?	Do the examples build a strong case?
How does this evidence compare with evidence from other sources?	What different and perhaps opposing arguments seem equally valid?

student PROFILE

Aneela Gonzales

GOLDEN WEST COLLEGE, HUNTINGTON BEACH, CALIFORNIA

About me:

I was born into a bicultural family: Hispanic American and Pakistani. My dad left the family when I was 3 months old and my mother became ill with cancer when I was 6. She passed away when I was 11, and the next few years were very difficult. I had to move to a new state to live with my aunt and uncle.

What I focus on:

Ever since I was a child, I dreamed of being a nurse. However, once I finally got to college to study nursing, I found that remembering what I read was a problem and I struggled to pass exams. I had to come up with specific techniques to help. One technique that worked well for me was using different colored highlighters while I read (pink for somewhat important and yellow for very important), typing out all the very important points, and then reviewing that sheet several times. To figure out what to highlight, I paid close attention to what the instructor lectured about and reread those topics in the text.

I also learned it was important for me was to read in a quiet environment with few distractions. I read much better in the library with my phone off. When I didn't understand something I was reading, I went to the Tutoring Center. I found it useful to talk about the reading assignment one-on-one with another person. Finally, I realized that outside stresses, such as having to work to support myself through school, had an effect on my reading skills. Learning to manage my stress helped me better remember what I read.

What will help me in the workplace:

I just graduated from college and started work as a nurse. I have much to read at work so it helps to apply some of the techniques I learned in college. First, I find a quiet place to read. Then I skim the material to find out if it is relevant for me. Finally, I slow down and read only those portions I need. I find this saves me a lot of time.

Evaluate Every Source

Because the reliability of Internet content varies widely, your Internet research is only as strong as your critical thinking. Robert Harris, professor and Web expert, has developed a system for evaluating Internet information called the CARS test for information quality (Credibility, Accuracy, Reasonableness, Support). Use the information in Key 5.12 to question sources as you conduct research. You can also use it to test the reliability of non-Internet sources.

Your future demands that you be able to read, understand, and critically evaluate information on a daily basis in school, on the job, and in life (your 401[k] retirement plan, local and world news, the fine print in a cell phone contract). Develop the ability to read with focus, purpose, and follow-through, and you will never stop enjoying the benefits.

Use the CARS test to determine information quality on the Internet.

CREDIBILITY	ACCURACY	REASONABLENESS	SUPPORT
Examine whether a source is believable and trustworthy.	*Examine whether information is correct—i.e., factual, comprehensive, detailed, and up to date (if necessary).*	*Examine whether material is fair, objective, moderate, and consistent.*	*Examine whether a source is adequately supported with citations.*
What are the author's credentials? Look for education and experience, title or position of employment, membership in any known and respected organization, reliable contact information, biographical information, and reputation.	**Is it up to date, and is that important?** If you are searching for a work of literature, such as Shakespeare's play *Macbeth*, there is no "updated" version. However, you may want reviews of its latest productions. For most scientific research, you will need to rely on the most updated information you can find.	**Does the source seem fair?** Look for a balanced argument, accurate claims, and a reasoned tone that does not appeal primarily to your emotions.	**Where does the information come from?** Look at the site, the sources used by the person or group who compiled the information, and the contact information. Make sure that the cited sources seem reliable and that statistics are documented.
Is there quality control? Look for ways in which the source may have been screened. For example, materials on an organization's website have most likely been approved by several members; information coming from an academic journal has to be screened by several people before it is published.	**Is it comprehensive?** Does the material leave out any important facts or information? Does it neglect to consider alternative views or crucial consequences? Although no one source can contain all of the available information on a topic, it should still be as comprehensive as is possible within its scope.	**Does the source seem objective?** While there is a range of objectivity in writing, you want to favor authors and organizations who can control their bias. An author with a strong political or religious agenda or an intent to sell a product may not be a source of the most truthful material.	**Is the information corroborated?** Test information by looking for other sources that confirm the facts in this information—or, if the information is opinion, sources that share that opinion and back it up with their own citations. One good strategy is to find at least three sources that corroborate each other.
Is there any posted summary or evaluation of the source? You may find abstracts of sources (summary) or a recommendation, rating, or review from a person or organization (evaluation). Either of these—or, ideally, both—can give you an idea of credibility before you decide to examine a source in depth.	**For whom is the source written, and for what purpose?** Looking at what the author wants to accomplish will help you assess whether it has a bias. Sometimes biased information will not be useful for your purpose; sometimes your research will require that you note and evaluate bias (such as if you were to compare Civil War diaries from Union soldiers with those from Confederate soldiers).	**Does the source seem moderate?** Do claims seem possible, or does the information seem hard to believe? Does what you read make sense when compared to what you already know? While wild claims may turn out to be truthful, you are safest to check everything out.	**Is the source externally consistent?** Most material is a mix of both current and old information. External consistency refers to whether the old information agrees with what you already know. If a source contradicts something you know to be true, chances are higher that the information new to you may be inconsistent as well.
Signals of a potential lack of credibility: Anonymous materials, negative evaluations, little or no evidence of quality control, bad grammar or misspelled words	*Signals of a potential lack of accuracy:* Lack of date or old date, generalizations, one-sided views that do not acknowledge opposing arguments	*Signals of a potential lack of reasonableness:* Extreme or emotional language, sweeping statements, conflict of interest, inconsistencies or contradictions	*Signals of a potential lack of support:* Statistics without sources, lack of documentation, lack of corroboration using other reliable sources

Source: Harris, Robert. "Evaluating Internet Research Sources." VirtualSalt, November 22, 2010. From http://www.virtualsalt.com/evalu8it.htm

Reading and Information Literacy

revisit RISK AND REWARD

What happened to Gary? Gary's perseverance earned him the reward of a career in health care management and strategic planning, as a consultant with clients that include Fortune 500 insurance companies. However, he lives every day with the challenge of dyslexia. Because of the time and effort required to read, Gary works in small private offices or a home office. The support of his wife, Lynne, a gifted writer and public speaker, has proven essential. Armed with knowledge about learning differences, Gary and Lynne tested their children early, and were able to provide their son with an academic environment that addressed his reading challenges. With their support, their son has developed a level of self-confidence that Gary still strives for.

What does this story mean for you? Most people have a "big secret," or perhaps a "small secret" that causes challenges in school or on the job. Whether the secret is a learning disability like dyslexia, a negative attitude toward reading or math, or a dysfunctional home life, it becomes an obstacle to your success. Think about one secret you have, and put it in writing. Then write the name of a person whom you trust to support you. Finally, risk having a conversation with this person. Together, come up with ideas of how to address your "secret" in a way that can bring productive rewards.

What risk may bring reward beyond your world? The more the world's citizens know how to read, the more they will be able to solve the problems facing our future. To start exploring what is happening in the promotion of literacy, go to www.roomtoread.org and explore what this organization is doing to build schools, stock libraries, and support education. Click the Get Involved tab to see how to support its initiatives. Perhaps you will want to get involved yourself— or, if not, look into ways you can support literacy in your community, at your college, or even within your own family. Be a part of the solution in a way that brings reward to others.

CHAPTER 5

RISK ACTION
FOR COLLEGE, CAREER, AND LIFE REWARDS

Complete the following on paper or in digital format.

KNOW IT *Think Critically*
Study a Text Page

Build basic skills. The facing page is from the chapter "Groups and Organizations" in the sixth edition of John J. Macionis's *Sociology.* Skim the excerpt. Identify the headings on the page and the relationships among them. Mark primary-level headings with a numeral 1, secondary headings with a 2, and tertiary (third-level) headings with a 3.

SOCIAL GROUPS

Virtually everyone moves through life with a sense of belonging; this is the experience of group life. A social group refers to *two or more people who identify and interact with one another*. Human beings continually come together to form couples, families, circles of friends, neighborhoods, churches, businesses, clubs, and numerous large organizations. Whatever the form, groups encompass people with shared experiences, loyalties, and interests. In short, while maintaining their individuality, the members of social groups also think of themselves as a special "we."

Groups, Categories, and Crowds

People often use the term "group" imprecisely. We now distinguish the group from the similar concepts of category and crowd.

Category

A *category* refers to people who have some status in common. Women, single fathers, military recruits, homeowners, and Roman Catholics are all examples of categories.

Why are categories not considered groups? Simply because, while the individuals involved are aware that they are not the only ones to hold that particular status, the vast majority are strangers to one another.

Crowd

A *crowd* refers to a temporary cluster of individuals who may or may not interact at all. Students sitting in a lecture hall do engage one another and share some common identity as college classmates; thus, such a crowd might be called a loosely formed group. By contrast, riders hurtling along on a subway train or bathers enjoying a summer day at the beach pay little attention to one another and amount to an anonymous aggregate of people. In general, then, crowds are too transitory and impersonal to qualify as social groups.

The right circumstances, however, could turn a crowd into a group. People riding in a subway train that crashes under the city streets generally become keenly aware of their common plight and begin to help one another. Sometimes such extraordinary experiences become the basis for lasting relationships.

Primary and Secondary Groups

Acquaintances commonly greet one another with a smile and the simple phrase, "Hi! How are you?" The response is usually a well scripted, "Just fine, thanks, how about you?" This answer, of course, is often more formal than truthful. In most cases, providing a detailed account of how you are *really* doing would prompt the other person to beat a hasty and awkward exit.

Sociologists classify social groups by measuring them against two ideal types based on members' genuine level of personal concern. This variation is the key to distinguishing primary from secondary groups.

According to Charles Horton Cooley (1864–1929), a **primary group** is a *small social group whose members share personal and enduring relationships*. Bound together by primary relationships, individuals in primary groups typically spend a great deal of time together, engage in a wide range of common activities, and feel that they know one another well. Although not without periodic conflict, members of primary groups display sincere concern for each other's welfare. The family is every society's most important primary group.

Cooley characterized these personal and tightly integrated groups as *primary* because they are among the first groups we experience in life. In addition, the family and early play groups also hold primary importance in the socialization process, shaping attitudes, behavior, and social identity.

Source: John J. Macionis, *Sociology*, 6th ed., p. 145, © 1997 Prentice-Hall, Inc. Reproduced by permission of Pearson Education, Inc., Upper Saddle River, NJ.

Reading and Information Literacy

Take it to the next level. Analyze the headings and text by answering the following questions.

1. Which heading serves as an umbrella for the rest?
2. What do the headings tell you about the content of the page?
3. Name three concepts that seem important to remember.
4. Based on the three concepts you pulled out, write three study questions that you can review with an instructor, a teaching assistant, or a fellow student.

Move toward mastery. Read the excerpt, putting SQ3R to work. Use a marker pen to highlight key phrases and sentences. Write short marginal notes to help you review the material later. After reading this page thoroughly, write a short summary paragraph.

WRITE IT *Communicate*

Emotional intelligence Journal: Reading challenges. Which current course presents your most difficult reading challenge? Describe what makes the reading tough: the type of material, the length of the assignments, the level of difficulty, or something else. What feelings come up for you when you read, and what effect do they have on your reading? Describe techniques you learned in this chapter that can help you get into a growth mindset and read productively.

Real-life writing: Ask for help. Self-help plans often involve reaching out to others. Draft an email to your instructor that describes the difficulties you are facing in your challenging course, as well as specific help you need to move to the next step. Make sure your message is clear and accurate; your grammar, spelling, and punctuation are correct; and your tone is appropriate. (See the Quick Start for guidelines on communicating with instructors.) Whether you send the email is up to you. In either case, writing it will help you move forward in your reading-improvement plan.

WORK IT *Build Your Brand*

Reading Skills on the Job

21st Century Learning Building Blocks

- Information literacy
- Media literacy
- ICT literacy

Excellent reading skills are a requirement for almost every 21st century job. Employers expect you to read independently and master new skills to keep up with change. For example, working in the field of sociology requires you to keep on top of case reports, government regulations, court documents, and research materials. Plus, nearly every job requires you to read memos, emails, and reports from your co-workers and managers.

Prepare by assessing your practical skills *right now*. Copy the following list on your paper or in your document. For each item, rate your ability on a scale of 1 to 10, with 10 being the highest:

- Concentrate, no matter the distractions.
- Define your reading purpose and use it to guide your focus and pace.
- Use specific vocabulary-building techniques to improve comprehension.
- Use every aspect of SQ3R to master content.
- Skim and scan.
- Use analytical thinking skills when reading.
- Use highlighting and notes to help you master content.

Identify the two skill areas where you rated yourself lowest and think about how you can improve. Make a problem-solving plan for each (you may want to use a flowchart like the one on page 104). Check your progress in one month and again at the end of the term. Finally, write one short paragraph describing how you anticipate using reading skills in your chosen career.

6

Good listening allows you to figure out what is important to write down, and taking effective notes rewards you with the ability to recall and

Listening and Note Taking

TAKING IN AND RECORDING INFORMATION

What Would You Risk? *Norton Ewart*

THINK ABOUT THIS SITUATION AS YOU READ, AND CONSIDER WHAT ACTION YOU WOULD TAKE. THIS CHAPTER INTRODUCES YOU TO LISTENING AND NOTE-TAKING SKILLS THAT WILL HELP YOU SUCCESSFULLY TAKE IN AND WRITE DOWN USEFUL KNOWLEDGE.

Norton Ewart struggled starting in fourth grade. In high school, overwhelmed by the work and the level of independence, he avoided risk by doing the least amount of work possible. He enrolled in a local college out of a desire to please his parents. Uninterested in his courses and not ready to work for the rewards of college life, Norton hitchhiked home each weekend to work as a housepainter and left school 10 weeks later. He then moved to his aunt's house in Colorado, where he skied black diamond runs, worked as a ski technician, and tried to figure out who he was and what he wanted.

After two years, Norton decided he wanted to return to college and moved back home. Thinking he might follow the path of engineering, as had three generations before him, he decided to pursue an associate's degree in math and science at Hudson Valley Community College in Troy, New York. Despite his newfound confidence and the fun of a state-of-the-art calculator his father had given him, he could not quickly put his inconsistent study habits behind him. He received Cs and Ds in his calculus and physics courses during his first year.

Norton was behind, but for the first time he was determined to excel. He found himself enjoying the creativity and beauty of math and how the mind interacts with it. On the advice of an academic advisor, he spent a year in a civil technology program while retaking every calculus and physics course. Aware that he was more motivated when working with others, he risked reaching out to a group of fellow engineering students. They created a study group called the "Engineering Defense League" and met daily to work through problems, drill one another on formulas and problem-solving steps, and experience the struggle together.

To be continued...

SKIING AND WORKING IN COLORADO GAVE NORTON A SENSE OF OWNERSHIP OF HIS SUCCESS AS WELL AS A DESIRE—AND A REASON—TO GET BACK TO COLLEGE. YOU'LL LEARN MORE ABOUT NORTON, AND THE REWARD RESULTING FROM HIS ACTIONS, WITHIN THE CHAPTER.

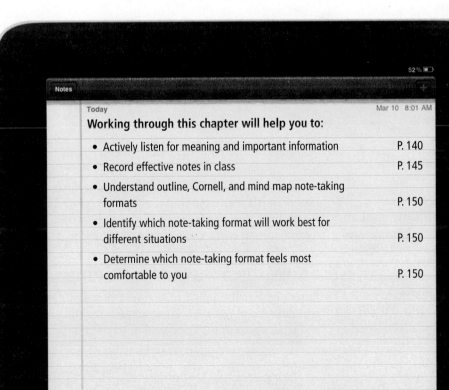

52% 🔋

Notes

Today — Mar 10 8:01 AM

Working through this chapter will help you to:

status CHECK

How Developed Are Your Listening and Note-Taking Skills?

For each statement, fill in the number that feels right to you, from 1 for "not true for me" to 5 for "very true for me."

1. I know and understand the stages of listening. ① ② ③ ④ ⑤

2. I arrive early for class, prepared to absorb information because I read the required textbook ahead of time. ① ② ③ ④ ⑤

3. I ask questions during lectures and listen for verbal clues to identify important information. ① ② ③ ④ ⑤

4. I understand the differences between internal and external distractions and work to control my learning environment whenever possible. ① ② ③ ④ ⑤

5. I use different note-taking formats depending on my instructors' teaching styles and the subject matter. ① ② ③ ④ ⑤

6. I know how to use visuals in my notes to clarify tough concepts discussed in class. ① ② ③ ④ ⑤

7. I believe that good preparation is a necessary first step toward taking comprehensive notes. ① ② ③ ④ ⑤

8. I use note-taking strategies to make sense of and record class discussions. ① ② ③ ④ ⑤

9. I review notes within 24 hours of taking them. ① ② ③ ④ ⑤

10. I use shorthand to take notes faster. ① ② ③ ④ ⑤

Each of the topics in these statements is covered in this chapter. Note those statements for which you filled in a 3 or lower. Skim the chapter to see where those topics appear, and pay special attention to them as you read, learn, and apply new strategies.

REMEMBER: NO MATTER HOW DEVELOPED YOUR LISTENING AND NOTE-TAKING SKILLS ARE, YOU CAN IMPROVE THEM WITH EFFORT AND PRACTICE.

HOW CAN YOU BECOME
a better listener?

The act of hearing is not the same as the act of **listening**. *Hearing* refers to sensing spoken messages from their source. You can hear things but not understand or remember all of them, as Norton found out in the beginning of his college career. Listening starts with hearing, but then continues with focused thinking about what you hear. Listening is a learnable skill that engages your analytical, creative, and practical thinking abilities. It extends far beyond the classroom and rewards you with increased ability to relate to work and school colleagues, friends, and family.

Know the Stages of Listening

Listening is made up of four stages that build on one another: sensing, interpreting, evaluating, and reacting. These stages take the message from the speaker to the listener and back again to the speaker (see Key 6.1).

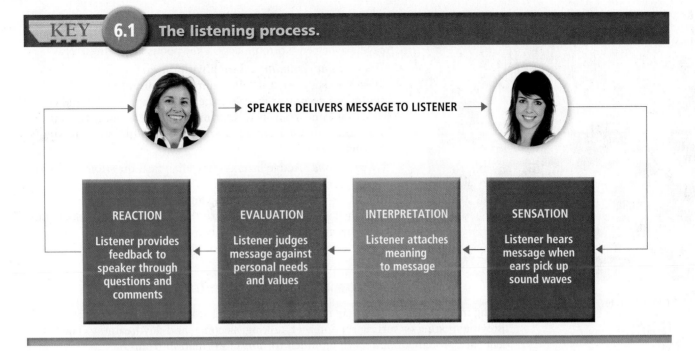

SPEAKER DELIVERS MESSAGE TO LISTENER

REACTION
Listener provides feedback to speaker through questions and comments

EVALUATION
Listener judges message against personal needs and values

INTERPRETATION
Listener attaches meaning to message

SENSATION
Listener hears message when ears pick up sound waves

- During the *sensing* stage (also known as *hearing*), your ears pick up sound waves and transmit them to the brain. For example, you are sitting in class and hear your instructor say, "The only opportunity to make up last week's test is Tuesday at 5:00 p.m."

- In the *interpreting* stage, you attach meaning to a message: You understand what is said and link it to what you already know. You relate this message to your knowledge of the test, whether you need to make it up, and what you are doing on Tuesday at 5:00.

- In the *evaluating* stage, you compare the message with your needs and values. If the message goes against your values or does not fulfill your needs, you may reject it, stop listening, or argue in your mind with the speaker. In this example, if you need to make up the test but have to work Tuesday at 5:00, you may not like the message.

- The final stage of listening is a *reacting* to the message through direct feedback. In a classroom, direct feedback often means asking questions and making comments. For example, your reaction may be to ask the instructor if she can schedule another test time.

You will become a better listener by recognizing and managing listening challenges and becoming actively involved with the material.

Become an Active Listener

On the surface, listening seems like a passive activity: You sit back as someone else speaks. In reality, *effective* listening is an active process. Risk the following actions to earn the reward of greater retention and understanding:

- *Be there.* Being an active listener starts with showing up on time, preferably a few minutes before class begins. Instructors often make important announcements in the first few minutes of class and may also summarize the last lecture.

- *Set purposes for listening.* Before every class, establish the reward you are aiming for, such as understanding a concept. Many instructors start class with a statement of purpose, so listen carefully and write it at the top of your notes to help

Listening to other students can be as important as listening to instructors. These students may learn something useful from their fellow student's perspective.

you focus. If you read assignments before class and review previous notes, you may be able to follow along more easily. This technique may have helped Norton focus on key points more effectively.

■ *Focus on understanding.* Listen with the goal of being able to say to yourself, "I get it!" If you miss important material, make an obvious comment in your notes, such as [WHAT?] and come back to it later. Your instructor may repeat the point you missed or another student's comment may help you fill in the missing information.

■ *Ask questions.* Active listeners ask analytical questions, such as "What is this part of?" or "How is it similar to yesterday's topic?", to clarify understanding and associate new ideas with what they already know. Get into the habit of jotting down your questions and coming back to them during a discussion period so they don't interfere with listening.

Manage Listening Challenges

Sitting in your classes, you may notice students engaged in activities that interfere with listening: texting or surfing the Internet, talking, sleeping, and daydreaming. These students are probably not absorbing much (or any) information from the instructor, and may be distracting you as well. Read on to learn how to address this challenge and others on your path to better listening.

Issue #1: Distractions that divide your attention

Common distractions that interfere with listening include *internal distractions* (worry, anticipation, hunger, feeling too hot or too cold, or hungry) and *external distractions* (chatting, texting, computer use, any kind of movement or noise). These distractions prevent you from paying full attention to what is said. As a result, you can easily miss or misunderstand things.

Fix #1: Focus, focus, focus

First of all, remind yourself you're risking the effort of college for the reward of education, which at the moment means learning the material for this course. You may even want to remind yourself how much it costs to sit in this classroom. Find practical ways to minimize distractions, such as the following:

■ Sit near the front of the room.

■ Move away from talkative classmates.

■ Turn off your cell phone or put it in silent mode, and don't text during class time.

■ Consider writing your notes by hand, rather than using a laptop.

■ If you do use a computer to take notes, stay on task—no gaming, Facebook, Twitter, or surfing during class.

■ Get enough sleep to stay alert.

■ Eat enough so you're not hungry—or bring small snacks if allowed.

It's important to try to put stray thoughts and worries aside while in class. "Switch-tasking"—switching back and forth between tasks—reduces focus and increases the chance of making mistakes. In a study at Stanford, people switching between fewer tasks (low multitaskers) actually outperformed people switching between more tasks (high multitaskers) on all tasks.[1] Even when it is hard, risk keeping your focus on one thing at a time.

Issue #2: Listening lapses

Even the most fantastic instructor cannot *make* you listen. Only you can do that. If you decide that a subject is too difficult or uninteresting, you may tune out and miss what comes next. Or, you may focus on only certain points and shut out everything else. Either way, you may miss valuable information and not gain much reward for your time spent.

Fix #2: An I-can-do-it attitude

- *Start with a productive mindset.* If the class is hard, you have more incentive to pay attention. Instructors are generally more sympathetic to, and eager to help, students who've obviously been trying even when the subject matter is difficult.
- *Concentrate.* Work to take in the whole message so you can later review with your textbook notes and think critically about what is important. Making connections between ideas can reduce both the difficulty of the material in some cases, and boredom if you're familiar with the concepts.
- *Refocus.* If you experience a listening lapse, try to get back into the lecture quickly instead of worrying about what you missed. After class, look at a classmate's notes to fill in the gaps.
- *Be aware.* Pay attention to verbal signposts. These are words or phrases that call attention to what comes next, help organize information, connect ideas, and indicate what is important and what is not. See Key 6.2 for examples.

> **VERBAL SIGNPOSTS**
> Spoken words or phrases that call attention to information that follows.

Issue #3: Rushing to judgment

It's common to stop listening when you hear something you don't like, don't agree with, or don't understand. Unfortunately, that type of emotional reaction may cause you to miss important information, which can hurt you at test time. Judgments also involve reactions to speakers themselves. If you do not like your instructors or have preconceived notions about their race, ethnicity, gender, physical characteristics, or disability, you may dismiss their messages and miss out on your opportunity to learn.

Fix #3: Recognize and correct your patterns

Emotions are very powerful. They can warp what you hear or prevent you from hearing completely. College is about broadening your horizons and looking for what different people can teach you, even though their beliefs may differ from yours. So, what do you do if you react emotionally to a speaker or a message?

KEY 6.2 Pay attention to verbal signposts.

SIGNALS THAT POINT TO KEY CONCEPTS	SIGNALS THAT SUPPORT
A key point to remember …	A perfect example …
Point 1, point 2, etc. …	Specifically, …
The impact of this was …	For instance, …
The critical stages in the process are …	Similarly, …

SIGNALS THAT POINT TO DIFFERENCES	SIGNALS THAT SUMMARIZE
On the contrary, …	From this you have learned …
On the other hand, …	In conclusion, …
In contrast, …	As a result, …
However, …	Finally, …

- *Recognize your pattern so you can change it.* When you feel yourself reacting to something, stop and take a deep breath. Count to ten. Take one more breath and see how you feel.
- *Know that you cannot hear or learn from others if you are filled with preconceived notions about them and their ideas.* Put yourself in their shoes: Would you want them to stop listening to you if they disagreed with you, or would you want to be heard completely?
- *Stop it.* It's as simple as that. Risk listening with an open mind. Even when you disagree or have a negative reaction about an instructor, keep listening. Being open to the new and different, even when it makes you a bit uncomfortable, can bring the reward of learning that changes you for the better.

Issue #4: Partial hearing loss and learning disabilities

If you have a hearing loss or a learning disability, listening effectively in class may prove challenging. Learning disabilities come in a variety of forms affecting different parts of cognition.

Fix #4: Get help

If you have a hearing loss, find out about available equipment. For example, listening to a taped lecture at a higher-than-normal volume can help you hear things you missed in class. Ask instructors if digitalized recordings are available for download to a computer or iPod. Meet with your instructor outside of class to clarify your notes or sit near the front of the room.

If you have, or think you have, a learning disability, learn what services are available. Seek connections with people who can reward you with productive help. Talk to your advisor and instructor about your problem, seek out a tutor, visit academic centers that can help (such as the writing center, if you have a writing issue), scan the college website, and connect with the office of students with disabilities.

Issue #5: Comprehension difficulties for non-native English speakers

If English is not your first language, it may be challenging to listen and understand material in the classroom. Specialized vocabulary, informal language, and the rate of speech can add to the challenge. Succeeding in the classroom will require concentration, dedication, and patience.

Fix #5: Take a proactive approach to understanding

Talk to your instructor as soon as possible about your situation. Discussing your needs with your instructor early in the course keeps the instructor informed and shows your dedication. In some cases, your instructor will give you a list of key terms to review before class. During class, keep a list of unfamiliar words and phrases to look up later, but try not to let the terms prevent you from understanding the main ideas. Focus on the main points of the lecture and meet with classmates after class to fill in the gaps in your understanding.

If, after several weeks, you're still having difficulties, consider enrolling in an English refresher course, getting a tutor, or visiting the campus advising center for more assistance. Be proactive about your education.

Listening isn't always easy and it isn't always comfortable. Keeping an open, engaged mind takes practice and sometimes exposes you to information that you disagree with or that even upsets you. However, only by taking the risk to listen well can you be rewarded with the ability to focus on and remember the most important information.

get analytical

DISCOVER YOURSELF AS A LISTENER

Complete the following on paper or in digital format.

Answer the questions as you focus on your personal listening habits:

1. Analyze how present you are as a listener. Are you easily distracted, or can you focus well? Do you prefer to listen or do you tend to talk?

2. When you are listening, what distracts you?

3. What happens to your listening skills when you become confused?

4. How do you react when you strongly disagree with something your instructor says? When you are convinced you are right and your instructor is wrong?

5. Thinking about your answers, list two strategies from the chapter that will help you improve your listening skills.

Effective listening skills are the basis for effective note taking—an essential and powerful study tool.

HOW CAN YOU IMPROVE
your note-taking skills?

Taking notes makes you an active class participant, even when you don't say a word. Notes also provide you with study materials. Note taking is key to your academic success.

Taking Notes in Class

Class notes serve two primary purposes: (1) they record what happened in class, and (2) they provide study materials. Because it is virtually impossible to write or type every word you hear, note taking encourages you to use your analytical intelligence to critically evaluate what is worth remembering—the main challenge for Norton and for so many other college students. Exploring the strategies outlined next helps you prepare for class, take notes in class, and review notes after class.

Prepare

Showing up for class on time is just the start. Here's more about preparing to take notes:

- *Preview your reading material.* Reading assigned materials before class will give you the background to take effective notes, and is one of the most rewarding possible study strategies. Check your class syllabi daily for assignment due dates, and plan your reading time with these deadlines in mind.

Good listening powers note taking. When taking notes in class, stop to listen to the information before deciding what to write down.

- *Review what you know.* Taking 15 minutes before class to review previous notes and reading will help you to follow the lecture from the start.
- *Set up your environment.* Find a comfortable seat, away from friends if sitting with them distracts you. Set up your notebook or, if you use a laptop, open the file containing your class notes. Be ready to write (or type) as soon as the instructor begins speaking.
- *Gather support.* In each class, set up a support format with one or two students so you can meet to discuss questions you have or look at their notes after an absence. Find students whose work you respect.

Record information effectively during class

The following practical suggestions will help you record information to review later:

- Write down all key terms and definitions.
- For difficult concepts, note relevant examples, applications, and links to other material.
- If questions are welcome during class, ask them. If you prefer to ask questions after class, jot down questions as you think of them through the class period.
- Write down every question your instructor raises, since these questions may be on a test.
- Be organized, but not fussy. Remember that you can always improve your notes later.
- Draw pictures and diagrams to illustrate ideas.
- Be consistent. Use the same system to show importance—such as indenting, spacing, or underlining—on each page.
- If you have trouble with a concept, leave space for an explanation and flag it with a question mark. After class, consult your text or ask a classmate or instructor for help.
- Go beyond the PowerPoint. When instructors use electronic resources, expand on the main points listed there with details from the lecture.
- Consider learning preferences. The Multiple Intelligences table in this chapter (see page 147) suggests MI-related note-taking strategies.

Finally, don't stop taking notes when your class engages in a discussion. Even though it isn't part of the instructor's planned presentation, it often includes important information. Key 6.3 has suggestions for how to take notes during class discussions.

Review and revise

The process of note taking is not complete when you put your pen down or close your computer at the end of the class period. Notes are only useful to you if you review and revise them, and within as short a time period as you can manage. The longer you wait to review those notes, the less likely it is that you will understand them.

Class notes often have sections that are incomplete, confusing, or illegible. Review and revise your notes as soon as possible after class to fill in gaps while the material is still fresh, clarify sloppy handwriting, and raise questions. Rewriting or retyping notes is a great way to reinforce what you heard in class, review new ideas, and create easy-to-read study aids. It also prepares you for the rewarding strategy of combining class and textbook notes.

multiple intelligence strategies

Name an upcoming class meeting (date, time, course): _____.
In the right-hand column, record specific ideas for how MI strategies can help you take notes in this class.

INTELLIGENCE	USE MI STRATEGIES TO IMPROVE YOUR NOTES	IDENTIFY MI STRATEGIES THAT CAN HELP YOU TAKE NOTES
Verbal-Linguistic	• Rewrite your class notes in an alternate note-taking style to see connections more clearly. • Combine class and textbook notes to get a complete picture.	
Logical-Mathematical	• When reviewing or rewriting notes, put information into a logical sequence. • Create tables that show relationships.	
Bodily-Kinesthetic	• Think of your notes as a crafts project with "knowledge layers" of different colors. Use colored pens to texture your notes. • Study with your notes spread in sequence around you so that you can see knowledge building from left to right.	
Visual-Spatial	• Take notes using colored markers or pens. • Rewrite lecture notes as a mind map, focusing on the most important points.	
Interpersonal	• Try to schedule a study group right after a lecture to discuss class notes. • Review class notes with a study buddy and compare notes to see what each of you missed.	
Intrapersonal	• Schedule some quiet time soon after a lecture to review and think about your notes. • As you review your notes, decide whether you grasp the material or need help.	
Musical	• To improve recall, recite concepts in your notes to rhythms. • Write a song that includes material from your class and text notes. Use the refrain to emphasize what is important.	
Naturalistic	• Notice similarities and differences in concepts by organizing material into natural groupings.	

- Listen to everyone; you never know when something important will be said.

- Listen for threads that weave through comments. They may signal an important point.

- Listen for ideas the instructor likes and for encouraging comments, such as "You make a great point" or "I like your idea."

- Take notes when the instructor rephrases and clarifies a point.

Taking Notes from Books

Note taking is not only useful in class, it can also help you decide and reinforce what is most important to remember when you read textbooks, articles, or any other materials assigned for class or used for research. You may decide to take separate notes on reading material if the book is a library copy or borrowed from a classmate. Or, you might do so when you don't have enough room to take notes in the margin. Some students simply prefer to take separate notes on reading material as a study strategy.

Start the process by identifying what you want to get from the notes. Are you looking for the basic topics from a chapter? An in-depth understanding of a particular concept? Once you've established the goal, then you can identify the best format. For instance, mind maps work well to understand broad connections, overall relationships, or how your text works in relation to your instructor's lecture. On the other hand, formal outlines make sense of complicated information in a structured way that can provide clarity. Later in the chapter you will read about different note-taking formats and try different approaches to see which ones work for you.

After choosing a format, read and take notes on the material using the Survey, Question, and Read stages of SQ3R:

- Survey to get an overview of what the material can offer you.
- Question to focus your attention what is important enough to record in your notes.
- Read and record your notes on paper or an electronic file.

Finally, remember that many of the in-class note-taking strategies you just explored will help you take effective notes on reading materials. For example, you can note key terms and definitions, re-create important diagrams, use consistent formatting, and flag areas of confusion with a question mark.

get $mart

ACQUIRING FINANCIAL INFORMATION

Complete the following on paper or in digital format.

When you set yourself up to access financial information effectively, you will be more able to make the most of money-oriented resources on campus. Explore how you prefer to acquire financial information.

1. Which style of reading is most comfortable to you—print or electronic?

2. Rewrite this list of information sources according to how you would rank them, from 1 (I respond best to this) to 7 (I respond least to this).

   a. In-person conversations

   b. Magazines/newspapers

   c. Books

   d. Websites

   e. YouTube

   f. Blog posts

   g. Twitter feeds

3. Given these preferences, identify three specific sources that will best help you stay informed. Name each source and give a brief description of what it offers. *Note:* Use the library and Internet to locate the sources.

4. What are two of your most pressing questions about personal finances right now?

5. Using the three sources you identified, find and write answers to these questions.

talk risk and reward . . .

Risk asking tough questions to be rewarded with new insights. Use the following questions to inspire discussion with classmates, either in person or online.

- Think about what typically plays on your brain's "soundtrack" during a class meeting—words, music, anything that streams through. Be honest: How much of it relates to the class and how much is unrelated? What effect does it have on your focus?

- Focus is an ongoing challenge for many students. What are you willing to risk to be more focused in the classroom?

CONSIDER THE CASE: How do you respond when, like Norton, you have no interest in what you are studying? Do you attempt to find meaning, do the minimum, give up? What is the effect on your behavior, your grades, your commitment?

Listening and Note Taking

WHAT NOTE-TAKING *formats can you use?*

Now that you have gathered some useful strategies for what goes into your notes and how to study that material, take a look at different note-taking formats. As you read, keep some questions in mind:

- What class or type of instruction is this format best suited for? Why?
- How could I make use of this format?
- Which format seems most comfortable to me?
- What format might be most compatible with my learning preferences? Why?

This section discusses different note-taking formats. As Norton found, different formats may suit different courses, so don't assume that the format that seems most comfortable to you will be the best choice for every academic subject. To select a format that works best in each class, take the following into account:

- *The instructor's style* (which will be clear after a few classes). In the same term, you may have an instructor who is organized, another who jumps around and talks rapidly, and a third who goes off topic in response to questions. Be flexible as you adapt.
- *The course material.* You may decide that an informal outline works best for a highly structured lecture and that a mind map (discussed later in the chapter) is right for a looser presentation. Try one note-taking format for several classes, then adjust if necessary.
- *Your learning preferences.* For the greatest reward in exchange for your effort, choose strategies that make the most of your strengths and compensate for weaknesses.

Now look at examples of various note-taking formats and how they work.

Outlines

Outlines use a standard structure to show how ideas interrelate. *Formal outlines* indicate idea dominance and subordination with Roman numerals, uppercase and lowercase letters, and numbers. In contrast, *informal outlines* show the same associations but replace the formality with a format of consistent indenting and dashes.

When a lecture seems well organized, an informal outline can show how ideas and supporting details relate and can indicate levels of importance. Key 6.4 shows how the structure of an informal outline could help a student take notes on the topic of tropical rain forests. During class time, it is usually easier and faster to use an informal outline than to carefully construct a formal outline using letters and numbers to identify pieces of information.

From time to time, an instructor may give you a guide, usually in outline form, to help you take notes in class. This outline, known as *guided notes*, may be on the board, on an overhead projector, or on a handout that you receive at the beginning of class. Guided notes do *not* replace your own notes. Designed to be sketchy and limited, they require you to fill in the details during class, which helps you to pay attention. In addition, the act of writing helps anchor your memory of information (you may learn more about memory strategies elsewhere in your text).

When an instructor's presentation is disorganized, it may be difficult to use an outline. Focus instead on taking down whatever information you can as you try to connect key topics. The following note-taking methods can be beneficial in such situations.

Tropical Rain Forests

What are tropical rain forests?

— Areas in South America and Africa, along the equator

— Average temperatures between 25° and 30° C (77°–86° F)

— Average annual rainfalls range between 250 and 400 centimeters (100–160 inches)

Rain forests are the Earth's richest, most biodiverse ecosystem.

— A biodiverse ecosystem has a great number of organisms co-existing within a defined area.

— Examples of rain forest biodiversity

– 2½ acres in the Amazon rain forest has 283 species of trees

– a 3-square-mile section of a Peruvian rain forest has more than 1,300 butterfly species and 600 bird species

— Compare this biodiversity to what is found in the entire U.S.

– only 400 butterfly species and 700 bird species

How are humans changing the rain forest?

— Humans destroy an estimated 50,000 square miles of rain forest a year (10 times the area of Connecticut).

– Cutting down trees for lumber

– Clearing the land for ranching or agriculture

— Rain forest removal is also linked to the increase in atmospheric carbon dioxide, which worsens the greenhouse effect (where gases such as carbon dioxide trap the sun's energy in the Earth's atmosphere as heat resulting in global warning).

Source: Audesirk, Teresa, Gerald Audesirk, and Bruce E. Byers. *Life on Earth,* 9th ed. Upper Saddle River, NJ: Prentice Hall, 2011, pp. 559–561.

Cornell T-Note Format

The Cornell note-taking format, also known as the *T-note format,* consists of three sections on ordinary notepaper:[2]

- *Notes,* the largest section, is on the right. Record your notes here in whatever form you choose. Skip lines between topics so you can clearly see where a section begins and ends.

- The *cues* column goes on the left side of your notes. Leave it blank while you read or listen, and then fill it in later while you review. You might insert key words or comments that highlight ideas, clarify meaning, add examples, link ideas, or draw diagrams. Many students use this column to raise questions, which they answer when they study.

- The *summary* goes at the bottom of the page. Here you reduce your notes to critical points, a process that helps you learn the material. Use this section to provide an overview of what the notes say.

Create this note-taking structure *before* class begins by following these directions:

- Start with a sheet of 8.5-by-11-inch lined paper. Label it with the date and lecture title.

- To create the cues column, draw a vertical line about 2.5 inches from the left side of the paper. End the line about 2 inches from the bottom of the sheet.

- To create the summary area, start at the point where the vertical line ends (about 2 inches from the bottom of the page) and draw a horizontal line that spans the entire paper.

Cues	Notes

Summary

Label a sheet of paper with the date and title of the lecture.

Create the cue column by drawing a vertical line about 2-½ inches from the left side of the paper. End the line about 2 inches from the bottom of the sheet.

Create the summary area by starting where the vertical line ends (about 2 inches from the bottom of the page) and drawing a horizontal line across the paper.

October 3, 2014, p. 1

Understanding Employee Motivation

Why do some workers have a better attitude toward their work than others?

Some managers view workers as lazy; others view them as motivated and productive.

Maslow's Hierarchy

self-actualization needs (challenging job)
esteem needs (job title)
social needs (friends at work)
security needs (health plan)
physiological needs (pay)

Purpose of motivational theories
— To explain role of human relations in motivating employee performance
— Theories translate into how managers actually treat workers

2 specific theories
— Human resources model, developed by Douglas McGregor, shows that managers have radically different beliefs about motivation.
— Theory X holds that people are naturally irresponsible and uncooperative
— Theory Y holds that people are naturally responsible and self-motivated
— Maslow's Hierarchy of Needs says that people have needs in 5 different areas, which they attempt to satisfy in their work.
— Physiological need: need for survival, including food and shelter
— Security need: need for stability and protection
— Social need: need for friendship and companionship
— Esteem need: need for status and recognition
— Self-actualization need: need for self-fulfillment
Needs at lower levels must be met before a person tries to satisfy needs at higher levels.
— Developed by psychologist Abraham Maslow

Two motivational theories try to explain worker motivation. The human resources model includes Theory X and Theory Y. Maslow's Hierarchy of Needs suggests that people have needs in 5 different areas: physiological, security, social, esteem, and self-actualization.

Key 6.5 shows how the Cornell format was used to take notes in a business course.

Mind Map

A mind map, also known as a *think link* or *word web*, is a visual form of note taking that encourages flexible thinking and making connections. When you draw a mind map, you use shapes and lines to connect ideas with supporting details and examples. The visual design makes the connections easy to see, and shapes and pictures extend the material beyond words.

To create a mind map, start by circling or boxing your topic in the middle of the paper. Next, draw a line from the topic and write the name of one major idea at the end of the line. Circle that idea. Then, jot down specific facts related to the idea, linking them to the idea with more lines. Continue the process, identifying thoughts with words

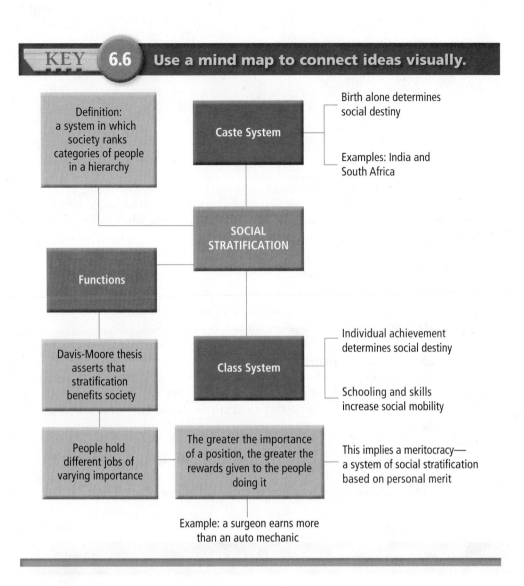

and circles, and connecting them to one another with lines. Key 6.6 shows a mind map illustrating the sociological concept called stratification.

A mind map does not have to include circles and lines; it can take on a number of different forms, such as a "jellyfish" (main idea at the top with examples dangling down below) or a series of stairs with examples building to the idea at the top. Engage your creativity to develop a shape that works for you. If a mind map is difficult to construct in class, consider transforming your notes into a mind map format later when you review.

Charting Method

Sometimes instructors deliver information in such quanities and at such speeds that taking detailed notes becomes nearly impossible. When there is a lot of material coming at you very quickly, the charting method might prove useful, and can provide a useful memorization tool. It is also excellent for information presented chronologically or sequentially.

To create charting notes, look ahead in your syllabus to determine the topics of the day's lecture or contact your instructor. Then separate your paper into distinct columns, such as definitions, important phrases, and key themes. As you listen to the lecture, fill in the columns. Here is an example showing a section of a set of charting notes for a history class:

TIME PERIOD	IMPORTANT PEOPLE	EVENTS	IMPORTANCE
1969–1974	Richard Nixon	Watergate, Vietnam War	Ended Vietnam War, opened relations with China, first president to resign

Other Visual Strategies

There are other strategies that help organize information for visual learners, although they may be too involved to complete during class. Use them when taking textbook notes or combining class and textbook notes for review.

- *Timelines.* Use a timeline to organize information into chronological order. Draw a vertical or horizontal line on the page and place tic marks on the line in order, noting the dates and filling in basic event descriptions.
- *Tables.* Use the columns and rows of a table to organize information as you condense and summarize your class and textbook notes.
- *Branch diagrams.* This type of diagram, also called a *tree chart,* shows how items that come from a single source are related to one another. Typical examples of branch diagrams include family trees, evolutionary charts, and organizational charts (for people or files). Key 6.7 illustrates a partial branch diagram representing the structure of a chemistry department website in a small college.
- *Flowchart.* This diagram shows a set of ordered steps that make up a process. The diagram often includes points where you have to make a decision before proceeding in a particular direction. For example, Key 6.8 illustrates a flowchart that could help you remember the steps to learning a new software program.

KEY 6.7 A branch diagram shows relationships.

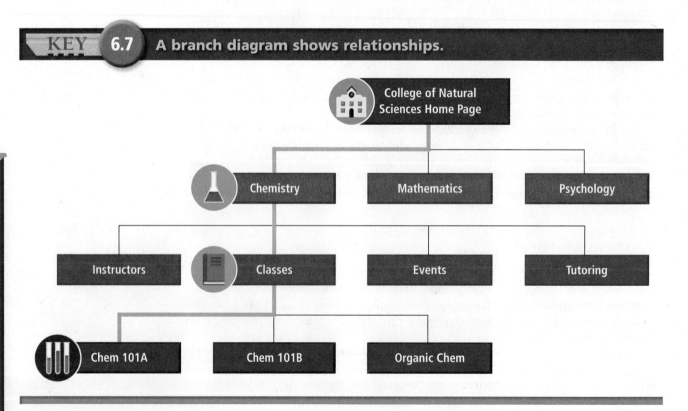

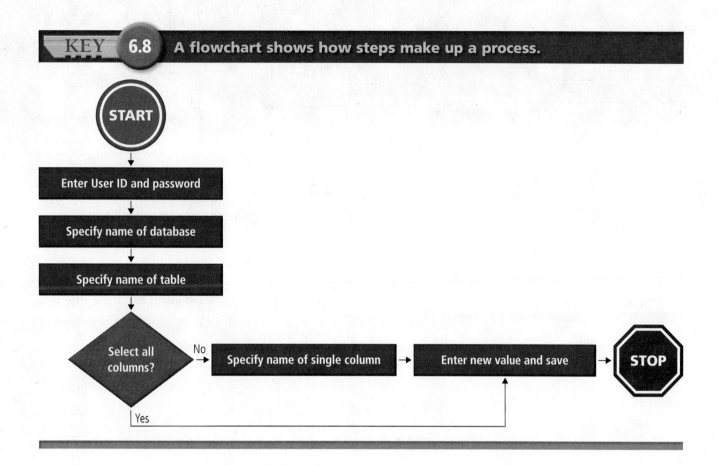

Electronic Strategies

If you take notes using an electronic device, saving them safely is essential. You can save notes on your device or on a remote server (known as "the cloud") connected to the Internet. Evernote is a software package that lets you take notes using any computer or Android phone. These notes include text, webpage URLs and content, photographs, or voice memos—all of which can have attachments. You can save your notes on your own computer or on a special Evernote server.

GoogleDocs is another example of a documentation and note-taking tool that lets you save text to the cloud. With GoogleDocs, you need only connect to the Internet, open GoogleDocs and start typing. When you're done, you save your work to a collection (folder) of your choice, hosted on a Google server. You can also download the file to your own computer. You can allow other people in a study group to access your file in GoogleDocs and edit it, adding new information where necessary.

Finally, recent note-taking technology has added recording capabilities to your arsenal. The Livescribe "smartpen" records exactly what you hear and write with the pen on a specialized notebook which saves everything electronically, enabling you to store and review the lecture and your notes on a computer. SoundNote is a similar application that works with tablet computers. When you type notes on a tablet, SoundNote will record everything you type as well as what you are hearing during the class.[3]

get practical

FACE A NOTE-TAKING CHALLENGE

Complete the following on paper or in digital format.

Get set to take in and record information in your most difficult class.

1. What is the name of the course that is most challenging for you right now?

2. Consult your syllabus for this course. What do you have to read (text sections and/or other materials) before your next class?

3. Where will you sit in class to focus your attention and minimize distractions?

4. Which note-taking format is best suited for the class and why?

5. Who are two classmates whose notes you can borrow if you miss a class or are confused about material? Include phone numbers and/or email addresses.

HOW CAN YOU
take notes faster?

Personal shorthand is a practical intelligence strategy for writing faster. Because you are the only intended reader, you can misspell and abbreviate words in ways that only you understand. A risk of using shorthand is that you might forget what your own writing means. To avoid this problem, review your notes shortly after class and properly spell any words that are confusing.

The following suggestions will help you master shorthand. Many will be familiar and you may already use them in your emails, texts, and instant messages. As useful as they are for note taking, make sure you do not use them in assignments that you turn in.

SHORTHAND
A format of rapid handwriting that employs symbols, abbreviations, and shortened words to represent words and phrases.

1. Use standard abbreviations in place of complete words.

w/, w/o	with, without	Cf	compare, in comparison to
Ur	you are	Ff	following
→	means; resulting in	Q	question
←	as a result of	gr8	great
↑	increasing	Pov	point of view
↓	decreasing	<	less than
∴	therefore	>	more than
b/c	because	=	Equals
≈	approximately	b&f	back and forth
+ *or* &	and	Δ	change
Y	why	2	to; two; too
No. *or* #	number	Afap	as far as possible
i.e.	that is,	e.g.	for example
cos	change of subject	c/o	care of
Ng	no good	lb	pound
POTUS	President of the United States	hx	history

student PROFILE

Tomohito Kondo
DE ANZA COMMUNITY COLLEGE, CALIFORNIA

About me:

I came here in the spring of 2009 right after I graduated from high school in Japan. I am on the De Anza Community College soccer team and I'm majoring in political science. I plan to transfer to a four-year university next fall.

What I focus on:

In college, most professors move from topic to topic when they want to, no matter where students may be in their note taking. It is important to take good notes, but it can be hard to do so when you are trying to keep up with the professor. The point is to take notes that *you* can understand.

I focus on listening and I like to write down key words as I listen. When I later read my notes, those keywords help me remember what the teacher was talking about. Even if your handwriting is really awful, it doesn't matter as long as you can read it. I think my note-taking skills help me succeed in my classes, and also to save me time so I can enjoy the fun side of college life.

What will help me in the workplace:

At any time of your life, you may need to remember key points. For example, I want to be an international meeting coordinator, so I will have to remember everything representatives from other countries say. Whatever your future job will be, taking good notes will help you remember important information, which will help you get into a better position. You want to move to the next stage, right? Good listening and note-taking skills will give you the boost to do so.

2. Shorten words by removing vowels from the middle of words.

   prps = purpose
   lwyr = lawyer
   cmptr = computer

3. Substitute word beginnings for entire words.

   assoc = associate; association
   info = information
   subj = subject

4. Form plurals by adding s to shortened words.

   prblms = problems
   envlps = envelopes
   prntrs = printers

5. Make up your own symbols and use them consistently.

   b/4   = before
   4tn   = fortune
   2thake = toothache

get creative

CRAFT YOUR OWN SHORTHAND

Complete the following on paper or in digital format.

Customize your shorthand to suit your needs.

1. Identify a class where you take a lot of notes or would like to take better notes.

2. Next, write 10 terms used often in this class. For instance, if you were creating a list of shorthand terms for your psychology class, you might include terms like Sigmund Freud, child development, or neuropsychology.

3. Last, create a list of shorthand terms for the items you chose. Be creative, but make sure they are easy to remember and use. Thus, your shorthand should not be longer or more complex than the word itself. Your shorthand could include numbers, symbols, or even small images (like a heart or smiley face). For the list of psychology terms, the shorthand might look like the following:

   - Sigmund Freud = SigFrd

   - Child development = ChDev

   - Neuropsychology = nro-psych

6. Use standard or informal abbreviations for proper nouns such as places, people, companies, scientific substances, and events.

   DC = Washington, D.C.
   H_2O = water
   Moz. = Wolfgang Amadeus Mozart

7. If you will be repeating a word or phrase frequently, write it once and then establish an abbreviation. For example, the first time your political science instructor mentions the Iraq Study Group, the 2006 bipartisan commission that issued recommendations to the president on the Iraq War, write the name in full. After that, use the initials ISG.

In life, you never know where you may need to take notes—at the doctor's office, in a business meeting, or during a presentation. The ability to listen well means you will be able to figure out what is important to write down, and the ability to take effective notes rewards you with the ability to recall and use that information in the future.

revisit RISK AND REWARD

What happened to Norton? As a result of his increased efforts and help from his study group, Norton was rewarded with academic success and returned to the pre-engineering program, later transferring to Union College where he graduated with a bachelor's in electrical engineering. He was hired by Hewlett-Packard after college and worked his way up to management over 20 years. After several years at a different job in the area of product management, he is back at HP. He is still an expert skier and remains just as willing to take productive risks in his personal life and career as he is on double black diamond slopes.

What does this mean for you? Every student experiences different levels of motivation and interest for different courses. Your challenge is to find a way to do the work well when your interest doesn't provide the energy. Choose the course you are taking right now that interests you the least. Make three lists with the following headers: Study Strategies That Can Help, How I Will Use What I Learn in This Course, and What Reward Will Result If I Persist in This Course. Then fill each list with as many items as you can and put them where you can refer to them as you make your way through the term.

What risk may bring reward beyond your world? The demands of your everyday life may be so pressing you cannot see how you will have the time to help out. Think, though, about a person, place, thing, idea, or situation that has sparked your interest and emotion. Find an organization that relates to it and investigate to see how you can help in some small way. One action now, no matter how small, can help. Who knows? Maybe you can make time for more action in the future.

Complete the following on paper or in digital format.

KNOW IT *Think Critically*

Your Best Listening and Note-Taking Conditions

Build basic skills. Think of a recent class where you were able to listen and take notes effectively.

1. Describe the environment (course title, classroom setting, and so on).
2. Describe the instructor's style (lecture, group discussion, question and answer).
3. Describe your level of preparation and attitude toward the class.
4. Describe the note-taking style you typically use in the class and note how effective it is.
5. Describe any barriers to effective listening in the class.

Now think of a recent class in which you found it hard to listen and take notes.

1. Describe the environment (course title, classroom setting, and so on).
2. Describe the instructor's style (lecture, group discussion, question and answer).
3. Describe your level of preparation and attitude toward the class.
4. Describe the note-taking style you typically use in the class, and note how effective it is.
5. Describe any barriers to effective listening in the class.

Take it to the next level. Examining the two situations you identified, identify three conditions that seem to be crucial for you to effectively listen and take notes.

Move toward mastery. Think about the more difficult listening and note-taking situation. For each of the three conditions you identified, describe how to either (a) to make sure the condition occurs, or (b) compensate for the condition if it is out of your control.

WRITE IT *Communicate*

Emotional intelligence journal: Understanding your needs and making changes.
Think about a situation in which you had trouble taking effective notes. Was it the teacher's pace? The subject matter of the class? How did you feel about the situation and what did you do? After you describe the situation, identify three note-taking strategies from this chapter that could help you in the future. How might they help you create a more positive outcome?

Real-life writing: Determining the best method for you. Over the next week, commit to trying at least three types of note-taking formats in your classes. If possible, choose a different format for each subject. Before entering the class, prepare by readying your notebook with the correct formatting for the particular note-taking format. Take your class notes using the new format. When the week is over, think about which style worked best for you and which would be the most beneficial going forward.

WORK IT *Build Your Brand*

Learn More About Career Success

21st Century Learning Building Blocks

- Financial, economic, business, and entrepreneurial literacy
- Information literacy
- Media literacy

1. Put your listening and note-taking skills to work as you investigate what brings success in the workplace. Name two or three career areas that interest you.

2. Next, visit an Internet website, such as YouTube.com, that hosts user-loaded videos. Search for an interview with someone working in a career of your choice. You might try search terms like "marketing interview," "what's it like to be a dental technician," or "what does a movie producer do." Once you find a usable video (one with credible, realistic information), take notes on the interview using one of the note-taking techniques from this chapter.

   a. Watch the video once all the way through, concentrating on main points and overall themes.

   b. Watch it again to fill in gaps, understand key terms and concepts, and gather interesting extras. Remember to use shorthand when necessary.

   c. After you watch the video twice and have thorough notes, write a one-page summary of the career for your portfolio. Include important information discussed in the video, such as what training is required, salary expectations, daily duties, challenges, and rewards. Keep the summary in your portfolio for future career searches.

Whatever you study, your goal is to anchor important information in long-term memory so that you can use it – for both short-term goals like tests and long-term goals like performing effectively on the job.

Memory and Studying

RETAINING WHAT YOU LEARN

What Would You Risk? *Cindy Estrada*

THINK ABOUT THIS SITUATION AS YOU READ, AND CONSIDER WHAT ACTION YOU WOULD TAKE. THIS CHAPTER SHOWS YOU HOW MEMORY WORKS AND THEN HELPS YOU USE IT EFFECTIVELY TO REMEMBER WHAT YOU STUDY. ALTHOUGH IT'S EASIER TO REMEMBER THINGS THAT YOU WANT TO KNOW, THE STRATEGIES YOU LEARN WILL HELP YOU STUDY MATERIALS NO MATTER HOW YOU FEEL ABOUT THEM.

Cindy Estrada never knew a carefree childhood. Her father was a ground medic during the Vietnam War, and post-traumatic stress disorder took its toll on him after the war. By the time Cindy reached age 6, he was no longer a presence in the Estrada household. While her mom worked, Cindy watched over her three younger brothers. "At an early age, I was there for them after school until my mom got home in the evenings," Cindy recalls. "It was a very nontraditional household." But Cindy had plenty of ambition. She aimed for the reward of being first in her family to go to college, so she worked hard and explored four-year college options.

At age 17, Cindy got pregnant. Her newborn son, Jeramie, was the new joy in her life. However, she wondered how she would be able to support her new son and herself without even a high school diploma. She transferred to an alternative high school in her hometown, Cheyenne, Wyoming, to complete her high school education. But as a single mom, she knew she needed to risk more in order to provide for her son.

Cindy enrolled at Laramie County Community College while working as an operator with Mountain Bell. Two years later, she transferred to the University of Wyoming in Laramie, 50 miles away. Aiming for a telecommunications degree required her to risk balancing a full-time job with mom duties and 100 miles of daily commuting, all while retaining information from classes and study sessions.

To be continued . . .

DRIVEN TO FORGE A SOLID LIFESTYLE FOR HER YOUNG FAMILY, CINDY WAS DETERMINED TO PULL OFF AN ASTOUNDING JUGGLING ACT. TO DO SO, SHE WOULD NEED TO MAXIMIZE STUDY TIME. YOU'LL LEARN MORE ABOUT CINDY, AND THE REWARD RESULTING FROM HER ACTIONS, WITHIN THE CHAPTER.

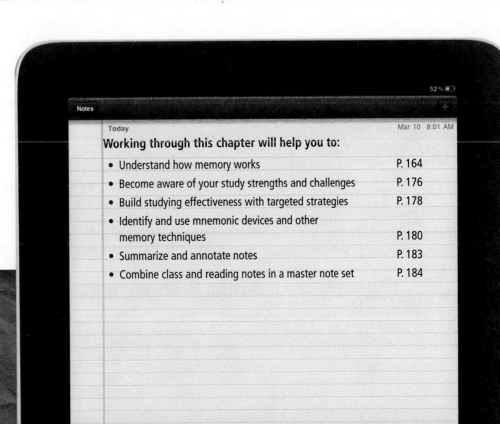

Notes

Today — Mar 10 8:01 AM

Working through this chapter will help you to:

status CHECK

How Developed Are Your Memory and Studying Skills?

For each statement, fill in the number that best describes how often it applies to you.

1 = never   2 = seldom   3 = sometimes   4 = often   5 = always

1. I know that not everything that I hear and read will necessarily stay in my memory for long—or at all.   ① ② ③ ④ ⑤

2. When I am studying, I try to choose what is most important to remember.   ① ② ③ ④ ⑤

3. Through trial and error, I have figured out study locations and times that work best for me.   ① ② ③ ④ ⑤

4. I write, rewrite, and summarize information to remember it.   ① ② ③ ④ ⑤

5. I use flash cards and other active memory strategies to remember what I study.   ① ② ③ ④ ⑤

6. I create mnemonic devices with images and associations as memory hooks.   ① ② ③ ④ ⑤

7. I try to review material in several sessions over time rather than cram the night before a test.   ① ② ③ ④ ⑤

8. If I find myself looking up something over and over again, I make an effort to memorize it.   ① ② ③ ④ ⑤

9. I know how to study class and text notes effectively to prepare for tests.   ① ② ③ ④ ⑤

10. My study strategies work for me; after a test or presentation is over, I retain much of what I had to know.   ① ② ③ ④ ⑤

Each of the topics in these statements is covered in this chapter. Note those statements for which you filled in a 3 or lower. Skim the chapter to see where those topics appear, and pay special attention to them as you read, learn, and apply new strategies.

REMEMBER: NO MATTER HOW DEVELOPED YOUR MEMORY AND STUDYING SKILLS ARE, YOU CAN IMPROVE WITH EFFORT AND PRACTICE.

HOW DOES
memory work?

All learning and performance depends on memory, because the information you remember—concepts, facts, processes, formulas, and more—is the raw material with which you think, write, create, build, and perform your day-to-day actions in school and out. Memorization also forms a foundation for higher-level thinking, because you need to recall and understand information before you can apply, analyze, synthesize, or evaluate it.

Through the effort of studying and a positive attitude, you earn the reward of a memory that can help you move toward your goals. This chapter provides memory-improvement techniques that you can make your own. First, explore how memory works.

The Information Processing Model of Memory

Memory refers to the way the brain stores and recalls information or experiences that are acquired through the five senses. While you take in thousands of pieces of information every second—everything from the shape and color of your chair to how your

MyStudentSuccessLab

(www.mystudentsuccesslab.com) is an online solution designed to help you "Start Strong, Finish Stronger" by building skills for ongoing personal and professional development.

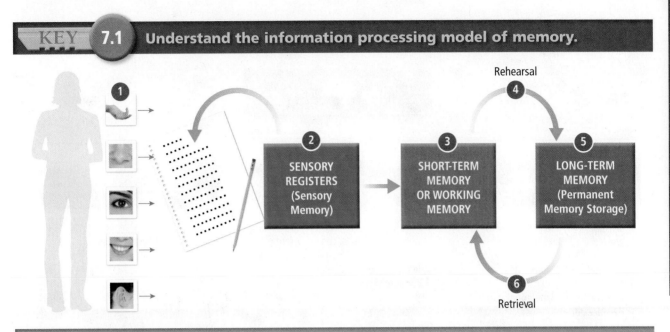

history text describes Abraham Lincoln's presidency—you remember few. Unconsciously, your brain sorts through stimuli and stores only what it considers important.

Learning and memories occur through chemical and structural changes in the brain—neurons (brain cells) growing new dendrites, strengthening synapses or forming new ones, and communicating information over those synapses using chemicals called *neurotransmitters*. Look at Key 7.1 as you read how the brain forms lasting memories:

1. Raw information, gathered through the five senses, reaches the brain (for example: the tune of a song you're learning in your jazz ensemble class).

2. This information enters **sensory registers**, where it stays for only seconds (as you play the notes for the first time, the sounds stop in short-term memory).

SENSORY REGISTER
Brain filters through which sensory information enters the brain and is sent to short-term memory.

3. You then pay attention to the information that seems most important to you. This moves it into **short-term memory**, or working memory, which contains what you are thinking at any moment and makes information available for further processing (the part of the song that you're responsible for—for example, the clarinet solo—will likely take up residence in your working memory). To do this, your brain improves the functioning of synapses (the gaps between cells across which electrical pulses carry messages), but doesn't yet make more permanent changes to neurons.[1] You can temporarily keep information in short-term memory through *rote rehearsal*—the process of repeating information to yourself or even out loud.

SHORT-TERM MEMORY
The brain's temporary information storehouse in which information remains for a limited time (from a few seconds to half a minute).

4. Information moves to **long-term memory** through focused, active rehearsal repeated over time (as you practice the song, your brain stores the tone, rhythm, and pace in your long-term memory where you will be able to draw on it again). To create these memories, brain cells grow new dendrites and build new synapses, which grow stronger the more times the same electrical signal passes through them (created by your repetition).[2] Long-term memory is the storage house for everything you know, from Civil War battle dates to the location of your grade school. Most people retain memories of personal experiences and procedures longer than concepts, facts, formulas, and dates.

LONG-TERM MEMORY
The brain's permanent information storehouse from which information can be retrieved.

Long-term memory has three separate storage houses, as shown in Key 7.2.

When you need a piece of information from long-term memory, the brain retrieves it and places it in short-term memory. On test day, this enables you to choose the right answer on a multiple-choice question or lay out a fact-based argument for an essay question. This movement of information in your brain from short-term to long-term memory and then back again strengthens synapses much in the same way as repetition does.

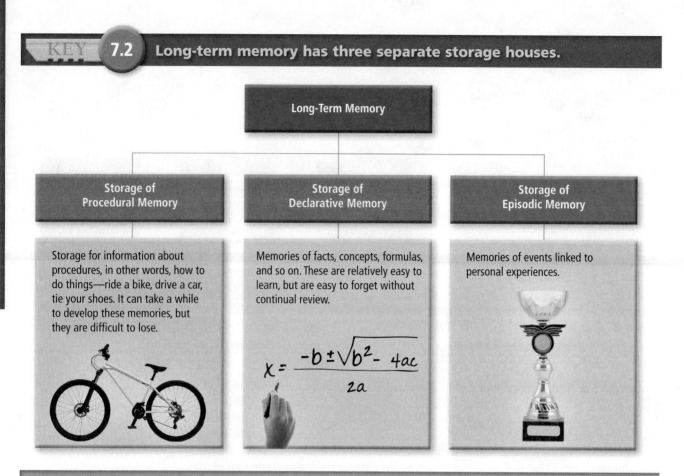

Long-Term Memory

Storage of Procedural Memory

Storage for information about procedures, in other words, how to do things—ride a bike, drive a car, tie your shoes. It can take a while to develop these memories, but they are difficult to lose.

Storage of Declarative Memory

Memories of facts, concepts, formulas, and so on. These are relatively easy to learn, but are easy to forget without continual review.

$$x = \frac{-b \pm \sqrt{b^2 - 4ac}}{2a}$$

Storage of Episodic Memory

Memories of events linked to personal experiences.

Why You Forget

Issues with health, nutrition, and stress can cause memory problems. Research shows that even short-term stress can interfere with cell communication in the learning and memory regions of the brain.[3] However, the most common reason that information fails to stay in long-term memory is ineffective studying—not risking the effort necessary to earn the reward of retention.

Retaining information requires continual review. If you review the material over time—after 24 hours, a week, a month, six months, and more—your reward is knowledge retention. If you do not review, the neural connections will weaken, and eventually you will forget. In a classic study conducted in 1885, researcher Herman Ebbinghaus memorized a list of meaningless three-letter words such as CEF and LAZ. He then examined how quickly he forgot them. Within one hour he had forgotten more than 50% of what he had learned; after two days, he knew less than 30% of the memorized words. His experiment shows how fragile memory can be without regular review.[4]

In his studies of how the brain remembers, neuroscientist Karim Nader has made groundbreaking discoveries about the effort necessary to retain accurate memories. Once a memory is solidified in the brain, Nader has shown that it is to some extent rebuilt each time it is remembered, and can be altered by environment or circumstances when it is rebuilt.[5] For example, most people have had an experience where they realize that they've recalled an event from the past inaccurately because they've been influenced by how someone else told the story or by their desire to forget some aspect of it.

For your purposes as a college student, this emphasizes the importance of both regular repetition and studying in as consistent an environment as you can manage. Because Cindy is in her car every day, for example, she could benefit from recording important information and listening to it on her commute.

get analytical

LINK MEMORY AND ANALYTICAL THINKING

Complete the following on paper or in digital format.

1. Identify the course that interests you the most this term.

2. Analyzing the material for the course, name a set of information you believe you will have to memorize.

3. Describe specific ways you can use analytical thinking to learn this material (look at the analytical thinking actions and Bloom's Taxonomy on page 116 to get ideas).

4. Will this material you have to remember be important to your working and/or personal life after college? If so, describe the connection. If your first response is "no," think carefully about it, and describe how the experience of learning it might be useful to you in your future.

Now that you know more about how memory works, get down to the business of how to retain the information you think is important, and access that information when you need it.

HOW CAN YOU REMEMBER
what you study?

Whatever you study—textbooks, course materials, notes, primary sources—your goal is to anchor important information in long-term memory so that you can *use it*, for both short-term goals like tests and long-term goals like being an information technology specialist. Take a productive risk and try out a variety of strategies to see which will reward you with the most retention. One great way to do this is to use *journalists' questions*—six questions journalists tend to ask as a writing aid:

1. **When, where,** and **who:** Determine the times, places, and company (or none) that suit you.
2. **What** and **why:** Choose what is important to study, and set the rest aside.
3. **How:** Find the specific tips and techniques that work best for you.

When, Where, and Who: Choosing Your Best Setting

Figuring out the when, where, and who of studying is all about self-management. You analyze what works best for you, create ideas about how to put that self-knowledge to work, and use practical thinking to implement those ideas as you study.

When

The first part of *when* is *how much*. Having the right amount of time for the job is crucial. One formula for success is this: For every hour you spend in the classroom each week, spend at least two to three hours preparing for the class. For example, if you are carrying a course load of 15 credit hours, you should spend 30 hours a week studying outside of class. Check your syllabus for the dates reading assignments are due, and give yourself enough time to complete them.

The second part of *when* is *what time*. If two students go over their biology notes from 8 to 9 A.M., but one is a morning person who went to bed at 11 P.M. and one is a night owl who hit the sack around 2 A.M., you can guess who has more of a chance of remembering the information. First, determine what time is available to you in between classes, work, and other commitments. Then, thinking about when you function best, choose your study times carefully. You may not always have the luxury of being free during your peak energy times, especially if, like Cindy, you are responsible for one or more children, but do the best you can.

The third part of *when* is *how close to original learning*. Because most forgetting happens right after learning, the review that helps you retain information most effectively happens close to when you first learn the material. If you can, review notes the same day you took them in class, make an organizer of important information from a text chapter shortly after you read it, or write a summary of a group study session within 24 hours of the meeting.

The final part of *when* is *when to stop*. Take a break, or go to sleep, when your body is no longer responding. Forcing yourself to study when you're not focused won't reward you with increased retention, and may in fact have detrimental effects.

Where

Where you study matters. As with time, consider your restrictions first—there may be only so many places that are available to you, close by, and open when you have study time free. Also, analyze the effectiveness of the locations of previous study sessions. If you spent too much time blocking out distractions at a particular location, try someplace different.

Many students like to study in a library. Your main library may have a variety of possibilities such as quiet rooms that don't allow talking, social areas where study groups can discuss materials, rooms where computer terminals are available for research, and so on. Also, keep in mind that many discipline-specific buildings have their own smaller libraries where you might consider spending some study time.

Dorms or other living spaces (rooms or common areas) and outdoor areas can be useful study spots. Where you live, find times to study when distractions are at a minimum. Explore your campus to find outdoor locations that are secluded enough to allow you to focus. An empty classroom is another great option. If you know a classroom will be unused for a period of time, it can provide a quiet space with room to spread out materials.

The study location that works for you depends on individual needs and preferences. These students have found that they can concentrate effectively at individual desks in the library.

Who

Some students prefer to study alone, and some in pairs or groups. Many mix it up, doing some kinds of studying (such as first reading) alone, and others (such as problem sets) with one or more people. Some find that they prefer to study certain subjects alone and others with a group.

Even students who prefer to study alone might consider the risk of working with others from time to time. Besides the reward of greater communication and teamwork skills, group study enhances your ability to remember information because it:[6]

- Gets you to say what you know out loud, which solidifies your understanding
- Exposes you to the ideas of others and gets you thinking in different ways
- Increases the chance that all of the important information will be covered

- Motivates you to study in preparation for a group meeting
- Subjects you to questions about your knowledge, and maybe even some challenges, that make you clarify and build on your thinking

Instructors sometimes initiate student study groups, commonly for math or science courses, known as *peer-assisted study sessions* or *supplemental instruction*. However, don't wait for your instructor—or for exam crunch time—to benefit from studying with others. As you begin to get to know students in your classes, start exchanging phone numbers and emails, form groups, and schedule meetings. Here are some strategies for study group success:

- *Limit group size.* Groups of five or fewer tend to experience the most success.
- *Set long-term and short-term goals.* At your first meeting, determine what the group wants to accomplish, and set mini-goals at the start of the first meeeting.
- *Determine a regular schedule and leadership rotation.* Determine what your group needs and what the members' schedules can handle. Try to meet weekly or, at the least, every other week. Rotate leadership among members willing to lead.
- *Create study materials for one another.* Give each person a task of finding a piece of information to compile and share with the group. Teach material to one another.
- *Share the workload and pool note-taking resources.* The most important factor is a willingness to work, not knowledge level. Compare notes with group members and fill in information you don't have.
- *Know how to be an effective leader.* The leader needs to define projects, assign work, set schedules and meeting goals, and keep people focused, motivated, and moving ahead.
- *Know how to be an effective participant.* Participants are "part owners" of the team process with a responsibility for, and a stake in, the outcome. Participants need to fulfill the tasks they promise to do, be organized, and stay open to discussion.
- *Be creative with technology if it's tough to meet in person.* Use Skype, a chat room or discussion board, a Wiki, or other tech tool to gather virtually.

One final part of *who* is dealing with *who might be distracting.* You may have friends who want you to go out. You may have young children or other family members who need you. You may have work responsibilities. Think carefully about your choices. Do you want to head out with friends you can see anytime, even if it compromises your focus on an important course? Can you schedule your study time when your kids are occupied for an hour or so?

Tell your friends and family members why studying is important to you. People who truly care about you are likely to support your goals. Tell your kids (if they are old enough to understand) what it will mean to you, and to them, for you to have an education and a degree. Children may be more able to cope if they see what lies at the end of the road. Key 7.3 shows some ways parents or others caring for children can maximize their efforts.

What and Why: Evaluating Study Materials

It is impossible, inefficient, and unnecessary to study every word and bit of information. Before you study, engage your analytical thinking skills: Decide *what* is important to study by examining *why* you need to know it. Here's how:

Choose materials to study. Put away materials or notes you know you do not need to review. Looking at the notes, textbooks, and other materials left, determine what chapters or sections are important to know for your immediate goal (for example, studying for a test) and why. Thinking about the "why" can increase your focus.

get $mart

STAY AWARE OF YOUR MONEY

Complete the following on paper or in digital format.

How good is your memory when it comes to bills and due dates? Find out by answering the following questions. First, create a hard-copy or digital table with headers as shown.

BILL	EST. AMOUNT	ACTUAL AMOUNT	EST. DUE DATE	ACTUAL DUE DATE

1. Off the top of your head, list your typical monthly bills, their estimated amount and estimated due date. Do this quickly and do NOT worry if you are wrong.
2. Now go through your actual bills to fill in the actual amount and actual due date. Then complete the following:

   a. Name any bills you forgot to include in your first list.

   b. For any bill where your estimate did not match the actual values, identify how far off you were in dollars and whether your estimate was high or low.

Prioritize materials. Determine what you need the most work on and put it first, then save easier materials for later. Almost every student has more steam at the beginning of a study session than at the end; plus, fatigue or an interruption may prevent you from covering everything.

Set specific goals. Look at what you need to cover and the time you have available, and decide what you will accomplish—for example, you will read pages of a certain textbook

KEY 7.3 Manage children while studying.

STUDYING WITH CHILDREN

- **Keep them up-to-date on your schedule.** Kids appreciate being involved, even though they may not understand entirely. Let them know when you have a big test or project due and what they can expect of you.
- **Find help.** Know your schedule and arrange for child care if necessary. Consider offering to help another parent in exchange for babysitting, hiring a sitter, or using a day care center.
- **Utilize techonology.** You may be able to have a study session over the phone, through instant messaging, by email, or over social networking sites. Additionally, some sites offer tools that allow multiple users to work on a document or project remotely.
- **Be prepared and keep them active.** Consider keeping some toys, activities, or books that only come out during study time. This will make the time special for children.
- **Plan for family time.** Offset your time away from your children with plans to do something together such as a movie or ice cream. Children may be more apt to let you study when they have something to look forward to.

STUDYING WITH INFANTS

- **Utilize your baby's sleeping schedule.** Study at night if your baby goes to sleep early or in the morning if your baby sleeps late.
- **Make time in the middle.** Study during nap times if you aren't too tired yourself.
- **Talk to your baby.** Recite your notes to the baby. The baby will appreciate the attention, and you will get work done.
- **Keep them close.** Put your baby in a safe and fun place while you study, such as a playpen, motorized swing, or jumping seat.

chapter, review three sets of class notes, and create a study sheet from both the book and your notes. Make a list so you can check things off as you go.

Within the sections you study, separate main points from unimportant details. Ask yourself, "What is the most important information?" Highlight only the key points in your texts, and write notes in the margins about main ideas.

How: Using Study Strategies

Now that you have figured out the *when*, *where*, *who*, *what*, and *why* of studying, focus on the *how*—the strategies that will anchor the information you need in your brain. You may already use several of them. Try as many as you can, and keep what works. Key 7.4 shows all of the strategies that follow.

Have purpose, intention, and emotional connection

Often, when you can remember the lyrics to dozens of popular songs but not the functions of the pancreas, emotion (usually positive) is involved. When you care about something, your brain responds differently, and you learn and remember more easily.

To achieve the same reward in school, try to create a purpose and will to remember by becoming emotionally involved with what you are studying. For example, an accounting student might think of a friend who is running a small business and needs

KEY 7.4 The *how* of study success.

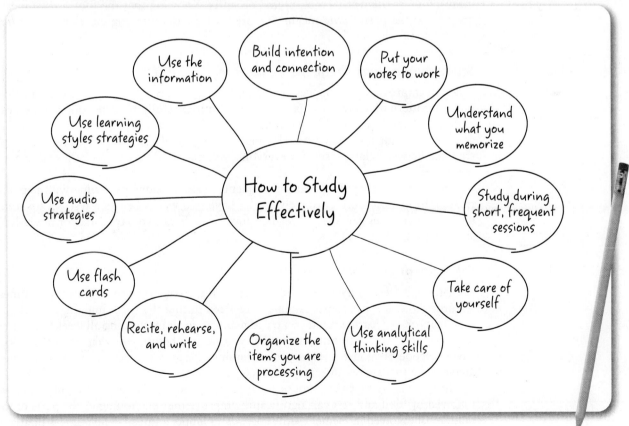

to keep his records in order—to pay bills on time, to record income, to meet tax payments. Putting himself in the position of his friend's accountant, the student connects learning accounting principles with making a difference in a friend's life.

Often, keeping a larger reward in mind can motivate you to take calculated risks. Being determined to give her son a good life helped Cindy persist in her studies in the face of time pressures and other challenges.

Put your notes to work

It is common to let notes sit in a notebook unread until just before midterms or finals. Even the most comprehensive, brilliant notes offer no reward if you don't refer back to them. Regularly reread your notes in batches (for example, every one or two weeks) to build your recall of information. As you reread, do the following:

- Fill in any gaps or get help with trouble spots.
- Mark up your notes by highlighting main ideas and key supporting points.
- Add recall or practice test questions in the margins.
- Add relevant points from homework, text, and labwork into your notes.

Understand what you memorize

It sounds obvious, but something that has meaning is easier to recall than something that makes little sense. This basic principle applies to everything you study. Figure out logical connections, and use these connections to help you learn. For example, in a plant biology course, memorize plants in family groups; in a history course, link events in a cause-and-effect chain.

When you have trouble remembering something new, think about how the new idea fits into what you already know. A simple example: If you can't remember what a word means, look at the word's root, prefix, or suffix. Knowing that the root *bellum* means "war" and the prefix *ante* means "before" will help you recognize that *antebellum* means "before the war."

Study during short, frequent sessions

You can improve your chances of remembering material if you learn it more than once. A pattern of short sessions, say three 20-minute study sessions followed by brief periods of rest, is more effective than continual studying with little or no rest. Try studying on your own or with a classmate during breaks in your schedule. Although studying between classes isn't for everyone, you may find that it can help you remember more.

In addition, scheduling regular, frequent review sessions over time will help you retain information more effectively. If you have two weeks before a test, set up study sessions three times per week instead of putting the final two days aside for hours-long study marathons.[7]

Take care of yourself

Even though sleep may take a back seat with all you have to do in crunch times, research indicates that shortchanging your sleep during the week impairs your ability to remember and learn, even if you try to make up for it by sleeping all weekend.[8] Sleep improves your ability to remember what you studied before you went to bed. So does having a good breakfast. Even if you're running late, grab something quick so that you aren't going to class on an empty stomach.

Exercise is another key component. The latest research shows that regular exercise followed by food and rest can significantly improve the functioning of the parts of the brain most involved in memory—the cortex and hippocampus.[9] When time is tight and you have trouble scheduling workouts, remember that those workouts can improve your academic performance.

Use analytical thinking skills

Analytical, or critical, thinking encourages you to associate new information with what you already know. Imagine you have to remember information about the signing of the Treaty of Versailles, which ended World War I. How can critical thinking help?

- Recall everything that you know about the topic.
- Think about how this event is similar to other events in history.
- Consider what is different and unique about this treaty in comparison to other treaties.
- Explore the causes that led up to this event, and look at the event's effects.
- Evaluate how successful you think the treaty was.

This critical exploration makes it easier to remember the material you are studying.

When you study with a classmate, you can help each other understand difficult concepts as well as fill in the holes in each other's notes.

Organize the items you are processing

There are a few ways to do this:

- *Divide material into manageable sections.* Master each section, put all the sections together, and then test your memory of all the material.
- *Use the chunking strategy.* Chunking increases the capacity of short-term and long-term memory. For example, while it is hard to remember these 10 digits—4808371557—it is easier to remember them in three chunks—480 837 1557. In general, try to limit groups to 10 items or fewer. The eight-day study plan in Key 7.5 relies on chunking.

> CHUNKING
> Placing disconnected information into smaller units that are easier to remember.

- *Use organizational tools.* Put your note-taking knowledge to work using an outline, a think link, or another tool to record material and make connections among the elements.
- *Be careful when studying more than one subject.* When studying for several tests at once, avoid studying two similar subjects back-to-back. Your memory may be more accurate when you study history after biology rather than chemistry after biology.
- *Notice what ends up in the middle, and practice it.* When you are studying, you tend to remember what you study first and last. The weak link is likely to be what you study in the middle. Knowing this, try to give this material special attention.

Recite, rehearse, and write

The more you can repeat, and the more ways you can repeat, the more likely you are to remember. Reciting, rehearsing, and writing help you diversify your repetition and maximize memory. When you *recite* material, you repeat key concepts aloud, in your own words, to aid memorization. *Rehearsing* is similar to reciting but is done silently. *Writing* is reciting on paper. Use these steps to get the greatest benefit:

- As you read, focus on *main ideas*, which are usually found in the topic sentences of paragraphs. Then recite, rehearse, or write the ideas down.
- Convert each main idea into a key word, phrase, or visual image—something that is easy to recall and that will set off a chain of memories that will bring you back to the original material. Write each key word or phrase on an index card.
- One by one, look at the key words on your cards and recite, rehearse, or write all the associated information you can recall. Check your recall against the original material.

KEY 7.5 Study plan success depends on a good memory.

DAY 8 (IN EIGHT DAYS, YOU'LL BE TAKING A TEST)

PLANNING DAY
- List everything that may be on the exam. (Check your syllabus and class notes; talk with your instructor.)
- Divide the material into four learning chunks.
- Decide on a study schedule for the next 7 days—when you will study, with whom you will study, the materials you need, and so on.

DAY 7 (COUNTDOWN: SEVEN DAYS TO GO)

- Use your preferred study techniques to study chunk A.
- Memorize key concepts, facts, formulas, and so on that may be on the test.
- Take an active approach to learning: take practice tests, summarize what you read in your own words, use critical thinking to connect ideas.

DAY 6 (COUNTDOWN: SIX DAYS TO GO)

- Use the same techniques to study chunk B.

DAY 5 (COUNTDOWN: FIVE DAYS TO GO)

- Use the same techniques to study chunk C.

DAY 4 (COUNTDOWN: FOUR DAYS TO GO)

- Use the same techniques to study chunk D.

DAY 3 (COUNTDOWN: THREE DAYS TO GO)

- Combine and review chunks A and B.

DAY 2 (COUNTDOWN: TWO DAYS TO GO)

- Combine and review chunks C and D.

DAY 1 (COUNTDOWN: ONE DAY TO GO)

PUT IT ALL TOGETHER: REVIEW CHUNKS A, B, C, AND D
- Take an active approach to review all four chunks.
- Make sure you have committed every concept, fact, formula, process, and so on to memory.
- Take a timed practice test. Write out complete answers so that concepts and words stick in your memory.
- Create a sheet with important information to memorize (again) for test day.

TEST DAY—DO YOUR BEST WORK

- Look at your last-minute study sheet right before you enter the test room so that difficult information sticks.
- As soon as you get your test, write down critical facts on scrap paper.

Source: Adapted from the University of Arizona. "The Eight-Day Study Plan." From http://ulc.arizona.edu/documents/8day_074.pdf

These steps are part of the process of consolidating and summarizing lecture and text notes as you study—a key study strategy you will read more about later in this chapter.

Reciting, rehearsing, and writing involve more than rereading material and then parroting words out loud, in your head, or on paper. Because rereading does not necessarily require involvement, you can reread without learning. However, you cannot help but think and learn when you convert text concepts into key points, rewrite main ideas as key words and phrases, and assess what you know and what you still need to learn.

Use flash cards

Flash cards give you short, repeated review sessions that provide immediate feedback. Use the front of a 3-by-5-inch index card to write a word, idea, or phrase you want to remember or find an online site on which you can create electronic flash cards. Use the back for a definition, explanation, example, and other key facts. Key 7.6 shows two flash cards used to study for a psychology exam.

Here are some suggestions for making the most of your flash cards:

- *Use the cards as a self-test.* As you go through them, divide them into two piles—the material you know and the material you are learning.
- *Carry the cards with you and review them frequently.* You'll learn the most if you start using cards early in the course, well ahead of exam time.
- *Shuffle the cards and learn the information in various orders.* This will help you avoid putting too much focus on some items and not enough on others.
- *Test yourself in both directions.* First, look at the terms and provide the definitions or explanations. Then turn the cards over and reverse the process.
- *Reduce the stack as you learn.* Eliminate cards when you know them well. As the pile shrinks, your motivation may grow. Do a final review of all the cards before the test.

Use audio strategies

Although all students can benefit from these strategies, they are especially useful if you learn best through hearing.

- *Create audio flash cards.* Record short-answer study questions by leaving 10 to 15 seconds between questions blank, so you can answer out loud. Record the correct answer after the pause to give yourself immediate feedback. For example, part of a recording for a writing class might say: "Three elements that require analysis before writing are . . . [pause] topic, audience, and purpose."
- *Use podcasts.* An increasing amount of information is presented in podcasts—knowledge segments that are downloadable to your computer of MP3 player. Ask your instructors if they intend to make any of their lectures available in podcast format.

KEY 7.6 **Flash cards help you memorize important facts.**

Theory

- Definition: Explanation for a phenomenon based on careful and precise observations
- Part of the scientific method
- Leads to hypotheses

Hypothesis

- Prediction about future behavior that is derived from observations and theories
- Methods for testing hypotheses: case studies, naturalistic observations, and experiments

get practical

ANSWER YOUR JOURNALISTS' QUESTIONS

Complete the following on paper or in digital format.

Think about a study session you've had in the past that you believe did not prepare you well for a test, and recall what strategies you used—if any. Now, plan a study session that will take place within the next seven days—one that will help you learn something important to know for one of your current courses. Answer the questions below to create your session:

1. *When* will you study, and for how long?

2. *Where* will you study?

3. *Who* will you study with, if anyone?

4. *What* will you study?

5. *Why* is this material important to know?

6. *How* will you study it—what strategy (or strategies) do you plan to use?

7. How do you think the journalists' questions, and this structure, would have helped you get more out of your previous study session?

8. Final step—put this plan to work. Name the date you will use it.

Use learning preference strategies

Thinking about any learning preference self-assessments you have completed in this course, identify your strongest areas and locate study techniques applicable for each. For example, if you scored highly in bodily-kinesthetic learning, try reciting material aloud while standing or listening to it on an MP3 player while walking.

Be open to trying something new—even if it sounds a little odd to begin with. The Multiple Intelligences table in this chapter (see page 177) suggests MI-related memory strategies. Try ones that relate to your strengths—or, if you want to develop in areas that are more challenging for you, try strategies that relate to those intelligences.

Use the information

In the days after you learn something new, try to use the information in every way you can. Apply it to new situations and link it to problems. Explain the material to a classmate. Test your knowledge to make sure the material is in long-term memory. "Don't confuse recognizing information with being able to recall it," says learning expert Adam Robinson. "Be sure you can recall the information without looking at your notes for clues. And don't move on until you have created some sort of sense-memory hook for calling it back up when you need it."[10]

multiple intelligence strategies

FOR MEMORY

Name a set of information that you have to know for a particular course: _____.
In the right-hand column, record specific ideas for how MI strategies can help you retain that information.

INTELLIGENCE	USE MI STRATEGIES TO REMEMBER MORE EFFECTIVELY	IDENTIFY MI STRATEGIES THAT CAN HELP YOU RETAIN INFORMATION
Verbal-Linguistic	• Develop a story line for a mnemonic first; then work on the visual images. • Write out answers to practice essay questions.	
Logical-Mathematical	• Create logical groupings that help you memorize knowledge chunks. • When you study material in the middle, link it to what comes before and after.	
Bodily-Kinesthetic	• Reenact concepts physically if you can to solidify them in memory. • Record information onto a digital recorder and listen as you walk between classes.	
Visual-Spatial	• Focus on visual mnemonics such as mental walks. • Use markers to add color to the images you use in your mnemonics.	
Interpersonal	• Do flash card drills with a study partner. • Recite important material to a study partner.	
Intrapersonal	• Listen to an audio podcast that reviews test material. • Create vocabulary cartoons and test yourself on the material.	
Musical	• Play music while you brainstorm ideas. • Create a mnemonic in the form of a musical rhyme.	
Naturalistic	• Organize what you have to learn so you see how everything fits together. • Sit outside and go through your flash cards.	

WHAT WILL HELP YOU REMEMBER
math and science material?

The strategies you've just explored apply to all sorts of academic areas. However, recalling what you learn in math and science courses can demand particular attention and specific techniques.

Here's the key overarching strategy for math and science: Avoid falling behind at all costs. In a world religions course, for example, missing a lecture on Buddhism is not likely to cause serious problems with understanding the coverage of Taoism a few weeks later. Not so with math and math-based sciences such as chemistry and physics. These topics are presented sequentially with earlier concepts forming the foundation for later ones. You cannot effectively understand a later concept without a clear grasp of the concepts that precede it. Take calculated risks for the reward of staying on top of your work:[11]

- Before class, read what will be covered. You are more likely to grasp what your instructor covers if you have a baseline understanding of the concepts.
- Read slowly and note symbols. Go step by step through each process and description. Work to understand symbols—they are as important as numbers.
- Stay on top of homework assignments. Doing your homework is as important as reading when it comes to staying caught up.
- When you have trouble, seek help fast. Every day you wait can put you that much more behind. Consult your instructor, a tutor, or an experienced classmate.

Review processes and procedures. Much of math and science work involves knowing how to work through each step of a proof, a problem-solving process, or a lab experiment. Look at your notes with the textbook alongside and compare the lecture information to the book. Fill in missing steps in the instructor's examples before you forget them. You may want to write the instructor's examples in the book next to the corresponding topics. Review your class notes as soon as possible after each class.

Do problems, problems, and more problems. Rework problems that appear in your text, on your own paper, as well as doing problems found in exercises. Working through problems provides examples that will help you understand concepts and formulas. Plus, becoming familiar with a group of problems and related formulas will help you apply what you know to similar problems on other assignments and tests.

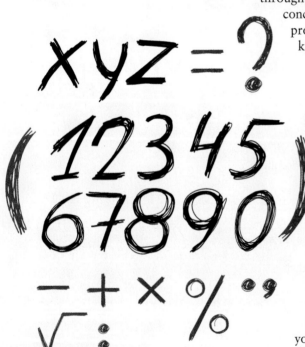

Fight frustration with action. If you are stuck on a problem, go on to another one. If you repeatedly get a wrong answer, look at the steps you've taken and see if anything doesn't make sense. If you hit a wall, take a break to clear your head. If you have done the assigned homework but still don't feel secure, do additional problems or ask for help.

Work with others. Working with one or more classmates can be particularly helpful when trying to figure out math and science problems. Do as much of your homework as you can on your own, and then meet to discuss it and work through additional problems. Be open to other perspectives, and ask others how they arrived at answers, especially if they used different approaches. When the work is really tough, try to meet daily.

Focus on learning preferences. Use strategies that activate your strengths. A visual learner might draw pictures to illustrate problems, and an interpersonal learner might organize a study group.

"HOW MUCH IS THAT *X* IN THE EQUATION?"

(to the tune of "How Much Is That Doggie in the Window?")

How much is that *x* in the equation?
What value will make it be true?
To find the *x* and get the solution
The numbers attached we **undo**.

The **connector** is plus or minus seven,
To find *x* we have to **undo**.
Just write below both sides—make it even.
We **undo** to find the *x* value.

If multiply or divide is showing,
The **connector** tells what has been done.
To **undo** is where we still are going—
We're trying to get *x* alone.

Source: Reprinted with permission. Aaker, Barbara. *Mathematics: The Musical.* Denver: Crazy Broad Publishing, 1999.

Musical learners might create songs describing math concepts. Barbara Aaker wrote 40 songs for her students at the Community College of Denver to help musical learners retain difficult concepts. Key 7.7 presents one of her algebra songs.

Strive for accuracy. Complete a step of an algebra problem or biology lab project inaccurately, and your answer will be incorrect. In class, the consequences of inaccuracy are reflected in low grades. In life, the consequences could show in a patient's health or in the strength of a bridge. Check over the details of your work and always try to get it exactly right.

Because many math and science courses require you to memorize sets and lists of information, one key tool is the *mnemonic device*. As you will see next, mnemonic devices create sense-memory hooks that are difficult to forget.

talk risk and reward . . .

Risk asking tough questions to be rewarded with new insights. Use the following questions to inspire discussion with classmates, either in person or online.

- Every student experiences the frustration of needing to work hard to remember something that you think is completely unimportant and irrelevant to your life. How do you handle this, and what is the result? How *should* you handle it?

- What memorization techniques do you resist trying? Is it because they seem too unrelated to the information, or too goofy? What would you be willing to risk to see if they work?

CONSIDER THE CASE: Whether you combine work and parenting with school or not, you have many demands on your time. Are you able to juggle it all? If not, what trips you up? If you were Cindy's advisor, how would you suggest she stay on top of her studies?

HOW CAN MNEMONICS
boost recall?

Memory techniques known as **mnemonic devices** (pronounced neh-MAHN-ick) can help you learn and recall information. Mnemonics make information unforgettable through unusual mental associations and visual pictures. Instead of learning new facts by *rote* (repetitive practice), associations give you a "hook" on which to hang these facts and retrieve them later.

Because mnemonics take effort to create and motivation to remember, use them only when necessary—for instance, to distinguish confusing concepts that consistently trip you up. Also, know that no matter how clever they are and how easy they are to remember, mnemonics have nothing to do with understanding. Their sole objective is to help you memorize.

Mnemonics all involve some combination of *imagination* (coming up with vivid images that are meaningful to you), *association* (connecting information you need to know with information you already know), and *location* ("locating" pieces of information in familiar places). They offer the reward of lasting memory in exchange for the risk of getting a little wacky. Here are some common types to try.

MNEMONIC DEVICES
Memory techniques that use vivid associations and acronyms to link new information to what you already know.

Visual Images and Associations

Turning information into mental pictures helps improve memory, especially for visual learners. To remember that the Spanish artist Picasso painted *The Three Women*, you might imagine the women in a circle dancing to a Spanish song with a pig and a donkey (pig-asso). The best images involve bright colors, three dimensions, action scenes, inanimate objects with human traits, and humor.

Here is another example: Say you are trying to learn some Spanish vocabulary, including the words *carta, libro,* and *dinero.* Instead of relying on rote learning, you might come up with mental images such as those in Key 7.8.

The Method of Loci

This technique involves imagining storing new ideas in familiar locations. Say, for example, that on your next biology test you have to remember the body's major endocrine glands. Think of the route you travel through campus to the library. You pass the college theater, the physics building, the bookstore, the cafeteria, the athletic center, and the social science building before reaching the library. At each spot along the way, you "place" a concept you want to learn. You then link the concept with a similar-sounding word that brings an image to mind (see Key 7.9):

- At the campus theater, you imagine bumping into the actor Brad Pitt (pituitary gland).
- At the science center, you visualize a body builder with bulging thighs (thyroid gland).
- At the campus bookstore, you envision a second body builder with his thighs covered in mustard (thymus gland).
- In the cafeteria, you bump into Dean Al (adrenal gland).

KEY 7.8 Visual images aid recall.

SPANISH WORD	DEFINITION	MENTAL IMAGE
carta	letter	A person pushing a shopping cart filled with letters into a post office.
dinero	money	A man eating lasagna at a diner. The lasagna is made of layers of money.
libro	book	A pile of books on a table at a library.

- At the athletic center, you think of the school team, the Panthers—nicknamed the Pans—and remember the sound of the cheer "Pans-R-Us" (pancreas).
- At the social science building, you imagine receiving a standing ovation (ovaries).
- And at the library, you visualize sitting at a table taking a test that is easy (testes).

KEY 7.9 A mental walk helps you remember items in a list.

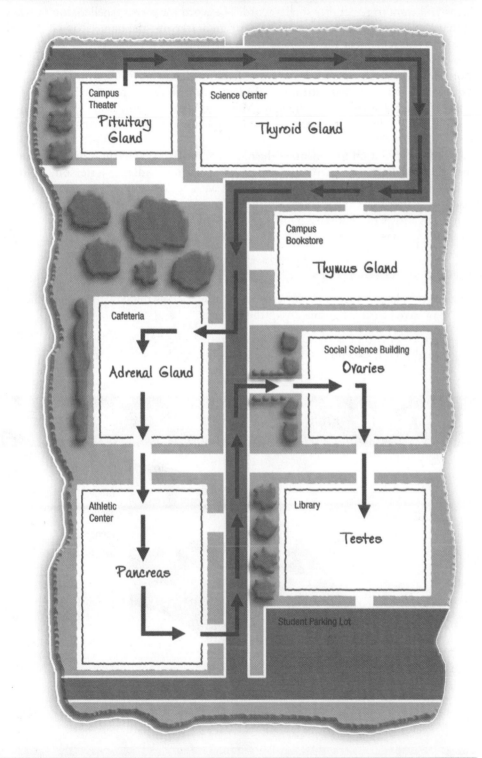

You can use all kinds of locations with the method of loci. Try locating information at buildings in a city you know well, places in your bedroom, or locations on a familiar game board.

Acronyms

Another helpful association method involves acronyms. In history class, you can remember the Allies during World War II—Britain, America, and Russia—with the acronym BAR. This is an example of a *word acronym,* because the first letters of the items you want to remember spell a word. The word (or words) spelled don't necessarily have to be real words. See Key 7.10 for an acronym—the name Roy G. Biv—that will help you remember the colors of the spectrum.

Other acronyms take the form of an entire sentence, in which the first letter of each word in each sentence stands for the first letter of the memorized term. This is called a *list order acronym.* When astronomy students want to remember the list of planets in order of their distance from the sun (Mercury, Venus, Earth, Mars, Jupiter, Saturn, Uranus, and Neptune), they might learn this sentence: My very elegant mother just served us nectarines.

Suppose you want to remember the names of the first six U.S. presidents. You notice that the first letters of their last names—Washington, Adams, Jefferson, Madison, Monroe, and Adams—together read W A J M M A. To remember them, first you might insert an e after the J and create a short nonsense word: *wajemma.* Then, to make sure you don't forget the nonsense word, visualize the six presidents sitting in a row and wearing pajamas.

Songs and Rhymes

Some of the classic mnemonic devices are rhyming poems that stick in your mind. One you may have heard is the rule about the order of "i" and "e" in spelling:

> I before E, except after C, or when sounded like "A" as in "neighbor" and "weigh." Four exceptions if you please: either, neither, seizure, seize.

ACRONYM
A word formed from the first letters of a series of words created to help you remember the series.

KEY 7.10 Use this acronym to remember the colors of the spectrum.

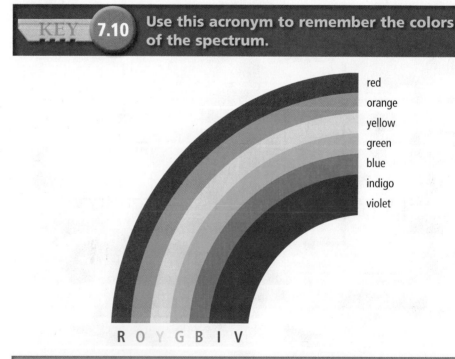

red
orange
yellow
green
blue
indigo
violet

R O Y G B I V

get creative

CRAFT YOUR OWN MNEMONIC

Complete the following on paper or in digital format.

Create a mnemonic to help you remember some facts.

1. Identify a group of facts that you have to memorize—for example, the names of all the world's major religions, or a series of elements in the periodic table.

2. Now create your own mnemonic to remember the grouping, using any of the devices in this chapter. Write the mnemonic out in detail.

3. Describe your mnemonic. Is it focused on images or sounds – or both? Is it humorous, ridiculous, colorful?

4. Considering your learning style preferences, describe why you think this particular device will help you retain the information.

Music can be an exceptional memory tool. For example, a whole generation of children grew up in the 1970s knowing the Preamble to the Constitution because of the Schoolhouse Rock Preamble Song (look it up on YouTube and see if it doesn't stick in your head). Make up your own poems or songs, linking familiar tunes or rhymes with information you want to remember.

For example, thinking back to the "wajemma" mnemonic, imagine that you want to remember the presidents' first names as well. You might set those first names—George, John, Thomas, James, James, and John—to the tune of "Happy Birthday." Or, to extend the history theme, you might use the first musical phrase of the National Anthem.

Improving your memory requires energy, time, and work. It also helps to master the SQ3R the textbook study technique. By going through the steps in SQ3R and using the specific memory techniques described in this chapter, you will be able to learn more in less time, remember what you learn long after exams are over, and build memory skills that will serve you well in the workplace.

WHAT STUDY STRATEGIES HELP *you put it all together?*

Especially in the later stages of review, strategies that help you combine and condense materials provide significant reward for the extra time they require. They help you connect information in new ways and boost analytical and creative thinking, which is especially important for essay exams.

Create a Summary of Reading Material

When you summarize main ideas in your own words, you engage analytical thinking, considering what is important to include as well as how to organize and link it together. To construct a summary, focus on the main ideas and examples that support them. Don't include your own ideas or evaluations at this point. Your summary should simply condense the material, making it easier to focus on concepts and interrelationships when you review.

Here are suggestions for creating effective summaries:

- Choose material to summarize—a textbook chapter, for example, or an article.
- Before you summarize, identify the main ideas and key supporting details by highlighting or annotating the material.
- Wherever possible, use your own words. When studying a technical subject with precise definitions, you may have little choice but to use text wording.
- Try to make your writing simple, clear, and brief. Eliminate less important details.
- Consider creating an outline of your notes or the portion of the text so you can see the interrelationship among ideas.
- Include information from tables, charts, photographs, and captions in your summary; these visual presentations may contain important information not written in the text.
- Combine word-based and visual note-taking forms that effectively condense the information, such as a concept map, timeline, chart, or outline.
- Use visual strategies such as a color-coding system to indicate different ideas or different colored pens to indicate levels of importance for information.

Combine Class and Reading Notes into a Master Set

Studying from either text or class notes alone is not enough, since your instructor may present material in class that is not in your text or may gloss over topics that your text covers in depth. The process of combining class and text notes enables you to see patterns and relationships among ideas, find examples for difficult concepts, and much more. It strengthens memory and offers a cohesive and comprehensive study tool, which is especially useful at midterm or finals time. Follow these steps to use a master note set:

MASTER NOTE SET
The complete, integrated note set that contains both class and text notes.

Step 1: Condense down to what's important. Combine and reduce your notes so they contain only main ideas and key supporting details, such as terms, dates, formulas, and examples. Tightening and summarizing forces you to critically evaluate which ideas are most important. Key 7.11 shows a comprehensive outline and a reduced key term outline of the same material.

Step 2: Recite what you know. As you approach exam time, use the terms in your bare-bones notes as cues for reciting what you know about a topic. Many students assume that they know concepts simply because they understand what they read. What they are actually demonstrating is a passive understanding that doesn't necessarily mean that they can re-create the material on an exam or apply it to problems. Make the process more active by reciting out loud during study sessions, writing your responses on paper, making flash cards, or working with a partner.

Step 3: Use critical thinking. Reflect on ideas as you review your combined notes:

- Generate examples from other sources that illustrate central ideas. Write down new ideas or questions that come up as you review.
- Think of ideas from your readings or from class that support or clarify your notes.

Different Views of Freedom and Equality in the American Democracy

I.   U.S. democracy based on 5 core values: freedom and equality, order and stability, majority rule, protection of minority rights, and participation.

A. U.S. would be a "perfect democracy" if it always upheld these values.

B. U.S. is less than perfect, so it is called an "approaching democracy."

II.   Freedom and Equality

A. Historian Isaiah Berlin defines freedom as either positive or negative.

1. Positive freedoms allow us to exercise rights under the Constitution, including right to vote.

2. Negative freedoms safeguard us from government actions that restrict certain rights, such as the right to assemble. The 1st Amendment restricts government action by declaring that "Congress shall make no law . . ."

B. The value of equality suggests that all people be treated equally, regardless of circumstance. Different views on what equality means and the implications for society.

1. Equality of opportunity implies that everyone has the same chance to develop inborn talents.

a. But life's circumstances—affected by factors like race and income—differ. This means that people start at different points and have different results. E.g., a poor, inner-city student will be less prepared for college than an affluent, suburban student.

b. It is impossible to equalize opportunity for all Americans.

2. Equality of result seeks to eliminate all forms of inequality, including economic differences, through wealth redistribution.

C. Freedom and equality are in conflict, say text authors Berman and Murphy: "If your view of freedom is freedom from government intervention, then equality of any kind will be difficult to achieve. If government stays out of all citizen affairs, some people will become extremely wealthy, others will fall through the cracks, and economic inequality will multiply. On the other hand, if you wish to promote equality of result, then you will have to restrict some people's freedoms—the freedom to earn and retain an unlimited amount of money, for example."*

KEY-TERM OUTLINE OF THE SAME MATERIAL

Different Views of Freedom and Equality in the American Democracy

I.   America's 5 core values: freedom and equality, order and stability, majority rule, protection of minority rights, and participation.

A. "Perfect democracy"

B. "Approaching democracy"

II.   Value #1—Freedom and equality

A. Positive freedoms and negative freedoms

B. Different views of equality: equality of opportunity versus equality of result

C. Conflict between freedom and equality centers on differing views of government's role

---

Source: Larry Berman and Bruce Allen Murphy, *Approaching Democracy: Portfolio Edition,* Upper Saddle River, NJ: Prentice Hall, 2005, pp. 6–8.

student PROFILE

Alexis Zendejas

BRIGHAM YOUNG UNIVERSITY, PROVO, UTAH

About me:

I am a Native American woman from Omaha, Nebraska. I am the seventh of eight children. Growing up in a big family was a lot of fun as well as challenging; my personal goal was to keep up with my older brothers and sisters educationally and mentally. I plan to major in business marketing with a minor in American history. After completing my undergraduate degree, I hope to earn a joint juris doctorate (law degree) and master's of business administration (MBA).

What I focus on:

When I started high school, I didn't have to work that hard to do well. That all changed junior year when I took three advanced placement classes and three honors classes. I had to apply myself beyond just completing my assigned homework.

Here is how I approach studying: I give myself a short break after my day of classes, setting a time to return to my studies. When I go back, I start by reading my notes from my classes for about 15 minutes or sometimes a bit longer, depending on the class and my ability to understand the material. Then I spend the rest of my time studying my materials. I make and use a lot of flash cards (my studying salvation!) for subjects where repetitive learning is required to grasp the words and their meanings. I make sure to apply what I've learned after memorizing from flash cards. For example, I would make flash cards for Spanish, then speak the vocabulary words in my day-to-day speech. I work hard to focus and not let myself get distracted during my study time. I do take short 10-minute breaks to get a drink of water, listen to a song, or move around.

What will help me in the workplace:

One of my sisters works in a law firm and I see that she has to do a lot of research. It's easy to imagine that all a lawyer does is work in a courtroom pleading the case to a judge or showcase evidence to persuade a grand jury, but I see her spending more time gathering information than anything else. I know that the study skills I practice will come in handy during my intended career whenever I need to learn and focus.

- Consider what in your class notes differed from your reading notes and why.
- Apply concepts to problems at the ends of text chapters, to problems posed in class, or to real-world situations.

Step 4: Create study sheets. This step puts your master notes in their shortest, most manageable (and portable) form. A study sheet is a one-page synthesis of all key points on one theme, topic, or process. Use critical thinking skills to organize information into themes or topics that you will need to know on an exam.

Step 5: Review and review again. To ensure learning and prepare for exams, review your condensed notes, study sheets, and critical thinking questions until you know every topic cold. Try to vary your review methods, focusing on active involvement. Recite the material to yourself, have a Q and A session with a study partner, create and take a practice test. Another helpful technique is to summarize your notes in writing from memory after you review them. This will give you a fairly good indication of your ability to recall the information on a test.

revisit RISK AND REWARD

What happened to Cindy? Working nights allowed Cindy to attend college during the day. Without compromising her work duties, she was able to find time on the night shift to review that day's lessons. Writing out classroom notes in longhand helped her retain information. After graduating with her bachelor's from Wyoming, Cindy's company paid for her to get her master's degree, and ultimately her hard work earned her the reward of a promotion to senior manager. "Being a Hispanic woman was a hurdle," she says. "I needed fortitude. I had to gain the customers' trust and confidence. For me it's always been about building relationships."

Cindy's willingness to take targeted risks is evident in her recreational pursuits, too. She is an accomplished marathon runner, having tackled the famed Boston Marathon, as well as road treks in Honolulu and at the foot of Mount Everest. Now a director of program management at Goodman Networks, Cindy recently conquered a new challenge—breast cancer. "It's taking things one day at a time, reaching within and really discovering what type of inner strength you have," she says of beating cancer. "Believe me, it was like a hundred Everest marathons."

What does this mean for you? A strong work ethic, a supportive family, and an open-minded employer helped Cindy study and retain information for her coursework while holding down a job to support her young son. What are your two biggest time commitments outside of schoolwork? Name them; then, for each, identify the times you are committed to and how much time you spend per week total. Now describe how each affects your study time and your ability to retain information. Finally, determine what risks you need to take to maximize your retention—adjusting commitments, studying during work, reshuffling your schedule, and so on.

What risk may bring reward beyond your world? Everything that students accomplish in college owes a debt to someone who helped somewhere along the way. Even if you need support, keep in mind that your own help and expertise can offer rewards to others. Perhaps you could be the one to help someone else adjust a schedule, improve memory skills, or study more effectively. Check your school's website to see what tutoring services are offered and whether there is a peer advising or mentoring group you can consider.

Complete the following on paper or in digital format.

KNOW IT *Think Critically*

Evaluate Your Memory

Build basic skills. For each of these classifications of information in long-term memory, write down an example from your personal experience:

- *Episodic memory (events).* Example: I remember the first time I conducted an experiment in chemistry class.
- *Declarative memory (facts).* Example: I know that the electoral college must vote before a new U.S. president is officially elected.
- *Procedural memory (motion).* Example: I know how to type without looking at the keyboard.

Take it to the next level. Answer the following:

1. Which type of information (events, facts, motion) is easiest for you to remember? Why?
2. Which type of information is hardest for you to remember? Why?

Move toward mastery. Address the type of information that you said you find most difficult to remember.

1. Name an example, from your life, of some information in this category that you need to be able to recall and use.
2. Name two actions from the chapter that you believe will help you strengthen it.
3. Now use both during your next study session. Afterward, identify the one that worked best.

WRITE IT *Communicate*

Emotional intelligence journal: How feelings connect to study success. Think about how you were feeling at times when you were most able to recall and use information in a high-stress situation—a test, a workplace challenge, a group presentation. What thought, action, or situation put you in this productive mindset that helped you succeed? Did you go for a run, talk to your best friend, take 30 minutes for yourself? Create a list of thoughts or actions you can call on when you will be faced with a challenge to your memory and want the best possible outcome.

Real-life writing: Combining class and text notes. Choose a course for which you have a test coming up in the next four weeks. Create a master set of notes for that course that combines one week's classes and reading assignments (make sure it is material you need to know for your test). Your goal is to summarize and connect all the important information covered during the period.

WORK IT *Build Your Brand*

Memory and Networking

21st Century Learning Building Blocks

- Communication and collaboration
- Social and cross-cultural skills

Your ability to remember people you meet or interact with in the workplace—their names, what they do, other relevant information about them—is an enormous factor in your career success. Consider this scenario: You are introduced to your supervisor's new boss, someone who could help you advance in the company, and you exchange small talk for a few minutes. A week later you run into him outside the building. What if you greet him by name and ask if his son is over the case of the flu he had? You have made a good impression that is likely to help you in the future. What if you call him by the wrong name, realize your mistake, and slink off to work? You've set up a bit of a hurdle for yourself as you try to get ahead.

With what you know about memory strategies and what works for you, set up a system to record and retain information about people you meet whom you want to remember. For your system, decide on a tool (address book, set of notecards, electronic organizer, computer file), what to record (name, phone, email, title, how you met, important details), and how you will update. Choose a tool that you are most likely to use and that will be easy for you to refer to and update.

1. Name your tool of choice.
2. List the information you will record for each entry.
3. Describe when you will record information and how often you will check/update it.

Finally, get started by putting in information for all of the people you consider to be important networking contacts at this point. These could be family, friends, instructors and advisors, or work colleagues and supervisors. Make this the start of a database that will serve you throughout your career.

The best test preparation is learning, *because the goal of a test is to see what you have learned. As you attend class, work on assignments, and participate in discussions, you become ever more ready to succeed in testing situations.*

Test Taking

SHOWING WHAT YOU KNOW

What Would You Risk? *Jay Dobyns*

THINK ABOUT THIS SITUATION AS YOU READ, AND CONSIDER WHAT ACTION YOU WOULD TAKE. THIS CHAPTER HELPS YOU USE PREPARATION, PERSISTENCE, AND STRATEGY TO CONQUER TEST ANXIETY, SHOW WHAT YOU KNOW, AND LEARN FROM TEST MISTAKES.

Raised in a solid middle-class home, Jay Dobyns had every-thing a boy could want—a bike, a baseball glove, and a safe place to play. His parents were great role models, blue-collar workers who inspired Jay to overachieve. By high school, Jay was taking risks calculated to bring a specific reward—being a wide receiver in the National Football League.

Never the biggest or strongest or fastest, Jay was the hardest worker on the playing field, with a "gracious confidence" that fueled his sports aspirations. At the University of Arizona, Jay earned Pac-10 all-conference honors. Academically, Jay was uninspired but got the job done, earning a degree in public administration. "All I cared about was catching footballs and school was simply a means for me to get to do that," Jay says. The big test for him was whether he could catch a football with 70,000 people watching. As with many student athletes, his dream was derailed by the harsh reality of professional sports.

Next test: Map out a new career. Eager for the reward of serving others in an exciting atmosphere, Jay risked embarking on a career in federal law enforcement, as an undercover officer for the Bureau of Alcohol, Tobacco and Fire-arms. "As an undercover agent, every day is a test," Jay says. "They aren't written tests or multiple choice. Your instructor is the criminal. You're trying to pass the test in the eye of the criminal."

Just four days into his ATF career, Jay was taken hos-tage by a drug addict and was shot point blank in the back, the bullet piercing Jay's lung and exiting his chest. Once an athlete destined for NFL greatness, Jay was lying in the dirt, bleeding to death. Jay's risk had presented him with the ultimate test—and no guarantee if a reward would follow.

To be continued . . .

JAY'S LIFE TESTS HAVE REQUIRED FOCUS, PASSION, AND GRACE UNDER PRESSURE. YOUR TESTS MIGHT BE OF A VASTLY DIFFERENT NATURE, BUT YOU WILL NEED SKILL AND FORTITUDE TO PASS THEM. YOU'LL LEARN MORE ABOUT JAY, AND THE REWARD RESULTING FROM HIS ACTIONS, WITHIN THE CHAPTER.

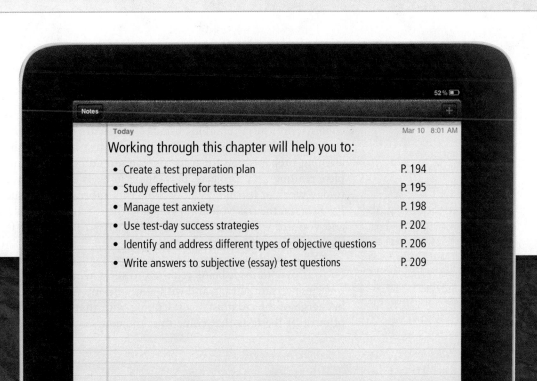

Today   Mar 10 8:01 AM

Working through this chapter will help you to:

statusCHECK

How Prepared Are You for Taking Tests?

For each statement, fill in the number that best describes how often it applies to you.

1 = never   2 = seldom   3 = sometimes   4 = often   5 = always

1. I use strategies to help me predict what will be on tests.   ① ② ③ ④ ⑤

2. I actively prepare and review before taking exams.   ① ② ③ ④ ⑤

3. I do anything to avoid cramming.   ① ② ③ ④ ⑤

4. When I recognize signs of test anxiety, I use relaxation methods to calm down.   ① ② ③ ④ ⑤

5. I read test directions before beginning.   ① ② ③ ④ ⑤

6. I use certain strategies to answer questions for which I'm unsure of the answers.   ① ② ③ ④ ⑤

7. I don't think cheating is worth the price.   ① ② ③ ④ ⑤

8. I know the difference between objective and subjective questions and how to answer each.   ① ② ③ ④ ⑤

9. I look for action verbs when answering essay questions.   ① ② ③ ④ ⑤

10. I learn from my testing mistakes and actively grow from them.   ① ② ③ ④ ⑤

Each of the topics in these statements is covered in this chapter. Note those statements for which you filled in a 3 or lower. Skim the chapter to see where those topics appear, and pay special attention to them as you read, learn, and apply new strategies.

REMEMBER: NO MATTER HOW PREPARED YOU ARE FOR TAKING TESTS, YOU CAN IMPROVE WITH EFFORT AND PRACTICE.

HOW CAN PREPARATION IMPROVE
test performance?

Many students approach tests and exams with dread, seeing them as roadblocks, contests, or insurmountable obstacles. If you are one of these students, shift your mindset by considering this idea: The goal of a test is to see what you have learned—and learning prepares you for tests. As you attend class, stay on top of assignments, complete readings and projects, participate in class discussions, and generally do the day-to-day work of learning, you become ever more ready to succeed in testing situations. Re-envision the risk you are taking and the reward you seek. If learning is your reward and you are willing to risk time and energy to earn it, effective test performance is likely to come along with the package.

What makes a testing situation more challenging than demonstrating knowledge on your own terms is being required to show what you know during a preset period of time, in a certain setting, and with—or without—particular tools. You are generally not in charge of the circumstances. Coping with that is a crucial life skill, as it will be true of most of the tests that come over the course of your life, and you often won't even

MyStudentSuccessLab

(www.mystudentsuccesslab.com) is an online solution designed to help you "Start Strong, Finish Stronger" by building skills for ongoing personal and professional development.

know a test is coming, as was the case with Jay's life-threatening injury. The following strategies engage your analytical, creative, and practical thinking skills and help you prepare for the challenge of test taking.

Gather Information

Before you begin studying, find out as much as you can about the test.

What type of test?

Investigate the following.

- *Types of questions.* Will the questions be objective (multiple choice with only one correct answer, multiple choice with more than one correct answer, true–false, sentence completion), subjective (essay), or a combination?
- *Test logistics.* What is the date, time, and location of the test? Is it an in-class or a take-home exam? Will you complete it in person or online?
- *Supplemental information and tools.* Is the test open-book (meaning you can use your class text), open note (meaning you can use any notes you've taken), both, or neither? Can you use a graphing calculator or any other tool?
- *Value of the test.* All tests are not created equal in terms of how they affect your final course grade. For example, a quiz is not as important as a midterm or final, although accumulated quiz grades do add up. Plan and prioritize your study time and energy according to the value of the quiz or test.

Don't fall into the trip of thinking that online tests and open-book tests should be easier than traditional tests in the classroom. In reality, the fact that you have access to resources usually leads instructors to create challenging tests that require more critical thinking. If you prepare for an online or open book exam as you would any other test, chances are you will have a more successful result.

What are you expected to know?

Read your syllabus and talk to your instructor to get a clear idea of the following.

- *Topics that will be covered.* Will the test cover everything since the term began or will it be more limited?
- *Material you will be tested on.* Will the test cover only what you learned in class and in the text or will it also include outside readings?

What else can you do to predict what will be on a test?

- *Use your textbook.* Check features such as summaries, vocabulary terms, and study questions for clues about what's important to remember.
- *Listen at review sessions.* Many instructors offer review sessions before midterms and finals. Bring your questions to these sessions and listen to the questions others ask.
- *Make an appointment to see your instructor.* Spending a few minutes talking about the test one-on-one may clarify misunderstandings and help you focus on what to study.
- *Get information from people who already took the course.* Try to get a sense of test difficulty, whether tests focus primarily on assigned readings or class notes, what materials are usually covered, and the types of questions that are asked.

- *Examine old tests, if the instructor makes them available.* You may find old tests in class, online, or on reserve in the library. Old tests will help you answer questions like:
  - Do tests focus on examples and details, general ideas and themes, or a combination?
  - Are the questions straightforward or confusing and sometimes tricky?
  - Will you be asked to apply principles to new situations and problems?

Experience is a great teacher when it comes to test taking. After taking the first exam in a course, you will have a better idea of what to expect from that instructor over the rest of the term.

What materials should you study?

With your understanding of what you need to know for the test, you can decide what to study.

- *Sort through materials.* Go through your notes, texts, related primary sources, and handouts. Choose what you need to study, and set aside materials you don't need.
- *Prioritize materials.* Arrange your chosen materials in order of priority so that you focus the bulk of your time on the information you most need to understand.

Use Time Management Strategies to Schedule Study Time

Want to be as ready as possible for a test? Don't wait until the night before to study for it, and don't assume that paying attention during class time is enough. The most effective studying takes place in consistent segments over time. Use time management skills to lay out a study schedule.

- *Consider relevant factors.* Note the number of days until the test, when in your days you have time available, and how much material you have to cover.
- *Schedule a series of study sessions.* If you need to, define what materials you will focus on for each session.
- *Enter study sessions in your planner.* Do this ahead of time, just as you would for a class, a work commitment, or any other important appointment. Then stick to your commitment.

Use Goal-Setting Strategies to Complete Your Plan

Here again, the skills you have built will prove essential to your success. Make getting ready for a test a SMART goal by making it:

- *Specific.* Get clear on what you will be tested on and what you need to study.
- *Measurable.* Acknowledge what you accomplish each study session.
- *Achievable.* Stay up-to-date with your coursework so that you can feel confident on test day.
- *Realistic.* Give yourself enough time and resources to get the job done.
- *Time frame.* Anchor each step toward the test in your schedule.

A comprehensive study plan will help you work SMART. Try using a plan like the one in Key 8.1. Consider making several copies and filling one out for each major test you have this term. You may prefer to create your own version, perhaps using Key 8.1 as a model and modifying it according to your specific needs. Format your version on a computer so that you can print out copies.

Complete the following checklist for each exam to define your study goals, get organized, and stay on track:

Course: _____ Instructor: _____

Date, time, and place of test: _____

Type of test (Is it a midterm or a minor quiz?): _____

What instructor said about the test, including types of test questions, test length, and how much the test counts toward your final grade:

_____

_____

Topics to be covered on the test, in order of importance (information should also come from your instructor):

1. _____

2. _____

3. _____

4. _____

5. _____

Study schedule, including materials you plan to study (texts, class notes, homework problems, and so forth) and dates you plan to complete each:

Material	**Completion Date**
1. _____	_____
2. _____	_____
3. _____	_____
4. _____	_____
5. _____	_____

Materials you are expected to bring to the test (textbook, sourcebook, calculator, etc.):

_____

_____

_____

Special study arrangements (such as planning study group meeting, asking the instructor for special help, getting outside tutoring):

_____

_____

_____

Life-management issues (such as rearranging work hours):

_____

_____

_____

Source: Adapted from Ron Fry, *"Ace" Any Test*, 3rd ed., Franklin Lakes, NJ: Career Press, 1996, pp. 123–124.

Review Using Study Strategies

Put your plan and schedule to work. Use what you have learned about learning, thinking, reading, memory, and studying during this course to understand and remember material.

Test Taking

195

get creative

WRITE YOUR OWN TEST

Complete the following on paper or in digital format.

Create a pretest that helps you prepare for a specific upcoming test in one of your courses. Use the tips in this chapter to predict the material that will be covered, the types of questions that will be asked (multiple choice, essay, etc.), and the nature of the questions (a broad overview of the material or specific details). Then be creative. Write interesting questions that tap into what you have learned and make you think about the material in different ways. Go through the following steps:

1. Create your questions on paper or in a digital file.

2. Use what you created as a pretest. Set up test-like conditions—a quiet, timed environment—and see how you do.

3. Evaluate your pretest answers against your notes and the text. How did you do?

4. Finally, after you take the actual exam, evaluate whether you think this exercise improved your performance. Would you use this technique again? Why or why not?

- *Think analytically.* College exams often ask you to analyze and apply material in more depth than you experienced in high school. For example, your history instructor may ask you to place a primary source in its historical context. Prepare by continually asking analytical thinking questions and using the higher levels of Bloom's taxonomy.

- *Use SQ3R.* This reading method provides an excellent structure for reviewing your reading materials.

- *Consider your learning preferences.* Use study strategies that engage your strengths. When necessary, incorporate strategies that boost your areas of challenge.

- *Remember your best settings.* Use the locations, times, and company that suit you best.

- *Employ specific study strategies.* Consider your favorites. Use flash cards, audio strategies, chunking, anything that suits you and the material.

- *Create mnemonic devices.* These work exceptionally well for remembering lists or groups of items. Use mnemonics that make what you review stick.

- *Actively review your combined class and text notes.* Summaries and master sets of combined text and class notes provide comprehensive study tools.

- *Make and take a pretest.* Use end-of-chapter text questions to create a pretest. If your course doesn't have a text, develop questions from notes, assigned readings, and old homework problems. Some texts provide a website with online activites and pretests to help you review. Answer questions under test-like conditions—in a quiet place, with no books or notes (unless the exam is open book), and with a clock to tell you when to quit.

Prepare Physically

Most tests ask you to work at your best under pressure, so try to get a good night's sleep before the exam. Sleep improves your ability to remember what you studied before you went to bed. By contrast, research has shown that sleep deprivation, which is rampant among college students, results in lower levels of recall, impaired contextual memory (you might remember a fact but can't recall how it connects to other information), and a decrease in cognitive performance.[1] Taking a test while sleep deprived can be compared to driving drunk; although it may not endanger your life, it involves a similar level of impairment and is likely to bring unwanted consequences.

Eating a light, well-balanced meal that is high in protein (eggs, milk, yogurt, meat and fish, nuts, and peanut butter) will keep you full longer than carbohydrates (breads, candy, and pastries). When time is short, don't skip breakfast—grab a quick meal such as a few spoonfuls of peanut butter, a banana, or a high-protein energy bar.

Make the Most of Last-Minute Cramming

Cramming—studying intensively and around the clock right before an exam—often results in information going into your head and popping right back out when the exam is over. If learning is your goal, cramming will not help you reach it. The reality, however, is that you are likely to cram for tests, especially midterms and finals, from time to time in your college career. You may also cram if anxiety leads you to avoid studying. Use these hints to make the most of your time:

- *Focus on crucial concepts.* Summarize the most important points and try to resist reviewing notes or texts page by page.
- *Create a last-minute study sheet to review right before the test.* Write down key facts, definitions, and formulas on a single sheet of paper or on flash cards.
- *Arrive early.* Review your study aids until you are asked to clear your desk.

After your exam, step back and evaluate your performance. Did cramming help, or did it load your mind with disconnected details? Did it increase or decrease anxiety at test time? If you find that in a few days you remember very little, know that this will work against you in advanced courses and careers that build on this knowledge. Plan to start studying earlier next time.

Prepare for Final Exams

Studying for final exams, which usually take place the last week of the term, is a major commitment that requires careful time management. Your college may schedule study days (also called a "reading period") between the end of classes and the beginning of finals. Lasting from a day or two to a couple of weeks, these days give you time to prepare for exams and finish papers. As tempting as it may be to blow off work for a portion of your reading period, try to take advantage of this precious study time. With classes no longer in your calendar, you have that much more time to work and prepare, and you will benefit from the extra effort.

Plan out your reading period at least a week before it starts, beginning with a look at your final exam schedule. Note exactly when each final takes place, and plan several study sessions in the days before each final exam time, setting aside blocks of time assigned to specific subject areas. If you have a day when you are taking more than one final, make sure you factor that into your study plan for the days leading up to it. If you have family responsibilities, let children and other family members know how your schedule will change during reading period and finals, and try to arrange for extra child care or other support ahead of time.

End-of-year studying requires flexibility. Libraries are often packed, and students may need to find alternative locations. Consider outdoor settings (if weather permits), smaller libraries (many departments have their own libraries), and empty classrooms. Set up times and places that will provide the atmosphere you need.[2]

HOW CAN YOU WORK *through test anxiety?*

A moderate amount of stress can have a positive effect, making sure you are alert, ready to act, and geared up to do your best. Some students, however, experience incapacitating stress before and during exams, especially midterms and finals. *Test anxiety* can cause sweating, nausea, dizziness, headaches, and fatigue. It can reduce concentration and cause you to forget everything you learned. Sufferers may get lower grades because their performance does not reflect what they know or because their fear has affected their ability to prepare effectively.

Two Sources of Test Anxiety

Test anxiety has two different sources, and students may experience one or both:[3]

- *Lack of preparation:* Not having put in the work to build knowledge of the material
- *Dislike of testing situations:* Being nervous about a test because of its very nature

For anxiety that stems from being unprepared, the answer is straightforward: Get prepared. All of the information in this chapter about creating and implementing a study plan and schedule is designed to give you the best possible chance of doing well on the test. If you are able to stay calm when you feel ready for a test, effective preparation is your key test anxiety strategy.

Unfortunately, being prepared doesn't necessarily ensure confidence. For students who dread the event no matter how prepared they are, having a test—any test—causes anxiety. Because testing is unavoidable, this anxiety is more challenging to manage. Such students need to shift their mindset and build a positive attitude that says: "I know this material and I'm ready to show it," although this is often easier said than done. To gear up for the next life test, for example, Jay had to overcome the disappointment of failing to make it in the NFL.

Anxiety is defined as an emotional disturbance, meaning that it tends to be based on an imagined risk rather than an actual one, and often leads you away from your goals rather than toward them.[4] If you experience test anxiety, analyze your situation to build a more realistic view of your risk and get back on track toward your goal of test success:

- Reconceive the negative risk and costly result you think you are facing, looking at the risk in a positive sense with a focus on the potential reward. Downplay the negative by considering the possibility that you may be more prepared than you realize, or that the test is not as important as it seems, or not as difficult as you believe it to be.
- Define your goal for this test. Identify the physical and mental issues affecting your ability to reach that goal, and see which of them you can attribute to your anxiety.
- Build a realistic, positive, and productive attitude that says "I know this material and I'm ready to show it." Key 8.2 provides several ways to do this.
- Assess your level of anxiety around test-taking situations. Use the test anxiety assessment on page 201 to determine if you have anxiety that preparation alone cannot eliminate.

See tests as opportunities to learn. Think of tests as signposts along the way to mastering material.

Take care of yourself. The better your physical health, the more able you will be to think positively. Exercise, sleep, and good nutrition all combat anxiety.

Remind yourself of your goals. Focusing on how the test will help you reach your long-term goals will help you calm down.

Ways to build a positive attitude

Seek positive study partners. Find people who inspire you to do your best and don't trigger negativity or anxiety in you.

Understand that tests measure performance, not personal value. Grades don't reflect your ability to succeed or your self-worth.

Engage your instructors' help. Your instructors want you to succeed, no matter how challenging the tests they give you. Contact them for help and advice as you are preparing.

talk risk and reward . . .

Risk asking tough questions to be rewarded with new insights. Use the following questions to inspire discussion with classmates, either in person or online.

- What did you learn about yourself from the test anxiety questionnaire? If you experience test anxiety, what effect do you think it will have on your future?

- Which suggestions for reducing test anxiety are you likely to use? How do you think they will help you feel more comfortable at test time? What other risks, however small, might reward you with better test performance?

CONSIDER THE CASE: The test that Jay faced was one of life or death. What in Jay's life before that time, do you think, prepared him to face this test? Talk about the greatest test life has given you so far. How did you handle it? What risk did you take that can inform how you can aim for rewards at test time?

Test Time Strategies to Address Anxiety

It's test time, and you have arrived at the testing location (ideally a few minutes early) and are waiting for the cue to begin. How can you be calm and focused? These strategies may help.

Manage your environment. Make a conscious effort to sit away from students who might distract you. If it helps, listen to relaxing music on an MP3 player while waiting for class to begin.

Reassure yourself with positive self-talk. Tell yourself that you can do well and that it is normal to feel anxious, particularly before an important exam.

Write down your feelings. Researchers have found that if students take a few minutes before an exam to put their feelings in writing, they post higher grades and have less anxiety. Without worrying about the quality of your writing, express your fears and anxieties about the test on a piece of paper or your computer. "It's almost as if you empty the fears out of your mind," says researcher and psychology professor Sian Beilock.[5]

Practice relaxation. Close your eyes, breathe deeply and slowly, and visualize positive mental images like finishing the test with confidence. Or, try a more physical tensing-and-relaxing method:[6]

1. Put your feet flat on the floor.
2. With your hands, grab underneath the chair.
3. Push down with your feet and pull up on your chair at the same time for about five seconds.
4. Relax for 5 to 10 seconds.
5. Repeat the procedure two or three times.
6. Relax all your muscles except the ones that are actually used to take the test.

Bring a special object. If an object has special meaning for you—a photograph, a stone or crystal, a wristband, a piece of jewelry, a hat—it may provide comfort at test time. Bring it along and hold it, look at it, or wear it during the test. Let its presence settle and inspire you.

Some of these strategies may seem odd or embarassing. However, they might also make a difference for you. Consider whether you are willing to risk a little embarassment for the reward of doing well on a test. It just might be worth it.

Math Anxiety

For some students, math exams cause more anxiety than other academic areas. A form of test anxiety, *math anxiety* is often based on common misconceptions about math, such as the notion that people are born with or without an ability to think quantitatively or that men are better at math than women. Students who feel that they can't do math may give up without asking for help. At exam time, they may experience test anxiety symptoms that reduce their ability to concentrate and leave them feeling defeated.

All of the test anxiety strategies in this section will help combat math anxiety. In addition, math anxiety sufferers should focus heavily on problem solving and should seek help from instructors and tutors early and often.

Test Anxiety and the Returning Student

If you're returning to school after years away, you may wonder how well you will handle exams. To deal with these feelings, focus on what you have learned through life experience, including the ability to handle work and family pressures. Without

get practical

ASSESS TEST ANXIETY WITH THE WESTSIDE TEST ANXIETY SCALE

The first step toward becoming a fearless test-taker is understanding your personal level of test anxiety. Answer the questions below as honestly as possible.

Rate how true each of the following is of you, from extremely or always true, to not at all or never true. Use the following 5 point scale. Circle your answers.

1 = never true   2 = seldom true   3 = sometimes true   4 = usually true   5 = always true

1. The closer I am to a major exam, the harder it is for me to concentrate on the material.	1 2 3 4 5
2. When I study for my exams, I worry that I will not remember the material on the exam.	1 2 3 4 5
3. During important exams, I think that I am doing awful or that I may fail.	1 2 3 4 5
4. I lose focus on important exams, and I cannot remember material that I knew before the exam.	1 2 3 4 5
5. I finally remember the answer to exam questions after the exam is already over.	1 2 3 4 5
6. I worry so much before a major exam that I am too worn out to do my best on the exam.	1 2 3 4 5
7. I feel out of sorts or not really myself when I take important exams.	1 2 3 4 5
8. I find that my mind sometimes wanders when I am taking important exams.	1 2 3 4 5
9. After an exam, I worry about whether I did well enough.	1 2 3 4 5
10. I struggle with written assignments, or avoid doing them, because I want them to be perfect.	1 2 3 4 5

Sum of the 10 questions _____.

Now divide the sum by 10. Write it here _____. This is your test anxiety score.

Compare your score against the scale below. How does your level of test anxiety rate? In general, students that score a 3.0 or higher on the scale tend to have more test anxiety than normal and may benefit from seeking additional assistance.

1.0–1.9 Comfortably low test anxiety
2.0–2.5 Normal or average test anxiety
2.5–2.9 High normal test anxiety
3.0–3.4 Moderately high (some items rated 4)
3.5–3.9 High test anxiety (half or more of the items rated 4)
4.0–5.0 Extremely high anxiety (items rated 4 and 5)

Reflect on your results. Are you considered to have high levels of test anxiety? Normal levels? On paper or in a digital file, write a paragraph describing your anxiety-management plan for your next test, using what you've learned about yourself and test anxiety-reducing strategies.

Source: "Westside Test Anxiety Scale" from Test Anxiety Instrument by Richard Driscoll. Copyright © 2004 by Richard Driscoll, Ph.D. Used by permission of Richard Driscoll.

Test Taking

even thinking about it, you may have developed time-management, planning, organizational, and communication skills needed for test success and college success in general. You may also know yourself well, which will help you choose strategies that work for you.

Furthermore, your life experiences can give real meaning to abstract classroom ideas. For example, workplace relationships may help you understand social psychology concepts, and refinancing your home mortgage may help you grasp a key concept in economics—how the actions of the Federal Reserve Bank influence interest rate swings.

WHAT GENERAL STRATEGIES CAN *help you succeed on tests?*

Even though every test is different, there are general strategies that will help you handle almost all tests, including short-answer and essay exams.

Test Day Strategies

Choose the right seat. Find a seat that will help you maximize focus and minimize distractions. Know yourself—for many students, it's smart to avoid sitting near friends.

Write down key facts. Before you even look at the test, write down key information, including formulas, rules, and definitions, that you don't want to forget. (Use the back of the question sheet so your instructor knows that you made these notes after the test began.)

Start with the big picture. Scan the questions—how many in each section, types, difficulty, point values—and use what you learn to schedule your time. For example, if for a two-hour test you think the writing section will take you more time than the short-answer section, you can budget an hour and a quarter for the essays and 45 minutes for the short-answer questions.

Directions count, so read them. Reading test directions carefully can save you trouble. For example, you may be required to answer only one of three essay questions; you may also be told that you will be penalized for incorrect responses to short-answer questions.

QUALIFERS
Words and phrases that can alter the meaning of a test question and that require careful attention.

Mark up the questions. Mark up instructions and key words to avoid careless errors. Circle qualifiers such as *always, never, all, none, sometimes,* and *every;* verbs that communicate specific instructions; and concepts that are tricky or need special attention.

Be precise when taking a machine-scored test. Use the right pencil (usually a #2) on machine-scored tests, and mark your answer in the correct space, filling it completely. Periodically, check the answer number against the question number to make sure they match.

Work from easy to hard. Begin with the easiest questions and answer them quickly without sacrificing accuracy. This will boost your confidence and leave more time for harder questions. Mark tough questions as you reach them, and return to them after answering the questions you know.

Watch the clock. If you are worried about time, you may rush through the test and have time left over. When this happens, check over your work instead of leaving early. If, on the other hand, you are falling behind, be flexibile about the best use of the remaining time.

Take a strategic approach to questions you cannot answer. Even if you are well prepared, you may face questions you do not understand or cannot answer. Key 8.3 has ideas to consider.

Use special techniques for math tests. In addition to these general test-taking strategies, the techniques in Key 8.4 can help you achieve better results on math exams.

Maintain Academic Integrity

While cheating has the immediate gain of possibly passing a test or at the least getting a few answers right, its long-term consequences aren't so beneficial. If you cheat, you may be caught and disciplined (with consequences that can go as far as expulsion). Furthermore, cheating that goes on your record can damage your ability to get a job.

In recent years, cheating has become high-tech, with students putting all kinds of devices to dishonest uses. Examples include:[7]

- Texting answers from cell phones or smartphones
- Using in-phone cameras to take pictures of tests to send to friends or sell online

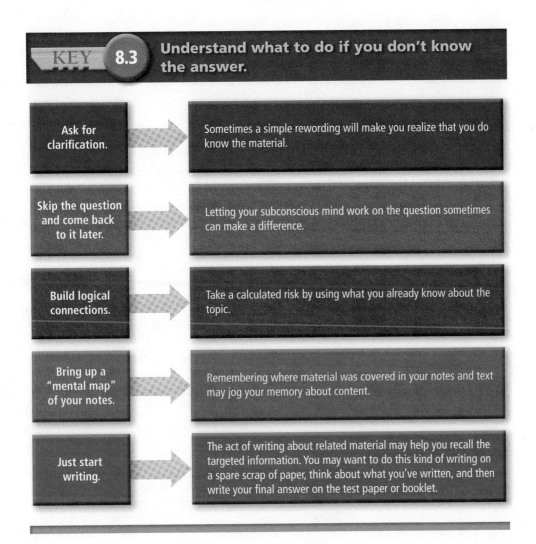

KEY 8.3 Understand what to do if you don't know the answer.

Ask for clarification.	Sometimes a simple rewording will make you realize that you do know the material.
Skip the question and come back to it later.	Letting your subconscious mind work on the question sometimes can make a difference.
Build logical connections.	Take a calculated risk by using what you already know about the topic.
Bring up a "mental map" of your notes.	Remembering where material was covered in your notes and text may jog your memory about content.
Just start writing.	The act of writing about related material may help you recall the targeted information. You may want to do this kind of writing on a spare scrap of paper, think about what you've written, and then write your final answer on the test paper or booklet.

- Using graphing calculators to save formulas that were supposed to have been memorized
- With an Internet connection, finding answers on crowd-sourcing sites such as Quora
- Sharing answers on private all-student groups connected to learning management systems

Because this type of cheating can be difficult to discover when exams are administered in large lecture halls, some instructors ban all electronic devices from the room.

Valid concerns can put students under pressure: "I have to do well on the final. I am in a time crunch. I need a good grade to qualify for the next course in my major. I can't fail because I'm already in debt and I have to graduate and get a job." Compounded, these worries can often drive students to thoughts of academic dishonesty. However, feeling the drive to cheat generally means you haven't learned the material. Ask yourself: Am I in college to learn information that I can use? Or to cheat my way to a decent GPA and breathe a sigh of relief when the term is done? Retention of knowledge is necessary both to complete future coursework and to thrive in jobs that require you to use it. Only one course of action will earn you that reward.

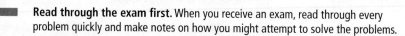

KEY 8.4 Try these techniques to succeed on math exams.

Read through the exam first. When you receive an exam, read through every problem quickly and make notes on how you might attempt to solve the problems.

Analyze problems carefully. Categorize problems according to type. Take the "givens" into account, and write down any formulas, theorems, or definitions that apply. Focus on what you want to find or prove.

Estimate to come up with a "ballpark" solution. Then work the problem and check the solution against your estimate. The two answers should be close. If they're not, recheck your calculations.

Break the calculation into the smallest possible pieces. Go step-by-step and don't move on to the next step until you are clear about what you've done so far.

Recall how you solved similar problems. Past experience can provide valuable clues.

Draw a picture to help you see the problem. Visual images such as a diagram, chart, probability tree, or geometric figure may help clarify your thinking.

Be neat. Sloppy numbers can mean the difference between a right and a wrong answer. A 4 that looks like a 9 will be marked wrong.

Use the opposite operation to check your work. Work backward from your answer to see if you are right.

Look back at the question to be sure you did everything. Did you answer every part of the question? Did you show all required work?

The risk of cheating may bring a starkly different reward than the risk of staying honest even in the face of a lack of preparation. The next time you are tempted to break the rules of academic integrity, remember: The choice is yours, and so are the consequences. Your decisions will have lasting impacts on your future and your life. Key 8.5 shows you some choices and potential consequences of cheating on a final exam.

KEY 8.5 **Think through the consequences of cheating.**

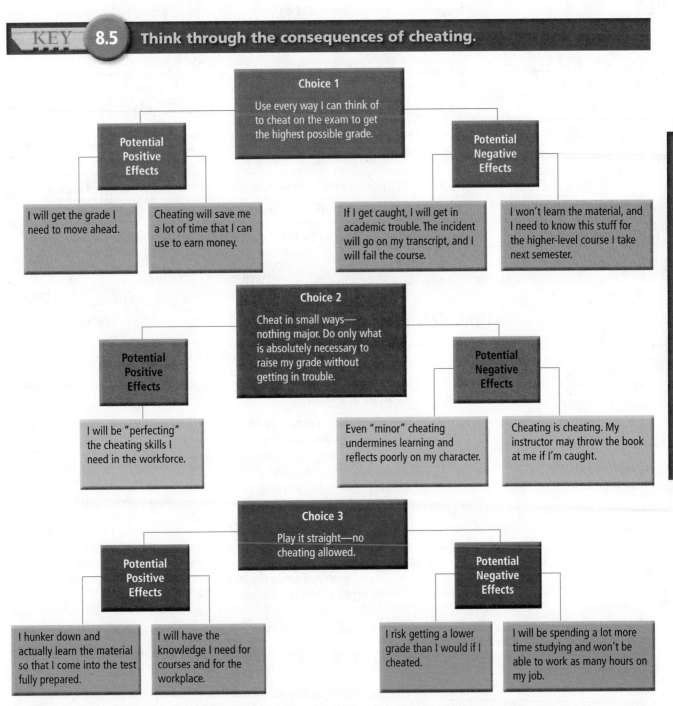

Choice 1
Use every way I can think of to cheat on the exam to get the highest possible grade.

Potential Positive Effects

I will get the grade I need to move ahead.

Cheating will save me a lot of time that I can use to earn money.

Potential Negative Effects

If I get caught, I will get in academic trouble. The incident will go on my transcript, and I will fail the course.

I won't learn the material, and I need to know this stuff for the higher-level course I take next semester.

Choice 2
Cheat in small ways—nothing major. Do only what is absolutely necessary to raise my grade without getting in trouble.

Potential Positive Effects

I will be "perfecting" the cheating skills I need in the workforce.

Potential Negative Effects

Even "minor" cheating undermines learning and reflects poorly on my character.

Cheating is cheating. My instructor may throw the book at me if I'm caught.

Choice 3
Play it straight—no cheating allowed.

Potential Positive Effects

I hunker down and actually learn the material so that I come into the test fully prepared.

I will have the knowledge I need for courses and for the workplace.

Potential Negative Effects

I risk getting a lower grade than I would if I cheated.

I will be spending a lot more time studying and won't be able to work as many hours on my job.

get $mart

TEST YOUR FINANCIAL LITERACY

As with any academic area of study, knowledge of basic terms is a necessary foundation on which to build understanding. Test your knowledge of some financial literacy terminology with this matching exercise.

1. ____ finance charge	A. A number assigned to you based on your credit activity—higher numbers are better.
2. ____ net worth	B. Using more money than you have available in a bank account.
3. ____ IRA	C. Your total financial assets—cash, savings, property—minus your debt.
4. ____ debit card	D. A percentage charged annually on the amount of a loan or credit card debt.
5. ____ overdraft	E. A first payment on a large purchase that you cannot cover all at once.
6. ____ credit score	F. When someone acquires and uses your personal information without your consent.
7. ____ interest	G. When you use it, the purchase amount is subtracted from your bank account.
8. ____ APR	H. A percentage that you earn on savings or pay on borrowed money or credit.
9. ____ down payment	I. What it costs you to use credit; can be a percentage of what you owe, or a flat fee.
10. ____ identity theft	J. An account designed to help you save money for retirement.

HOW CAN YOU MASTER DIFFERENT
types of test questions?

Every type of test question has a different way of finding out how much you know. The two main forms of questions are:

- *Objective questions.* These generally have you choose or write a short answer, often selecting from a limited number of choices. They can include multiple-choice, fill-in-the-blank, matching, and true-or-false questions.
- *Subjective questions.* These demand the same information recall as objective questions, but they also require you to plan, organize, draft, and refine a response. All essay questions are subjective.

As you review the sample questions in the following section, look also at the Multiple Intelligence Strategies for Test Taking on page 207. Harness the strategies that fit your learning strengths to prepare for exams. Note that some suggestions are repeated in the following sections, in order to reinforce the importance of these suggestions and their application to different types of test questions.

Multiple-Choice Questions

Multiple-choice questions are the most popular type of question on standardized tests. The following analytical and practical strategies will help you answer them:

- *Read the directions carefully and try to think of the answer before looking at the choices.* Then read the choices and make your selection.
- *Underline key words and phrases.* If the question is complicated, try to break it down into small sections that are easy to understand.

multiple intelligence strategies

FOR TEST PREPARATION

Describe an upcoming exam (date, course, exam type): _____.
In the right-hand column, record specific ideas for how MI strategies can help you prepare for it.

INTELLIGENCE	USE MI STRATEGIES TO IMPROVE TEST PREPARATION	IDENTIFY MI TEST-PREP STRATEGIES THAT CAN HELP YOU PREPARE
Verbal-Linguistic 	• Write test questions your instructor might ask. Answer the questions and then try rewriting them in a different format (essay, true/false, and so on). • Underline important words in review or practice questions.	
Logical-Mathematical 	• Logically connect what you are studying with what you know. Consider similarities, differences, and cause-and-effect relationships. • Draw charts that show relationships and analyze trends.	
Bodily-Kinesthetic 	• Use text highlighting to take a hands-on approach to studying. • Create a sculpture, model, or skit to depict a tough concept that will be on the test.	
Visual-Spatial 	• Make charts, diagrams, or think links illustrating concepts. • Make drawings related to possible test topics.	
Interpersonal 	• Form a study group to prepare for your test. • In your group, come up with possible test questions. Then use the questions to test each other's knowledge.	
Intrapersonal 	• Apply concepts to your own life; think about how you would manage. • Make up test questions and then take the sample "test" you developed.	
Musical 	• Recite text concepts to rhythms or write a song to depict them. • Explore relevant musical links to reading material.	
Naturalistic 	• Try to notice similarities and differences in objects and concepts by organizing your study materials into relevant groupings.	

Test Taking

207

- *Make sure you read every word of every answer.* Focus especially on qualifying words such as *always, never, tend to, most, often,* and *frequently.* Look also for negatives in a question ("Which of the following is *not . . .*").
- *When questions are linked to a reading passage, read the questions first.* This will help you focus on the information you need to answer the questions.

The following examples show the kinds of multiple-choice questions you might encounter in an introductory psychology course (the correct answer follows each question):

1. Although you know that alcohol is a central nervous system depressant, your friend says it is actually a stimulant because he does things that he wouldn't otherwise do after having a couple of drinks. He also feels less inhibited, more spontaneous, and more entertaining. The reason your friend experiences alcohol as a stimulant is that

  a. Alcohol has the same effect on the nervous system as amphetamines.
  b. Alcohol has a strong placebo effect.
  c. The effects of alcohol depend almost entirely on the expectations of the user.
  d. Alcohol depresses areas in the brain responsible for critical judgment and impulsiveness.

(answer: d)

2. John drinks five or six cups of strong coffee each day. Which of the following symptoms is he most likely to report?

  a. nausea, loss of appetite, cold hands, and chills
  b. feelings of euphoria and well-being
  c. anxiety, headaches, insomnia, and diarrhea
  d. time distortion and reduced emotional sensitivity

(answer: c)

Source: Charles G. Morris and Albert A. Maisto, *Understanding Psychology,* 10th ed., p. 145. © 2013 Pearson Education, Inc. Reprinted by permission of Pearson Education, Inc., Upper Saddle River, NJ.

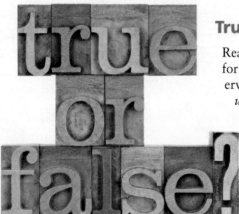

True-or-False Questions

Read true-or-false questions carefully to evaluate what they are asking. Look for absolute qualifiers (such as *all, only,* and *always* that often make an otherwise true statement false) and conservative qualifiers (*generally, often, usually,* and *sometimes* that often make an otherwise false statement true).

For example, "The grammar rule 'I before E except after C' is *always* true" is false, whereas "The grammar rule 'I before E except after C' is *usually* true" is true.

Be sure to read *every* word of a true-or-false-question to avoid jumping to an incorrect conclusion. Common problems in reading too quickly include missing negatives (*not, no*) that would change your response and deciding on an answer before reading the complete statement.

The following examples show the kinds of true–false questions you might encounter in an introductory psychology course (the correct answer follows each question):

Indicate whether the following statements are true (T) or false (F):

1. Alcohol is implicated in more than two-thirds of all automobile accidents.   *(true)*

2. Caffeine is not addictive.   *(false)*

3. Recurring hallucinations are common among users of hallucinogens.   *(true)*

4. Marijuana interferes with short-term memory.   *(true)*

Source: Charles G. Morris and Albert A. Maisto, *Understanding Psychology,* 10th ed., p. 145. © 2013 Pearson Education, Inc. Reprinted by permission of Pearson Education, Inc., Upper Saddle River, NJ.

Matching Questions

Matching questions ask you to match the terms in one list with the terms in another list. For example, the directions may tell you to match a communicable disease with the microorganism that usually causes it. The following strategies will help you handle these questions.

- *Make sure you understand the directions.* The directions tell you whether each answer can be used only once (common practice) or more than once.
- *Work from the column with the longest entries.* The column on the left usually contains terms to be defined or questions to be answered, while the column on the right has definitions or answers. As a result, entries on the right are usually longer than those on the left. Reading those items only once will save time.
- *Start with the matches you know.* On your first run-through, pencil in these matches.
- *Finally, tackle the matches of which you're not sure.* Think back to your class lectures, text notes, and study sessions as you try to visualize the correct response. If one or more phrases seem to have no correct answer and you can use answers only once, consider the possibility that one of your sure-thing answers is wrong.

Fill-in-the-Blank Questions

Fill-in-the-blank questions, also known as sentence completion questions, ask you to supply one or more words or phrases. These strategies will help you make successful choices.

- *Be logical.* Insert your answer, then reread the sentence from beginning to end to be sure it makes sense and is factually and grammatically correct.
- *Note the length and number of the blanks.* If two blanks appear right after one another, the instructor is probably looking for a two-word answer. If a blank is longer than usual, the correct response may require additional space.
- *If there is more than one blank and the blanks are widely separated, treat each one separately.* Answering each as if it is a separate sentence-completion question increases the likelihood that you will get at least one answer correct.
- *If you are uncertain, guess.* Have faith that after hours of studying, the correct answer is somewhere in your subconscious mind and that your guess is not completely random.

The following examples show fill-in-the-blank questions you might encounter in an introductory psychology course (correct answers follow questions):

1. Our awareness of the mental processes of our everyday life is called _____. *(consciousness)*

2. The major characteristic of waking consciousness is _____. *(selective attention)*

3. In humans, sleeping and waking follow a _____ cycle. *(circadian)*

4. Most vivid dreaming takes place during the _____ stage of sleep. *(REM)*

Source: Charles G. Morris and Albert A. Maisto, *Understanding Psychology*, 10th ed., p. 130. © 2013 Pearson Education, Inc. Reprinted by permission of Pearson Education, Inc., Upper Saddle River, NJ.

Essay Questions

Essay questions ask you to express your knowledge and views in a less structured way than short-answer questions. With freedom of thought and expression comes the challenge to organize your ideas and write well under time pressure. These steps are a shortened version of the writing process (see Appendix A)—will help you plan, draft, revise, and edit your responses.

Source: Charles G. Morris and Albert A. Maisto, *Understanding Psychology*, 10th ed., pp. 196, 260, 385. © 2013 Pearson Education, Inc. Reprinted by permission of Pearson Education, Inc., Upper Saddle River, NJ.

1. *Read every question.* Decide which to tackle (if there's a choice). Read carefully, and use critical thinking to identify exactly what the question is asking.

2. *Map out your time.* Schedule how long to allot for each answer, and then break your time down into smaller segments for each part of the process; for example, if you have 20 minutes to answer a question, use 5 to plan, 10 to draft, and 5 to review and finalize. Be flexible and ready to adjust how you use your time if things don't go as planned.

3. *Focus on action verbs.* Action verbs like those in Key 8.6 tell you what to do to answer the question. Underline these words and use them to guide your writing.

4. *Plan.* Thinking about what the question is asking and what you know, define your goal—what you intend to say in your answer. On scrap paper, outline or map your ideas and supporting evidence. Then develop a thesis statement that outlines the goal you've set, illustrating both the content and, if applicable, your point of view. Don't skimp on planning: Not only does planning result in a better essay, it also reduces stress because it helps you get in control.

5. *Draft.* Note the test directions before drafting your answer. Your essay may need to be of a certain length, for example, or may need to take a certain format. Then, use the following guidelines as you work:

   - State your thesis, and then get right to the evidence that backs it up.
   - Structure your essay so that each paragraph presents an idea that supports the thesis.
   - Use clear language and tight logic to link ideas to your thesis and to create transitions between paragraphs.
   - Look back at your planning notes periodically to make sure you cover everything.
   - Wrap it up with a short, to-the-point conclusion.

6. *Revise.* Although you may not have the time to rewrite your entire answer, you can improve it with minor changes. Check word choice, paragraph structure, and style. If you notice anything missing, use editing marks to insert it (neatly so it remains legible) into the text. When you're done, make sure it's the best possible representation of your ideas.

   As you check over your essay, ask yourself these questions:

   - Have I answered the question?
   - Does my essay begin with a clear thesis statement, and does each paragraph start with a strong topic sentence that supports the thesis?

- Have I provided adequate support—in the form of examples, statistics, and relevant facts—to prove my argument? Have I used tight logic?
- Have I covered all the points in my original outline or map?
- Is my conclusion an effective wrap-up?

7. *Edit.* Check for mistakes in grammar, spelling, punctuation, and usage. Correct language—and neat, legible handwriting—leaves a positive impression and helps your grade.

Even the most prepared student can hit a wall during an essay test and have trouble continuing, or even starting, an essay. This is a common occurrence. If it happens to you, your best bet is just to start writing, even if you are unsure of what you want to say. You don't want to be sitting in front of an empty page when time is called. One way to get moving is to begin writing on the second page of your test booklet, leaving

KEY 8.6   **Focus on action verbs in essay tests.**

ANALYZE	Break into parts and discuss each part separately.
COMPARE	Explain similarities and differences.
CONTRAST	Distinguish between items being compared by focusing on differences.
CRITICIZE	Evaluate the issue, focusing on its problems or deficiencies.
DEFINE	State the essential quality or meaning.
DESCRIBE	Paint a complete picture; provide the details of a story or the main characteristics of a situation.
DIAGRAM	Present a drawing, chart, or other visual.
DISCUSS	Examine completely, using evidence and often presenting both sides of an issue.
ELABORATE ON	Start with information presented in the question, and then add new material.
ENUMERATE/LIST/IDENTIFY	Specify items in the form of a list.
EVALUATE	Give your opinion about the value or worth of a topic and justify your conclusion.
EXPLAIN	Make meaning clear, often by discussing causes and consequences.
ILLUSTRATE	Supply examples.
INTERPRET	Explain your personal views and judgments.
JUSTIFY	Discuss the reasons for your conclusions or for the question's premise.
OUTLINE	Organize and present main and subordinate points.
PROVE	Use evidence and logic to show that a statement is true.
REFUTE	Use evidence and logic to show that a statement is not true or tell how you disagree with it.
RELATE	Connect items mentioned in the question, showing, for example, how one item influenced another.
REVIEW	Provide an overview of ideas and establish their merits and features.
STATE	Explain clearly, simply, and concisely.
SUMMARIZE	Give the important ideas in brief, without comments.
TRACE	Present a history of a situation's development, often by showing cause and effect.

Test Taking

the first page blank so that you can go back and create an introduction once you have a clearer idea of what you want to say.[8]

Key 8.7 shows a student's completed response to an essay question on body language including word changes and inserts she made while revising her draft.

Before she began writing the answer to this essay question, this student created the planning outline shown in Key 8.8. Notice how abbreviations and shorthand are involved.

KEY 8.7 **Response to an essay question with revision marks.**

QUESTION: Describe three ways that body language affects interpersonal communication.

Body language plays an important role in interpersonal communication and helps shape the impression you make. *, especially when you meet someone for the first time* Two of the most important functions of body language are to contradict and reinforce verbal statements. When body language contradicts verbal language, the message ~~conveyed~~ *delivered* by the body is dominant. For example, if a friend tells you that she is feeling "fine," but her posture is slumped, *her eye contact minimal,* and her facial expression troubled, you have every reason to wonder whether she is telling the truth. If the same friend tells you that she is feeling fine and is smiling, walking with a bounce in her step, and has direct eye contact, her body language is ~~telling the truth.~~ *accurately reflecting and reinforcing her words.*

The nonverbal cues that make up body language also have the power to add shades of meaning. Consider this statement: "This is the best idea I've heard all day." If you were to say this three different ways—in a loud voice while standing up; quietly while sitting with arms and legs crossed and looking away; and while ~~maintening~~ *maintaining* eye contact and taking the receiver's hand—you might send three different messages.

Finally, the impact of nonverbal cues can be greatest when you meet someone for the first time. When you meet someone, you tend to make assumptions based on nonverbal behavior such as posture, eye contact, gestures, and speed and style of movement.

In summary, nonverbal communication plays a ~~crucial~~ *crucial* role in interpersonal relationships. It has the power to send an accurate message that may ~~destroy~~ *belie* the speaker's words, offer shades of meaning, and set the tone of a first meeting.

Although first impressions emerge ~~from a combination of nonverbal cues, tone of voice, and choice of words,~~ nonverbal elements (cues and tone) ~~usually come~~ across first and strongest.

---

get analytical

Complete the following on paper or in digital format.

Focusing on the action verbs in essay test instructions can mean the difference between giving instructors what they want and wandering off track. Get to know action verbs a litle more closely. Choose three verbs from Key 8.6 that you've seen used in essay questions. List each verb. Then, for each, write out what the verb inspires you to do *without reusing the verb*. In other words, avoid saying that "Describe" asks you to describe.

Now put your choices to work.

1. Name a topic you learned about in this text—for example, the concept of successful intelligence or different barriers to listening.

2. Put yourself in the role of instructor. Write an essay question on this topic, using one of the action verbs you listed. For example, "List the three aspects of successful intelligence" or "Analyze the classroom-based challenges associated with internal barriers to listening."

3. Now rewrite your original question twice more, using the other two action verbs you chose, and adjusting the question to the verb each time.

4. Finally, analyze how each new verb changes the focus of the essay. Describe the goal of each essay question and note how they differ.

KEY **8.8**   **Create an informal outline during essay tests.**

> Essay question: Describe three ways in which body language affects interpersonal communication.
>
> Roles of BL in IC
>
>   1. To contradict or reinforce words
>   —e.g., friend says, "I'm fine"
>   2. To add shades of meaning
>   —saying the same sentence in 3 diff. ways
>   3. To make lasting 1st impression
>   —impact of nv cues and voice tone greater than words
>   —we assume things abt person based on posture, eye contact, etc.

Neatness is crucial. No matter how good your ideas are, if your instructor can't read them, your grade will suffer. If your handwriting is a problem, try printing or skipping every other line, and be sure to write on only one side of the page. Students with illegible handwriting might ask to take the test on a computer.

The purpose of a test is to see how much you know, not merely to get a grade. Embrace this attitude to learn from your mistakes.

WHAT CAN YOU LEARN
from test mistakes?

Congratulations! You've finished the exam, handed it in, gone home to a well-deserved night of sleep. At the next class meeting you've returned refreshed, rejuvenated, and ready to accept a perfect score. As you receive the test back from your instructor, you look wide-eyed at your grade. *How could that be?*

No one aces every test or understands every piece of material perfectly. Making mistakes on tests and learning from them is an essential part of the academic experience. Instead of beating yourself up about a bad grade, take the risk of looking realistically at what you could have done better. Identify what you can correct, and you may be rewarded with better study choices and an improved performance on your next exam. Jay certainly found out from his experiences that learning from mistakes is essential to growth and development in life. Here are some helpful actions to take:

Ask yourself global questions that may help you identify correctable patterns. Honest answers can help you change the way you study for the next exam.

- What were your biggest problems? Did you get nervous, misread the question, fail to study enough, study incorrectly, focus on memorizing material instead of on understanding and applying it?
- Did your instructor's comments clarify where you slipped up? Did your answer lack specificity? Did you fail to support your thesis well? Was your analysis weak?
- Were you surprised by the questions? For example, did you expect them all to be from the lecture notes and text instead of from your notes and text and supplemental readings?

- Did you make careless errors? Did you misread the question or directions, blacken the wrong box on the answer sheet, skip a question, write illegibly?
- Did you make conceptual or factual errors? Did you misunderstand a concept? Did you fail to master facts or concepts?

Rework the questions you got wrong. Based on instructor feedback, try to rewrite an essay, recalculate a math problem from the original question, or redo questions following a reading selection. If you discover a pattern of careless errors, redouble your efforts to be more careful, and save time to double-check your work.

student PROFILE

Kevin Ix

**BERGEN COMMUNITY COLLEGE,
PARAMUS, NEW JERSEY**

About me:

After high school, I attended college for three semesters studying to become an electrician. Later, seeing the way the housing market has plummeted and the direction the economy is heading, I decided a business major made more sense. I am now working toward a degree in business. I keep busy during the summer with one full-time and one part-time job.

How I faced a challenge:

Taking the time to read directions has never been my strong point. Whether it's setting up a new television or taking a final exam, I jump right into the task without paying attention to instructions. On one particular occasion I remember being given a test and started answering the questions without even glancing at the directions. At the end of the test, the teacher began collecting the exams and occasionally laughed as she made her way around the room. As it turned out, the directions on the top of the test clearly read, "If you're reading these directions, please do not fill in the answer sheet." Clearly she intended to test our ability to follow directions. While I was not the only one to make this mistake, I did not fare too well on that particular test! I work to combat my tendencies by paying careful attention to directions.

What will help me in the workplace:

The expression "measure twice, cut once" was instilled into my mind while I was enrolled in technical college. If you didn't pay particular attention to measurements and directions, your mistake could become extremely expensive in material costs. This simple saying reminds me to focus on directions, making sure that I avoid the costly mistakes that come from ignoring or just glancing at them.

After reviewing your mistakes, fill in your knowledge gaps. If you made mistakes because you didn't understand important concepts, develop a plan to learn the material.

Talk to your instructor. Focus on specific mistakes on objective questions or a weak essay. The fact that you care enough to review your errors will make a good impression. If you are not sure why you were marked down on an essay, ask what you could have done better. If you feel that an essay was unfairly graded, ask for a rereading. When you use your social intelligence and approach your instructor in a non-defensive way, you are likely to receive help.

Rethink the way you studied. Make changes to avoid repeating your errors. Use varied techniques to study more effectively so that you can show yourself and your instructors what you are capable of doing. The earlier in the term you make positive adjustments the better, so make a special effort to analyze and learn from early test mistakes.

If you fail a test, don't throw it away. Use it to review troublesome material, especially if you will be tested on it again. You might also want to keep it as a reminder that you can improve. When you compare a failure to later successes, you'll see how far you've come.

A final word: Tests reflect your ability to *show* what you know. They do not necessarily indicate what you know, and certainly they do not define who you are. Understand the limitations of tests. Learn from them and take from them what reward you can as you move into the greater test of life in the 21st century.

revisit RISK AND REWARD

What happened to Jay? Saved by a skilled trauma surgeon, Jay went on to become one of the most legendary agents in ATF history. "Being shot empowered me," Jay says. "It showed me that . . . I did want to be the guy that would stand up to the violence on behalf of my community." Known on the streets and in the law enforcement community as "Jaybird," he risked infiltrating the Hells Angels motorcycle gang as an undercover agent, earning the extraordinary reward of being the first law enforcement officer to defeat the gang's multilayered security measures to become a full patched member. His 2009 memoir, *No Angel: My Harrowing Undercover Journey to the Inner Circle of the Hells Angels,* became a *New York Times* bestseller. Jay retired with 12 ATF Special Act Awards for excellence in criminal investigations. Now married and the father of two, Jay is a motivational speaker. "My presentations are not hero stories," Jay says. "I spend more time talking about the mistakes I made and the failures and regrets. . . . I hope people listen to my stories and don't make the same mistakes I made."

What does this mean for you? To ace the "test" of being an undercover agent, Jay armed himself with knowledge. "I studied criminals. How they talked, walked, looked, dressed, what they drove, where they lived, how they interacted. Crime environments were my school room." Knowledge and experience are the keys to passing school tests as well as life tests such as relationships or career challenges. Risk revisiting your most recent tests. Describe how you prepared for a school test; then, list up to three things you could have done to prepare more effectively. Now do the same for a recent "life" test. How would you grade yourself on this test?

What risk may bring reward beyond your world? Jay's 17 years of undercover street work came at a price. "It darkened my outlook and personality. I had lost faith in people," Jay says. Jay then met Ed Harrow, the founder of Heartbeat for Africa, a faith-based nonprofit that provides clean water systems and medical care to children and orphans in the Volta Region of Ghana, West Africa. Reluctantly, Jay traveled to Africa on a Heartbeat mission, witnessing extreme poverty but encountering people full of spirit and hope. "They restored my faith in humanity," Jay says. Visit www.heartbeatforafrica.org to learn more about the organization's mission. Then consider how you can risk moving past your own ups and downs to create reward for someone else—locally, nationally, or internationally. What cause inspires emotions in you and makes you wish you could help? Research online and turn that wish into reality.

Complete the following on paper or in digital format.

KNOW IT *Think Critically*

Effectively Prepare for Tests

Take a careful look at your performance on and preparation for a test you took recently.

Build basic skills. Think about how you did on the test. Were you pleased or disappointed with your performance and grade? Explain your answer.

List any of the problems below that you feel you experienced in this exam. If you experienced one or more problems not listed here, include them in your document. For each problem you identified, think about why you made mistakes.

- Incomplete preparation
- Fatigue
- Feeling rushed during the test
- Shaky understanding of concepts
- Poor guessing techniques
- Feeling confused about directions
- Test anxiety
- Poor essay organization or writing

Take it to the next level. Be creative about test-preparation strategies. If you had all the time and materials you needed, how would you have prepared for this test? Describe briefly what your plan would be and how it would address your problem(s).

Now think back to your actual test preparation—the techniques you used and amount of time you spent. Describe the difference between the ideal study plan you just described and what you actually did.

Move toward mastery. Improve your chances for success on the next exam by coming up with specific changes in your preparation.

1. Actions I took this time, but do *not* intend to take next time:
2. Actions I did *not* take this time, but do intend to take next time:

Test Taking

WRITE IT *Communicate*

Emotional intelligence journal: Test types. What type of test do you feel most comfortable with, and what type brings up more negative feelings? Thinking of a particular situation involving the test type that challenges you, describe how it made you feel and how that feeling affected your performance. Discuss ways in which you might be able to shift your mindset in order to feel more confident about this type of test.

Real-life writing: Ask your instructor for feedback on a test. Nearly every student has been in the position of believing that the response written for an essay exam was marked down unfairly. The next time this happens to you—when you have no idea why you lost points or disagree with the instructor's assessment of your work—draft a respectful email to your instructor explaining your position and asking for a meeting to discuss the essay. (See email etiquette guidelines in Quick Start.) Use clear logic to defend your work and refer back to what you learned in class and in the text. It is important to specifically address any comments or criticisms the instructor made on the test paper. Before sending the email, analyze your argument: Did you make your case effectively or was the instructor correct? When you have the meeting, the work you did on the email will prepare you to defend your position.

WORK IT *Build Your Brand*

On-the-Job Testing

21st Century Learning Building Blocks

- Information literacy
- Initiative and self-direction
- Productivity and accountability

You may encounter different tests throughout your career. For example, if you are studying to be a nurse you are now tested on subjects like anatomy and pharmacology. After you graduate you will be required to take certification and recertification exams that gauge your mastery of the latest information in different aspects of nursing.

Some post-graduate tests are for entry into the field; some test proficiency on particular equipment; some move you to the next level of employment. Choose one career you are thinking about and investigate what tests are involved as you advance through different career stages.

Create a document with your chosen career area as the title. On your document, create a grid that has several rows and the following five headers:

- Test name
- When taken
- What it covers
- How to prepare
- Web resources

Finally, search for the information you need to fill in the grid. Use one row for every test that you find.

Answers to Get $mart quiz:

1. I
2. C
3. J
4. G
5. B
6. A
7. H
8. D
9. E
10. F

Much of your school and work experience will involve teamwork, both in person and virtually. Interacting effectively with all kinds of people is crucial to your

Diversity and Communication

MAKING RELATIONSHIPS WORK

What Would You Risk? *Louise Gaile Edrozo*

THINK ABOUT THIS PROBLEM AS YOU READ, AND CONSIDER WHAT ACTION YOU WOULD TAKE. THIS CHAPTER FOCUSES ON THE DIVERSITY OF TODAY'S STUDENT BODY, EFFECTIVE COMMUNICATION, AND CONNECTING WITH OTHERS.

In her native Philippines, Gaile Edrozo was on track to earn a biology degree and begin medical school. However, financial difficulties derailed her plans. Seeking more opportunity to work and earn a living, she and her family took the calculated risk of coming to the United States. Gaile enrolled as a nursing student at Highline Community College in the fall of 2004. She was considered an international student because she was not yet a U.S. citizen.

As Gaile worked toward her goal to become a nurse, the financial burden of her education caused excessive stress and sleepless nights. The cost of her education was too high for her family to manage, even with the many sacrifices her parents had made. Even more frightening was the possibility that Gaile would lose her status in the United States if she was unable to stay in school, and she would have to return to the Philippines without her family.

Gaile feared that the reward of becoming a nurse, having a career she loved, and financially contributing to her family would be out of reach as it had been in the Philippines. She threw herself into her schoolwork, hoping to be eligible for scholarships or other aid. However, no scholarship she explored was available to an international student. Ready to risk reaching out for help, Gaile registered for Honors 100, a course at Highline for both citizens and international students that helps students explore scholarship opportunities, prepare portfolio and résumé materials, and look at four-year institutions. She hoped her instructor, Dr. Barbara Clinton, could help her avoid losing her dream a second time.

To be continued . . .

CONNECTING WITH OTHERS OPENS UP POSSIBILITIES AND CAN HELP YOU LIVE YOUR DREAMS. YOU'LL LEARN MORE ABOUT GAILE, AND THE REWARD RESULTING FROM HER ACTIONS, WITHIN THIS CHAPTER.

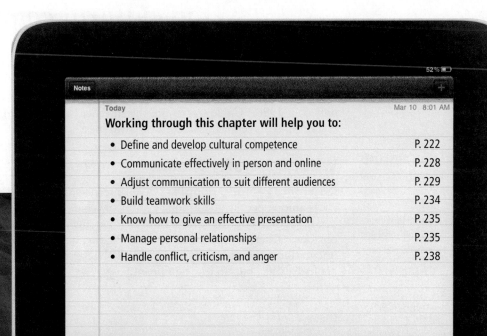

52%

Notes

Today   Mar 10 8:01 AM

Working through this chapter will help you to:

status CHECK

How Developed Are Your Cultural Competence and Communication Skills?

For each statement, fill in the number that feels right to you, from 1 for "not at all true for me" to 5 for "very true for me."

1. I consistently work to develop cultural competence. ① ② ③ ④ ⑤

2. I seek to incorporate diverse people and cultures into my life. ① ② ③ ④ ⑤

3. I believe even positive stereotypes can hurt my ability to get to know someone. ① ② ③ ④ ⑤

4. I understand the difference between tolerating those different from me and accepting and celebrating those differences. ① ② ③ ④ ⑤

5. I can adjust my communication style to more effectively connect with others. ① ② ③ ④ ⑤

6. I pay attention to and interpret meaning from nonverbal and body language. ① ② ③ ④ ⑤

7. I participate effectively when working with a group or team. ① ② ③ ④ ⑤

8. I use positive relationship strategies to strengthen my personal connections. ① ② ③ ④ ⑤

9. I manage electronic communication effectively and do not let it run my life. ① ② ③ ④ ⑤

10. I am able to receive constructive criticism and use it to improve. ① ② ③ ④ ⑤

Each of the topics in these statements is covered in this chapter. Note those statements for which you filled in a 3 or lower. Skim the chapter to see where those topics appear, and pay special attention to them as you read, learn, and apply new strategies.

REMEMBER: NO MATTER HOW DEVELOPED YOUR CULTURAL COMPETENCE AND COMMUNICATION SKILLS ARE, YOU CAN IMPROVE WITH EFFORT AND PRACTICE.

HOW CAN YOU
develop cultural competence?

A century ago it was possible to live an entire lifetime surrounded only by people from your own culture. Not so today. American society consists of people from a multitude of countries and cultural backgrounds. In fact, in the 2000 census, American citizens described themselves in terms of 63 different racial categories, compared with only 5 in 1990.[1] Cable television, the Internet, social networking sites, and the global marketplace have increased cultural awareness.

What *Diversity* Means

Differences among people. On an interpersonal level, *diversity* refers to the differences among people and among groups of which people are a part. Differences in gender, skin color, ethnicity and national origin, age, and physical characteristics are most obvious. Differences in cultural and religious beliefs and practices, education, sexual orientation, socioeconomic status, family background, and marital and parental status are less visible, but no less significant.

Differences within people. Another layer of diversity lies within each person. Among the factors defining this layer are personality traits, learning preferences, strengths and weaknesses, and talents and interests. No one else has been or ever will be exactly like you.

In college, at work, and as you go about your daily life, you are likely to meet people who reflect America's growing diversity, including:

- Biracial or multiracial individuals
- People from families with more than one religious tradition
- Non-native English speakers, like Gaile, who may have emigrated from outside the United States
- Nontraditional students who are older than "traditional" 18- to 22-year-old students
- People living with various kinds of disabilities
- Gay, lesbian, bi, or transgender individuals
- People practicing different lifestyles, which are often expressed by the way they dress, their interests, their friends, or their leisure activities

Interacting effectively with all kinds of people is crucial to your school and life success and is the goal of *cultural competence*—the ability to understand and appreciate differences among people and adjust your behavior in ways that enhance, rather than detract from, relationships and communication. Risking becoming culturally competent carries significant rewards promoting both school and life success. According to the National Center for Cultural Competence, developing cultural competence involves these five actions:[2]

1. Value diversity.
2. Identify and evaluate personal perceptions and attitudes.
3. Be aware of what happens when different cultures interact.
4. Build knowledge about other cultures.
5. Use what you learn to adapt to diverse cultures as you encounter them.

As you get to know people you collaborate with, you will discover both visible and invisible characteristics and qualities.

In developing cultural competence, you develop practical skills that help you connect to others, bridging the gap between who you are and who they are.[3]

Action #1: Value Diversity

Valuing diversity means having a basic respect for the differences among people and an understanding of what is positive about those differences. You may not like everyone you meet, but if you value diversity, you will tolerate and respect people whether you like them or not, avoid assumptions, and grant them the right to think, feel, and believe without being judged. This attitude helps you to take emotionally intelligent actions, as shown in Key 9.1.

Valuing diversity is about more than just passive *tolerance* of the world around you (not causing conflict but not seeking harmony either). The reward of productive teamwork and deep friendship demands a more significant risk than that. Valuing diversity is about moving toward *acceptance* by actively celebrating differences as an enriching part of life.

Action #2: Identify and Evaluate Personal Perceptions and Attitudes

Bringing emotional intelligence into play, you identify perceptions and attitudes by first noticing your feelings about others, and then evaluating these attitudes by looking at

YOUR ROLE	SITUATION	CLOSED-MINDED RESPONSE	EMOTIONALLY INTELLIGENT RESPONSE
Fellow student	For an assignment, you are paired with a student old enough to be your mother.	You assume the student will be clueless about the modern world. You get ready to react against her preaching about how to do the assignment.	You acknowledge your feelings but try to get to know the student as an individual. You stay open to what you can learn from her experiences and realize you have things to offer as well.
Friend	You are invited to dinner at a friend's house. When he introduces you to his partner, you realize that he is gay.	Uncomfortable with the idea of two men in a relationship, you pretend you have a cell phone call and make an excuse to leave early. You avoid your friend after that.	You have dinner with the two men and make an effort to get to know more about them, both individually and as a couple. You compare your immediate assumptions to what you learned about them at dinner.
Employee	Your new boss is of a different racial and cultural background than yours.	You assume that you and your new boss don't have much in common. Thinking he will be distant and uninterested in you, you already don't like him.	You acknowledge your stereotypes but set them aside to build a relationship with your boss. You adapt to his style and make an effort to get to know him better.

the effect they have on you and others. Many who value the *concept* of diversity experience negative feelings about the *reality* of diversity in their own lives. This disconnect reveals prejudices and stereotypes.

PREJUDICE
A preconceived judgment or opinion formed without just grounds or sufficient knowledge.

Prejudice Almost everyone has some level of **prejudice**, usually on the basis of gender, race, sexual orientation, disability, and religion. People judge others without knowing anything about them because of factors like the following:

- *Influence of family and culture.* Children learn attitudes—including intolerance, superiority, and hate—from their parents, peers, and community.
- *Fear of differences.* It is human to fear and make assumptions about the unfamiliar.
- *Experience.* One bad experience with a person of a particular race or religion may lead someone to condemn all people with the same background.

STEREOTYPE
A standardized mental picture that represents an oversimplified opinion or uncritical judgment.

Stereotypes Prejudice is usually based on **stereotypes**—assumptions made without proof or critical thinking, about the characteristics of a person or group of people, based on factors such as the following:

- *Desire for patterns and logic.* People often try to make sense of the world by using the labels, categories, and generalizations that stereotypes provide.
- *Media influences.* The more people see stereotypical images—the beautiful blonde airhead, the jolly fat man—the easier it is to believe that stereotypes are universal.
- *Laziness.* People often find it easier to group members according to a characteristic they seem to have in common than to ask questions about who each individual really is. It takes conscious thinking to overcome the stereotypes that quickly come to mind.

Stereotypes derail personal connections and block effective communication because pasting a label on a person makes it hard for you to see the real person underneath. Even stereotypes that seem "positive" may be untrue and get in the way of perceiving uniqueness. Key 9.2 lists some "positive" and "negative" stereotypes.

POSITIVE STEREOTYPE	NEGATIVE STEREOTYPE
Women are nurturing.	Women are too emotional for business.
African Americans are great athletes.	African Americans struggle in school.
Hispanic Americans are family oriented.	Hispanic Americans have too many kids.
White people are successful in business.	White people are cold and power hungry.
Gay men have a great sense of style.	Gay men are overly effeminate.
People with disabilities have strength of will.	People with disabilities are bitter.
Older people are wise.	Older people are set in their ways.
Asian Americans are good at math and science.	Asian Americans are poor leaders.

Risk identifying your stereotypical or prejudicial thinking on the way to the reward of cultural competence. Ask analytical questions about your own ideas and beliefs:

- How do I react to differences?
- What prejudices or stereotypes come to mind when I see people, in real life or in the media, who are a different color than I am? From a different culture? Making different choices?
- Where did my prejudices and stereotypes come from?
- Are these prejudices fair? Are these stereotypes accurate?
- How does having prejudices and believing stereotypes harm me?

With the knowledge you gain as you answer these questions, move on to the next stage: looking carefully at what happens when people from different cultures interact.

Action #3: Be Aware of What Happens When Cultures Interact

Interaction among people from different cultures can promote learning, build mutual respect, and broaden perspectives. However, as history has shown, such interaction can also produce problems caused by lack of understanding, prejudice, and stereotypic thinking. At their mildest, these problems create roadblocks that obstruct relationships and communication. At their worst, they set the stage for acts of discrimination and hate crimes.

Discrimination Federal law says you cannot be denied basic opportunities and rights because of your race, creed, color, age, gender, national or ethnic origin, religion, marital status, potential or actual pregnancy, or potential or actual illness or disability (unless the illness or disability prevents you from performing required tasks, and unless accommodations are not possible). Despite these

get creative

EXPAND YOUR PERCEPTION OF DIVERSITY

Complete the following on paper or in digital format.

The ability to respond to people as individuals requires you to become more aware of diversity that is not always on the surface. Start by examining your own uniqueness. Brainstorm 10 words or phrases that describe you. The challenge: Keep references to your ethnicity or appearance to a minimum (brunette, Cuban American, wheelchair dependent, and so on), and fill the list with characteristics others cannot see at a glance (laid-back, only child, 24 years old, drummer, marathoner, interpersonal learner, and so on).

Next, pair up with a classmate whom you do not know well. First list any characteristics you think you know about him or her—chances are most of them will be visible. Then talk with the classmate. As you talk, fill out and correct your lists about each other with what you have discovered from your conversation. Finally, answer two questions.

1. What stands out to you about what you learned about your classmate, and why?

2. Looking at your description of yourself, what would you like people to focus on more often, and why?

DISCRIMINATION
Actions that deny people equal employment, educational, and housing opportunities, or treat people as second-class citizens.

legal protections, discrimination is common and often appears on college campuses. For example, members of campus clubs may reject prospective members because of religious differences, or instructors and students may judge one another according to weight, accent, or body piercings.

Hate crimes When prejudice turns violent, it often manifests itself in *hate crimes*—crimes motivated by a hatred of a specific characteristic thought to be possessed by the victim, usually based on his or her race, ethnicity, or religious or sexual orientation. Because hate crime statistics include only reported incidents, they tell just a part of the story. Many more crimes likely go unreported by victims fearful of what might happen if they contact authorities.

Focusing on the positive aspect of intercultural interaction starts with awareness of the ideas and attitudes that lead to discrimination and hate crimes. With this awareness, you will be better prepared to push past negative possibilities and risk opening your mind to positive ones. Dr. Martin Luther King, Jr., believed that careful thinking could change attitudes. He said:

> The tough-minded person always examines the facts before he reaches conclusions: in short, he postjudges. The tender-minded person reaches conclusions before he has examined the first fact; in short, he prejudges and is prejudiced. . . . There is little hope for us until we become tough minded enough to break loose from the shackles of prejudice, half-truths, and down-right ignorance.[4]

Action #4: Build Cultural Knowledge

The successfully intelligent response to discrimination and hate is to gather knowledge. Taking the risk to learn about people who are different from you, especially those you are likely to meet on campus or on the job, sets you up for productive relationships. How can you begin?

- Read newspapers, books, magazines, and websites that expose you to different perspectives.
- Ask questions of all kinds of people, about themselves and their traditions.

- Observe how people behave, what they eat and wear, how they interact with others.
- Travel internationally to unfamiliar places where you can experience different ways of life.
- Travel locally to equally unfamiliar, but close-by, places where you will encounter a variety of people.
- Build friendships with fellow students or coworkers you would not ordinarily approach.

Some colleges have international exchange programs that can help you appreciate the world's cultural diversity. Engaging with students from other countries, whether they have come to your college or you have chosen to study abroad, can provide a two-way learning experience, helping each of you learn about the other's culture.

Building knowledge also means exploring yourself. Talk with family, read, and seek experiences that educate you about your own cultural heritage; then share what you know with others.

Action #5: Adapt to Diverse Cultures

Now put what you've learned to work with practical actions. Taking the risk to open your mind can bring the reward of extraordinary relationships and new understanding. Let the following suggestions inspire more ideas about what you can do to improve how you relate to others.

- *Look past external characteristics.* If you meet a woman with a disability, get to know her. She may be an accounting major, a guitar player, and a mother. She may love baseball and politics. These characteristics—not just her physical person—describe who she is.
- *Move beyond your feelings.* Engage your emotional intelligence to note what different people make you feel, and then examine the potential effect of those feelings. By working to move beyond feelings that could lead to harmful assumptions and negative outcomes, you will improve your chances for successful communication.
- *Risk putting yourself in other people's shoes.* Ask questions about what other people feel, especially if there's a conflict. Offer friendship to someone new to your class. Seek the reward of mutual understanding.
- *Adjust to cultural differences.* When you understand someone's way of being and put it into practice, you show respect and encourage communication. For example, if a study group member takes offense at a particular kind of language, avoid it when you meet.
- *Climb over language barriers.* When speaking with someone who is struggling with your language, choose words the person is likely to know, avoid slang expressions, be patient, and use body language to fill in what words cannot say. Invite questions, and ask them yourself.
- *Help others.* There are countless ways to make a difference, from providing food or money to a neighbor in need, to sending relief funds to nations devastated by natural disasters. Every act, no matter how small, makes the world that much better. Remember Gaile's story and how she needed help to complete her education so she could help others as a nurse.
- *Stand up against prejudice, discrimination, and hate.* When you hear a prejudiced remark, notice discrimination taking

Risk asking tough questions to be rewarded with new insights. Use the following questions to inspire discussion with classmates, either in person or online.

- What stereotypes seem to stay in your head whether or not you want them to? For each one you can name, identify a person who reinforces it *and* a person who contradicts it.

- Has a point of difference ever kept you from connecting with someone? What makes you hesitate? What reward might you gain from the risk of connection?

CONSIDER THE CASE: Fellow students led Gaile to the course and person who helped her most. When have fellow students helped you—or not—when you needed it? When have you chosen to help or to avoid helping? What resulted from your choice?

place, or suspect a hate crime, make a comment or get help from an authority such as an instructor or dean. Support organizations that encourage tolerance. The reward of keeping someone safe is worth the risk.

- *Recognize that people everywhere have the same basic needs.* Everyone loves, thinks, hurts, hopes, fears, and plans. When you are trying to find common ground with diverse people, remember that you are united through your essential humanity.

Just as there is diversity in skin color and ethnicity, there is also diversity in the way people communicate. Effective communication helps people of all cultures make connections.

HOW CAN YOU
communicate effectively?

Clearly spoken communication promotes success at school, at work, and in personal relationships. Thinking communicators analyze and adjust to different communication styles, learn to give and receive criticism, analyze and make practical use of body language, and work through communication problems.

Adjust to Communication Styles

When you speak, your goal is for listeners to receive the message as you intended. Problems arise when one person has trouble "translating" a message coming from someone using a different communication style. Your knowledge of learning preferences can help you understand and analyze the ways diverse people communicate. Following is a set of communication styles based on the dimensions of the Personality Spectrum self-assessment.

Identifying your styles

Successful communication depends on understanding your personal style and becoming attuned to the styles of others. Following are styles associated with the four dimensions of the Personality Spectrum. No one style is better than another. As you read, keep in mind that these are generalizations—individuals will exhibit a range of variations within each style.

- *Thinkers communicate by focusing on facts and logic.* As speakers, they tend to rely on logical analysis to communicate ideas and prefer a factual, quantitative approach, rather than a conceptual or emotional one. As listeners, they often do best with logical messages. Thinkers also need time to process what they hear before responding (you may have to wait more than a few seconds). Written messages, on paper or by email, are useful because creating them allows time to logically put ideas together.

- *Organizers communicate by focusing on structure and completeness.* As speakers, they tend to deliver well-thought-out, structured messages that fit into an organized plan. As listeners, they often appreciate a well-organized message that defines practical tasks in concrete terms. As with Thinkers, a written format is often an effective form of communication to or from an Organizer.

- *Givers communicate by focusing on concern for others.* As speakers, they tend to cultivate harmony, analyzing what will promote closeness in relationships. As listeners, they often appreciate messages that emphasize personal connection and address the emotional side of an issue. Whether speaking or listening, Givers often favor in-person talks over written messages.

- *Adventurers communicate by focusing on the present.* As speakers, they focus on creative ideas, conveying a message as soon as the idea arises and moving on to the next activity. As listeners, they appreciate up-front, short, direct messages that don't get sidetracked. Like Givers, Adventurers tend to communicate and listen more effectively in person.

What is your style? Use this information as a jumping-off point for your self-exploration. Just as people tend to demonstrate characteristics from more than one dimension of a learning preferences assessment, communicators may demonstrate different styles.

Put your knowledge of communication style to use

Compare these communication styles to your own tendencies and consider how others seem to respond to you. Your practical thinking skills can help you figure out what works well for you, and your creative skills will help you shift your perspective to think about what the other person is thinking or feeling.

Speakers adjust to listeners. Listeners may interpret messages in ways you never intended. For example, consider the following interaction between a Giver (instructor) and a Thinker (student):

Instructor: "Your essay didn't communicate any sense of your personal voice."

Student: "What do you mean? I spent hours writing it. I thought it was on the mark."

- *Without adjustment:* The instructor ignores the student's need for detail and continues to generalize. Comments like, "You need to elaborate. Try writing from the heart. You're not considering your audience" might confuse or discourage the student.

- *With adjustment:* Greater logic and detail will help. For example, the instructor might say: "You've supported your central idea clearly, but you didn't move beyond the facts into your interpretation of what they mean. Your essay reads like a research paper. The language doesn't sound like it is coming directly from you."

Listeners adjust to speakers. As a listener, improve understanding by being aware of differences and translating messages so they make sense to you. For example, consider the following interaction between an Adventurer (employee) and an Organizer (supervisor):

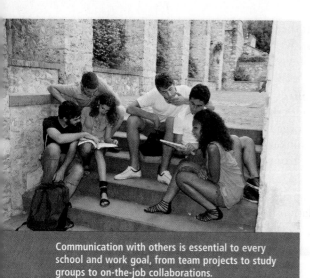

Communication with others is essential to every school and work goal, from team projects to study groups to on-the-job collaborations.

Employee: "I'm upset about the email you sent me. You never talked to me directly and you let the problem build into a crisis. I haven't had a chance to defend myself."

■ *Without adjustment:* If the Organizer supervisor is annoyed by the employee's insistence on direct personal contact, he or she may become defensive: "I told you clearly what needs to be done. I don't know what else there is to discuss."

■ *With adjustment:* In an effort to improve communication, the supervisor responds by encouraging the in-person exchange that is best for the employee. "Let's meet after lunch so you can explain to me how you believe we can improve the situation."

Multiple Intelligences can also provide clues about communication style. The Multiple Intelligence strategies grid for communication on page 231 provides ideas about communication strategies that align with strengths in different intelligences.

Knowing yourself is an important aspect of successful communication. However, adapting to differences between yourself and others, such as generational differences, is essential as well.

Adjust to communication styles within generations

Generations come with personal and lifestyle characteristics that can affect intergenerational communication. Recognizing and adapting to differences caused by generation gaps can help you communicate successfully. Key 9.3 contains helpful communication tips for interacting with various generations.

Although adjusting to communication styles helps you speak and listen more effectively, you also need to understand, and learn how to effectively give and receive criticism.

KEY 9.3 — Communicate with intergenerational awareness.

GENERATION	CHARACTERISTICS	COMMUNICATION CHALLENGES	TIPS FOR COMMUNICATING
Baby Boomers (1946–1964)	• Communication style focuses on personal growth and achievement • Political correctness • Inclined to use both face-to-face and electronic communication	• Can easily misunderstand instant electronic communication (texts, IMs, blogs, etc.) • Uncomfortable with conflict • Judgmental	• Be open and direct (Baby Boomers are the "show me" generation) • Use face-to-face or electronic communication • Provide details
Generation X (1965–1980)	• Communication style is casual, pragmatic, skeptical • Unimpressed by authority • Prefers email	• Impatient • Cynical • Often limits communication to email or other noninteractive forms of communication	• Use email as primary communication • Ask for feedback • Keep it short to maintain their attention • Use an informational communication style
Generation Y (a.k.a. Millennials) (1980–1994)	• Self-expression over self-control • Respect must be earned • Comfortable with online communication • Spend a lot of time online	• Too much information readily accessible • Teaching older generations to use technology • Eroding sense of respect for elders • Inexperienced dealing with others in person	• Use email, voicemail, and texts • Communicate with visuals • Use humor • Respect their knowledge • Encourage them to break rules when thinking

Note: The majority of people from all generations prefer face-to-face communication to written or electronic communication.

Source: Some information is from a table on different generations by Hammil, Greg. "Mixing and Managing Four Generations of Employees." *FDU Magazine,* Winter/Spring 2005. From http://www.fdu.edu/newspubs/magazine/05ws/generations.htm

multiple intelligences strategies

Describe an upcoming study group meeting or team project (course, topic): _____.
In the right-hand column, record specific ideas for how MI strategies can help you make the most of it.

INTELLIGENCE	USE MI STRATEGIES TO IMPROVE COMMUNICATION	IDENTIFY MI COMMUNICATION STRATEGIES THAT CAN HELP YOU WORK WELL WITH OTHERS
Verbal-Linguistic	• Find opportunities to express your thoughts and feelings to others—either in writing or in person. • Keep in mind that listening to words is at least as important as speaking them.	
Logical-Mathematical	• Allow yourself time to think through a problem before discussing it. Write out an argument on paper and rehearse it. • When communicating with others whose styles are not as logic-focused, ask specific questions to learn the facts you need.	
Bodily-Kinesthetic	• Have an important talk while walking, running, or performing a task that does not involve concentration. • Work out to burn off excess energy before having an important discussion.	
Visual-Spatial	• Make a drawing or diagram of points you want to communicate during an important discussion. • If you are in a formal classroom or work setting, use visual aids to explain your main points.	
Interpersonal	• If you tend to dominate group conversation, focus more on listening. • If you tend to prioritize listening to others, work on becoming more assertive about expressing your opinion.	
Intrapersonal	• Be as clear as possible when expressing what you know about yourself, and recognize that not all communicators may be self-aware. • When you have a difficult encounter, take time alone to decide how to communicate more effectively next time.	
Musical	• Before communicating difficult thoughts or feelings, work through them by writing a poem or song. • Be sensitive to the rhythms of a conversation. Sense when to voice your opinion and when to hang back.	
Naturalistic	• Use your ability to recognize patterns to evaluate communication situations. Employ patterns that work well and avoid those that do not. • When appropriate, make an analogy from the natural world of plants or animals to clarify a point in a conversation.	

Diversity and Communication

Know How to Give and Take Criticism

Criticism can be either constructive or unconstructive. **Constructive criticism** is a practical problem-solving strategy involving goodwill suggestions for improving a situation. In contrast, unconstructive criticism focuses on what went wrong, doesn't offer alternatives to help solve the problem, and is often delivered negatively, creating bad feelings.

Constructive criticism can help bring about important changes. Consider someone who is continually late for study group sessions. Which comment from the group leader would encourage a change in behavior?

■ *Constructive.* The group leader talks privately with the student: "I've noticed you've been late a lot. We count on you to contribute. Is there a problem that is keeping you from being on time? Can we help?"

■ *Unconstructive.* The leader watches the student arrive late and says, in front of everyone, "If you can't start getting here on time, there's really no point in your coming."

At school, instructors criticize classwork, papers, and exams. On the job, criticism may come from supervisors, coworkers, or customers. No matter the source, constructive comments can help you grow. Be open to what you hear, and remember that most people want you to succeed.

Offering constructive criticism. Use the following strategies to be effective:

■ *Criticize the behavior, not the person.* Avoid personal attacks. "You've been late to five group meetings" is preferable to "You're lazy."

■ *Define the specific problem.* Try to focus on the facts, backing them up with specific examples and minimizing emotions.

■ *Suggest new approaches and offer help.* Talk about practical ways to handle the situation. Generate creative options. Help the person feel supported.

■ *Use a positive approach and hopeful language.* Express your belief that the person can turn the situation around.

Receiving criticism. Being open to criticism is a challenging risk, but the potential rewards of positive change make it worth the discomfort. When receiving criticism:

■ *Analyze the comments.* Listen carefully and then evaluate what you heard. What does it mean? What is the intent? Try to let unconstructive comments go without responding.

■ *Ask for suggestions on how to change your behavior.* Be open to what others say.

■ *Summarize the criticism and your response.* The goal is for all to understand the situation.

■ *Use a specific strategy.* Use problem-solving skills to analyze the problem, brainstorm ways to change, choose a strategy, and take practical action to make it happen.

Criticism, as well as other thoughts and feelings, may be communicated nonverbally. You will become a more effective communicator if you understand body language.

Understand Body Language

Body language has an extraordinary capacity to express people's real feelings through gestures, eye movements, facial expressions, body positioning and posture, touching behaviors, vocal tone, and use of personal space. Why is it important to know how to analyze body language?

■ **Nonverbal cues shade meaning.** What you say can mean different things depending on body positioning or vocal tone. The statement "That's a great idea" sounds positive. However, said while sitting with your arms and legs crossed and looking away, it may communicate that you dislike the idea. Said sarcastically, the tone may reveal that you consider the idea a joke.

get analytical

GIVE CONSTRUCTIVE CRITICISM

Complete the following on paper or in digital format.

Think of a situation that could be improved if you were able to offer constructive criticism to a friend or family member.

1. Describe the situation and name the improvement you seek.

2. Imagine that you have a chance to speak to this person. First describe the setting—time, place, and atmosphere—where you think you would be most successful.

3. Now develop your "script." Analyze the situation and decide on what you think would be the most constructive approach. Free write what you would say. Keep in mind the goal you want your communication to achieve. Revise what you wrote as necessary.

4. Finally, if you can, make your plan a reality. Will you do it?

5. If you do have the conversation, analyze the result. Was it worth it?

- *Different cultures use body language differently.* Be aware that ways of standing, sitting, or looking may mean different things in different countries. For example, in the United States, looking away from someone during a conversation may be a sign of anger or distress; elsewhere, the same behavior can signify respect.

- *Nonverbal communication strongly influences first impressions.* Nonverbal elements including tone of voice, posture, eye contact, and speed and style of movement usually have a bigger impact than the actual words you say.

Although reading body language is not an exact science, the following practical strategies will help you use it to improve communication.

- *Pay attention to what is said through nonverbal cues.* Focus on your tone, your body position, and whether your cues reinforce or contradict your words. Then look for meaning in the physical behavior of your listeners. For example, if their arms are crossed, they may be resisting what you are saying.

- *Adjust behavior based on cultural differences.* In cross-cultural conversation, discover what seems appropriate by paying attention to what others do and how they react to you. Then consider changes based on your observations. For example, when meeting someone from Japan for the first time, a nod or a small bow might be the most appropriate gesture.

- *Adjust body language to the person or situation.* What body language might you use when making a presentation in class? In a meeting with your advisor? When confronting an angry coworker? Think through how to use your physicality. For example, when making suggestions, you might consider opening your arms or hands to show you are open to ideas.

Effective verbal and nonverbal communication play a big part in your success in school and work, especially when you are part of a team.

Work in Teams

Much of your school and work experience will involve teamwork, both in-person and virtually. Being part of a team means knowing how to collaborate as well as how to lead.

Know how to collaborate

Collaboration means working effectively with others to achieve a common goal. It is built on trust, which can only be achieved through the following:

- *Honesty.* Team members tell one another the truth, not just what each wants to hear, so they can work together to solve problems and overcome obstacles.
- *Openness.* Team members risk saying what is on their minds and share information because they understand the reward of productivity depends on it.
- *Consistency.* Each team member works and interacts in a consistent manner, and team members consistently do what they say they will do.
- *Respect.* Team members see one another as vital parts of the team and speak, listen, and behave respectfully toward one another.

Know how to lead

You may be called upon to lead your team, as well as participate in it. Being a leader is a risk, but the reward for effective leadership is getting things done. Here are some tips for being an effective leader:

- Communicate clearly so your team understands what you are trying to accomplish and why, and how they fit into your vision.
- Set goals for yourself and your team so everyone knows what to do and when.
- Be clear on the skills and talents you have and those that others have so you know how to best contribute and how to delegate the right tasks to others.
- Manage your own time and help others stay on track so your team completes tasks on time.
- Follow through—finish what you start.

Effective team meetings

To ensure you accomplish your goals during a meeting, follow good meeting etiquette:

- *Show up on time.* If you cannot avoid being late, call, text, or email to let people know. Then apologize briefly when you arrive.
- *Be prepared.* Make sure you have all necessary materials. Do a "tech check" ahead of time to make sure your equipment is working (computer, software, and video projector).
- *Use an agenda and take notes.* Communicate the goal of the meeting, the items that will be covered, and how long it will last. Then stick to that agenda and have someone take notes.
- *Listen and don't interrupt.* Listen to what the person is saying instead of planning your response or interrupting. When it's your turn, you will appreciate not being interrupted.
- *Practice civility.* No matter how angry or frustrated you feel, do not get overly emotional. Also, if you have an issue with someone, talk to him or her privately after the meeting.
- *Avoid distractions.* If you text or take phone calls during a meeting, you will seem rude and may miss important information. Give your full attention to the meeting and your teammates.
- *Meet virtually.* If you encounter scheduling conflicts, keep in mind that you can use virtual meeting technology to communicate when your group cannot gather in person.

Make an Effective Presentation

Some courses require individual students or teams of students to give a presentation at some point in the term. Many people dread this event, but if you think of a presentation as a friendly conversation with a group of people, it may be less stressful. Building this important workplace skill requires the risk of trying it over and over again. To prepare for a presentation that will resonate with your listeners, do the following:

- *Identify your audience.* Because you give a presentation to other people, you need to know who they are and why they would want to listen to you. Understanding their motivation will help you choose your topic, words, and tone.
- *Identify your goal.* Get clear on the outcome you hope to achieve. Do you want your audience to do something? Do you want to change the way they think about something? Do you want to solve a problem? This goal becomes the purpose of the presentation and drives its content.
- *Identify your speaking points.* To achieve your goal, what points do you need to make? Certain information will be necessary to inform, educate, or persuade your audience.
- *Add visual aids.* Images draw people's attention, explain complicated concepts, and help people remember important information. You can use a flip chart or a white board to draw or write as you go, or use prepared slides, videos, or animation—anything that enhances your audience's understanding of the topics in the presentation.
- *Keep text to a minimum.* If you choose to use slides, do *not* put down every word you plan to say. Simply note important points you want people to remember and then elaborate on them with your own words. For helpful advice, check out www. presentationzen.com.
- *Tell a story.* If you really want people to remember what you say, weave in stories throughout your presentation. People remember stories better than they remember individual facts. Give real examples. Share personal experiences. Break up your talk with humorous anecdotes. Your presentation will stick with people when you tell stories.

Whether you work by yourself, one-on-one with individuals, or in large groups, a primary goal of successful communication is to build and maintain good relationships with family, friends, and others you encounter in your daily life. All the communication and cultural competence strategies you've read about will contribute to that goal. Read on for more ways to navigate your relationships successfully.

HOW DO YOU MAKE THE MOST
of personal relationships?

Personal connections with friends, classmates, spouses, partners, and parents can be sources of great satisfaction and inner peace. Good relationships can motivate you to do your best in school and on the job. Commitment requires risk, however, and the reward doesn't always last. When conflicts arise or relationships fall apart, it can affect your ability to function in all areas of your life. Relationships have enormous power.

Following are some straightforward ways to make your personal relationships as good as they can be, and to manage problems when things move in the wrong direction.

Use Positive Relationship Strategies

When you devote time and energy to education, work, and activities you enjoy, you get positive results. The same is true of human connections. Here are a few ways to nurture relationships:

- *Approach people and conversations with emotional intelligence.* The more you can notice feelings, understand what they mean, and handle them in ways that bring people closer to you instead of pushing them away, the better your relationships will be.

YOUR PERSONAL RELATIONSHIP WITH MONEY

Complete the following on paper or in digital format.

Think about how you relate to money and why. Answer the following questions.

1. Do members of your family discuss finances? If they do, what do they talk about? If they do not discuss finances, why do you think that is?
2. Do you spend money on things you want but do not need? If and when you do, how do you feel before, during, and after the purchase? One week later?
3. How does the topic of money make you feel?
4. How often, and how regularly, do you actively manage your money?
5. What do you feel are your biggest problems with money?
6. Do you borrow money from friends or family? If so, how do you pay it back—on time or not, all at once or in smaller amounts, not at all?
7. Do you talk with friends and family about money problems? Why or why not?
8. Based on your answers, how would you summarize your relationship with money in a short paragraph?

- *If you want a friend, be a friend.* If you treat others with the kind of loyalty and support that you appreciate, you are likely to receive the same in return.
- *Spend time with people you respect and admire.* Life is too short to hang out with people who bring you down or encourage you to ignore your values.
- *Work through tensions.* Negative feelings can fester when left unspoken. Risk discussing a problem as early as you can for a better chance at the reward of solving it; then compromise, forgive, or move on.
- *Risk revealing yourself.* It can be frightening to expose your dreams and frustrations, to devote yourself to a friend, or to fall in love. However, if you open yourself up, you stand to gain the incredible rewards of companionship.
- *Find a relationship style that suits you.* Some students date exclusively and commit early, and others date casually. Some students prefer to socialize in groups. Some are in committed long-term partnerships. Be honest with yourself and others about what you want in a relationship.
- *If a relationship fails, find ways to cope.* When an important relationship with an individual or a group becomes strained or breaks up, analyze the situation and choose practical strategies to move on. Some people need time alone; others need to be with friends and family. Some need a change of scene; some need to let off steam with exercise or other activities. Whatever you do, in time you will emerge from the experience stronger.

Plug into Communication Technology without Losing Touch

Modern technology has revolutionized the way people communicate. You can call or text on a mobile phone; write a note via email, instant message, or Twitter; communicate through blogs and chat rooms; use social networking sites such as Facebook, Instagram, and more. Although communication technology allows you to communicate faster, more

KEY 9.4 Electronic communication has positive and negative effects.

Advantages of electronic communication	Disadvantages of electronic communication
Able to communicate faster	Easy to reveal information that is inappropriate or too personal, potentially having a negative impact on jobs or careers
Able to communicate with many people at one time	Without hearing a voice or seeing facial expression, easy to misunderstand or misinterpret messages
Messages can be revised before sending and can be forwarded easily to others	Can be addictive, encouraging procrastination during study time and making it tough to sustain focus on important tasks
Can build confidence for those who struggle in face-to-face situations	Can limit interpersonal abilities and face-to-face interaction skills such as the ability to read nonverbal cues
Enables communication anytime and makes near-instant responses possible	Being reachable at all times can increase stress and anxiety

frequently, and with more people than ever before, it has its drawbacks. Key 9.4 shows some positive and negative aspects of communication technology.

As freeing and convenient as it may be to communicate electronically in a faceless environment, its low-risk feeling matches its limited potential for reward. Real life demands that people effectively interact face-to-face. It's important to keep up your interpersonal communication skills and fine-tune your ability to read nonverbal cues. It's also crucial to make sure that you don't prioritize electronic communication over in-person, real-time interaction (think about how you feel when a friend you are with spends half your time together texting). In addition, elecronic communication can compromise your privacy. See Key 9.5 for seven strategies for safeguarding your privacy and personal information.

Aim for electronic communication to *enhance* real-time interaction rather than *replace* it. Ask questions to develop your own personal communication "recipe": How do you prefer to communicate with others? What forms of communication do you use, and what are the effects? Consider keeping a time journal. Whenever you use an electronic device, log the time you start and the time you stop. Review the log after a week, think about the results, and consider whether you need to make changes to improve the balance in your life.

Whether online or in person, conflict occurs within nearly every relationship, and it can cause anger. With effort, you can manage both conflict and anger (and stay away from those who cannot).

1.

Password-protect your devices.
Make sure only you can access personal information on your smartphone, tablet, or computer, and don't give out your password

7.

Don't spread gossip online.
Information online moves at breakneck speed and remains available indefinitely, and gossip you spread will be easily traced to you and can cause trouble.

2.

Use theft-recovery applications.
Apps such as Find My Phone can locate a lost or stolen device.

Take Steps to Protect Your Privacy

6.

Shop securely.
Look for websites with URLs starting with https, which are the most secure.

3.

Use conservative social networking privacy settings.
Make sure you are not letting information roam too far from your close network.

5.

Be wary of revealing your location.
Instead of using Foursquare or other location apps, consider texting your location to only those few people who need to know it.

4.

Protect your online reputation.
Make sure that everything you post on a blog, social network, or chat forum is something you would be comfortable with an instructor or employer seeing

Source: Maier, Fran. "Back to School: 10 Privacy Tips for the Connected Student" (Retitled: "Take Steps to Protect Your Privacy"). *Mashable,* September 7, 2011. From http://mashable.com/2011/09/07/privacy-back-to-school. Copyright (c) 2011 by Fran Maier. Used by Permission of Fran Maier.

Manage Conflict

Conflicts, both large and small, arise when there is a clash of ideas or interests. You may have small conflicts with a housemate over a door left unlocked. You may have a major conflict with your partner about finances or with an instructor about a failing grade. Conflict, as unpleasant as it can be, is a natural element in the dynamic of getting along with others. Prevent conflict when you can—and when you can't, use problem-solving strategies as soon as possible to resolve it.

Conflict prevention strategies

The following two strategies can help prevent conflict from starting in the first place.

Send "I" messages. "I" messages communicate your needs rather than attacking someone else. Creating these messages involves some simple rephrasing: "You didn't lock the door!" becomes "I was worried when I came home and found the door unlocked." "I" statements soften the conflict by highlighting the effects the other person's actions have on you, rather than focusing on the person or the actions themselves.

Be assertive. Most people tend to express themselves in one of three ways—aggressively, assertively, or passively. *Aggressive* communicators focus primarily on their own needs and become impatient when needs are not satisfied. *Passive* communicators focus primarily on the needs of others and often deny themselves power, causing frustration. *Assertive* communicators are able to declare and affirm their opinions while respecting the rights of others to do the same. Assertive behavior strikes a balance between aggres-

student PROFILE

Jad El-Adaimi

CALIFORNIA POLYTECHNIC STATE UNIVERSITY,
SAN LUIS OBISPO, CALIFORNIA

About me:

I went to school in Lebanon. Then I came to Cupertino, California, where I attended De Ana College for two years and attained my A.S. degree in biological sciences. I then transferred to Cal Poly in San Luis Obispo and graduated in June of 2010 with a B.S. in molecular and cellular biology. I started my master's program in September of 2010.

What I focus on:

I grew up in Lebanon, where almost everyone was Lebanese. I was open and friendly with everyone, but had never lived with people from other cultures. When I came to college in the U.S. that all changed. I met people from around the world. I worked and studied with people from different backgrounds. In the beginning I felt disconnected and tried finding friends from my area of the world. This did not help me adjust; instead, I felt homesick. However, as soon as I started broadening my perspective of cultures and communicating with everyone, everything changed.

We learn from everyone around us. I started being less secluded and more outgoing, and became closer to people from all over the U.S. and the world. This meant I learned a few words from each person's language, ate their food, celebrated some of their holidays, and respected their traditions. Broadening my communication allowed me to adjust to different cultures and people, and helped me transfer successfully from De Anza to Cal Poly.

What will help me in the workplace:

We build our personality and experiences through the people around us. When you start a new job you meet new people. Learn to adjust to individuals and accept them for who they are, within your limits. This way you can do your work at the highest standard and still remain social and enjoy your workplace. Accepting people or at least adjusting to them in some manner will help in any situation.

---

sion and passivity and promotes the most productive communication. Key 9.6 contrasts these three communication styles.

What can aggressive and passive communicators do to move toward an assertive style? Aggressive communicators might take time before speaking, use "I" statements, listen to others, and avoid giving orders. Passive communicators might acknowledge their anger, express opinions, exercise the right to make requests, and know that their ideas and feelings are important.

KEY 9.6 — Assertiveness fosters successful communication.

AGGRESSIVE	ASSERTIVE	PASSIVE
Blaming, name-calling, and verbal insults: "You created this mess!"	Expressing yourself and letting others do the same: "I have thoughts about this— first, what is your opinion?"	Feeling you have no right to express anger: "No, I'm fine."
Escalating arguments: "You'll do it my way, no matter what it takes."	Using "I" statements to defuse arguments: "I am uncomfortable with that choice and want to discuss it."	Avoiding arguments: "Whatever you want to do is fine."
Being demanding: "Do this."	Asking and giving reasons: "Please consider doing it this way, and here's why. ... "	Being noncommittal: "I'm not sure what the best way to handle this is. ...."

get practical

CONFLICT PREVENTION STRATEGIES

Complete the following on paper or in digital format.

1. Name two ways to manage conflict and anger that seem effective to you.

2. Think of a conflict you were involved in over the past year—one that was not resolved well. Choose which of the two listed strategies you believe would have helped you prevent it or at least manage it more effectively. Describe the impact you think the strategy would have had on the situation. What might the other party's reaction have been?

3. Now, ask yourself *why* the technique would have been beneficial. What issue in the conflict does this technique address or improve?

4. Name two other situations in which this technique might prove useful. For each, describe how you think it would play out.

Conflict resolution

All too often, people deal with conflict through *avoidance* (a passive tactic that shuts down communication and may cause problems to fester and worsen) or *escalation* (an aggressive tactic that often leads to fighting). Conflict resolution demands calm communication, motivation, and careful thinking. Use analytical, creative, and practical thinking skills to apply a problem-solving plan. Thinking through conflict using the steps that a problem-solving plan provides will help you step back from it and focus on the issue that underlies the anger.

Trying to calm anger is an important part of resolving conflict. All people get angry at times—at people, events, and themselves. However, excessive anger can contaminate relationships, stifle communication, and turn friends and family away.

Manage Anger

Strong emotions can get in the way of happiness and success. It is hard to concentrate on American history when you are raging over a nasty email or a bad grade. Psychologists report that angry outbursts may actually make things worse. The first and most important strategy for anger management is to take time before you react. Then, with a cooler attitude, you can address the problem more productively. Here are some ways to pause when you feel yourself losing control.

- *Try to calm down.* Breathe slowly. Slowly repeat a phrase like "Relax" or "Let it go."
- *Change your environment.* Take a break from what's upsetting you. Take a walk, go to the gym, or see a movie. Come up with a creative idea that will help you settle down.
- *Think before you speak.* When angry, people tend to say the first thing that comes to mind, even if it's hurtful. Instead, wait until you are in control before you say something.
- *Problem solve.* Instead of blowing up, analyze a challenging situation, make a plan, and begin. Even if it doesn't work, making the effort may help cool your anger.

Finally, get help if you need it. If you can't keep your anger in check, you may need help from a counselor. Many schools have mental health professionals available to students.

What happened to Gaile? Gaile's Honors 100 course instructor Dr. Barbara Clinton, also the head of the Highline honors program, helped her express her strengths in her portfolio and résumé and take productive risks toward the rewards she sought. After Gaile shared her financial concerns, Dr. Clinton helped her find and win scholarships for which she was eligible. With newfound confidence, Gaile took risks that rewarded her with employment authorization from the Immigration and Naturalization Service and a job as a critical care nurse technician. She graduated in 2007 and started working as a registered nurse. She has completed a bachelor's in nursing from the University of Washington at Tacoma, and will soon have permanent resident status.[5]

What does this mean for you? Everyone needs a person who can be a "resource for life," like Dr. Clinton was for Gaile. This person can help bring out strengths and provide support and encouragement as you take risks. Who could be your resource for life? Make two lists, each with at least five people's names (friends, family, faculty, work acquaintances, anyone you know personally). One list identifies people who you know well, who already support you and care about you. The other list identifies people you don't know as well but that you admire and feel you could learn from. Choose one person from each list and brainstorm a short paragraph about what you think you need from that person as a mentor.

What risk may bring reward beyond your world? Your needs are important and so are the needs of others. Risk reaching beyond your world to mentor someone who could use your help. Check out www.mentoring.org as a start to find out more about what mentoring involves and what kinds of programs are already in place for people who want to mentor others. Look into a program from that website, a program at your college or in your community, or start making more regular contact with someone in need on your own. Your presence will reward the person you mentor, as well as yourself.

RISK ACTION
FOR COLLEGE, CAREER, AND LIFE REWARDS

Complete the following on paper or in digital format.

KNOW IT *Think Critically*

Build basic skills. Review the five actions for cultural competence earlier in this chapter. Reread the suggestions for Action 5: Adapt to Diverse Cultures on pages 227–228. For the three strategies listed at the top of the next page, give a real-life version (something you've done or know someone else has done). For example, by choosing to wear a blindfold for an entire day as part of a "Blind for a Day" experience, students put themselves in other people's shoes.

Diversity and Communication

1. Put yourself in other people's shoes.
2. Adjust to cultural differences.
3. Help others in need.

Take it to the next level. Make these three strategies into personal plans. Rewrite them as specific actions you are willing to take in the next six months. For example, "help others in need" might become "Sign up as a tutor for the Writing Center."

Move toward mastery. Choose one of the three plans to put into action in the next 30 days (or even tomorrow, if you can). Choose wisely—recall your knowledge of SMART goals and pick the one that is most attainable and realistic. Name your choice. Describe your goal with this action—how you want to make a difference.

Finally, do it. Name the date by which you plan to have taken action.

WRITE IT *Communicate*

Emotional intelligence journal: Your experience with prejudice. Have you ever been discriminated against or experienced any other type of prejudice? Have you been on the other end and acted with prejudice yourself? Describe what happened and your feelings about the situation. If you have no personal experience, describe a situation you have seen or heard about. Outline an emotionally intelligent response that you feel would bring something positive or helpful out of the situation.

Real-life writing: Improve communication. Few students make use of the wealth of ideas and experience that academic advisors can offer. Think of a question you have regarding a specific course, major, or academic situation that your advisor might help you answer. Craft an email in appropriate language to your advisor, and send it. Then, to stretch your communication skills, rewrite the same email twice more: once in a format you would send to an instructor, and once in a format appropriate for a friend. Send either or both of these if you think the response would be valuable to you.

WORK IT *Build Your Brand*

Write a Job Interview Cover Letter

21st Century Learning Building Blocks

- Communication and collaboration
- Financial, economic, business, and entrepreneurial literacy
- Leadership and responsibility

To secure a job interview, you will have to create a cover letter to accompany your résumé. With this key communication tool, you can pull out your best selling points from your résumé and highlight them to a potential employer so the employer wants to read your résumé.

Write a one-page, three-paragraph cover letter to a prospective employer, describing your background and explaining your value to the company. Be creative—you may use fictitious names, but select a career and industry that interest you. Use the format shown in Key 9.7.

- *Introductory paragraph:* Start with a statement that convinces the employer to read on. You might name a person the employer knows who suggested you write, or refer to something positive about the company that you read in the newspaper or on the Internet. Identify the position for which you are applying, and tell the employer why you are interested in working for the company.
- *Middle paragraph:* Sell your value. Try to convince the employer that hiring you will help the company in some way. Center your "sales effort" on your experience in school and the workplace. If possible, tie your qualifications to the needs of the company. Refer indirectly to your enclosed résumé.
- *Final paragraph:* Close with a call to action. Ask the employer to call you or tell the employer to expect your call to arrange an interview.

First_name Last_name
1234 Your Street
City, ST 12345

March 15, 2015

Ms. Prospective Employer
Prospective Company
3432 Their Street
City, ST 54321

Dear Ms. Employer:

Mr. X, career center advisor at Y college, recommended I write to you about the position of production assistant at KWKW Radio. I read the description of the job and your company on the career center's employment-opportunity bulletin board, and I would like to apply for the position. I have greatly admired your station's programming over the past four years and believe I would be a good fit for the position.

I am a senior at Y College and will graduate this spring with a degree in communications. Ever since I declared my major in my sophmore year, I have wanted to pursue a career in radio. For the last year I have worked as a production intern at KCOL Radio, the college's station, and have occasionally filled in as disc jockey after the evening news show. I enjoy being on the air, but my primary interest is production and programming. My enclosed résumé will tell you more about my background and experience.

I would enjoy talking with you in person so I can learn more about your station and the position, and you can learn more about me. You can reach me anytime at 555/555-5555 or by email at xxxx@xx.com. Thank you for your consideration, and I look forward to meeting you.

Sincerely,

Sign Your Name Here

First_name Last_name

Enclosure: Résumé *[use this notation if you have included a résumé or other item with your letter]*

Exchange your first draft of the cover letter with a classmate. Read each other's letters and make marginal notes to improve impact and persuasiveness, writing style, grammar, punctuation, and spelling. Discuss and then make corrections. Create a final draft for your portfolio.

10

Because stress and health are linked, every action you take to improve your physical and mental health can also increase your ability to cope with stress.

Wellness and Stress Management

STAYING HEALTHY IN MIND AND BODY

What Would You Risk? *Kelly Addington and Becca Tieder*

THINK ABOUT THIS SITUATION AS YOU READ, AND CONSIDER WHAT ACTION YOU WOULD TAKE. THIS CHAPTER EXAMINES WAYS TO MANAGE STRESS THROUGH HEALTH MAINTENANCE, HANDLE PHYSICAL AND MENTAL HEALTH ISSUES, AND MAKE EFFECTIVE DECISIONS ABOUT SUBSTANCES AND SEX.

Kelly and Becca were typical students and close friends. They studied hard and enjoyed the nonacademic side of the college experience. One Saturday night, they were socializing and drinking moderately at a local beach bar. Kelly accepted a ride home from a designated driver, a male friend with whom she felt secure.

The next morning, Kelly felt ill with what she thought was simply a hangover. She couldn't remember what had happened the previous night. But the headaches persisted, and she had nightmares and visions of someone on top of her and of feeling suffocated. She took a pregnancy test and it was positive, even though she had not had sexual intercourse in a year. After confiding in Becca, Kelly took another pregnancy test to be sure. It, too, was positive.

Becca and Kelly put the pieces together: Kelly was a victim of date rape. Her male friend had slipped a date rape drug into her drink, then sexually assaulted her. She called the friend, who claimed that Kelly was "begging" for sex that night. "I had a lot of trust issues from that," Kelly says, "because this is someone I cared about and someone I thought I could trust."

Kelly later suffered a miscarriage. Physically, she would recover. Mentally, however, she was shaken and vulnerable. Did she do something to deserve this? What would her parents think? What would she need to risk to be able to have healthy self-esteem or a positive sexual relationship? "Within six months to a year after being sexually assaulted," Kelly says, "the only thing I was trying to do was forget what happened."

To be continued . . .

KELLY AND BECCA'S DETERMINATION HAS LED THEM TO DISCOVER PERSONAL EMPOWERMENT AND DELIVER A POWERFUL MESSAGE TO THE COLLEGE POPULATION. YOU'LL LEARN MORE ABOUT KELLY AND BECCA, AND THE REWARDS RESULTING FROM THEIR ACTIONS, WITHIN THE CHAPTER.

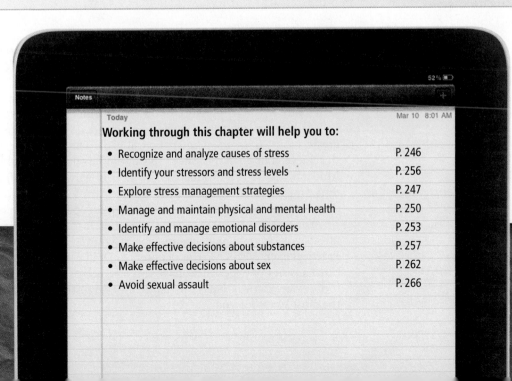

Working through this chapter will help you to:

statusCHECK

How Effectively Do You Maintain Your Personal Wellness?

For each statement, fill in the number that best describes how often it applies to you.

1 = never   2 = seldom   3 = sometimes   4 = often   5 = always

1. I know that my health is a major factor in my success as a college student. ① ② ③ ④ ⑤

2. I am able to delay gratification when I know the reward is worth it. ① ② ③ ④ ⑤

3. I eat a healthy, balanced diet, and rarely overeat or undereat. ① ② ③ ④ ⑤

4. I make it a point to exercise regularly in some way. ① ② ③ ④ ⑤

5. I consistently get eight to nine hours of sleep per night. ① ② ③ ④ ⑤

6. I understand what constitutes sexual abuse, avoid abusive behaviors, and work to stay safe. ① ② ③ ④ ⑤

7. When I am feeling "out of it," I use healthy methods to elevate my mood. ① ② ③ ④ ⑤

8. I know the ways in which addiction can affect my life. ① ② ③ ④ ⑤

9. I understand the potential consequences of substance use and make choices based on that knowledge. ① ② ③ ④ ⑤

10. I understand the potential consequences of sexual activity and feel comfortable with my choices. ① ② ③ ④ ⑤

Each of the topics in these statements is covered in this chapter. Note those statements for which you filled in a 3 or lower. Skim the chapter to see where those topics appear, and pay special attention to them as you read, learn, and apply new strategies.

REMEMBER: NO MATTER HOW WELL YOU TAKE CARE OF YOURSELF, YOU CAN IMPROVE WITH EFFORT AND PRACTICE.

HOW CAN FOCUSING ON HEALTH
help you manage stress?

If you're feeling high levels of *stress*—the physical or mental strain that occurs when your body reacts to pressure—you're not alone. Stress levels tend to be high among college students, who are frequently overloaded with activities and responsibilities. The greater your stress, the greater the toll it may take on your health and on your ability to achieve your goals. However, this doesn't mean you should try to get rid of *all* stress. Moderate stress is a productive risk that rewards you with motivation to do well on tests, finish assignments on time, and prepare for presentations. Key 10.1 shows that stress can increase or decrease performance, depending on how much you experience.

Your ability to manage stress depends in part on your understanding of how it affects you. Certain assessments look at your level of exposure to stressors. In the Get Practical exercise later in this chapter, you will fill out an assessment that asks you how often a series of experiences have recently been part of your life. With the information it provides, you will have a better idea of how stressed you are and what factors cause the most stress for you.

CHAPTER 10

Wellness and Stress Management

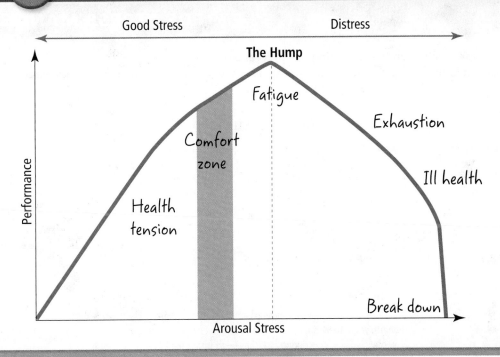

Source: The American Institute of Stress, "Stress, Definition of Stress, Stressor, What Is Stress? Eustress?" from The American Institute of Stress website, accessed on December 26, 2006 at www.stress.org/topic-definition-stress.htmn, 2006.

Although you cannot always control what happens to you, you can control your response. Being as physically and mentally healthy as possible is crucial to responding productively to stress. In fact, you are on your way to becoming more healthy by simply being in school. Scientists and researchers who study aging report that more education is linked to a longer life, perhaps because education teaches cause-and-effect thinking that helps people make better choices. Another link could be that educated people tend to be more able to **delay gratification**, which helps you to avoid harmful habits.[1]

No one is able to make healthy choices and delay gratification all the time. However, you can pledge to do your best to maintain your health. As you consider the range of choices, think through what risks you are willing to take to earn the reward of a healthy body and mind. Think also about stress-management techniques that may relate to different intelligences (see the Multiple Intelligence Strategies for Stress Management on page 248 for ideas).

DELAY GRATIFICATION
Putting aside an immediate pleasure or reward to gain a more substantial one later.

Eat Well

Making intelligent choices about what you eat can lead to more energy, better general health, and an improved quality of life. However, this is easier said than done. One reason is that the food environment in which most Americans live is characterized by an overabundance of unhealthy food choices, and the cheapest choices are usually not the best. College students often live on limited budgets, so such an environment does not support their efforts to choose well.[2]

Day-to-day college life is also an issue. Students spend hours sitting and tend to eat on the run, build social events around food, and eat as a reaction to stress. Even though recent research has shown that students average less weight gain than the "freshman 15," they still tend to put on weight, and may experience low energy and health issues related to food choices.[3]

multiple intelligence strategies

FOR STRESS MANAGEMENT

Name a current task or situation that is causing a high level of stress: _____.
In the right-hand column, record specific ideas for how MI strategies can help you manage that stress.

INTELLIGENCE	USE MI STRATEGIES TO MANAGE STRESS	IDENTIFY MI STRATEGIES THAT CAN HELP YOU MANAGE AND REDUCE STRESS
Verbal-Linguistic	• Keep a journal of what situations, people, or events cause stress. • Write letters or email friends about your problems.	
Logical-Mathematical	• Think through problems using a problem-solving process, and devise a detailed plan. • Analyze the negative and positive effects that may result from a stressful situation.	
Bodily-Kinesthetic	• Choose a physical activity that helps you release tension—running, yoga, team sports—and do it regularly. • Plan physical activities during free time—go for a hike, take a bike ride, go dancing with friends.	
Visual-Spatial	• Enjoy things that appeal to you visually—visit an exhibit, see an art film, shoot photos with your camera. • Use a visual organizer to plan out a solution to a stressful problem.	
Interpersonal	• Talk with people who care about you and are supportive. • Shift your focus by being a good listener to others who need to talk about their stresses.	
Intrapersonal	• Schedule downtime when you can think through what is causing stress. • Allow yourself 5 minutes a day of meditation where you visualize a positive way in which you want a stressful situation to resolve.	
Musical	• Listen to music that relaxes, inspires, and/or energizes you. • Write a song about what is bothering you.	
Naturalistic	• See whether the things that cause you stress fall into categories that can give you helpful ideas about how to handle situations. • If nature is calming for you, interact with it—spend time outdoors, watch nature-focused TV, read books or articles on nature or science.	

- Vary what you eat, focusing on local, organic fruits and vegetables, when possible.
- Choose foods with limited fat, cholesterol, and trans fats.
- Replace sugary snacks with fresh or dried fruit.
- Keep healthy snacks within reach to avoid temptation.
- Limit calorie-heavy alcoholic drinks and sugar-heavy sodas.
- Notice and reduce portion sizes.
- Plan meals and minimize late-night eating sprees.
- Substitute other activities for stress-related eating.
- Get help from weight-loss organizations and on-campus support.

Healthy eating requires balance (varying your diet) and moderation (eating reasonable amounts). Key 10.2 presents some ways to incorporate both into your life. Following are some additional details.

Evaluate your eating habits. Keep a food log for a week, writing down what you eat and when you eat it each day. Look over the log. What kinds of food are you eating? What time of day are you eating the most? Do you eat when you are hungry? Worried? Nervous? Are you eating more than you need? See Key 10.3 for some healthy alternatives to common foods you might be eating. If you consistently have reactions to a certain type of food, consult a doctor. You may have a condition such as celiac disease, lactose intolerance, or food allergy that requires you to change how you eat.

Eat a variety of foods. For guidance about the different types and amounts of food you should be eating, explore the information and helpful tools at www.choosemyplate.gov. The graphic shown on this website indicates an ideal balance of food groups. For example, half of your daily food intake should be fruits and vegetables—ideally, five servings a day. However, research at Oregon State University found that the average student barely

KEY 10.3 Explore healthier alternatives.

UNHEALTHY FOOD CALORIES AND NUTRIENT CONTENT	HEALTHY ALTERNATIVE CALORIES AND NUTRIENT CONTENT	BENEFITS OF HEALTHY ALTERNATIVE
Large cheeseburger from fast food restaurant (550 calories)	Whole grain sandwich with tuna fish, chopped celery, and tomato (390 calories)	More fiber, vitamins (B and E), and high-quality protein; less salt and fat
Fruit-flavored candy (80–100 calories)	Fresh or dried fruit such as organic apples, peaches, apricots, and strawberries (50–90 calories)	More fiber and vitamins (A and C); less sugar
Can of soda (90 calories)	Fresh juice from fruits or vegetables, such as apple, orange, or carrot juice (64–80 calories)	More vitamins and antioxidents (vitamins A and C); less sugar and phosphorous (phosphorous can leach calcium from your teeth and bones)
Milk shake from a fast food restaurant (750–1000 calories)	Fruit smoothie, glass of milk (cow, goat, soy, or rice), or yogurt (100–250 calories)	More protein, calcium, and magnesium; less sugar and fat
Canned vegetable soup (120–150 calories)	Fresh, lightly steamed, or stir-fried vegetables, such as spinach, chard, broccoli, carrots, or beets (50 calories)	More vitamins (A and B), more iron, and more fiber; much less salt
French fries from fast food restaurant (230 calories)	Baked potato (60 calories)	More vitamin C and fiber; much less fat and salt

Source: "The Fast Food Explorer." 2011. Retrieved October 28, 2011, from http://www.fatcalories.com

managed five servings of fruits and vegetables a *week*.[4] Work to balance your diet so that you get the nutrients you need.

Evaluate your food sources. Do you buy your food at a convenience store? The dining hall? A supermarket? A local farmer's market? Eat the highest quality food you can find (and afford). Your body breaks your food down into nutrients that allow you to think, move, and live. If the food is poor quality, your body won't get what it needs to keep you going.

Understand the effects of obesity. The term *obese* refers to a person with a body mass index (BMI) of 30 or more (overweight refers to having a BMI of 25–29). Overweight and obese people make up the majority of the U.S. population, with 66% currently falling into these two categories.[5] Obesity is a major factor in the development of adult-onset diabetes, coronary heart disease, high blood pressure, stroke, cancer, and other illnesses. Additional studies show that overweight job applicants and workers experience discrimination in interviews and on the job.[6]

BODY MASS INDEX (BMI)
The ratio of your weight to your height.

Target your ideal weight. Visit the Centers for Disease Control website at www.cdc.gov and use its BMI calculator to find out if you fall within a healthy range or would be considered overweight or obese. If you want to lose weight, set a reasonable goal and work toward it at a pace of approximately 1 to 2 pounds a week. You may also want to consult health professionals, enroll in a reputable and reasonable weight-loss program, and incorporate regular exercise into your life. Strive to reduce your BMI, which will improve not only your physical well-being, but also your mental health.

Get Exercise

Evidence increasingly points to exercise as a key element of your health. The Mayo Clinic reports numerous positive effects of exercise including easing depression, warding off illnesses, reducing fatigue, and maintaining a healthy weight.[7] During physical activity, the brain releases endorphins—chemical compounds that have a positive and calming effect on the body. In addition, regular exercise builds discipline, time-management skills, and motivation that can also contribute to academic success. Risking the time and effort to exercise brings enormous rewards.

Types of exercise

There are three general categories of exercise: cardiovascular (aerobic activity for your heart), strength, and flexibility (see Key 10.4). The type you choose depends on your exercise goals, personality, available equipment, your time and fitness level, and other factors.

Some exercises fall primarily into one category. For example weight lifting is a strength activity and biking is a cardiovascular activity. However, others, like power yoga or Pilates, combine elements of two or three categories. For maximum benefit, try cross-training (alternating types of exercise and combining elements from different types of exercise). For example, if you lift weights, use a stationary bike for cardiovascular work and add a stretching routine.

Always check with a physician before beginning an exercise program, and adjust your program to your physical needs and fitness level. If you are not currently exercising, don't immediately head to the track for a long run. Instead, begin with a daily walking program. Start with a 10-minute walk and increase your time gradually. Walking is gentle on your joints, burns calories, helps your heart, and can improve your mood as well.

KEY 10.4 Vary your exercise activities among three types of training.

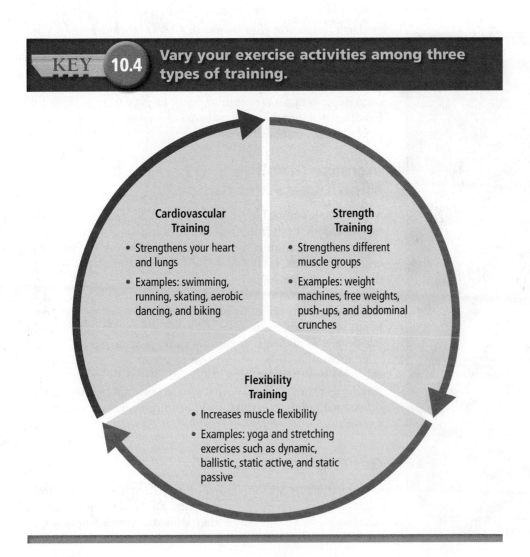

Cardiovascular Training
- Strengthens your heart and lungs
- Examples: swimming, running, skating, aerobic dancing, and biking

Strength Training
- Strengthens different muscle groups
- Examples: weight machines, free weights, push-ups, and abdominal crunches

Flexibility Training
- Increases muscle flexibility
- Examples: yoga and stretching exercises such as dynamic, ballistic, static active, and static passive

How much exercise do you need? Try to do both aerobic and muscle-strengthening activities and spread out your activity through the week. You may want to break it into smaller chunks of time throughout the day. Even 10 minutes at a time is just fine.[8] Dr. Mike Evans has a video on YouTube identifying 30 minutes of exercise a day as a more significant health intervention than any other. He asks a question: "Can you limit your sitting and sleeping to just 23½ hours a day?" When you think about it, that's a pretty minimal risk for a significant reward.[9]

Make exercise a priority

Busy students often have trouble getting to the gym, even if there is a fully equipped athletic center on campus. Use the following ideas to make exercise a priority, even in the busiest weeks.

- Walk to classes and meetings from the parking lot, bus stop, or your home. Use stairs whenever possible.
- Use your school's fitness facilities.
- Ride your bike instead of driving.
- Play team recreational sports at school or in your community.
- Use your school's fitness facilities.
- Take walks or bike rides for study breaks.
- Find activities you can do outside of a club, such as running or pickup basketball.
- Work out with friends or family to combine socializing and exercise.
- Do a routine on your own with a DVD or on-demand TV exercise program.

Being fit is a lifelong pursuit that is never "done." Furthermore, since your body is constantly changing, re-evaluate your exercise program on a regular basis to maximize its benefits. Finally, remember that taking charge of your well-being is part of your personal responsibility.

Increase Stability and Focus with Mindfulness Meditation

Many people's minds are overwhelmed with thoughts and worries on a daily basis. *Mindfulness* refers to paying focused attention, and meditation is a form of contemplation that helps you create that focus, reducing stress and anxiety and the damage they cause to your body.

Pick a quiet time of day and a location where you can be alone and comfortable. Sit on a cushion or in a chair. Rest your hands in your lap, palms up, and close your eyes. Start by breathing deeply, in and out, preferably through your nose. Listen to your breathing. Some people like to count as they inhale and exhale. When thoughts come up, let them pass by as if you were watching a movie. If you have a hard time sitting still, try an active meditation, breathing and counting while you walk, bike, or swim.

Get Enough Sleep

College students are often sleep deprived. While research indicates that students need eight to nine hours of sleep a night to function well, studies show that students average only six to seven hours—and often get much less.[10] Inadequate sleep hinders

How you meditate is up to you—it's your time. Some people like to set a timer and start with a one-minute meditation, then extend it to two, three, or more minutes.

your ability to concentrate, raises stress levels, and makes you more susceptible to illness. It can also increase the likelihood of auto accidents. According to Dr. Tracy Kuo at the Stanford Sleep Disorders Clinic, "A sleepy driver is just as dangerous as a drunk driver."[11]

Students, overwhelmed with responsibilities, often feel they have no choice but to prioritize schoolwork over sleep. Some regularly stay up until the wee hours of the morning to study. Others pull "all-nighters" from time to time to get through a tough project or paper. These habits affect your ability to learn and think, and can weaken your immune system. If you choose the risk of sleeping instead of putting in a few more hours of studying, you may experience a greater reward at test time than if you had studied all night.

For the sake of your health and your GPA, find a way to get enough sleep. Look for such tell-tale symptoms of sleep deprivation as being groggy in the morning, dozing off during the day, or needing caffeine to make it through the day. Sleep expert Gregg D. Jacobs, Ph.D., has the following practical suggestions for improving sleep habits:[12]

- *Reduce consumption of alcohol and caffeine.* Caffeine may make you hungry (it drops your blood sugar level) or keep you awake, especially if you drink it late. Alcohol causes you to sleep lightly, making you feel less rested when you awaken.
- *Exercise regularly.* Regular exercise, especially in the afternoon or early evening, promotes sleep.
- *Take naps.* Taking short afternoon naps can reduce the effects of sleep deprivation.
- *Be consistent.* Try to establish somewhat regular times to wake up and go to bed.
- *Create a ritual.* Wind down and transition from work to sleep with a bedtime ritual. Read a book, listen to calming music, or drink a cup of herbal tea.
- *Manage your sleep environment.* Wear something comfortable, turn down the lights, and keep the room cool. Use earplugs or white noise to deal with outside distractions.

Address Mental Health Issues

Staying positive about who you are, making hopeful plans for the future, and building resilience to cope with setbacks will help you cultivate good mental health. However, some people experience emotional disorders that make it more difficult than usual to calm the stress response and cope. If you recognize yourself in any of the following descriptions, take practical steps to improve your health. Most student health centers and campus counseling centers provide both medical and psychological help or referrals. Although asking for help may feel like a risk, most who do it find it is well worth the reward of feeling better and functioning more effectively.

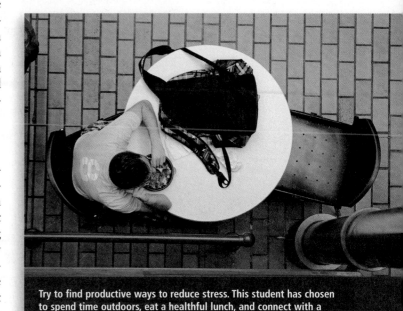

Try to find productive ways to reduce stress. This student has chosen to spend time outdoors, eat a healthful lunch, and connect with a friend on the phone.

Depression

Almost everyone has experienced sadness after setbacks such as breaking up with your partner or failing a course. However, a depressive disorder is an illness, not a temporary, pessimistic mental state that you can "snap out of." It is also fairly common among college students. Recent research reports that nearly half of surveyed students reported feelings of depression at some point, with over 30% saying that the level of depression made it difficult to function at times.[13] Key 10.5 shows possible causes of depression as well as some typical symptoms.

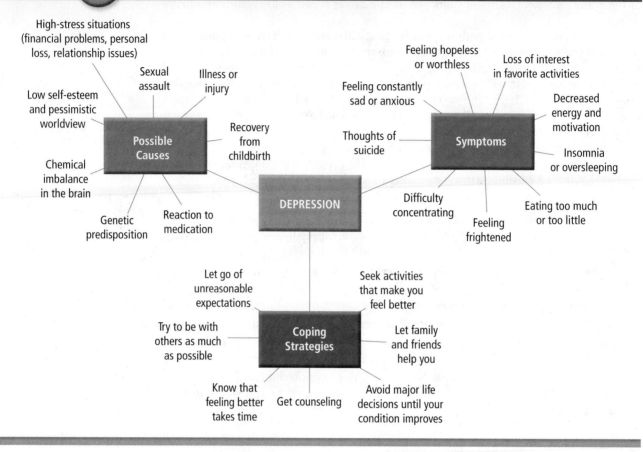

Source: "Depression." National Institutes of Health publication 02-3561. Bethesda, MD: National Institutes of Health, 2002.

If you recognize some of these symptoms in yourself, seek help from a professional. Depression is treatable, but diagnosis requires a medical evaluation. Most student health centers and campus counseling centers provide both medical and psychological help as well as referrals. For some people, adequate sleep, a regular exercise program, a healthy diet, and the passage of time are enough to lessen stress and ease the disorder. For others, behavioral modification therapy and medication are important.

At its worst, depression can lead to suicide. SAVE (Suicide Awareness Voices of Education) lists the warning signs of an impending suicide:[14]

- Statements about hopelessness or worthlessness: "The world would be better without me."
- Loss of interest in people, things, or activities.
- Preoccupation with suicide or death.
- Visiting or calling family and friends and giving things away.
- Sudden sense of happiness or calm. A decision to commit suicide often brings a sense of relief that convinces others that the person "seemed to be on an upswing."

If you recognize these symptoms in someone you know, begin talking with the person about his or her feelings. Then do everything you can to convince the individual to see a doctor or mental health professional. Don't keep your concerns a secret; risk sounding an alarm that may save someone. If you recognize these symptoms in yourself, get help. There are people who care and can assist you. The right help can change or even save your life.

Anxiety Disorders

As with depression, anxiety disorders have been on the rise among college students over the last decade. Potential causes include the struggling economy and job market, being constantly available via communication technology, and information overload—both in general and specifically regarding what everyone around you is doing and accomplishing. If factors like these cause a high stress response that won't settle down, an anxiety disorder can result.

Types of anxiety disorders include:

- Generalized anxiety disorder (GAD), characterized by a nearly constant state of worry that is difficult to control and not always related to a cause
- Obsessive-compulsive disorder (OCD), characterized by obsessive thoughts that lead to compulsive behaviors
- Post-traumatic stress disorder (PTSD), which is especially common in war veterans or survivors of abuse, and involves flashbacks, avoidance, and heightened emotion and awareness
- Panic disorder, characterized by "panic attacks" that feature increased heart and breathing rates, dizziness, and a sense of impending doom

Recognizing an anxiety disorder can be challenging. In fact, many students who ultimately are diagnosed do not initially believe they have a medical problem, figuring that the anxiety they are experiencing is normal. This is especially true for students who have experienced high levels of anxiety all of their lives up until this point without any medical intervention. Any student who feels that anxiety is affecting his or her ability to function in or out of class should consult with a professional to see if an anxiety disorder is to blame.

For general advice about mental health issues, visit the Campus Mental Health: Know Your Rights! website found at www.bazelon.org.

Eating Disorders

Millions of people develop serious and sometimes life-threatening *eating disorders* every year, including anorexia nervosa, bulimia, and binge eating disorder. Negative effects of these disorders range from fertility and obesity issues to digestive tract and other organ damage, heart failure, and even death. There are three basic types of eating disorders:[15]

- *Anorexia nervosa.* People with anorexia nervosa restrict their eating and become dangerously underweight. They may also engage in over-exercising, vomiting, and abuse of diuretics and laxatives. Eventually, without proper nourishment, their internal organs begin to shut down, ending in death if no intervention occurs. Anorexia nervosa is often linked to excessive anxiety and perfectionism or the desire for control.
- *Bulimia nervosa.* People with bulimia engage in "binge episodes," which involve eating excessive amounts of foods and feeling out of control. Following the binge, the person feels remorseful and attempts to purge the calories through self-induced vomiting, laxative abuse, excessive exercise, or fasting. Bulimia is often linked to emotional distress that causes so much pain that an individual tries to "numb" the feeling by overeating.
- *Binge eating disorder.* Binge eating disorder is the most common eating disorder. People with this condition eat large amounts of food and feel out of control, similar to those with bulimia, but they do not purge after a binge episode. However, just like bulimics, they eat unusually fast, eat in secret, eat until they feel uncomfortably full, and feel ashamed of their eating behaviors.

get practical

COLLEGE STRESS EXPLORATION

All sorts of situations and experiences can cause stress during college. Furthermore, everyone has a unique response to any potential stressor. One way to assess your individual situation is to look at the different areas of your life, and rate how much stress you are experiencing in each at the current time. Use a scale from 1 to 10, with 1 being the lowest possible level of stress, and 10 being the highest possible level:

_____ 1. Increased independence and responsibility

_____ 2. Family relationships

_____ 3. Friend relationships

_____ 4. Academic relationships (instructors, student peers, administration, etc.)

_____ 5. Boyfriend/girlfriend/spouse relationships

_____ 6. Managing time and schedule

_____ 7. Managing money

_____ 8. Performance on assignments

_____ 9. Performance on tests

_____ 10. Physical health and fitness

_____ 11. Mental health and balance

_____ 12. Academic planning (major, etc.)

_____ 13. Career planning and vision for future

_____ 14. Work situation, if you have a job on or off campus

_____ 15. Current living situation (home with family, apartment with a friend, etc.)

Total your points here: _____

The lowest possible score is 15, and the highest possible is 150. The higher your score, the more stress you perceive you are currently experiencing. Things to think about:

- Ponder what your total score says about your life at the moment. A score over 100 may indicate that reducing stress should be a top priority for you right now. A score under 50 may indicate that you are currently experiencing tolerable, and even productive, levels of stress.

- Take a look at how you rated each item, and consider putting particular energy into the areas that you rated the highest. There are two ways to determine where your energy would serve you best: One, focus on any area that you rated a 7 or higher. Two, focus on the five areas that you rated highest, no matter what number you gave them.

School and community resources can help you manage whatever level of stress you are experiencing. On a separate sheet of paper or digital file, write down names, locations, hours, phone numbers, URLs, and any other pertinent information for the following resources:

- Free counseling offered to students

- Exercise facility

- Sexual assault center

- Other resource

Source: Adapted in part from Kohn, P.M., K. Lafreniere, and M. Gurevich, "The Inventory of College Students Recent Life Experiences: A Decontaminated Hassles Scale for a Special Population." *Journal of Behavioral Medicine, 13*(6), 1990, pp. 619–630.

Eating disorders are very difficult to cope with on your own. If you suffer from an eating disorder, risk asking for help from a counselor who can offer the reward of care and understanding.

The stresses of college lead some students to experiment with alcohol, tobacco, and other potentially addictive substances. Although these substances may alleviate stress temporarily, they have potentially serious consequences.

HOW CAN YOU MAKE EFFECTIVE
decisions about alcohol, tobacco, and drugs?

Abusing alcohol, tobacco, and drugs adds significantly to stress levels and can cause financial struggles, emotional traumas, family and financial upheaval, health problems, and even death. As you read the information in this section, think about the effects of your actions on yourself and others. Measure the risk of substance use against the social risk of going against what others are doing, and decide which reward is more valuable to you. Continually look for ways to make positive, life-affirming choices.

The frontal lobe of your brain is responsible for "if-then" thinking and impulse control. It's the part that asks, "Is this really a good idea? What will happen if I take this action?" However, the frontal lobe does not reach full development until around the age of 25. This means that people under 25 are likely to perform an action, such as taking drugs, without considering potential consequences.[16] Worse, those drugs are more likely to impair brain development and result in addiction in a younger person than in an older one.[17] Keep this in mind, whether you are a younger student or an older student who interacts with younger students, and consider the information in this section.

Alcohol

Alcohol is a depressant and the most frequently abused drug on campus. Even a few drinks affect thinking and muscle coordination. Heavy drinking can damage the liver, digestive system, and brain cells, as well as impair the central nervous system. Prolonged use also leads to physical and emotional addiction, making it seem impossible to quit. In fact, alcohol contributes to the deaths of 75,000 people every year through both alcohol-related illnesses and accidents involving drunk drivers.[18]

ADDICTION The compulsive need for a habit-forming substance.

According to the Centers for Disease Control (CDC), your tolerance and reaction to alcohol depends on a variety of factors including, but not limited to, age, gender, race or ethnicity, physical condition, the amount of food consumed before drinking, how quickly alcohol was consumed, use of drugs or prescription medications, and family history.[19] Key 10.6 shows the varying levels of drinking behaviors defined by the CDC.

Of all alcohol consumption, *binge drinking* (see Key 10.6) is associated with the greatest problems, and is consistently an issue on college campuses, with over 42% of full-time students and over 35% of part-time students reporting a binge drinking episode in the month prior to the survey.[20] Students who binge drink are more likely to miss classes, perform poorly, experience physical problems (memory loss, headache, stomach issues), become depressed, and engage in unplanned or unsafe sex.[21]

If you drink, think carefully about the effects on your health, safety, and academic performance. The Get Analytical exercise on page 261 is a self-test that will help you analyze your habits.

Tobacco

In the United States, one in four men and one in five women smoke. Unfortunately, cigarette smoking still tops the list as the most preventable cause of death in the United States today, accounting for 438,000 deaths annually. That's like three jumbo jets filled to capacity crashing in the United States every single day, 365 days a year, killing everyone on board.[22]

Many students who use tobacco as a stress reliever become hooked on nicotine, a highly addictive drug found in all tobacco products. Nicotine's immediate effects may include an increase in blood pressure and heart rate, sweating, and throat irritation. Long-term effects may include high blood pressure, bronchitis and emphysema, stomach ulcers, heart disease, and cancer. Although advertisers spend millions of dollars a day trying to convince you smoking is sexy, an estimated 1 billion people will die from tobacco-related illnesses worldwide in the 21st century.[23]

KEY 10.6 Levels of alcohol consumption.

		Men	Women
Moderate Drinking	Lower-risk drinking pattern equaling "having no more than 1 drink per day for women and no more than 2 drinks per day for men."	per day	per day
Heavy Drinking	For men, heavy drinking is typically defined as consuming an average of three or more drinks per day. For women, heavy drinking is typically defined as consuming an average of two or more drinks per day.	+ per day	+ per day
Binge Drinking	"A pattern of alcohol consumption that brings the blood alcohol concentration (BAC) level to 0.08% or more. This pattern of drinking usually corresponds to five or more drinks on a single occasion for men or four or more drinks on a single occasion for women, generally within about two hours."	in 2 hrs.	in 2 hrs.

Source: Centers for Disease Control. "Alcohol and Public Health." Centers for Disease Control, October 14, 2011. Accessed on October 28, 2011, from http://www.cdc.gov/alcohol/index.htm

SECONDHAND SMOKE Smoke in the air exhaled by smokers or given off by cigarettes, cigars, or pipes.

In recent years, the health dangers of secondhand smoke have been recognized. Living with smokers or being around them on a regular basis is linked to about 3,000 lung cancer deaths and 46,000 heart disease deaths per year in nonsmokers.[24] This awareness has led many colleges (and local jurisdictions) to ban smoking in dorm rooms, classrooms, and other public spaces. More and more companies, aware of the problem, are banning smoking in the workplace or even refusing to hire people who smoke.[25]

If you smoke regularly, you can quit by being motivated, persevering, and seeking help. Practical suggestions for quitting include:[26]

- Try a nicotine patch or nicotine gum, and be sure to use them consistently.
- Get support and encouragement from a health care provider, a "quit smoking" program, a support group, and friends and family.

talk risk and reward . . .

Risk asking tough questions to be rewarded with new insights. Use the following questions to inspire discussion with classmates, either in person or online.

- When a friend has a substance problem or abusive tendencies, trying to help can be risky. How can you reach out without insulting the person? What reward do you think is possible?
- Consider how to approach health issues with your friends. What is worth the risk to discuss, and what should be off limits? Keeping a reward in mind, come up with effective ways to broach topics such as eating patterns, sleep patterns, and moods.

CONSIDER THE CASE: Imagine you are one of Kelly's best friends and you hear what happened to her. How would you help her cope and move ahead? Discuss a risk you would advise her to take and what reward she might earn from it.

- Avoid situations that increase your desire to smoke, such as being around other smokers and drinking heavily.
- Find other ways to lower stress, such as exercise or other activities you enjoy.
- Set goals. Set a quit date and tell friends and family. Make and keep medical appointments.

The positive effects of quitting—increased life expectancy, lung capacity, and energy, better skin, and less body odor, as well as significant financial savings—may inspire any smoker to make a lifestyle change. If you're interested in quitting, investigate quitting resources at the Centers for Disease Control (on its website, click on "S" to find "Smoking and Tobacco Use").

In order to assess the level of your potential addiction, you may want to take the self-test in the Get Analytical exercise on page 261, replacing the word "alcohol" or "drugs" with "cigarettes" or "smoking." Think about your results, weigh your options, and make a responsible choice.

Drugs

Illicit drug use is a perennial problem on college campuses. The NSDUH reports that 22% of college students surveyed had used illicit drugs in the year prior to the survey.[27] Some college students use drugs to relieve stress, others want to be accepted by peers, and other just want to try something new.

In most cases, however, the negative consequences of drug use outweigh any temporary high. Drug use violates federal, state, and local laws, and you may be arrested, tried, and imprisoned for possessing even a small amount of drugs. You can jeopardize your reputation, your student status, and your ability to get a job if you are caught using drugs or if drug use impairs your performance. Finally, long-term drug use can damage your body and mind. Key 10.7 has comprehensive information about the most commonly used illicit drugs.

KEY 10.7 Drugs have potent effects on the user.

DRUG	DRUG CATEGORY	USERS MAY FEEL . . .	POTENTIAL SHORT-TERM AND LONG-TERM PHYSICAL EFFECTS	DANGER OF DEPENDENCE
Alcohol	Depressant	Sedated, relaxed, loose	Impaired brain function, impaired reflexes and judgment, cirrhosis of the liver, impaired blood production, greater risk of cancer, heart attack, and stroke	Strong with regular, heavy use
Anabolic steroids (also called *roids, juice, hype*)	Steroid	Increased muscle strength and physical performance, energetic	Stunted growth, mood swings, male-pattern baldness, breast development (in men) or body hair development (in women), mood swings, liver damage, insomnia, aggression, irritability	Insubstantial
Cocaine (also called *coke, blow, snow*) and **crack** cocaine (also called *crack or rock*)	Stimulant	Alert, stimulated, excited, energetic, confident	Nervousness, mood swings, sexual problems, stroke or convulsions, psychoses, paranoia, coma at large doses	Strong
Ecstasy (also called *X, molly, XTC, vitamin E*)	Stimulant	Heightened sensual perception, relaxed, clear, fearless	Fatigue, anxiety, depression, heart arrhythmia, hyperthermia from lack of fluid intake during use	Insubstantial

Continued

KEY **10.7** **Drugs have potent effects on the user. (Continued)**

DRUG	DRUG CATEGORY	USERS MAY FEEL . . .	POTENTIAL SHORT-TERM AND LONG-TERM PHYSICAL EFFECTS	DANGER OF DEPENDENCE
Ephedrine (also called *chi powder, zest*)	Stimulant	Energetic	Anxiety, elevated blood pressure, heart palpitations, memory loss, stroke, psychosis, insomnia	Strong
Gamma hydroxyl butyrate (GHB) (also called *G, liquid ecstasy, goop*)	Depressant	Uninhibited, relaxed, euphoric	Anxiety, vertigo, increased heart rate, delirium, agitation	Strong
Glue, aerosols (also called *whippets, poppers, rush*)	Inhalants	Giddy, lightheaded, dizzy, excited	Damage to brain, liver, lungs, and kidneys, suffocation, heart failure	Insubstantial
Hallucinogenic mushrooms (psilocybin mushrooms or *amanita muscaria*) (also called *shrooms, magic mushrooms*)	Hallucinogen	Strong emotions, hallucinations, distortions of sight and sound, "out of body" experience	Paranoia, agitation, poisoning	Insubstantial
Heroin (also called *smack, dope, horse*) and **codeine**	Opiates	Warm, relaxed, without pain, without anxiety	Infection of organs, inflammation of the heart, convulsions, abscesses, risk of needle-transmitted diseases such as hepatitis and HIV	Strong, with heavy use
Ketamine (also called *K, Special K, vitamin K*)	Anesthetic	Dreamy, floating, having an "out of body" sensation, numb	Neuroses, disruptions in consciousness, reduced ability to move	Strong
Lysergic acid diethylamide (LSD) (also called *acid, blotter, trips*)	Hallucinogen	Heightened sensual perception, hallucinations, distortions of sight and sound, little sense of time	Impaired brain function, paranoia, agitation and confusion, flashbacks	Insubstantial
Marijuana and **hashish** (also called *pot, weed, herb*)	Cannabinol	Euphoric, mellow, little sensation of time, paranoid	Impaired judgment and coordination, bronchitis and asthma, lung and throat cancers, anxiety, lack of energy and motivation, hormone and fertility problems	Moderate
Methamphetamine (also called *meth, speed, crank*)	Stimulant	Euphoric, confident, alert, energetic	Seizures, heart attack, strokes, vein damage (if injected), sleeplessness, hallucinations, high blood pressure, paranoia, psychoses, depression, anxiety, loss of appetite, severe dental decay	Strong, especially if taken by smoking
Nicotine (also called *smokes, cigs*)	Stimulant and depressant	Causes a release of adrenaline, speeding up breathing and heartrate; also causes the release of dopamine into the brain, resulting in feelings of pleasure and well-being. Heroin and "crack" have the same effects on the brain.	Lung cancer, emphysema, asthma, stroke, heart attack, miscarriage, ear infections and respiratory problems (in children exposed to secondhand smoke)	High
OxyContin (also called *Oxy, OC, legal heroin*)	Analgesic (containing opiate)	Relaxed, detached, without pain or anxiety	Overdose death can result when users ingest or inhale crushed time-release pills, or take them in conjunction with alcohol or narcotics	Moderate, with long-term use

Source: Most information from "I Am a Parent." Drug Policy Alliance, 2011. Accessed on October 28, 2011, from http://www.safety1st.org/drugfacts.html; nicotine information from "NIDA InfoFacts: Cigarettes and Other Tobacco Products." National Institute on Drug Abuse, September, 2010. Accessed on October 25, 2011, from http://drugabuse.gov/infofacts/tobacco.html

get analytical

EVALUATE YOUR SUBSTANCE USE

Even one "yes" answer may indicate a need to look carefully at your habits. Three or more "yes" answers indicate that you may benefit from discussing your substance use with a counselor.

Within the last year:

Y N 1. Have you tried to stop drinking or taking drugs but found that you couldn't do so for long?

Y N 2. Do you get tired of people telling you they're concerned about your drinking or drug use?

Y N 3. Have you felt guilty about your drinking or drug use?

Y N 4. Have you felt that you needed a drink or drugs in the morning—as an "eye-opener"—to cope with a hangover?

Y N 5. Do you drink or use drugs alone?

Y N 6. Do you drink or use drugs every day?

Y N 7. Have you found yourself regularly thinking or saying you "need" a drink or any type of drug?

Y N 8. Have you lied about or concealed your drinking or drug use?

Y N 9. Do you drink or use drugs to escape worries, problems, mistakes, or shyness?

Y N 10. Do you find you need increasingly larger amounts of drugs or alcohol in order to achieve a desired effect?

Y N 11. Have you forgotten what happened while drinking or using drugs because you had a blackout?

Y N 12. Have you spent a lot of time, energy, or money getting alcohol or drugs?

Y N 13. Has your drinking or drug use caused you to neglect friends, your partner, your children, or other family members, or caused other problems at home?

Y N 14. Have you gotten into an argument or a fight that was alcohol or drug-related?

Y N 15. Has your drinking or drug use caused you to miss class, fail a test, or ignore schoolwork?

Y N 16. Have you been choosing to drink or use drugs instead of attending social events or performing other activities you used to enjoy?

Y N 17. Has your drinking or drug use affected your efficiency on the job or caused you to fail to show up at work?

Y N 18. Have you continued to drink or use drugs despite any physical problems that your use has caused or made worse?

Y N 19. Have you driven a car or performed any other potentially dangerous tasks while under the influence of alcohol or drugs?

Y N 20. Have you had a drug or alcohol-related legal problem or arrest (possession, use, disorderly conduct, driving while intoxicated, etc.)?

Source: Adapted from the Criteria for Substance Dependence and Criteria for Substance Abuse in the *Diagnostic and Statistical Manual of Mental Disorders,* Fourth Edition, published by the American Psychiatric Association, Washington, D.C., and from materials entitled "Are You An Alcoholic?" developed by Johns Hopkins University.

You are responsible for analyzing the potential consequences of what you introduce into your body. Ask questions like the following:

- What reward am I receiving from taking this risk, and it is worthwhile?
- Am I taking drugs to escape from other problems?
- What positive and negative effects might my behavior have?
- Why do others want me to take drugs, and what do I really think of these people?
- How would my drug use affect the people in my life?

Use the self-test to assess your relationship with drugs. If you believe you have a problem, read the following section on steps that can help you get your life back on track.

get creative

FIND MORE FUN

Complete the following on paper or in digital format.

Sometimes, college students get involved in potentially unsafe activities because it seems like there isn't anything else to do. Use your creativity to find enjoyable, safe activities to choose from when you hang out with friends. Check your resources: What possibilities can you find at your student union, student activities center, college or local arts organizations, athletic organizations, various clubs, nature groups? Could you go hiking? Take a walk or bike ride? Paint pottery? Check out a baseball game? Run a 5K? Try a new kind of cuisine? Volunteer at a children's hospital ward? See a play? Read a book? Watch a movie? List 10 specific activities available to you.

Facing Addiction

If you think you may be addicted, seek help through counseling and medical centers, detoxification centers, and support groups. Because substances often cause physical changes and psychological dependence, habits are tough to break and quitting may involve a painful withdrawal. Asking for help isn't a failure, but a risk calculated to earn you the reward of reclaiming your life.

Even one "yes" answer on the self-test may indicate a need to evaluate alcohol or drug use and monitor it more carefully. If you answered "yes" to three or more questions, you may benefit from talking to a professional about your substance use and the problems it may be causing.

Working through substance-abuse problems can lead to restored health and self-respect. Helpful resources can help you generate options and develop practical plans for recovery.

- *Counseling and medical care.* You can find help from school-based, private, government-sponsored, or workplace-sponsored resources. Ask your school's counseling or health center, your personal physician, or a local hospital for a referral.
- *Detoxification ("detox") centers.* If you have a severe addiction, you may need a controlled environment where you can separate yourself completely from drugs or alcohol, including the people and places associated with it.
- *Support groups.* Alcoholics Anonymous (AA) has led to other support groups for addicts such as Overeaters Anonymous (OA) and Narcotics Anonymous (NA). These groups are free, effective, anonymous, and meet in almost every city of the United States, almost every day of the week.

HOW CAN YOU MAKE EFFECTIVE
decisions about sex?

You choose what sexuality means to you and the role it plays in your life, and how you identify sexually is your personal business. However, the decisions you make go beyond the personal realm. Because sexual conduct can result in an unexpected pregnancy or passing on sexually transmitted infections (STIs), consequences can extend for years and can affect both the people involved in the act as well as their families.

Just as your success in school depends on your ability to manage time, your success in school also depends on making choices that maintain health and safety—yours as well as those of others with whom you may be involved. Analyze sexual issues carefully. Look at potential effects of your choices, determine what rewards hold value for you, and consider what calculated risks can move you safely toward those rewards. Ask questions like the following:

- Is this what I really want? Does it fit with my values?
- Do I feel ready or do I feel pressured? Does this choice cause stress for me?
- Is this the right person/moment/situation? Does my partner truly care for me and not just for what we might be doing? Will this enhance or damage our emotional relationship?
- Do I have what I need to prevent pregnancy and exposure to STIs? If not, is having unprotected sex worth taking the chance?

Sex needs to be a mutual decision. If you feel pressured and uncomfortable, the time is not right.

Birth Control

Using birth control is a choice that helps you decide when and if you want to be a parent. However, it is not for everyone. For some, using any kind of birth control goes against religious or personal beliefs. Others may want to have children. But many sexually active people who do not want children at the moment choose one or more methods of birth control.

Evaluate the pros and cons of each option for yourself and your partner. Consider cost, reliability, comfort, and protection against sexually transmitted infections (STIs). Communicate with your partner, then make a choice together. For more information, check your library, the Internet, or a bookstore; talk to your doctor; or ask a counselor at the student health center or local Planned Parenthood office. Key 10.8 describes established methods, with effectiveness percentages and STI prevention based on proper and regular use.

Sexually Transmitted Infections

STIs spread through sexual contact. This includes intercourse or other sexual activity (oral or anal) that involves contact with the genitals. All STIs are highly contagious. The only birth control methods that offer protection are the male and female condoms (latex or polyurethane only), which prevent skin-to-skin contact. Have a doctor examine any irregularity or discomfort as soon as you detect it. Key 10.9 describes common STIs.

AIDS and HIV

The most serious STI is AIDS (acquired immune deficiency syndrome), caused by the human immunodeficiency virus (HIV). AIDS has no cure and can result in death. Medical science continues to develop drugs to combat AIDS and related illnesses. Although the drugs can slow the progression of the infection and extend life expectancy, there is currently no known cure.

People acquire HIV through sexual relations, by sharing hypodermic needles for drug use, and by receiving infected blood transfusions. You cannot become infected unless one of those fluids is involved. Therefore, it is unlikely you can contract HIV from toilet seats, hugging, kissing, or sharing a glass. Other than not having sex at all, using condoms (latex only) is the best defense against AIDS. Avoid petroleum jelly, which can destroy latex. Be wary of "safe sex fatigue," where young and healthy people get tired of being vigilant about using condoms for every sexual encounter. Although some people dislike using condoms, using them is a small price to pay for preserving your life.

To be safe, get an HIV test at your doctor's office or at a government-sponsored clinic. Your school's health department may also administer HIV tests, and home HIV

KEY **10.8** **Make an educated decision about birth control.**

METHOD	APPROXIMATE EFFECTIVENESS	PREVENTS STIs?	DESCRIPTION
Abstinence	100%	Only if no sexual activity occurs	Just saying no. No intercourse means no risk of pregnancy. However, alternative modes of sexual activity can still spread STIs.
Condom (male)	85% (95% with spermicide)	Yes, if made of latex	A sheath that fits over the penis and prevents sperm from entering the vagina.
Condom (female)	95% if used correctly	Yes if used correctly	A pouch with flexible rings at each end. It is inserted into the vagina, with the ring at the open end staying outside the vagina.
Diaphragm, cervical cap, or **shield**	85%	No	A bendable rubber cap that fits over the cervix and pelvic bone inside the vagina (the cervical cap and shield are smaller and fit over the cervix only). The diaphragm and cervical cap must be fitted initially by a gynecologist. All must be used with a spermicide.
Oral contraceptives (the pill)	99% with perfect use, 92% for typical users	No	A dosage of hormones taken daily by a woman, preventing the ovaries from releasing eggs. Side effects can include headaches, weight gain, and increased chances of blood clotting. Various brands and dosages; must be prescribed by a gynecologist.
Injectable contraceptives (Depo-Provera)	97%	No	An injection that a woman must receive from a doctor every few months. Possible side effects may resemble those of oral contraceptives.
Vaginal ring (NuvaRing)	92%	No	A ring inserted into the vagina that releases hormones. Must be replaced monthly. Possible side effects may resemble those of oral contraceptives.
Spermicidal foams, jellies, inserts	71% if used alone	No	Usually used with diaphragms or condoms to enhance effectiveness, they have an ingredient that kills sperm cells (but not STIs). They stay effective for a limited period of time after insertion.
Intrauterine device (IUD)	99%	No	A small coil of wire inserted into the uterus by a gynecologist (who must also remove it). Prevents fertilized eggs from implanting in the uterine wall. May or may not have a hormone component. Possible side effects include increased or abnormal bleeding.
Tubal ligation	Nearly 100%	No	Surgery for women that cuts and ties the fallopian tubes, preventing eggs from traveling to the uterus. Difficult and expensive to reverse. Recommended for those who do not want any, or any more, children.
Vasectomy	Nearly 100%	No	Surgery for men that blocks the tube that delivers sperm to the penis. Like tubal ligation, difficult to reverse and only recommended for those who don't want any, or any more, children.
Rhythm method	Variable	No	Abstaining from intercourse during the ovulation segment of the woman's menstrual cycle. Can be difficult to time and may not account for cycle irregularities.
Withdrawal	Variable	No	Pulling the penis out of the vagina before ejaculation. Unreliable, because some sperm can escape in the fluid released prior to ejaculation. Dependent on a controlled partner.

Source: MayoClinic staff. "In-Depth birth control: Birth control basics." Mayo Clinic. Accessed on October 28, 2011, from http://www.mayoclinic.com/health/birth-control/MY01182/TAB=indepth

get $mart

THE RELATIONSHIP BETWEEN WELLNESS AND FINANCIAL FITNESS

Complete the following on paper or in digital format.

Wellness has its costs—fitness club fees and healthy food often aren't cheap, although they can save you medical costs down the line. Track health-related expenses (both positive and negative) for one week and enter your daily and weekly totals in a grid you create with headers as shown here. In the "Item" column, include a row for each of the following items: Food + (healthful food), Food − (junk food), Alcohol, Tobacco, Fitness, Other. For monthly fees such as fitness memberships, divide by four and enter your result in the TOTAL box for fitness.

ITEM	MON	TUES	WED	THURS	FRI	SAT	SUN	TOTAL

Looking at your grid when the week is over, answer the following questions.

1. Approximately how much did you spend on items that increase wellness?
2. Approximately how much did you spend on items that decrease wellness?
3. Are you spending more to increase or decrease wellness?
4. If you want to change how you spend money related to your wellness, describe your desired change and be specific about how you plan to put it into action.

KEY 10.9 To stay safe, know these facts about sexually transmitted infections.

DISEASE	SYMPTOMS	HEALTH PROBLEMS IF UNTREATED	TREATMENTS
Chlamydia	Discharge, painful urination, swollen or painful joints, change in menstrual periods for women	Can cause pelvic inflammatory disease (PID) in women, which can lead to sterility or ectopic pregnancies; infection; miscarriage; or premature birth.	Curable with full course of antibiotics; avoid sex until treatment is complete.
Gonorrhea	Discharge, burning while urinating	Can cause PID, swelling of testicles and penis, arthritis, skin problems, infections, sterility.	Usually curable with antibiotics; however, certain strains are becoming resistant to medication.
Genital herpes	Blister-like itchy sores in the genital area, headache, fever, chills	Symptoms may subside and then reoccur, often in response to high stress levels; carriers can transmit the virus even when it is dormant.	No cure; some antiviral medications can reduce and help heal the sores, as well as shorten outbreaks and reduce the chance of transmission.
Syphilis	A genital sore (often painless) lasting one to five weeks, followed by a rash, fatigue, fever, sore throat, headaches, swollen glands	If it lasts over four years, it can cause blindness, destruction of bone, dementia, or heart failure; can cause death or deformity of a child born to an infected woman.	Curable with full course of antibiotics. Important to receive treatment early; treatment will not reverse damage done by earlier stages of the disease.
Human Papilloma Virus (HPV, or genital warts)	Genital itching and irritation, small clusters of warts	Can increase risk of cancers including cervical cancer in women; virus may remain in body and cause recurrences even when warts are removed.	No treatment for virus, but warts are treatable with drugs or wart removal surgery. Vaccine available (three doses necessary); most effective when given before exposure to HPV.

tests are available over the counter. Consider requiring any of your sexual partners to be tested as well. If you are infected, inform all sexual partners and seek medical assistance. If you're interested in contacting support organizations in your area, call the National AIDS Hotline at 1-800-342-AIDS.

HOW CAN YOU STAY SAFE AND
avoid sexual assault?

Staying safe is part of staying well and reducing stress. Crime is a reality on campus as it is in any community. Alcohol- and drug-related offenses may occur more frequently than other crimes on campus. Women are particularly vulnerable to sexual assault. By law, colleges are required to report crime statistics yearly. For a link to statistics by school and for other helpful information, visit www.securityoncampus.org.

Personal Safety Strategies

Making intelligent choices is a crucial part of staying safe. Take these practical measures to prevent incidents that jeopardize your well-being.

Be aware of safety issues. Every college has its particular issues—problematic areas of the campus, particular celebrations that get out of hand, bad habits such as students propping open security doors. With awareness, you can steer clear of problems and even work to improve them.

Avoid situations that present clear dangers. Don't walk or exercise alone at night, especially in isolated areas. Don't work or study alone in a building. If a person looks suspicious, contact someone who can help.

Avoid drugs or overuse of alcohol. Anything that impairs judgment makes you vulnerable to assault. Avoid driving while impaired or riding with someone who has taken drugs or alcohol. Avoid attending large parties where people are binge drinking. It's too easy for rape to occur when someone is inebriated.

Avoid people who make you uneasy. If you feel threatened by anyone inside or outside of classes, tell an instructor or campus security. If you feel uncomfortable with someone, trust your intuition and get away from him or her. Stay alert and make no assumptions. As Kelly found out, danger can lurk even with a friend whom you think you can trust.

Be wary of dangers online. Don't give out personal information online to people whom you don't know well. If you have a Facebook page or Instagram, be careful about the text and photos you post. If you feel that someone is harassing you by email or IM, contact an advisor or counselor (you may want to save the messages as proof of harassment).

Review your immunizations. Your success in college also depends on your ability to fight off infections and diseases. College students living on campus should pay particular attention to the *meningococcal meningitis* vaccine (this protects you against an infection that results in the swelling and inflammation of the spinal cord and brain), and women under 26 should look into the HPV (*human papillomavirus*) vaccine (this protects you against an infection that attacks the skin and mucous membranes, often causing cervical cancer).

Take Steps to Avoid Sexual Assault

One in four females is likely to be sexually assaulted in her lifetime, as is one in six males. Approximately every two minutes, someone in the United States is sexually

student PROFILE

Andrew Willard

COLORADO STATE UNIVERSITY, FORT COLLINS

About me:

I am a senior attending Colorado State University. I always played sports growing up and I have always been very active. Though I have a busy schedule through college and work, I still make an effort to get some form of exercise in every day—forcing myself to be active relieves stress and allows me to be more productive academically and at work.

What I focus on:

School and work can be stressful and time-consuming, and it is hard to find time to stay active. Since daily exercise is a high priority for me, I have found that shortening my workouts to intense daily increments of a half hour allows me to get sufficient exercise while still having time to prioritize school and work obligations. Exercise allows me to clear my thoughts after a long day or organize them before the day begins—if I make time in my schedule to work out my productivity increases and I sleep better at night. Learning how to prioritize work out time without taking away from my academic and professional responsibilities is the most essential skill that I have learned during my college career. When I plan ahead to allow for time outside of work and school to work out and spend time by myself, I stay balanced and healthy.

What will help me in the workplace:

Being organized and able to prioritize will be useful in the workplace when managing various events and business projects. Making time for an active lifestyle in my off hours will help me stay healthy and fit, which in turn will allow me to maintain a high energy and performance level at work. I look forward to creating a working lifestyle that is both productive and healthy.

---

assaulted, and two-thirds of the people assaulted know their attacker—an acquaintance, a friend, or a family member.[28] Females between the ages of 18 and 24 are more likely to be stalked, harassed, or sexually assaulted than any other age group. In fact, most sexual assaults among that age range occur on college campuses or on dates.[29]

Sexual assault includes a wide range of behaviors, often called the "sexual violence continuum," ranging from obscene phone calls, to exhibitionism, to actual penetration or forced prostitution.[30] Unfortunately, many behaviors bordering on or involving sexual assault are actually advertised or condoned by society and the media. Kelly and Becca's program, One Student, provides resources, facts, and programs for students on campuses around the nation, aiming to educate students and create a future where sexual assaults no longer occur.

Rape is not about sex, it's about one person exerting power over another. Rape is not caused by the victim's behavior or clothing, any more than auto theft is caused by the owner of the car. Rape is about one person having nonconsensual sex (without permission) with another. It can happen on a date, at home, or at a party. And it's a crime.

If you find yourself in a situation where you feel powerless or threatened, leave immediately. If you feel afraid to leave by yourself, call a friend, or call a cab. And if you see that someone is being inappropriate or offensive toward another, show your disapproval and publicly interrupt the behavior as best you can. If necessary, call for help.

If you are assaulted, tell someone you trust right away. Call the Rape and Incest National Network (RAINN) hotline to find the phone number of a local rape crisis center so you can talk to someone. If you want to report the assault to the police, you can do that as well, preferably with a supportive person accompanying you. Get ongoing counseling to help you deal with your feelings and eventually move from being a victim to becoming a survivor. Rape-crisis centers specialize in this type of counseling.

revisit RISK AND REWARD

What happened to Kelly and Becca? With Becca's guidance, Kelly came to grips with the sexual assault. "Being a great leader is a choice," says Becca. "We were very average people who chose to respond to something in a way that was earnest." Choosing the risk of leading through education and communication, they founded Let's Talk About "IT" to uncover the truths about sexual assault and show how friendship and empathy help the recovery process. They decode the toxic language surrounding sex, and their work rewards students with innovative ways to address alcohol, sex under the influence, and date rape drugs.

Kelly and Becca continue to take risks that have brought great reward to students all over the country. They created the Sexversations card game to foster conversations about intimacy, sexuality, and sexual assault. In 2010, they founded One Student, an organization with a mission to combat sexual violence. Recently a filmmaker created a documentary about their journey and work (more information at YouAreTheOneFilm.org). They have shared their story and insight at more than 300 college campuses, taking special satisfaction when someone confides in them. Best of friends now for two decades, they have achieved personal fulfillment in relationships with loving husbands and supportive parents.

What does this mean for you? Most people think that sexual assault, like being struck by lightning, will never happen to them. Planning ahead and promoting a safe community can help. What are some specific steps you can take to reduce the likelihood that you will be a victim of, or be involved in, sexual assault? Kelly and Becca's case illustrates the importance of communication in the prevention and recovery processes. Who are some people in your life you could risk talking to about sexual assault? Are there other resources in your school, family, or community to which you can turn?

What risk may bring reward beyond your world? One Student's slogan is "One sexual assault is too many. One student can make a difference." Go to the website http://onestudent.org to learn how to take action. Then choose one or more risks that you think will bring rewards at your school. Consider ordering the free posters and post them in strategic locations, organizing a wristband campaign to symbolize a united front against sexual violence, or using the video "Take the First Step" to get a dialogue going with classmates, administrators, teachers, and parents. "We don't see the snow and the lack of life. We see the first blades of grass and the first blossom of flowers," Becca says. "Those are the students we hear from and their stories . . . we don't see the lack of success, we see the opportunity."

Wellness and Stress Management

Complete the following on paper or in digital format.

KNOW IT *Think Critically*

Move Toward Better Health

Build basic skills. Pick a behavior—eating, drinking, sleeping, sexual activity—that holds some kind of issue for you. Describe your behavior and your attitude toward what you do.

Example: *Issue:* binge drinking

      Behavior: I binge drink probably once a week.

      Attitude: I don't think it's any big deal. I like using it to escape.

    Question to think about: Is it worth it?

Take it to the next level. Examine whether your behavior is a problem by noting positive and negative effects. To continue the example above:

Positive effects: I have fun with my friends. I feel confident, accepted, social.

Negative effects: I feel foggy the next day. I miss class. I'm irritable.

Move toward mastery. Based on the effects of your behavior, think about where you want to make a difference, and why. Then describe changes you could make by answering the following questions. For example, the binge drinker might consider cutting back on one drinking outing a week and investigating one new social activity that does not involve drinking.

1. How might you change your behavior?
2. How might you change your attitude?
3. What positive effects do you think these changes would have?
4. Commit to these actions to put positive change in motion. Describe your plan, including specific steps and a time frame.

WRITE IT *Communicate*

Emotional intelligence journal: Addiction. Discuss how you feel about addiction in any form—to alcohol, drugs, food, sex, the Internet, gambling—whether or not it you have had direct or indirect experience with it. Imagine that a close friend or family member has a dangerous addiction of some kind. Use your emotional intelligence to describe how you would address the problem with that person to produce the best possible outcome.

Real-life writing: Health on campus. Think about what you consider to be the most significant health issue at your school—personal safety, alcohol or drug abuse, smoking, weight management, and so on. Write a 500-word editorial for your school paper on the topic, describing the details of the problem and proposing one or more solutions. For example, if weight control is a problem, you might suggest changing the contents of the drink vending machines. When you are done, consider submitting your editorial to the paper (have an instructor or peer review it before you send it in).

WORK IT *Build Your Brand*

Wellness at Work

21st Century Learning Building Blocks:

- Initiative and self-direction
- Critical thinking and problem solving
- Information literacy

Taking responsibility for your health can make you a more valuable employee, in part because many companies are putting pressure on their employees to do more in less time. Increased work burdens, late nights, and work calls during weekends or off-hours create a great deal of stress for workers. In addition, health care costs are on the rise for companies.

Part of your responsibility involves getting routine screenings from a doctor or health clinic. Below is a list of health items commonly tested during screening. Using the Internet or your library, research the listed items. For each, describe (1) what the item is and why it is important to your overall health; (2) what the normal range is for the item and what numbers (high, low, or both) indicate a concern; and (3) what to do if you have abnormal results for this item.

- Hemoglobin
- Hematocrit
- Glucose
- Potassium
- Magnesium
- Calcium
- Iron
- Cholesterol

11

When you understand the values and perspectives that lie behind your
financial decisions, you will be more able to take productive action
toward financial goals that are meaningful to you.

Managing Money

LIVING BELOW YOUR MEANS

What Would You Risk? *Torian Richardson*

THINK ABOUT THIS SITUATION AS YOU READ, AND CONSIDER WHAT ACTION YOU WOULD TAKE. THIS CHAPTER HELPS YOU GET TO KNOW YOURSELF AS A MONEY MANAGER. IT OFFERS STRATEGIES FOR USING MONEY WISELY IN THE PRESENT SO THAT YOU HAVE MORE FINANCIAL STABILITY IN THE FUTURE.

Despite growing up in a mentally, physically, and emotionally abusive, working-class household on the south side of Chicago, Torian Richardson developed strong work habits early on. His dad drove a bus and his mom worked at the post office to help send Torian and his sister to better schools. "Although my parents didn't have a college education—my mother graduated from high school and father earned a GED—they always talked about the value of education," he says.

Although a lackadaisical student in high school, Torian remained curious about how to overcome challenges, escape cycles of abuse, and succeed. Always observant and aware, he asked friends how they handled certain situations. To escape stress at home, he spent time on the playing fields, excelling in football, wrestling, and track. When he was 16, he moved from living with his mother on the south side to living with his father in the western suburbs of the city. He became aware of who had money and who didn't, and what budgeting was all about.

Torian earned a partial sports scholarship to college, and his grandmother helped cover expenses, but he struggled and was put on academic probation. Less than a year later, Torian lost that scholarship and transferred to a community college. He worked part-time at a fast-food drive through, trying to scrape together enough money to pay his tuition bills on his own. Friends and classmates who once looked up to him and anticipated his success in college saw the apparent lack of progress he had made, and his self-esteem took a hit. He doubted that he could take the needed risks to earn the reward of graduating from college and supporting his athletic pursuits on his own.

To be continued . . .

ECONOMIC CHALLENGES AND RAPIDLY DEVELOPING TECHNOLOGY HAVE CHANGED HOW PEOPLE MANAGE MONEY, AND PAYING FOR COLLEGE CONTINUES TO BE A CHALLENGE. YOU'LL LEARN MORE ABOUT TORIAN, AND THE REWARD RESULTING FROM HIS ACTIONS, WITHIN THE CHAPTER.

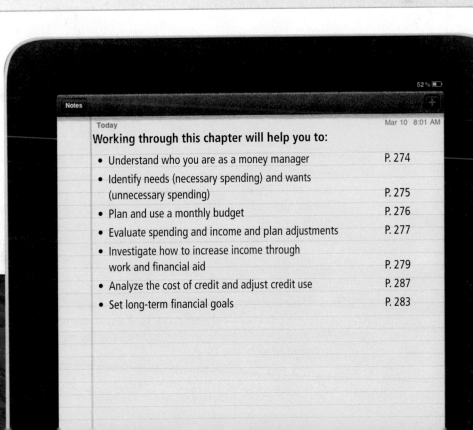

52% 🔋

Notes

Today   Mar 10   8:01 AM

Working through this chapter will help you to:

status**CHECK**

How Effectively Do You Manage Money?

For each statement, fill in the number that best describes how often it applies to you.

1 = never   2 = seldom   3 = sometimes   4 = often   5 = always

1. I am aware of my personal views on spending and saving money. ① ② ③ ④ ⑤
2. I know how much money I can spend each month. ① ② ③ ④ ⑤
3. I know the difference between things I want and things I need, and I shop accordingly. ① ② ③ ④ ⑤
4. I control my spending by using a monthly budget. ① ② ③ ④ ⑤
5. I successfully balance my responsibilities at work and at school. ① ② ③ ④ ⑤
6. I understand the benefits and responsibilities of financial aid. ① ② ③ ④ ⑤
7. I know the current interest rate, late fees, and balances on my credit cards. ① ② ③ ④ ⑤
8. I know my credit rating and its potential effect on my finances in the future. ① ② ③ ④ ⑤
9. I add to a savings account or CD regularly. ① ② ③ ④ ⑤
10. I have begun planning for my retirement. ① ② ③ ④ ⑤

Each of the topics in these statements is covered in this chapter. Note those statements for which you filled in a 3 or lower. Skim the chapter to see where those topics appear, and pay special attention to them as you read, learn, and apply new strategies.

REMEMBER: NO MATTER HOW EFFECTIVELY YOU MANAGE YOUR MONEY, YOU CAN IMPROVE WITH EFFORT AND PRACTICE.

WHAT DOES MONEY
mean in your life?

According to the American Psychological Association, nearly three out of four people in the United States cite money as the number one stressor in their lives.[1] The cost of college tuition continues to rise more quickly than the rate of inflation, and books and other college expenses take a toll on bank accounts. Self-supporting students have to pay for living and family expenses on top of college costs. Students who take longer than expected to complete a degree or certificate often pay more for the additional time in school. Add the recession that the United States is currently experiencing, and it adds up to challenging financial situations for the vast majority of college students.

Thinking analytically, creatively, and practically about money management can help you take calculated risks that reward you with increased control over your finances. First, analyze who you are as a money manager and examine the relationship between money and time.

MyStudentSuccessLab

(www.mystudentsuccesslab.com) is an online solution designed to help you "Start Strong, Finish Stronger" by building skills for ongoing personal and professional development.

How You Perceive and Use Money

How you interact with money is unique. Some people spend earnings right away, some save for the future. Some charge everything, some make cash purchases only, others do something in between. Some pay bills online and others mail checks. Some rewards people seek are measured in dollar amounts and others in nonmaterial terms. Your spending and saving behavior tend to reflect your values and goals. As you analyze who you are as a money manager, consider these influences in Key 11.1.

Improving how you handle money requires that you analyze your attitudes and behaviors. Says money coach Connie Kilmark, "If managing money was just about math and the numbers, everyone would know how to manage their finances sometime around the fifth grade."[2] Begin your analysis by looking at needs versus wants.

Needs Versus Wants

People often confuse what they *need* with what they *want*. True needs are absolutely essential for your survival: food, water, air, shelter (rent or mortgage, as well as home maintenance costs and utilities), family and friends, and some mode of transportation. Everything else is technically a want—something you would like but could live without. When people spend too much on wants, they may not have enough cash for needs. You might want to buy a $1,000 flat-screen TV, but might regret the purchase if your car broke down and needed a $1,000 repair.

Check your spending for purpose. What do you buy with your money? Are the items you purchase necessary? When you do spend on a want rather than a need, do you plan the expense into your budget with an eye toward a specific reward, or buy on the spur of the moment? With a clear idea of what you want and what you need, you

KEY 11.1 **Many factors affect how you manage money.**

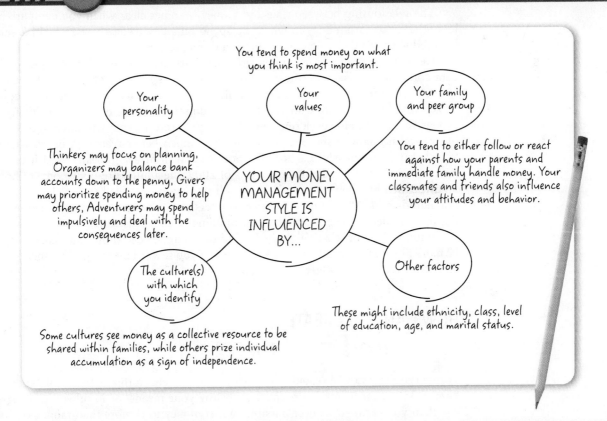

You tend to spend money on what you think is most important.

Your personality

Your values

Your family and peer group

YOUR MONEY MANAGEMENT STYLE IS INFLUENCED BY...

Thinkers may focus on planning, Organizers may balance bank accounts down to the penny, Givers may prioritize spending money to help others, Adventurers may spend impulsively and deal with the consequences later.

You tend to either follow or react against how your parents and immediate family handle money. Your classmates and friends also influence your attitudes and behavior.

Other factors

The culture(s) with which you identify

These might include ethnicity, class, level of education, age, and marital status.

Some cultures see money as a collective resource to be shared within families, while others prize individual accumulation as a sign of independence.

DAY-TO-DAY EXPENSE	APPROXIMATE COST	POTENTIAL SAVINGS
Gourmet coffee	$4 per day, 5 days a week, totals $20 per week	$80 per month; $960 for the year. Invested in a 5% interest account for a year, would amount to over $1,000.
Alcohol	Two drinks plus tip total about $20 per night, two nights per week amounts to $40 per week	$160 per month; $1,920 for the year. Invested in a 5% interest account for a year, would amount to over $2,000.
Ordering in meals	$15 per meal, twice per week, totals $30 per week	$120 per month; $1,440 for the year. Invested in a 5% interest account for a year, would amount to nearly $1,550.

can think through spending decisions more effectively. This is not to say that you should never spend money on wants. Just take calculated risks that satisfy your needs first, and then decide what to do with what is left over.

How Your Time Relates to Money

When you spend money from your paycheck, you exchange the time you spent earning that money for a product or service. For example, let's say you are thinking about spending $200 on a cell phone upgrade. If you have a part-time job that pays you $10 an hour after taxes, you need to work a full 20-hour week just to buy the phone ($200). Does the risk of the expense justify the reward? If the answer is no, put the money away and use it for something you value more. Exchange the risk of your work hours for rewards that matter most to you.

The relationship between time and money becomes clear when you compare how long it takes to earn money to what you spend on a day-to-day basis. Key 11.2 shows how reducing regular expenses can make a difference.

Getting a college education is a risk that costs many hours of work, and student debt continues to rise, with the mean debt burden for students graduating in 2011 at almost $18,000.[3] For many students, tuition costs are a significant factor in college choice, and more and more students are working to minimize debt by prioritizing less expensive schools. However, tuition and time spent reward you with improved chances of long-term financial success. "Education is a much better reason to borrow money than buying cars or McMansions," reports the *Wall Street Journal*, "and it endows people with economic advantages. . . . As of 2009, the annual pre-tax income of households headed by people with at least a college degree exceeded that of less-educated households by 101%."[4] *Opportunity cost* refers to what you give up to get something. For most students, the opportunity cost of going to college is worth it.

With an idea of what values lie behind the financial decisions you make, you will be more able to take productive risks that move you toward meaningful financial goals. Start with creating a budget.

HOW CAN YOU CREATE
and use a budget?

Everything you will read about money management in this chapter falls under the "umbrella" of one central concept: Live below your means, or in other words, spend less than you earn—whenever possible. When money in is more than money out, you will have extra to save or spend.

How can you find out the difference between what you spend and what you earn? Track your spending and earning, and create a (budget) that balances both. Torian was fortunate to develop an understanding of budgeting as a teenager, enabling him to look at his finances in that context as a college student. Because many expenses are billed monthly, most people use a month as a unit of time. Creating a budget involves several steps:

BUDGET
A plan to coordinate resources and expenditures; a set of goals regarding money.

1. Gather information about what you earn (money flowing in).
2. Figure out your expenditures (money flowing out).
3. Analyze the difference between earnings and expenditures.
4. Come up with creative ideas about how you can make changes.
5. Take practical action to adjust spending or earning so you come out even or ahead.

Your biggest expense right now is probably tuition. However, if you have taken out student loans that you don't begin to pay until after you earn your degree, that expense may not hit you fully until after you finish school. (Financial aid options will be explored later in the chapter.) For now, as you consider your budget, include only the part of the cost of your education you are paying for while you are still in school.

Figure Out What You Earn

To determine what is available to you on a monthly basis, start with the money you earn in a month's time at any regular job. Then, if you have savings set aside for your education or any other source of income, determine how much of it you can spend each month and add that amount. For example, if you have a grant for the entire year, divide it by 12 (or by how many months you are in school over the course of a year) to see how much you can use each month.

Figure Out What You Spend

First, note regular monthly expenses like rent, phone, and cable (look at past checks and electronic debits to estimate what the month's bills will be). Some expenses, like automobile and health insurance, may be billed only once or twice a year. In these cases, divide the yearly cost by 12 to see how much you spend every month. Then, over a month's time, keep a spending log in a small notebook to record each day's cash or debit card expenditures. Be sure to count smaller purchases if they are frequent (for example, one or two pricey coffees a day add up over time). By the end of the month, you will have a good idea of where your dollars go.

Key 11.3 lists common sources of income as well as expenses for students. Use the total of all your monthly expenses as a baseline for other months, realizing that spending will vary depending on events in your life or factors such as seasons. For example, if you pay for heating, that cost will be far greater in cold weather.

Personal finance software programs, such as Quicken, can help you track spending and saving and categorize expenses. With software, you can create reports about how much you spend on groceries in a one-month period or how much you earned from work in a year's time. Also, if you manage bank and credit accounts online, you can easily access information about what you are earning and spending over a period of time.

Evaluate the Difference

Once you know what you earn and what you spend, calculate the difference: Subtract your monthly expenses from your monthly income. Ideally, you have money left over to save or spend. However, if you are spending more than you take in, examine these areas of your budget.

Common Sources of Income	Common Expenses

Common Sources of Income

- Take-home pay from a full-time or part-time job
- Take-home pay from summer and holiday employment
- Money earned from work-study or paid internship
- Money from parents or other relatives
- Scholarships
- Grants
- Loans

Common Expenses

- Tuition you are paying now
- Books and other course materials
- Rent or mortgage
- Utilities (electric, gas, oil, water)
- Telephone (cell phone and/or landline)
- Food
- Clothing, toiletries, household supplies
- Transportation and auto expenses (gas, maintenance, service)
- Credit cards and other payments on credit (car payment)
- Childcare
- Entertainment (cable TV, movies, eating out, books and magazines, music downloads)
- Computer-related expenses, including online service costs
- Insurance (health, auto, homeowner's or renter's, life)
- Miscellaneous expenses

- *Expenses.* Did you forget to budget for recurring expenses such as the cost for semi-annual dental visits or car insurance? Or was your budget derailed by an emergency expense?
- *Spending patterns and priorities.* Did you spend money wisely during the month, or did you overspend on wants?
- *Income.* Do you bring in enough money? Do you need another income source or better job?

Adjust Spending or Earning

If you spend more than you are earning, you can earn more, spend less, or better yet, do both. You will explore ways to increase income through jobs and/or financial aid in the next section.

There are many ways to decrease spending. Perhaps the most important one is thinking before you buy: Do I really need this? Is the expense worth it? Just answering those questions will reduce unnecessary purchases. Here are other ways to manage spending:

Set up automatic payments. If you set up electronic monthly payments for bills and tuition and schedule regular automatic transfers of small amounts into your savings, you will take care of your needs first without thinking about it. Then, you can look at what is left over and decide how you want to spend or save it.

- Share living space.
- Rent movies or borrow them from friends or the library.
- Cook at home more often.
- Use grocery and restaurant coupons from the paper or online.
- Take advantage of sales, buy store brands, and buy in bulk.
- Walk, bike, carpool, or use public transport.
- Bring lunch from home.
- Shop in secondhand or consignment stores or swap clothing with friends.
- Communicate via email or snail mail rather than calling or texting (minutes and texts can add up fast).
- Ask a relative to help with childcare, or create a babysitting co-op.
- Reduce electricity costs by turning off lights when you leave a room, cut back on air conditioning, and switch to compact fluorescent bulbs (CFLs) in your lamps.

Comparison shop. Again, think before you buy. If you are in the market for an expensive item such as a cell phone, a computer, or a car, research prices at stores and online. Use websites such as ShopLocal, NexTag, and Woot to compare prices. Consider purchasing used items.

Show your student ID. Your student identification card is your ticket to savings for a variety of items such as movies, shows, concerts, restaurant meals and take out, book and clothing stores, travel services, electronics, and much more.

Finally, work to save money on a day-to-day basis. The effort of saving small amounts regularly can eventually bring significant reward. Key 11.4 has some suggestions.

Call on your dominant multiple intelligences when planning your budget. For example, logical-mathematical learners may choose a classic detail-oriented budgeting plan, visual learners may want to create a budget chart, and bodily-kinesthetic learners may want to make budgeting more tangible by dumping receipts into a big jar and tallying them at the end of the month. Personal finance software can accommodate different types of learners with features such as written reports (verbal-linguistic, logical-mathematical) and graphical reports (visual). Consider using online tools such as Mint.com or Thrive.com. See the Multiple Intelligence Strategies for Financial Management (page 280) for more MI-based ideas on how to manage your money.

HOW CAN YOU INCREASE INCOME
through work and financial aid?

If you reduce your spending and still come up short, you may need to look at ways to increase your income. The rising cost of education leads most students to seek additional dollars through work, financial aid, or both.

- According to a 2007 survey, nearly 50% of college freshmen add a job to their scheduled weekly responsibilities to earn money for tuition.[5]
- Statistics from the U.S. Department of Education show that in 2007–2008, fully two-thirds of undergraduates received some type of financial aid.[6]

Read on to find ways to get as much help as possible from these income sources.

Managing Money

multiple intelligence strategies

FOR FINANCIAL MANAGEMENT

Name a significant upcoming expense: _____.
In the right-hand column, record specific ideas for how MI strategies can help you afford it.

INTELLIGENCE	USE MI STRATEGIES TO MANAGE YOUR MONEY	IDENTIFY MI STRATEGIES THAT CAN HELP YOU MAKE A PURCHASE
Verbal-Linguistic	• Talk over your financial situation with someone you trust. • Write out a detailed budget outline. If you can, store it on a computer file so you can update it regularly.	
Logical-Mathematical	• Focus on the numbers; with a calculator and amounts that are as exact as possible, determine your income and spending. • Calculate how much you'll have in 10 years if you start now to put $2,000 in a 5% interest-bearing IRA account each year.	
Bodily-Kinesthetic	• Create a set of envelopes, each for a different budget item—rent, dining out, phone, and so on. Each month, put money, or a slip with a dollar amount, in each envelope to represent what you can spend. When the envelope is empty or the number on the paper is reduced to zero, stop spending.	
Visual-Spatial	• Set up a budgeting system that includes color-coded folders and colored charts. • Create color-coded folders for papers related to financial and retirement goals—investments, accounts, and so on.	
Interpersonal	• Whenever money problems come up, discuss them right away with a family member, partner, or roommate. • Brainstorm a 5-year financial plan with one of your friends.	
Intrapersonal	• Schedule quiet time to plan how to develop, follow, and update your budget. Consider financial management software, such as Quicken. • Think through where your money should go to best achieve your long-term financial goals.	
Musical	• Include a category of music-related purchases in your budget—going to concerts, buying CDs—but keep an eye on it to make sure you don't go overboard.	
Naturalistic	• Analyze your spending by using a system of categories. Your system may be based on time (when payments are due), priority (must-pay bills versus extras), or spending type (monthly bills, education, family expenses).	

get practical

MAP OUT YOUR BUDGET

Use this exercise to see what you take in and what you spend. Then decide what adjustments you need to make. Consider using an online calculator for this task, such as Calculatorweb.com.

Before You Begin. Keep a spending log for one week or one month, whatever you have time for (if you use one week, multiply it by four to determine estimated monthly expenses in Step 1). Note purchases made by cash, check, debit card, and credit card.

Step 1: Expenses. Based on your spending log, estimate your current expenses in dollars per month, using the following table. The grand total is your total monthly expenses. If any expense comes only once a year, enter it in the "Annual Expenses" column and divide by 12 to get your "Monthly Expenses" figure for that item.

EXPENSES	MONTHLY EXPENSES	ANNUAL EXPENSES
School supplies including books and technology		
Tuition and fees		
Housing: Dorms, rent, or mortgage		
Phone (cell and/or landline)		
Cable TV, Internet		
Gas and electric, water		
Car costs: monthly payment, auto insurance, maintenance, repairs, registration, inspections		
Travel costs: gas, public transportation, parking permits, tolls		
Vacations, trips home		
Food: Groceries, meal plan cafeteria, eating out, snacks		
Health insurance		
Health maintenance costs: gym, equipment, sports fees, classes		
Medical costs: doctor and dentists visits, vision, prescriptions, counseling		
Entertainment: movies, music purchases, socializing		
Laundry costs: supplies, service		
Clothing purchases		
Household supplies		
Payments on credit card debt		
Student loan or other loan repayment		
Donations to charitable organizations		
Childcare		
Other: emergencies, hobbies, gifts		
TOTAL EXPECTED EXPENSES		

Managing Money

Continued

281

get practical

MAP OUT YOUR BUDGET (CONTINUED)

Step 2: Gross Income. Calculate your average monthly income. As with expenses, if any source of income arrives only once a year, enter it in the annual column and divide by 12 to get the monthly figure. For example, if you have a $6,000 scholarship for the year, your monthly income would be $500 ($6,000 divided by 12).

INCOME/RESOURCES	MONTHLY INCOME	ANNUAL
Employment (after federal/state taxes)		
Family contribution		
Financial Assistance: grants, federal and other loans		
Scholarships		
Interest and dividends		
Other gifts, income, and contributions		
Total Expected Income		

Step 3: Net Income (Cash Flow). Subtract the grand total of your monthly expenses from the grand total of your monthly income.

INCOME PER MONTH	
Total expected expenses	
Total expected income	
NET INCOME (INCOME – EXPENSES)	

Source: Adapted from Julie Stein, California State University, East Bay.

Step 4: Adjustments. If you have a negative cash flow, what would you change? Examine your budget and spending log to look for problem areas. Remember, you can increase income, decrease spending, or do both. Describe two ideas about how to get your cash flow back in the black.

Juggle Work and School

If you want or need to work, as Torian did and as many students do, try to balance it with your academic work and goals. Thinking analytically and creatively, come up with productive risks that bring your desired reward.

Establish your needs

Think about what you need from a job. Ask questions like these:

- How much money do I need to make—weekly, per term, per year?
- What time of day is best for me? Should I consider night or weekend work?
- Can my schedule handle a full-time job, or should I look for part-time work?
- Do I want hands-on experience in a particular field?

- How flexible do I need the job to be?
- Can I or should I find work at my school or as part of a work–study program?

Analyze the impact

Working while in school has both positive and negative effects. Think through these pros and cons when considering or evaluating any job.

PROS OF WORKING WHILE IN SCHOOL	CONS OF WORKING WHILE IN SCHOOL
• Gain general and career-specific experience.	• Have less time to study due to time commitment for your job.
• Develop contacts.	• Have less time for nonacademic activities.
• Enhance your school performance (although full-time work can be problematic, working up to 15 hours a week may actually improve efficiency).	• Must shift gears mentally from work to classroom.
	• Stretch yourself too thin; become fatigued and anxious.
• Earn money.	

Create and choose options

With the information you have gathered and analyzed, look carefully at what is available on and off campus, and apply for the job or jobs that suit your needs best. Sometimes work–study programs are a good place to start because they are flexible, typically provide employment on campus (less commute time), and may offer college credit along with pay.

Continue to evaluate whether the reward of your job is worth the risk. Are your studies suffering? Are you making enough money? Are you getting enough sleep? If the job doesn't benefit you as much as you anticipated, consider making a change—perhaps you can renegotiate your job duties and schedule, or maybe you need to change jobs. Make careful, well-considered choices that bring you the rewards you need most.

Explore and Apply for Financial Aid

Financing your education—alone or with the help of your family—involves gathering financial information and making decisions about what you can afford and how much help you need. Here are some roadblocks that stand in the way of getting help:

- **Students don't apply.** One recent report indicated that almost 40% of full-time community college students do not fill out a federal aid application, including 29% of students with incomes under $10,000 per year. These students may be intimidated by the application process or simply believe that they won't qualify for aid.[7]

- **The economy has an effect.** When the economy is struggling, private banks are less likely to grant loans, and federal programs like the Pell Grants have less money. Also, in tough economic times, more students apply for grants like the Pell (see Key 11.5 in the next section), resulting in more people getting smaller pieces of the pie.

- **Colleges vary in what they offer.** State colleges provide fewer opportunities for aid when their funding is reduced. In addition, some smaller colleges no longer offer federal loans to their students because they are concerned about students' ability to pay back loans.

Find your way around these roadblocks by becoming informed about what is available to you. Then be proactive and go out and get it.

Many students are able to fit part-time work into their schedules if they stay local. Look for jobs at nearby businesses such as restaurants and retailers.

get $mart

YOUR FINANCIAL LIFESTYLE

Examine your current financial lifestyle. Circle your answers to the following questions:

1. Which do you typically spend money on first?
   a. Needs
   b. Wants

2. Where do you tend to find yourself at the end of the month?
   a. With a little bit of spending money
   b. Down to zero

3. How do you typically use credit cards?
   a. Only when I know I can pay off the balance at the end of the month.
   b. Frequently, and I pay the minimum each month.

4. How aware are you of money coming in and going out?
   a. I check my finances regularly and stay aware.
   b. I don't pay much attention to my finances.

5. Where do you keep money that you've saved?
   a. In a checking or savings account
   b. I don't have savings

Add up the number of a and b answers: a_____ b_____

More a answers than b answers indicates *more* financial stability. More b answers indicates *less* financial stability. Whether you tend to be more or less stable is not a judgment on you, but an opportunity to assess the effects of your financial lifestyle and decide if you want to adjust it in order to increase your stability. What is your reaction to this small look at your habits? Describe your reaction in a short paragraph on a sheet of paper or digital file.

Types of aid

Aid comes in the form of student loans, grants, and scholarships. Never assume you are not eligible for aid. Almost all students are eligible for some kind of need-based or merit-based financial assistance.

- *Student loans.* Student loan recipients are responsible for paying back the amount borrowed, plus interest, according to a payment schedule that may stretch over a number of years. The federal government administers or oversees all student loans. To receive aid from a federal program, you must be a citizen or eligible non-citizen and be enrolled in a program that meets government requirements. According to the College Board Advocacy and Policy Center, from 2010 to 2011, approximately 10.3 million students received Stafford Loans.[8]

- *Grants.* Unlike student loans, grants do not require repayment. Grants are funded by federal, state, or local governments as well as private organizations. They are awarded to students who show financial need. According to the College Board Advocacy and Policy Center, from 2010 to 2011, 51% of all undergraduates' grant aid came from the federal government.[9]

Risk asking tough questions to be rewarded with new insights. Use the following questions to inspire discussion with classmates, either in person or online.

- What obstacles, reasonable or not, have kept you from applying for financial aid? Identify a risk you can take today to earn the reward of overcoming one or more of them.

- How good are you at differentiating between needs and wants? At prioritizing needs?

- Everyone has coping strategies that involve spending: some people like new clothes, others like expensive restaurants. What can you do to make the reward of saving money seem worth the risk of feeling deprived?

CONSIDER THE CASE: Torian had a sudden change in his finances when he lost his athletic scholarship. Are you prepared to handle a sudden drain on your bank account or loss of financial support from your family? What could you do to be ready? If you have experienced a financial crisis, how did you get through it?

- *Scholarships.* Scholarships are awarded to students who show talent or ability in specific areas (academic achievement, sports, the arts, citizenship, or leadership). They may be financed by government or private organizations, employers (yours or your parents'), schools, religious organizations, local and community groups, credit unions, or individuals. They do not require repayment.

Key 11.5 lists federal grant and loan programs. Additional information about each is available in various federal student aid publications, which you can find at your school's financial aid office, request by phone (800-433-3243), or access online at http://studentaid.ed.gov.

Looking for aid

Now that you understand the different types of financial aid, consider how to go about getting that aid. First you will need to find out what aid is available. Here are five actions to take in your quest to pay for college.[10]

- *Ask, ask, ask.* Visit the financial aid office regularly. Ask what you are eligible for. Alert the office to any change in your financial situation. Search libraries and the Web, including your school's website, for information on everything that is possible.

- *Seek government aid.* Fill out the Free Application for Federal Student Aid (FAFSA) form electronically. The form can be found through your college's financial aid office, the FAFSA website (www.fafsa.ed.gov), or the U.S. Department

Managing Money

KEY 11.5 **Understand federal loan and grant programs.**

GRANTS	LOANS
• **Pell.** Need-based, available to undergraduates with no other degrees. In 2010–2011, approximately 9.1 million undergraduates received Pell Grants.	• **Stafford.** For students enrolled at least half-time. In 2010–2011, approximately 10.3 million students received Stafford Loans.
• **Federal Supplemental Educational Opportunity (FSEOG).** Need-based, only available at participating schools.	• **Perkins.** For those with exceptional financial need.
• **Work–study.** Need-based, pays an hourly wage for selected jobs.	• **PLUS.** Available to students claimed as dependents by their parents.

Sources: "Student Aid on the Web." U.S. Department of Education, January 31, 2012. From http://studentaid.ed.gov/PORTALSWebApp/students/english/index. jsp; and College Board Advocacy and Policy Center. *Trends in Student Aid 2011.* New York, NY: The College Board, 2011, p. 3.

of Education's website (www.ed.gov/finaid.html). You will create a personal portfolio, called MyFSA, on the site. This is where you will enter and store information, including your FAFSA form and any other pertinent forms. The U.S. Department of Education has an online tool called FAFSA Forecaster to help you estimate how much aid you qualify for. You will need to reapply every year for federal aid. *Note:* This is a *free* tool. If you hear about services that charge a fee for completing your FAFSA for you, avoid them.

- *Seek private aid.* Thoroughly investigate what you may be eligible for. Search libraries and your school's website, go through books that list scholarships and grants, talk with a financial aid advisor on your campus, and check scholarship search sites such as Scholarships.com and Fastweb.com. Know details that may help you identify sources available to you (you or your family's military status, ethnic background, membership in organizations, religious affiliation, and so on). However, be wary of private loans, which can have higher interest rates than federal loans, less flexible terms of repayment, and tougher consequences for late payments or defaults.

- *Consider a range of options.* Stay open to risks that are not your first choice but may prove productive. For example, transferring to a less expensive school may provide you with a comparable education while helping you to minimize debt. Changing your major to something with better job prospects could earn you more money to help pay off loans.

Applying for aid

Apply by the deadline, or even better, early. The earlier you complete the process, the greater your chances of being considered for financial aid, especially when you are competing for part of a limited pool of funds. Here are some additional tips from financial aid experts Arlina DeNardo and Carolyn Lindley of Northwestern University:[11]

- *Know what applications you need to fill out.* All colleges require FAFSA, but some also require a form called the CSS/Financial Aid Profile (see Student. collegeboard.org).

- *Note the difference between merit-based and need-based aid.* While some aid is awarded based on financial need, other aid is merit based, linked to specifics such as academic performance, a particular major, or ethnic origin.

- *Be aware of the total cost of attending college.* When you consider how much money you need, add books, transportation, housing, food, and other fees to the cost of tuition.

- *If you receive aid, pay attention to the award letter.* Know whether the aid is a grant or a loan that needs to be repaid. Follow all rules, such as remaining in good academic standing. Pay attention to all reapplication deadlines and meet them (many require reapplication every year). If you're late, you won't be able to apply.

- *Spend the money you receive on your needs.* Especially if it comes in one big check, the money might look so good that you will be tempted to buy a car and do some extra shopping before you get to that tuition bill. Don't let your wants distract you from your needs. Put your aid toward coursework and related food and housing expenses first.

- *Don't take out more money than you need.* If you max out on your total aid too early in your college career, you could run into trouble as you approach graduation. Look at your needs year by year and make sure you are only taking out what is absolutely necessary. Keep future plans in mind if you want to transfer to another institution and earn a separate degree. Consider the statistics: Approximately 55% of students who graduate with a bachelor's degree carry $28,000 in debt.[12]

Finally, if you receive aid from your college or somewhere else, follow all rules and regulations closely. Also, take a new look each year at what's available. You may be eligible for different grants or scholarships than those you first applied for.

GENERATE DAY-TO-DAY WAYS TO SAVE MONEY

Complete the following on paper or in digital format.

Think about all the ways you spend money in a month's time. Where can you trim a bit? What expense can you do without? Where can you look for savings or discounts? Can you barter a product or service with a friend? Create a list of five to ten workable ideas.

Then, give some of your ideas a try and see how they can help you save. Describe a plan for how you will use three to five ideas right away.

Consider making the experiment tangible by putting cash into a jar daily or weekly in the amounts that these changes are saving you. See what you have accumulated at the end of one month—and bank it.

In response to rising education costs, students are borrowing ever-larger amounts of money. Consequently, the number of students *defaulting* on loans (walking away from them without paying) is on the rise, and even personal bankruptcy won't make student loans go away.[13] The consequences for defaulting on a loan are severe and include credit trouble, inability to apply for further aid, money taken from your salary or social security payment, and more. Borrow only what you need. For helpful information about managing loans, see www.finaid.org.

Student loans are one way of borrowing the money you need to live and study. Next, look at a much more expensive form of borrowing—credit cards.

WHAT WILL HELP YOU USE CREDIT
cards and debit cards wisely?

The typical college student receives dozens of credit card offers. These offers, and the cards that go with them, are a double-edged sword: They are a handy alternative to cash and can reward you with a strong credit history if used with a reasonable level of risk. But they also can plunge you into a hole of debt. Students are acquiring cards in droves. In fact, in 2009, only 2% of undergraduates had no credit history.[14]

Credit cards are a particular danger for students. Credit companies often target students by presenting a positive spin about credit cards, knowing that many students lack knowledge about how credit works. Too much focus on *what* they can purchase with credit cards (rather than *how much* it will really cost them) leads students into trouble because they spend more than they can afford. Recent statistics from a survey of undergraduates illustrate the situation.[15]

- 84% of all students have at least one credit card and 50% have four or more credit cards.
- Students who hold credit cards carry an average outstanding balance of $3,173, and seniors graduate with an average of $4,100 in credit card debt.
- 82% of students don't pay their cards in full each month, and therefore pay finance charges.
- 90% of students pay for some type of education expense on credit, including 76% who charge textbooks and 30% who use cards to pay tuition.

Managing Money

Many college students charge a wide variety of expenses like car repairs, food, and clothes in addition to school costs. Before they know it, they are deeply in debt. It's hard to notice trouble brewing when you don't see your wallet taking a hit.

How Credit Cards Work

To charge means to create a debt that must be repaid. The credit card issuer, such as Bank of America, Chase, CitiGroup, or Wells Fargo, earns money by charging interest on unpaid balances. The interest is usually 18% or higher. Here's an example: Say you have a $3,000 unpaid balance on your card at an annual interest rate of 18%. If you make the $60 minimum payment every month, it will take *eight years* to pay off your debt, assuming that you make no other purchases. The effect on your wallet is staggering:

Original debt	$3,000
Cost to repay credit card loan at an annual interest rate of 18 percent for 8 years	$5,760
Cost of using credit	**$2,760** ($5,760 – $3,000)

By the time you finish, you will repay almost *twice* your original debt.

Keep in mind that credit card companies are in the business to make money off card owners like you (as well as retailers, who pay a "swipe fee" each time a customer pays with credit). They do *not* have your financial best interests at heart. Focusing on what's best for your finances is *your* job, and the first step is to know as much as you can about credit cards. Start with the important concepts presented in Key 11.6, read the fine print about any card you are considering, and stay focused on productive rewards that are worth the risk of spending on credit.

Watch for Problems

In response to recent economic changes, credit card disclaimers and policies can cause problems unless you stay alert. Here are a few you should note, both when seeking a new card and when looking at existing card statements:[16]

- *New fees.* In addition to annual fees, a card may charge fees for reward programs, paying your bill by phone, or even checking your balance. Find out what the fees are, and switch cards if you feel they are excessive.
- *Shrinking or disappearing grace periods.* In the past, a "grace period" of a few days may have given you a chance to pay late but avoid fees. Now, even just slightly late payments result in a late fee. And in many cases, once you pay late, the credit card company immediately increases your interest rate.
- *Reward program changes.* A reward program you've enjoyed for a while, such as airline miles or cash back, may change, so keep checking your statements. Cards may charge for reward programs or may change or remove them if you are late with a payment.
- *"Fee harvesting" cards.* Some cards feature low credit limits and come loaded with extra fees. After the fees are tacked onto the low credit limit, very little is left to spend and consumers often end up going over their limit, resulting in more fees.
- *The universal default clause.* This increasingly common policy allows a creditor to increase your interest rates if you make a late payment to *any* account, not just the accounts you have with those creditors. This means that if you are late on your payment for an unrelated loan, your creditors can increase your credit card interest rate.

- *Phishing emails.* Phishing is a technique for obtaining private information illegally. An email appearing to come from a legitimate business such as your credit card company asks you to verify information such as your social security number or PIN number. If you click on the link in the e-mail, you are taken to a fraudulent website where any personal information you enter can be stolen. To avoid phishing scams, do not respond to any e-mail that asks you to enter personal financial information. Your real bank and credit card companies would never ask you for it via email.
- *Identity theft.* The downside of technology is that identity theft makes a mess of hundreds of thousands of people's finances each year. Do your best to prevent it by holding on to receipts, shredding documents when you are done with them,

KEY 11.6 Learn to use credit carefully.

WHAT TO KNOW ABOUT . . .	. . . AND HOW TO USE WHAT YOU KNOW
Account balance. A dollar amount that includes any unpaid balance, new purchases and cash advances, finance charges, and fees. Updated monthly.	Charge only what you can afford to pay at the end of the month. Keep track of your balance. Hold on to receipts and call customer service if you have questions.
Annual fee. The yearly cost that some companies charge for owning a card.	Look for cards without an annual fee or, if you've paid your bills on time, ask your current company to waive the fee.
Annual percentage rate (APR). The amount of interest charged yearly on your unpaid balance. This is the cost of credit if you carry a balance in any given month. The higher the APR, the more you pay in finance charges.	Shop around (check Studentcredit.com). Also, watch out for low, but temporary, introductory rates that skyrocket to over 20% after a few months. Always ask what the long-term interest rate is and look for fixed rates (guaranteed not to change).
Available credit. The unused portion of your credit line, updated monthly on your bill.	It is important to have credit available for emergencies, so avoid charging to the limit.
Cash advance. An immediate loan, in the form of cash, from the credit card company. You are charged interest immediately and may also pay a separate transaction fee.	Use a cash advance only in extreme emergencies because the finance charges start as soon as you complete the transaction and interest rates are greater than the regular APR. It is a very expensive way to borrow money.
Credit limit. The debt ceiling the card company places on your account (e.g., $1,500). The total owed, including purchases, cash advances, finance charges, and fees, cannot exceed this limit.	Credit card companies generally set low credit limits for college students. Owning more than one card increases the credit available, but most likely increases problems as well. Try to use only one card.
Delinquent account. An account that is not paid on time or one where the minimum payment has not been met.	Always pay on time, even if it is only the minimum payment. If you do not pay on time, you will you be charged substantial late fees and will risk losing your good credit rating, which affects your ability to borrow in the future. Delinquent accounts remain part of your credit records for years.
Due date. The date your payment must be received and after which you will be charged a late fee.	Avoid late fees and finance charges by paying at least a week in advance.
Finance charges. The total cost of credit, including interest, service fees, and transaction fees.	The only way to avoid finance charges is to pay your balance in full by the due date. If you keep your balance low, you will be more able to pay it off.
Minimum payment. The smallest amount you can pay by the statement due date. The amount is set by the credit card company.	Making only the minimum payment each month can result in disaster if you charge more than you can afford. When you make a purchase, think in terms of total cost.
Outstanding balance. The total amount you owe on your card.	If you carry a balance over several months, additional purchases are hit with finance charges. Pay cash for new purchases until your balance is under control.
Past due. Your account is considered "past due" when you fail to pay the minimum required payment on schedule.	Look for past due accounts on your credit history by getting a credit report from one of the credit bureaus (Experian, TransUnion, and Equifax) or myFICO or Credit Karma.

To maintain an accurate perspective on where your money goes, keep credit card receipts and include those purchases as you track expenses.

making sure no one sees you enter a PIN, only using secure sites when shopping with your credit card online (they begin with an "https" instead of "http"), and avoiding giving out your Social Security number unless absolutely necessary.[17]

The best way to avoid problems is to read the fine print, pay attention to your balances, and pay your bills on time. Keep in mind that using a *debit card* is a smart alternative to paying on credit. A debit card is connected directly to your checking account. When you use it to withdraw cash from an ATM or to pay for your purchases at the register, the money comes right out of your checking account, so every purchase made with your debit card appears on your bank statement. This helps you track your purchases.

Manage Credit Card Debt

Many older students are familiar with the pros and cons of credit, and may already work hard to focus credit card use on items they or their families can't do without. However, even if you limit your card use to needs, you can still get into trouble. Debt can escalate quickly and can even lead to personal bankruptcy—a major blot on your credit that can last for years, and one to avoid at all costs. A few basics will help you stay in control.

- *Choose your card wisely.* Look for cards with low interest rate cards, no annual fee, a rewards program, and a grace period.
- *Ask questions before charging.* Would you buy that item if you had to pay cash? Can you pay the balance at the end of the billing cycle?
- *Pay bills regularly and on time, and try to make more than the minimim payment.* Set up a reminder system that activates a week or so before the due date. You can create an e-mail alert through your card account, make a note in your datebook, or set an alarm on your electronic planner.
- *If you get into trouble, call the credit company and ask to set up a payment plan.* You may even be able to make partial payments or get a reduced interest rate. Then, going forward, try to avoid the same mistakes. If you still need help, contact the following organizations for such help: National Foundation for Credit Counseling or American Financial Solutions. *Note:* These organizations do not charge for their services.
- *Shred credit cards when you close an account* or if you feel you have too many cards. Remember, even though you've destroyed the card, the debt attached to it remains until you've paid it off in full and sent a written statement to the company asking to close the account.

Build a Good Credit Score

CREDIT SCORE
A measure of how likely you are to pay your bills, calculated from a credit report using a standarized formula.

Your credit score is a prediction of your ability to pay back debt. If you've ever bought a car, signed up for a credit card, or purchased insurance, the deal you got was related to your credit score. If you rent an apartment, sign up for a cell phone plan, connect utilities at your home, or apply for a job where you are required to handle money, someone will examine your credit score.

CREDITOR
A person or company to whom a debt is owed, usually money.

Most credit scores are called FICO scores, determined by the Fair Isaac Company from a credit-scoring scale running from 300 to 850. Your number gives creditors an idea of how reliable you are. In general, having a higher score is related to getting better interest rates. For instance, suppose you have a score of 520 and another person has a score of 720, and both of you have a $100,000 30-year mortgage. Because of your lower credit

get analytical

EXAMINE CREDIT CARD USE

Complete the following on paper or in digital format.

Take a careful look at who you are as a credit consumer. Gather your most recent credit card statements to prepare for this exercise. Answer questions 1 through 5.

1. How many credit cards do you have? For each, list the following:
   - Name of card and who issued it (for example, VISA from Home State Bank)
   - Current interest rate
   - Current balance
   - Late fee if you do not pay on time
   - Approximate due date for card payment each month

2. Add your balances together. This total is your current credit debt.

3. How much did you pay last month in finance charges? Total your finance charges from the most recent statements of all cards.

4. Do you pay on time, do you tend to pay late, or does it vary?

5. Estimate how many times a year you pay a late fee. Looking at how much your cards charge for late fees, estimate how much money you spent in the last year in late fees.

When you've gathered all your information, analyze how effectively you currently use credit. If you are satisfied with your habits, keep up the good work. If not, identify your bad habits and write specific plans about how to change those habits.

score, you will have a higher APR (annual percentage rate) on your loan, and will ultimately pay $110,325 more in interest charges—the cost of another whole mortgage.[18] Even if a creditor uses another type of credit score, such as a VantageScore, your ratings on different scoring systems will be comparable. Higher is better no matter what the system.

If you're trying to keep your score in good shape, or if you need to get your score back on track, look at Key 11.7 to get an idea of what affects it.

Many people go through periods when they have a hard time paying bills. However, paying late could lower your credit rating, resulting in several negative effects including:

- Increased rates of interest
- Difficulty getting a loan for a home or car
- Higher premiums with insurance companies
- Obstacles to renting an apartment
- An indication to a potential employer that you may be less trustworthy
- Extra charges from utilities, such as a required deposit when opening an account

Building, maintaining, and repairing credit is an ongoing challenge. Three primary credit bureaus (Experian, TransUnion, and Equifax) will send you a report containing your credit score and credit history. You can obtain one free report per year, but charges are incurred for any additional reports. For more information, see AnnualCreditReport.com.

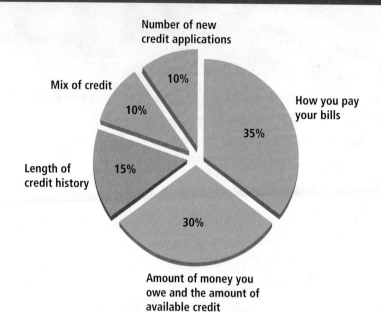

Number of new credit applications 10%

Mix of credit 10%

How you pay your bills 35%

Length of credit history 15%

30%

Amount of money you owe and the amount of available credit

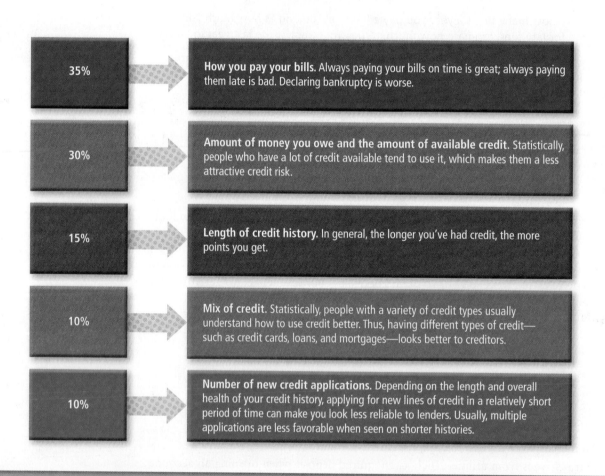

| 35% | **How you pay your bills.** Always paying your bills on time is great; always paying them late is bad. Declaring bankruptcy is worse. |

| 30% | **Amount of money you owe and the amount of available credit.** Statistically, people who have a lot of credit available tend to use it, which makes them a less attractive credit risk. |

| 15% | **Length of credit history.** In general, the longer you've had credit, the more points you get. |

| 10% | **Mix of credit.** Statistically, people with a variety of credit types usually understand how to use credit better. Thus, having different types of credit—such as credit cards, loans, and mortgages—looks better to creditors. |

| 10% | **Number of new credit applications.** Depending on the length and overall health of your credit history, applying for new lines of credit in a relatively short period of time can make you look less reliable to lenders. Usually, multiple applications are less favorable when seen on shorter histories. |

HOW CAN YOU PLAN FOR A
solid financial future?

Being able to achieve long-term financial goals—buying a car or a house, taking a vacation, saving money for retirement and for emergencies—requires that you think critically about short-term risks that will bring long-term financial reward. The strategies you've examined so far contribute to your long-term goals because they help you spend wisely and maximize your savings.

Save and Invest Your Money

When you live below your means, the money left over can go into savings accounts and investments, which can help you with regular expenses, long-term financial plans, and emergencies (financial advisors recommend a cash "emergency fund" that will cover at least three months' worth of expenses). Savings accounts, CDs, and money market accounts can help your money grow.

> **COMPOUND INTEREST**
> Interest calculated on the principal (original investment) as well as the interest already added to the account.

Savings accounts. Most savings accounts have a fixed rate of *interest* (a sum paid for the use of your money while it is in the bank). Money in those accounts earns **compound interest**. Here's how it works: If you put $1,000 in an account that carries 5% interest, you will earn $50 over the course of the first year. Your account then holds $1,050. From that point on, interest is calculated on that $1,050, not just on the original $1,000. Imagine this: If you invested that $1,000 at the age of 22 and put a mere $50 in the account each month, by the time you turned 62 you would have over $100,000.

Certificates of deposit (CDs) and money market accounts. CDs deliver a fixed rate of interest on an amount of money that you put away for a specific period of time (three months, six months, one year). Money market accounts also deliver a fixed rate of interest and allow you to withdraw money, but tend to require a minimum balance and restrict you to a certain number of withdrawals per month. Both types of accounts earn slightly more than a regular savings account.

Begin Saving for Retirement

With so many workers switching jobs frequently and working freelance, fewer people are retiring with guaranteed retirement income other than social security. As more employers reduce or eliminate pension benefits, it is up to individual workers to put away money for retirement.

Some employers offer their full-time workers a 401(k) retirement savings plan. This is a "painless" savings plan where you agree to have a certain amount of money automatically withdrawn from your paycheck and deposited in a retirement account. Your employer will often match your contribution, which means if you contribute $100 each month, $200 will be deposited in the account. The money you deposit is tax-free (you can deduct it from your annual earnings) and the interest it earns is tax-free until you begin withdrawing it after retirement.

student PROFILE

Charlotte Buckley

HINDS COMMUNITY COLLEGE,
JACKSON, MISSISSIPPI

About me:

I am 39 years old. I dropped out of high school and didn't return to school for 20 years. I wanted to finish my education, but as a single mom raising two kids, I couldn't figure out how to go back to school. My teenage daughter helped me gain the courage to get my GED through Hinds' Dropout Recovery Initiative. I discovered I had an interest in nursing and was able to find a work–study program so I could continue attending college classes at Hinds. Now I am applying to a nursing school in Memphis.

My challenge and how I meet it:

I have a family to help support and I must balance working with going to school. First of all, the work–study program is amazing.

I believe everyone who needs financial aid should consider work–study. Although I sometimes feel very busy, I keep my goal right in front of me: A good education is a ticket to a better-paying job. Second, our family has to run on a tight budget. I did get married three years ago, so things aren't as tight as they were, but we all keep our long-term goals in view to resist spending money on things we don't need. I've always stressed to my two kids, and now to my two stepchildren, that a college education is a need, not a want.

What will help me in the workplace:

Living on a budget and sacrificing now for long-term goals later involve a lot of discipline. In the workforce, discipline allows you to make commitments to excellence even when the going gets tough. Discipline helps you weather some of the temporary storms in the working world and in life.

If no such plan is offered, or if you are self-employed, consider looking into Individual Retirement Accounts (IRAs) offered by financial institutions or banks. When you open an IRA, you can contribute to it monthly or at the end of each year. There are two kinds of IRAs. With a traditional IRA, the money you contribute is tax deductible, meaning you can deduct it from your annual earnings and lower your taxes. You cannot draw the money out without a penalty until you are 59-1/2 years old, and you must pay taxes upon withdrawal. With a Roth IRA, the money you contribute is considered part of your earnings and is not tax-deductible. However, once you are 59-1/2 years old and have had your Roth for at least five years, you can withdraw the money without paying taxes on it.

IRAs may be your best bet for investment. Key 11.8 shows the extraordinary earning potential of an IRA. The type of IRA you choose will depend on your employment, your income, and the money you have available to invest.

If you're feeling a bit overwhelmed about finances at this point in your life, you're not alone. Many college students, both those for whom financial responsibility is new and those for whom tuition is just one more addition to a stack of bills, have similar feelings. However, the University of Arizona reports that "the benefits of financial knowledge extend beyond having money into realms of physical and psychological well-being."[19] Keep learning about money management, take future risks based on the rewards you need most, and your actions will contribute to success for life.

Initial investment and contributions	Investment growth, based on 10% return, after . . .		
	10 years	25 years	40 years
$5,000 one-time investment	$12,969	$54,174	$226,296
$2,000 investment plus $2,000 annual contribution	$37,062	$218,364	$975,704

revisit RISK AND REWARD

What happened to Torian? Torian came to see that year juggling community college and his job as a turning point. "I knew if I didn't buckle down and put some structure into my life, I wouldn't reach my goals." The risks he took to refocus earned him the reward of a 3.7 grade-point average that year. He transferred to Benedictine University, which would meet his athletic and academic needs without putting him in loan debt. After earning his bachelor's in business administration, Torian embarked on a fast-rising career in finance, sales, and growth strategies for publishing industry leaders Houghton Mifflin and Pearson Education, working most recently as business solutions director for Pearson's Africa division. His latest risk involves working toward his master's in public administration and learning to speak Mandarin at Tsinghua University in Beijing, China, while maintaining his investment company, Torianite, Inc.

What does this mean for you? "I've done quite well over the past 10 years, but I've made it a point to keep budgeting," says Torian. "I haven't changed the way I live." Torian advises students to stick to a budget, avoid impulse purchases, keep debt low, and evaluate high-cost items by including interest payments in their analysis. How can you emulate Torian's financial restraint? Name one action you are willing to take in each area— sticking to a budget, avoiding impulse purchases, and keeping debt low—to work toward the reward of financial stability.

What risk may bring reward beyond your world? Torian's career has taken him to Africa, the Middle East, and Asia. Working in villages where food, water, and electricity are scarce, he has learned firsthand about the contrast between the opportunities that people have in the United States and the lack of opportunities elsewhere. You too can fight poverty, and in ways that won't jeopardize a college student's budget. Check out http://youthink.worldbank.org and click on the Get Involved tab; then explore the Resource Center. The site lists dozens of volunteer, internship, and activism opportunities. Find a cause that has appeals to you, then brainstorm cost-effective ways for you to make a difference.

Managing Money

Complete the following on paper or in digital format.

KNOW IT *Think Critically*

Your Relationship with Money

Getting a handle on money anxiety starts with an honest examination of how you relate to money.

Build basic skills. Analyze yourself as a money manager. Look back at page xxx for a description of what influences the way people handle money. Make some notes about your personal specifics in the following areas.

1. What do you most value spending money on?
2. How do you manage money?
3. How does your culture tend to view money?
4. How do your family and friends tend to handle money?

Take it to the next level. Generate ideas about what you want to do with your money. If you had enough money for your expenses and then some, what would you do with the extra? Would you save it, spend it, do a little of both? Describe what you would do if you had an extra $10,000 to spend this year.

Move toward mastery. Look for practical ways to move toward the scenario you imagined. Realistically, how can you make that $10,000 a reality over time? You may need to change how you operate as a money manager. You may need to make some sacrifices in the short term. Describe two specific plans involving changes and sacrifices that will move you toward your goal.

WRITE IT *Communicate*

Emotional intelligence journal: You and credit. First, describe yourself as a credit card user. Do you pay in full or run up a balance? Pay on time or pay late? Restrict use to emergencies or use your credit card (or cards) all the time? Describe how using credit cards makes you feel. Examine those feelings and their effect on how you use credit. Then describe a change in your thinking you could make that would help you handle money more wisely.

Real-life writing: Apply for aid. Use Internet or library resources to find two scholarships that are not federally funded, available through your college, and for which you are eligible. They can be linked to academic areas of interest, associated with particular talents you have, or offered by a group to which you or members of your family belong. Get applications for each and fill them out. Jot down notes about your personality, skills, talent, achievements, dreams, and contributions to others. Use the information from those notes to write a one-page cover letter for each application, telling the committee why you should receive this scholarship. Have someone proofread your work, *send the applications*, and see what happens.

WORK IT *Build Your Brand*

Be Specific About Your Job Needs

21st Century Learning Building Blocks

- Business literacy
- Initiative and self-direction

As you consider specific job directions and opportunities, begin thinking about a variety of job-related factors that may affect your job experience and personal life. These factors include the following:

- Benefits, including health insurance, vacation, 401(k)
- Integrity of company (its reputation)
- How the company deals with employees
- Promotion prospects (your chances for advancement)
- Job stability
- Training and educational opportunities (Does the company offer in-house training or fund job-related coursework?)
- Starting salary
- Quality of employees and physical environment
- Quality of management
- Nature of the work you will be doing (Will you be required to travel extensively? Will you be expected to work long hours? Will you be working in an office or in the field?)
- Your relationship with the company (Will you be a full-time or part-time employee or an independent contractor?)
- Job title
- Location of your primary workplace
- Company size
- Company's financial performance over time

Think about how important each factor is in your job choice. Then list them separately, giving each a rating on a scale of 1 to 10, with 1 being the least important and 10 being the most important. Keep in mind that even if you consider something very important, you may not get it right away if you are just beginning your career.

Finally, consider the results of a survey of college students conducted by the National Association of Colleges and Employers. According to students, their top two reasons for choosing an employer are *integrity of organization in its dealings with employees* as number one and *job stability* as number two. How do these top choices compare to your own?[20]

CHAPTER

12

College provides an extraordinary opportunity to explore yourself and the knowledge available to you. The earlier you risk thinking about career goals, the greater reward you can receive from your education and college resources, which can prepare you for work in both job-specific and general ways.

Careers and More

BUILDING A SUCCESSFUL FUTURE

What Would You Risk? *Stephen Oh*

THINK ABOUT THIS SITUATION AS YOU READ, AND CONSIDER WHAT ACTION YOU WOULD TAKE. THIS CHAPTER FOCUSES FIRST ON HOW TO PREPARE FOR SUCCESS ON THE JOB. THEN IT SHOWS HOW TO APPLY THE POWER OF SUCCESSFUL INTELLIGENCE TO YOUR LIFE NOW AND AFTER COLLEGE AND PROVIDES AN OPPORTUNITY FOR YOU TO ASSESS YOUR DEVELOPMENT OVER THE TERM.

For South Korean native Stephen Oh, realizing the "American Dream" required risk-taking, patience, and hard work. During the 1960s, Oh's father worked as a mechanic at a U.S. military base in South Korea. Taking advantage of his eligibility to obtain a U.S. immigration green card, his father moved the family—including Stephen and his five sisters—to the United States.

At the age of 10, Stephen lived in Virginia under the guidance of his second-oldest sister, about an hour away from his mom, dad, and oldest sister, who embarked on running a grocery store in Baltimore, Maryland. Just one week into the store's operation, Stephen's mother was shot and killed in a robbery attempt. "For my father, his American dream was shattered," Stephen says. "That was motivation for me, realizing the sacrifices that my parents had made."

Stephen saw how hard his father worked as a janitor at banks and churches. With a similar work ethic and willingness to risk, Stephen set out to become the first in his family to graduate college. His high school teacher convinced him to become a history major, which he planned to use as a springboard to a law career. But one of his friends who had graduated a year earlier urged Stephen to spend a year in the workforce, making money, and after that reevaluate whether he wanted to continue on to law school.

Stephen was torn. Making money right away—and paying off his student loan debt—was appealing, but Stephen had long envisioned a law career as his family's ticket to long-term stability. He wasn't sure which risk brought the more valuable reward.

To be continued . . .

THE DECISION TO DEVIATE FROM A CAREFULLY PLANNED CAREER PATH IS SOMETHING MANY PEOPLE STRUGGLE WITH. IF YOU KNOW YOURSELF WELL AND TAKE ADVANTAGE OF RESOURCES INSIDE AND OUTSIDE THE CLASSROOM, YOU ARE LIKELY TO DISCOVER A REWARDING CAREER BLUEPRINT. YOU'LL LEARN MORE ABOUT STEPHEN, AND THE REWARD RESULTING FROM HIS ACTIONS, WITHIN THE CHAPTER.

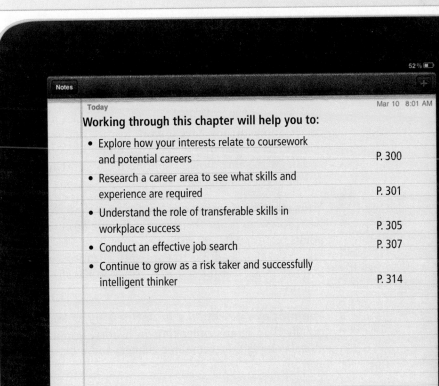

Notes

Today   Mar 10 8:01 AM

Working through this chapter will help you to:

statusCHECK

How Prepared Are You for Workplace and Life Success?

For each statement, fill in the number that best describes how often it applies to you.

1 = never   2 = seldom   3 = sometimes   4 = often   5 = always

1. I have thought about careers that may suit my interests and abilities. ① ② ③ ④ ⑤

2. I have looked into majors that match up with my career interests. ① ② ③ ④ ⑤

3. I have, or intend to get, hands-on experience through an internship, job, or volunteer work. ① ② ③ ④ ⑤

4. I understand the qualities that today's employers value most. ① ② ③ ④ ⑤

5. I save and update information about how to contact people with whom I network. ① ② ③ ④ ⑤

6. I am familiar with online job search, social networking, and career planning sites. ① ② ③ ④ ⑤

7. I know how to write an effective cover letter. ① ② ③ ④ ⑤

8. I have a current résumé to send out to prospective employers. ① ② ③ ④ ⑤

9. I am prepared to give a good impression during interviews. ① ② ③ ④ ⑤

10. Knowing how quickly the modern workplace changes, I'm ready to be flexible if a job or career choice doesn't last. ① ② ③ ④ ⑤

Each of the topics in these statements is covered in this chapter. Note those statements for which you filled in a 3 or lower. Skim the chapter to see where those topics appear, and pay special attention to them as you read, learn, and apply new strategies.

REMEMBER: NO MATTER HOW PREPARED YOU ARE TO SUCCEED IN THE WORKPLACE AND IN LIFE, YOU CAN IMPROVE WITH EFFORT AND PRACTICE.

HOW CAN YOU PREPARE FOR
career success?

Every student is in a unique position when it comes to preparing for a productive career. Some already have a work history, and others do not; some have known for a while exactly what they want to do, others have no idea at all, and still others are in the middle, with some thoughts but no focus yet. There are three things you should know as you begin this chapter:

Your starting point is not better or worse than anyone else's. Knowing exactly what you want is not "better" than having no clue—it's just different. Different starting points require different risks. Someone driven to pursue engineering, for example, may take risks that lead her toward specialization, while someone who has not yet pinpointed an area of interest may focus on risks that help clarify personal passions and abilities.

The modern workplace is defined by change. The working world shifts more rapidly than in any other time in history, responding to technological developments, global competition, economic change, and other factors. Although this brings a risk of frequent job changes, it also offers the reward of a myriad of opportunities to learn and reinvent yourself throughout your career. It also increases the importance of strong transferable skills such as thinking, teamwork, writing, goal setting, and more, which can make choosing a major a little less stressful.

Now is the time to think about careers. College provides a once-in-a-lifetime opportunity to explore yourself and the knowledge available to you. The earlier you take the risk to consider career goals, the greater reward you can receive from your education and college resources, which can prepare you for work in both job-specific and general ways.

Ideally, your career will reflect your values and talents and reward you with the income you need. The "right" career means something different to everyone, and, as Stephen found, what you think is best at one point may not be the path you ultimately take. With your self-discovery in this course, you are already on the road to discovering what makes the most sense for you. Read on about more career preparation strategies including considering your personality and strengths, exploring majors, investigating career paths, building knowledge and experience, knowing what employers want, and creating a strategic plan.

Taking courses in an area of interest can help you see how well a job in this area might suit you. These students get hands-on experience in respiratory therapy, as well as advice from an experienced instructor.

Consider Your Personality and Strengths

Because who you are as a learner relates closely to who you are as a worker, results from learning assessments provide clues in the search for the right career. For example, the Multiple Intelligences assessment points to information about your natural strengths and challenges, which can lead you to careers that involve these strengths. Look at Key 12.1 to see how those intelligences may link up with various careers.

The Personality Spectrum assessment is equally significant, because it focuses on how you work best with others, and career success often depends on your ability to function in a team. Key 12.2 links the four dimensions of the Personality Spectrum to career ideas and job search strategies. Look for your strengths and decide what you may want to keep in mind as you search. Look also at areas of challenge, and try to identify ways to boost your abilities in those areas. Even the most ideal job involves some tasks outside of your comfort zone. Remember to approach the information in Keys 12.1 and 12.2 as a guide, not a label. Your self-knowledge is a starting point for your goals about how you want to grow.

Finally, one other way to investigate how your personality and strengths may inform career choice is to take an inventory based on the Holland Theory. Theorizing that personality was related to career choice, psychologist John Holland came up with six different types that identify both personality and career areas: Realistic, Investigative, Artistic, Social, Enterprising, and Conventional (together known as RIASEC).[1] Holland developed two interest surveys that allow people to identify their order of preference for the six types and help them link their stronger types to career areas. Ask your career center about these surveys: the Vocational Preference Inventory (VPI®) or Self-Directed Search (SDS®).

Investigate Career Paths

Career possibilities extend far beyond what you can imagine. Talk to instructors, relatives, mentors, and fellow students about careers. Explore job listings, occupation lists, assessments, and other information at your school's career center. Check your library for

KEY 12.1 Multiple intelligences may open doors to careers.

MULTIPLE INTELLIGENCE	LOOK INTO A CAREER AS...
Bodily-kinesthetic	• Carpenter or draftsman • Physical therapist • Mechanical engineer • Dancer or actor • Exercise physiologist
Intrapersonal	• Research scientist • Computer engineer • Psychologist • Economist • Author
Interpersonal	• Social worker • PR or HR rep • Sociologist • Teacher • Nurse
Naturalistic	• Biochemical engineer • Natural scientist (geologist, ecologist, entymologist) • Paleontologist • Position with environmental group • Farmer or farm management
Musical	• Singer or voice coach • Music teacher • Record executive • Musician or conductor • Radio DJ or sound engineer
Logical-mathematical	• Doctor or dentist • Accountant • Attorney • Chemist • Investment banker
Verbal-linguistic	• Author or journalist • TV/radio producer • Literature or language teacher • Business executive • Copywriter or editor
Visual-spatial	• Graphic artist or illustrator • Photographer • Architect or interior designer • Art museum curator • Art teacher • Set or retail stylist

books on careers or biographies of people who worked in fields that interest you. Visit websites such as O*NET Online, which provides information about education and skills required for particular occupations, on-the-job tasks, possible salaries, and more. Look at Key 12.3 for the questions you might ask yourself as you conduct your research.

DIMENSION	JOB STRENGTHS	JOB CHALLENGES	WHAT TO LOOK FOR IN JOBS/CAREERS
Thinker	• Problem solving • Developing ideas • Keen analysis of situations • Fairness to others • Working efficiently through tasks • Innovating plans and systems • Ability to look strategically at the future	• A need for private time to think and work • A need, at times, to move away from established rules • A dislike of sameness—systems that don't change, repetitive tasks • Not always being open to expressing thoughts and feelings to others	• Some level of solo work/think time • Problem solving • Opportunity for innovation • Freedom to think creatively and to bend the rules • Technical work • Big picture strategic planning
Organizer	• High level of responsibility • Enthusiastic support of social structures • Order and reliability • Loyalty • Following through on tasks • Detailed planning skills with competent follow-through • Neatness and efficiency	• A need for tasks to be clearly, concretely defined • A need for structure and stability • A preference for less rapid change • A need for frequent feedback • A need for tangible appreciation • Low tolerance for people who don't conform to rules and regulations	• Clear, well-laid-out tasks and plans • Stable environment with consistent, repeated tasks • Organized supervisors • Clear structure of how employees nteract and report to one another • Value of, and reward for, loyalty
Giver	• Honesty and integrity • Commitment to putting energy toward close relationships with others • Finding ways to bring out the best in self and others • Peacemaker and mediator • Ability to listen well, respect opinions, and prioritize the needs of co-workers	• Difficulty handling conflict • Strong need for appreciation and praise • Low tolerance for perceived dishonesty or deception • Avoidance of people perceived as hostile, cold, or indifferent	• Emphasis on teamwork and relationship building • Indications of strong and open lines of communication among workers • Encouragement of personal expression in the workplace (arrangement of personal space, tolerance of personal celebrations, and so on)
Adventurer	• Skillfulness in many different areas • Willingness to try new things • Ability to take action • Hands-on problem-solving skills • Initiative and energy • Ability to negotiate • Spontaneity and creativity	• Intolerance of being kept waiting • Lack of detail focus • Impulsiveness • Dislike of sameness and authority • Need for freedom, constant change, and constant action • Tendency not to consider consequences of actions	• A spontaneous atmosphere • Less structure, more freedom • Adventuresome tasks • Situations involving change • Encouragement of hands-on problem solving • Travel and physical activity • Support of creative ideas and endeavors

Keep the following in mind as your investigate careers:

A wide array of job possibilities exists for most career fields. For example, the medical world consists of more than doctors and nurses. Administrators run hospitals, researchers test drugs, pharmacists prepare prescriptions, security experts ensure patient and visitor safety, and so on.

Within each job, there is a variety of tasks to perform. For instance, you may know that an instructor teaches, but you may not think about the fact that instructors may also write, research, study, design courses, give presentations, counsel, and coach. Take your career exploration beyond first impressions to get an accurate picture of the careers that interest you.

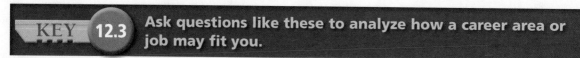

KEY 12.3 Ask questions like these to analyze how a career area or job may fit you.

What can I do in this area that I like and do well?	Do I respect the company or the industry? The product or service?
What are the educational requirements (certificates or degrees, courses)?	Does this company or industry accommodate special needs (child care, sick days, flex time)?
What skills are necessary?	Do I need to belong to a union? What does union membership involve?
What wage or salary and benefits can I expect?	Are there opportunities near where I live (or want to live)?
What personality types are best suited to this kind of work?	What other expectations exist (travel, overtime, and so on)?
What are the prospects for moving up to higher-level positions?	Do I prefer the service or production end of this industry?

Some career areas are growing more than others. If you have an interest in a growing career area, statistically you will have a better chance of finding a job. According to government data, careers projected to grow through the year 2014 include nursing, teaching, general and operations managers, accountants, and more.[2] Look up the U.S. Bureau of Labor's *Occupational Outlook Handbook* for projected growth, as well as average salary information, in different fields.

Explore Majors

You probably have explored majors at other times during this course, such as how choosing a major relates to goal setting and self-knowledge. Look to previous ideas and work for guidance as you continue and extend your exploration.

Focus on your interests and abilities. Countless sources of career advice make the point that pursuing a passion is a key element of career success. This doesn't mean that you'll love every aspect or every day of your job—no one does. However, you improve your chances of thriving if you spend the bulk of your job doing work that interests you and taps into your strengths.

Examine what your school offers. Even if you plan to transfer eventually, your school's major and certificate programs are an important aspect of your exploration. Look online and in the catalog to see what is offered. Meet with an advisor to discuss the options.

Consider career interests. If you are interested in one or more careers, investigate majors that may link to them—but don't narrow the field too much. An advisor can help you define which careers need specific majors and which are accessible from a broader range of educational backgrounds. For example, students going into medical professions usually need to major in a science or pre-med area, while students planning to pursue careers in business might major in anything from history, as Stephen did, to economics. Business owners are becoming more aware of how liberal arts majors bring value to the workplace through skills such as problem solving and writing.[3]

Build Knowledge and Experience

Even after comprehensive investigation, it's hard to choose the right path without knowledge or experience. Courses, internships, jobs, and volunteering are risks that promote those rewards.

Courses. Take a course or two in your areas of interest to determine if you like the material and excel in it. Find out what courses are required for a major in those areas. Check out your school's course catalogue for detailed information. Also, consider talking with the department chair, or an older student who has taken some of the courses, to gain more insight into the field.

Internships. An internship gives you a chance to work in your chosen field to see how you like it. Your career center may list summer or year-round internship opportunities. For more comprehensive guides, check out reference books like those published by Vault, as well as Internet sources like Internships.com and Princeton Review.

Jobs. You may discover career opportunities while earning money during a part-time job. Someone who takes a legal proofreading job to make extra cash might discover an interest in law. Someone who answers phones for a newspaper company might be drawn into journalism.

Volunteering. Helping others in need offers rewards including an introduction to careers, experience, new contacts, and a positive impression on potential employers. Many schools sponsor volunteer groups or have committees that organize volunteering opportunities. The federal government encourages volunteerism through AmeriCorps, a federal volunteer clearinghouse, which awards its volunteers money to pay for tuition or student loans.

Service learning. The goal of service learning is to provide the community with service and give students knowledge gained from hands-on experience.[4] Students in service learning programs enroll in credit-bearing courses where service and related assignments are required. Taking the risk of service learning can reward you with a sense of civic responsibility, opportunity to apply what you learn in the classroom, and personal growth. If you are interested, talk to your advisor about whether your school offers service learning programs.

INTERNSHIP
A temporary work program in which a student can gain supervised practical experience in a particular professional field.

Know What Employers Want

If you want to enter the job market or are already in it, know that prospective employers look for particular skills and qualities that mark you as a promising candidate. Most employers require you to have a skillset that includes specific technical know-how, but in this rapidly changing workplace, transferable skills may be even more crucial to your success.

Transferable skills

In the modern workplace, workers will hold an average of 11 jobs through their productive working years.[5] The high rate of job change means that abilities such as successful thinking and teamwork are crucial to workplace success and can transfer from one job or career to another. For example, you will need teamwork and writing skills for almost any job. Key 12.4 describes transferable skills employers seek.

SKILLSET
A combination of the knowledge, talent, and abilities that are needed to perform a specific job.

Emotional intelligence

Employers are also drawn to emotionally intelligent job candidates. Consider this scenario: You arrive at work distracted by a personal problem and tired from studying late the night before. Your supervisor is overloaded with a major project due that day. The person you work most closely with is coming in late due to a car problem. Everyone is stressed out. What does an emotionally intelligent person do?

KEY 12.4 Employers look for candidates with these important skills.

SKILL	WHY IS IT USEFUL?
Communication	Good listening, speaking, and writing skills are keys to working with others, as is being able to adjust to different communication styles.
Analytical thinking	Employees stand out when they can analyze choices and challenges, as well as assess the value of new ideas.
Creativity	The ability to come up with new concepts, plans, and products helps companies improve and innovate.
Practical thinking	No job gets done without employees who can think through a plan for achieving a goal, put it into action, and complete it successfully.
Teamwork	All workers interact with others on the job. Working well with others is essential for achieving workplace goals.
Goal setting	Teams fail if goals are unclear or unreasonable. Employees and companies benefit from setting realistic, specific goals and achieving them reliably.
Cultural competence	The workplace is increasingly diverse. Employees are valued when they can work with, adjust to, and respect people from different backgrounds and cultures.
Leadership	The ability to influence and motivate others in a positive way earns respect and career advancement.
Positive attitude	Other employees will gladly work with, and often advance, someone who completes tasks with positive, upbeat energy.
Integrity	Acting with integrity at work enhances value. This includes communicating promptly, being truthful and honest, following rules, and giving proper notice.
Flexibility	The most valuable employees understand the constancy of change and have developed the skills to adapt to its challenge.
Continual learning	The most valuable employees take personal responsibility to stay current in their fields.

- *Tune in to everyone's emotions first.* You: Tired and distracted. Your co-worker: Worried about the car and about being late. Your supervisor: Agitated about the project.
- *Pinpoint the thoughts that arise from these emotions.* People are likely to think that the deadline is in jeopardy.
- *Understand what the emotions are telling you.* Thinking that the deadline may not be met means that everyone is going to need an extra-focused and positive state of mind to get through the day and set aside distracted, negative thinking.
- *Manage the emotion with action.* You come up with several things you can do:
  - Prioritize your task list so that you can concentrate on what is most pressing.
  - Call your co-worker on his cell phone while he settles the car problem and let him know what's happening so he can prioritize tasks and support the supervisor when he arrives.
  - Ask another co-worker to bring in a favorite mid-morning snack to keep everyone going during the long day ahead.

The current emphasis on teamwork has highlighted emotional intelligence in the workplace. The more adept you are at working with others, the more likely you are to succeed.

get creative

YOUR STRATEGIC TIMELINE

Complete the following on paper or in digital format.

Considering your self-knowledge, experience, possible career paths, and understanding of the workplace, create a practical five-year timeline as a strategic plan to achieve a career goal. First, describe where you do want to be in five years. For each of the following time frames, write in the steps you think you will need to take toward that five-year goal. Include anything you envision in your path toward a career, such as steps related to declaring a major or a transfer to another school to pursue additional degrees.

- One month from now…
- Three months from now…
- Six months from now…
- One year from now…
- Two years from now…
- Three years from now…
- Four years from now…

Finally, create a timeline version of your plan, using a visual format you like and adding smaller goals as necessary. Keep your timeline where you can refer to it and revise it, since changes in the world and in your knowledge and experience may require adjustments in your plan.

Create a Strategic Plan

After your exploration has led you to jobs or careers that interest you, get specific and create a plan for how you will pursue one or more of them (see the Get Creative exercise for one way to do this). Establish the risks that make up this plan – whom you will talk to, what courses you will take, what skills you will work on, what jobs or internships you will investigate, and any other tasks. Be proactive in finding opportunities. But keep your plan flexible, seeing it as a structure to guide your actions, and knowing that there may be possibilities yet unknown to you.

With your knowledge of general workplace success strategies, you can effectively search for a job in a career area that works for you.

HOW CAN YOU CONDUCT
an effective job search?

Whether you are looking for a job now or planning ahead for a search closer to graduation, you have choices about how to proceed. In this challenging economy and struggling job market, finding the right job—or any job—may be tougher than you anticipated. Use resources available to you, know the basics about résumés and interviews, and plan strategically.

Careers and More

Use Available Resources

Use your school's career planning and placement office, your **networking** skills, classified ads, and online services to help you explore possibilities for career areas or specific jobs.

Your school's career planning and placement office

Generally, the career planning and placement office deals with post-graduation job opportunities, whereas the student employment office and financial aid office provide information about working during school. At either location you might find job listings, interview sign-up sheets, and company contact information. The career office may hold informational workshops on different topics. Your school may also sponsor job or career fairs where you can meet potential employers and explore job opportunities. Get acquainted with the career office early in your college career.

Take advantage of career fairs sponsored by your school or town. These career fair attendees pick up useful information and applications from a variety of employers.

NETWORKING
The exchange of information or services among individuals, groups, or institutions.

Networking

The most basic type of networking—talking to people about fields and jobs that interest you—is one of the most important job-hunting strategies. Networking contacts can answer questions regarding job hunting, job responsibilities and challenges, and salary expectations. Risk reaching out to friends and family members, instructors, administrators, counselors, alumni, employers, coworkers, and others for the reward of the help they can offer you.

Online social networking is another useful tool to help you in your job search. Tools like LinkedIn, Facebook, and Twitter allow members to connect with other individuals through groups, fan pages, and similar interests. During a job search, these sites can be used to meet people who work at companies you are interested in and showcase portfolio pieces. Businesses often search through LinkedIn profiles when they have job openings, so you never know who may contact you. However, online networking is no substitute for personal interaction; eventually you will have to talk to someone by phone or in person.

A word of caution: Your online presence is public. If you wouldn't want a potential employer (or your parents, instructor, or religious leader) to see something, don't post it. In fact, many employers review Facebook pages of applicants before inviting them for interviews.

Informational interviews and the hidden job market

When you find someone who is doing the job you want to do, teaching in your field of interest, or responsible for hiring in that field, try to set up an *informational interview* with this person—an opportunity for you to ask questions about what she does, how she got into the job, what she likes or doesn't like, and whom she knows. Since you are asking the questions and there is less at stake than in a traditional interview, you are likely to feel less nervous. Despite the lower risk, there is still potential for reward in the form of information and networking contacts.

To set up an interview, call or email the person. Introduce yourself and make it clear you are not looking for a job, just advice and support. Ask for 30 minutes of the person's time. Find out when he or she is are available and then suggest a meeting by phone, in the office, or at a coffee shop—whatever is most convenient. Prepare a set of questions ahead of time about things that matter to you. See Key 12.5 for a good list of informational interview questions.

On the day of the informational interview, dress professionally and arrive early. Have a copy of your résumé in case the person you are interviewing wants to see it.

1.	How did you find out about the job you are now in?	
2.	What skills do you have that are useful on the job?	
3.	Did you have those skills when you first started?	
4.	What are you good at?	
5.	Tell me about your typical day—what you do and who you work with.	
6.	What are your manager and co-workers like?	
7.	What's the communication style at your workplace?	
8.	What do you like about your job?	
9.	What makes your job difficult?	
10.	What is your educational and job background? Have you found it useful on the job?	
11.	What kind of education or experience do you recommend to get a job like the one you have?	
12.	What are the most important abilities you think someone needs to do your job well?	
13.	What is the starting salary range in your field?	
14.	About how many hours a week do you work?	
15.	Does your job have any benefits?	
16.	What do you think would prepare someone for your type of work?	
17.	Is there anything else you would like to share with me about your job?	
18.	Can you think of anyone else I should talk to?	

Take notes during the interview, and consider writing by hand so you do not distract the interviewee by typing. When you finish, express appreciation and ask if you can keep in touch. Provide your contact information (or a business card, if you have one) and ask for his or her card. Follow up with a personal thank-you note and send it by mail—handwritten notes get remembered. Then type up your notes and think about what they tell you about the job or career area you are investigating.

Through informational interviewing, you tap the "hidden job market"—unadvertised jobs that are filled through networking. More than 80% of new jobs are unadvertised.[6] Most companies would rather find a qualified person through word-of-mouth or a referral by one of their own employees. And the best way to get referred is to meet some of those employees through informational interviewing.

Online services and classified ads

When jobs get advertised, they generate a lot of competition. However, it doesn't hurt to look at job advertisements. Although classified ads are still helpful for local possibilities, the Internet—with its enormous information storage capabilities and low cost—is a better location for job postings. Many employers post detailed job openings through online job boards. In addition to a job description and salary information, most online postings will contain company information and a link to where you can submit an application. To get the most out of your virtual resources:

- Join a business-focused social networking site, like LinkedIn, and look at jobs posted there. Network with your contacts to find out about upcoming and existing openings.
- Check the web pages of individual associations and companies, which may post job listings and descriptions.

- Look up career-focused and job listing websites such as CareerBuilder.com, Monster.com, America's Job Bank, BilingualCareer.com, JobBankUSA, or futurestep.com. Many sites offer resources on career areas, résumés, and online job searching, in addition to job listings. *Note:* Competition is fierce on these large sites and you may not hear anything from them. Target companies where you think there is a fit, and try to find a specific person at that company to whom you can submit your résumé.
- Access job search databases such as the Career Placement Registry and U.S. Employment Opportunities.
- Do not hesitate to contact companies about jobs that are not advertised. For example, you see several jobs posted for a company you are interested in, but none for which you are qualified. Contact someone at the company and ask if there may be openings in your area of expertise in the near future. In addition, consider sending your résumé with a cover letter, to increase the chances that your name will come up when a position does become available.

If nothing happens right away, follow up with a short email, mail a hardcopy version of your résumé with a note that you are still interested, or call and ask the status of the application process. Keep in mind that statistically, networking results in far more hires than online posting. Some experts recommend you spend no more than 10 to 20% of your time responding to online job sites.[7] You don't risk much with this activity, but your chances for reward are likewise low.

Use an Organized, Consistent Strategy

Organize your approach according to what you need to do and when you have to do it. Do you plan to make three phone calls per day? Will you fill out one job application each week? Keep a record—on 3 by 5 cards, in a computer file or smartphone, or in a notebook—of the following:

- People you contact plus contact information and method of contact (email, snail mail, phone)
- Companies to which you apply
- Jobs for which you apply, including those you rule out (for example, a job that becomes unavailable)
- Responses to communications (phone calls to you, interviews, written communications), information about the person who contacted you (name, title), and the time and dates of contact

Keeping accurate records allows you to both chart your progress and maintain a clear picture of the process. Your records help you follow up and stay in touch. Key 12.6 shows you what part of a typical contact list might look like. If you don't get a job now but another opens up later at the same company, well-kept records will enable you to contact key personnel efficiently.

Your Résumé, Cover Letter, and Interview

"How-to" information about résumés, cover letters, and interviews fills entire books. To get you started, here are a few basic tips on giving yourself the best possible chance.

Cover letter and résumé

Cover letters and résumés are how you introduce yourself to prospective employers on paper so they will want to meet you in person. The purpose of the cover letter is to get the reader's attention so he or she will read your résumé. And the purpose of your résumé is to get the reader interested enough to call you in for an interview. You may have written a sample cover letter for an exercise earlier in this course.

CONTACT AND COMPANY	INITIAL PHONE CALL	LETTER / RESUME	FOLLOW-UP	INTERVIEW
Out Signals Jackson Fortnet PR Director 400 South Fields Street Suite 201 Chicago, IL 60622 312-505-0400 jfortnet@outsignals.com	SEPT. 13 Called and spoke briefly	SEPT. 14 Sent email to Jackson, along with résumé and job description.	SEPT. 21 Made follow-up call to find out if graphics design manager would be available for an informational interview. No such luck. Very unfriendly.	NO
Carto Net Scott de Frey 495-1000 scott.defrey@cartonet.com	SEPT. 15 Called Scott re: info. interview. He suggested sending in a résumé . . . but I don't know.	SEPT 19 Emailed Scott my letter and résumé.	SEPT. 22 Called Scott to set up info interview. Need to come up with list of questions	SEPT. 27 at 10:00 AM Informational interview with Scott by phone
Map Communication, Inc. Rachael and David Jacobson 203-0101 rjacobson@mapcomm.com	—	SEPT. 19 Responded to ad with résumé and cover letter	SEPT. 26 Called to check if my info. was received. Rachael said she liked what she saw and talked to me some more. She wants to interview me!	**SEPT. 28 At 3:30 PM** Interview at Map Communication

Keep your cover letter short, but attention-getting. Make sure it is focused on the job and company you are interested in. A good cover letter usually covers four main points:

1. The position for which you are applying and how you learned about it
2. Why you are the best person for the job (your abilities)
3. Why you want to work for the employer
4. A call to action (how you plan to follow up)

Design your résumé neatly, using a current and acceptable format (books or your career office can show you some standard formats). Make sure the information is accurate and truthful. Proofread it for errors and have someone else proofread it as well. Type or print it on high-quality paper (a heavier bond paper than is used for ordinary copies). Key 12.7 shows an example of a professional résumé.

Here are some general tips for writing a résumé:

- Always put your name and contact information at the top. Make it stand out.
- State an objective whenever possible. If your focus is narrow or you are designing this résumé for a particular interview or career area, keep your objective specific; otherwise, keep the objective more general.
- Provide a "core competencies" section that lists your key skills.
- List your post-secondary education, starting from the latest and working backward. This may include summer school, night school, seminars, and accreditations.
- List jobs in reverse chronological order (most recent job first). Include all types of work experience (full time, part time, volunteer, internship, and so on).
- When you describe your work experience, use action verbs and focus on what you have accomplished. Some people use the P + A = R formula when writing

Complete the following on paper or in digital format.

Name two career fields you would consider pursuing. Then, research résumé keywords that employers in these fields look for. To do so, enter the words "keyword," "resume," and a word or phrase related to the field ("chemical engineering," "criminal justice," etc.) into your favorite search engine. List at least five keywords for each field. Keep them on hand for tailoring your résumé to a job in either one of these fields.

their job tasks: They identify a problem, the action they took to solve it, and the results. For example: "Organized randomly filed client records in alphabetical and date order, reducing the time to access them by 80%."

■ Always make sure the descriptions in your job history demonstrate the skills listed in your core competencies section and relate to the job for which you are applying.

■ Include keywords that are linked to jobs for which you will be applying.

■ List references on a separate sheet (names, titles, companies, and contact information). You may want to put "References upon request" at the bottom of your résumé.

■ Use professional formatting and bullets to help the important information stand out. Stick with one font family for the body of the résumé and one for the headings (usually larger and bolded). Use italics sparingly because they are hard to read.

■ Get several people to look at your résumé before you send it out. Other readers will have ideas that you haven't thought of and may find errors that you have missed.

Prospective employers often use a computer to scan résumés, selecting the ones that contain keywords relating to the job opening or industry. Résumés without enough keywords probably won't even make it to the human resources desk. When you construct your résumé, make sure to include relevant keywords. For example, if you are seeking a computer-related job, list computer programs you use and other specific technical proficiencies. To figure out what keywords you need, look at the job descriptions and job postings and search online for examples of keywords related to your career interest.[8]

Interview

Be clean, neat, and appropriately dressed. Avoid tight or baggy clothing, extreme hairstyles, and flashy jewelry. Choose a nice pair of shoes—people notice (avoid spiky heels if you are a woman). You want interviewers to focus on you and your achievements, not your appearance.

Bring an extra copy of your résumé and any other materials that you want to show the interviewer, even if you sent a copy ahead of time. Avoid chewing gum and fidgeting. Don't text or check your Instagram—as a matter of fact, put all electronic devices away completely so you are not tempted to use them. Offer a confident handshake. Make eye contact. Show your integrity by speaking honestly about yourself.

Désirée Williams

237 Custer Street, San Francisco, CA 94101 • (415) 555-5252 (W) or (415) 555-7865 (H)
• email: desiree@comcast.net • website: www.DesireCulture.com

OBJECTIVE

Use my language, cross-cultural, and web skills to help children in an educational or corporate setting.

EDUCATION

2012 to present   San Francisco State University, San Francisco, CA

Pursuing a B.A. in the Spanish BCLAD (Bilingual, Cross-Cultural Language Acquisition Development) Education and Multiple Subject Credential Program.

Expected graduation: June 2016

SKILLS SUMMARY

Languages: Fluent in Spanish and English.

Proficient in Italian and Shona (majority language of Zimbabwe).

Computer: Programming ability in HTML, PHP, Javascript, .Net, and Silverlight.

Multimedia design expertise in Adobe Photoshop, Netobjects Fusion, Adobe Premiere, Macromedia Flash, and other visual design programs.

Personal: Perform professionally in Mary Schmary, a women's a cappela quartet.

Climbed Mt. Kilimanjaro.

PROFESSIONAL EMPLOYMENT

Sept. 2013 to present

Research Assistant, Knowledge Media Lab

San Francisco State University, San Francisco, CA

Develop ways for teachers to share their teaching practices online, in a collaborative, multimedia environment.

June 2013 to present

Webmaster/web Designer

Quake Net, San Mateo, CA (Internet service provider and Web commerce)

Designed several sites for the University of California, Berkeley, Graduate School of Education, as well as private clients, such as A Body of Work and Yoga Forever

Sept. 2012 to June 2013

Literacy Coordinator (internship)

Prescott School, Oakland, CA

Coordinated, advised, and created literacy curriculum for an America Reads literacy project.

Worked with nonreader 4th graders on writing and publishing, incorporating digital photography, Internet resources, and graphic design.

June 2012 to August 2012

Bilingual Educational Consultant (volunteer)

Children's Television Workshop, San Francisco, CA

Field-tested bilingual materials. With a research team, designed bilingual educational materials for an ecotourism project run by an indigenous rain forest community in Ecuador.

June 2009 to Sept. 2009

Children's Recreation Director: After-School Program

San Francisco Recreation and Parks Department

Performed playground supervision, taught arts and cultural activities, provided homework assistance, and managed summer reading program.

Worked primarily with low-income, Hispanic children, grades 1 to 5.

References and Portfolio of Work

Available upon request

get $mart

FIND WORK THAT COMBINES EARNINGS AND FULFILLMENT

Complete the following on paper or in digital format.

Investigate which jobs in your areas of interest can earn you what you need. Answer the following questions:

1. What are your most significant interests and skills?

2. What are three possible careers you feel would suit your interests and skills?

3. Identify three people you could talk to who work in, or know about, any of these careers. For each, write down the name, career, and contact information.

4. Contact an individual from the list to set up an informational interview. *Note:* Refer to "Informational Interviews and the Hidden Job Market" in this chapter for assistance.

5. Develop a list of questions to ask the individual about his or her job, making sure to focus on the question of how to balance passion and earnings. Save the list on a computer and print it.

6. Attend the informational interview, taking notes on your printed list. Send a follow-up thank you note. If you can, repeat the informational interview process with the other two people.

After the interview, no matter what the outcome, follow up right away with a formal but pleasant thank you note.

Being on time to your interview makes a positive impression—and being late will almost certainly be held against you. Finally, if you do not consider being late a sign of disrespect, remember that your interviewer may not agree.

HOW CAN YOU CONTINUE TO GROW
as a risk taker and thinker?

Much as finding a job is the beginning of your career adventure, finishing this course is the beginning of your life as a calculated risk taker and successfully intelligent learner. How can you stay motivated to keep thinking and risking? Earlier in this text, you may have completed a self-assessment to examine your levels of development in 20 characteristics that promote action and productive risks. According to Sternberg, successfully intelligent people:[9]

1. *Motivate themselves.* They make things happen, spurred on by a desire to succeed and a love of what they are doing. They rarely need others to tell them what to do.

2. *Learn to control their impulses.* Instead of going with their first quick response, they sit with a question or problem. They take time to let ideas surface before making a decision.

3. *Know when to persevere.* When the reward is worth the effort, they push past frustration and stay on course. They also recognize when they've hit a dead end and shift gears in response.

Risk asking tough questions to be rewarded with new insights. Use the following questions to inspire discussion with classmates, either in person or online.

- As one saying goes, "Do what you love and the money will follow." Do you agree that this risk will bring financial reward, or disagree? Support your opinion with examples.

- People who work freelance jobs make their own schedules but need to be careful money managers in order to save, pay for health insurance, and pay taxes. People who are employed by companies may have less freedom but are more likely to enjoy benefits such as insurance, savings plans, and having taxes taken out. Which suits you better?

- Have you had a job application rejected, failed to get a job after an interview, or been fired from a job? How did you cope? What reward resulted from your risk taking?

CONSIDER THE CASE: Stephen wasn't sure that a short-term career solution would provide stability for his family as effectively as his long-term plan to become a lawyer. If you knew him, which risk would you advise him to take? Would your advice change if you were his father? When should you deviate from what you consider to be a rewarding career plan?

4. *Know how to make the most of their abilities.* They understand what they do well and capitalize on those skills and abilities in school and work.

5. *Translate thought into action.* Not only do they have good ideas; they are able to turn those ideas into practical actions.

6. *Have a product orientation.* They want results. They focus on the reward they are aiming for first, then figure out what risks will get them there.

7. *Complete tasks and follow through.* With determination, they finish what they start. They also follow through to make sure loose ends are tied and the goal has been achieved.

8. *Are initiators.* They commit to people, projects, and ideas. They risk action rather than sitting back and waiting for things to happen to them.

9. *Are not afraid to fail.* Because their risks don't always bring the rewards they seek, they often learn from mistakes, build brain power, and enjoy greater success down the road.

10. *Don't procrastinate.* They are aware of the negative effects of putting things off, and they avoid it. They create schedules that allow them to accomplish what's important on time.

11. *Accept fair blame.* They strike a balance between never accepting blame and taking the blame for everything. If something is their fault, they accept responsibility.

12. *Reject self-pity.* When something goes wrong, they find a way to solve the problem. They don't get caught in the energy drain of feeling sorry for themselves.

13. *Are independent.* They can work on their own and think for themselves. They take responsibility for their own schedule and tasks.

14. *Seek to surmount personal difficulties.* They keep things in perspective, looking for ways to remedy personal problems and separate them from their professional lives.

15. *Focus and concentrate to achieve their goals.* They create an environment in which they can best avoid distraction and they focus steadily on their work.

get analytical

EVALUATE YOUR SELF-ACTIVATORS

To see how you use successful intelligence in your daily life, assess your perceived development on Sternberg's activators. Circle the number that best represents your answer, with 1 being "not at all like me" and 5 being "definitely like me."

1. I motivate myself well.   1 2 3 4 5
2. I can control my impulses.   1 2 3 4 5
3. I know when to persevere and when to change gears.   1 2 3 4 5
4. I make the most of what I do well.   1 2 3 4 5
5. I can successfully translate my ideas into action.   1 2 3 4 5
6. I can focus effectively on my goal.   1 2 3 4 5
7. I complete tasks and have good follow-through.   1 2 3 4 5
8. I initiate action—I move people and projects ahead.   1 2 3 4 5
9. I have the courage to risk failure.   1 2 3 4 5
10. I avoid procrastination.   1 2 3 4 5
11. I accept responsibility when I make a mistake.   1 2 3 4 5
12. I don't waste time feeling sorry for myself.   1 2 3 4 5
13. I independently take responsibility for tasks.   1 2 3 4 5
14. I work hard to overcome personal difficulties.   1 2 3 4 5
15. I create an environment that helps me concentrate on my goals.   1 2 3 4 5
16. I don't take on too much or too little work.   1 2 3 4 5
17. I can delay gratification in order to receive the benefits.   1 2 3 4 5
18. I can see both the big picture and the details in a situation.   1 2 3 4 5
19. I am able to maintain confidence in myself.   1 2 3 4 5
20. I balance my analytical, creative, and practical thinking skills. 1 2 3 4 5

If you completed this self-assessment at the beginning of the course, look back at your original scores. On a piece of paper or digital file, describe three changes over the course of the term that feel significant to you.

Finally, choose one self-activator that you feel still needs work. Analyze the specific reasons why it remains a challenge. For example, if you are still taking on too much work, is it because you want to please others? Write a one-paragraph analysis, and let this analysis guide you as you work to build your strength in this area.

16. *Spread themselves neither too thin nor too thick.* They strike a balance between doing too many things, which results in little progress on any of them, and too few things, which can reduce the level of accomplishment.
17. *Have the ability to delay gratification.* They risk effort in the present for the reward of gratifying goal achievement in the future.
18. *Have the ability to see the forest and the trees.* They are able to see the big picture and get a sense of the specifics, without getting bogged down in each and every tiny detail.

19. *Have a reasonable level of self-confidence and a belief in their ability to accomplish their goals.* They believe in themselves enough to get through the tough times, while avoiding the kind of overconfidence that stalls learning and growth, and alienates others.

20. *Balance analytical, creative, and practical thinking.* They sense what to use and when to use it. When problems arise, they combine all three skills to arrive at solutions.

These characteristics are "self-activators"—your personal motivational tools. Consult them when you need a way to get moving. You may even want to post them somewhere in your home, in the front of a notebook, or as a note in your smartphone. Use the "Get Analytical" exercise to see how you have developed the self-activators over the course of the term.

Lifelong Learning and the Growth Mindset

Knowledge in many fields is doubling every two to three years, and your personal interests and needs are changing all the time. With a growth mindset—the attitude that you can always grow and learn—you are as ready to achieve the goals you set out for yourself today as you are to achieve future goals you cannot yet anticipate.

You leave this course with a set of tools, skills, and attitudes that open the door to success in the 21st century. Throughout the term, you have built skills and knowledge in each quadrant of the 21st Century Learning grid. As you continue your educational journey, you will further develop these tools that benefit you in everything you do. See Key 12.8 for details.

What risks will reward you with learning throughout your life? Here are some:

Spend time with interesting people. When you meet someone new who inspires you and makes you think, keep in touch. Form a book club, get a pickup basketball game together, join a local volunteer organization. Learn something new from everyone you meet.

Talk to people from different generations. Younger people can learn from the broad perspective of those belonging to older generations; older people can learn from the fresh perspective of those younger than themselves. Communication builds mutual respect.

Investigate new interests. When information and events catch your attention, take your interest one step further and find out more. Instead of dreaming about it, just do it.

Read, read, read. Reading expert Jim Trelease says that people who don't read "base their future decisions on what they used to know. If you don't read much, you really don't know much."[10] Ask friends which books have changed their lives. Keep up with local, national, and world news through newspapers, magazines, and Internet sources.

Keep on top of changes in your career. After you complete your degree and move into the workforce, stay on top of ideas, developments, and new technology in your field. Seek out continuing education courses. Sign up for career-related seminars. Some companies offer additional on-the-job training or pay for their employees to take courses that will improve their knowledge and skills.

CONTINUING EDUCATION
Courses that students can take without having to be part of a degree program.

ACQUIRED SKILL	IN COLLEGE, YOU'LL USE IT TO . . .	IN CAREER AND LIFE, YOU'LL USE IT TO . . .
Investigating resources	. . . find who and what can help you have the college experience you want	. . . get acclimated at a new job or in a new town—find the people, resources, and services that can help you succeed
Knowing and using your learning styles	. . . select study strategies that make the most of your learning styles	. . . select jobs, career areas, and other pursuits that suit what you do best
Setting goals and managing stress	. . . complete assignments and achieve educational goals; reduce stress by being in control	. . . accomplish tasks and reach career and personal goals; reduce stress by being in control
Managing time	. . . get to classes on time, juggle school and work, turn in assignments when they are due, plan study time	. . . finish work tasks on time or before they are due, balance duties on the job and at home
Analytical, creative, and practical thinking	. . . think through writing assignments, solve math problems, analyze academic readings, brainstorm paper topics, work through academic issues, work effectively on team projects	. . . find ways to improve product design, increase market share, present ideas to customers; analyze life issues, come up with ideas, and take practical action
Reading	. . . read course texts and other materials	. . . Read operating manuals, user guides, employee handbooks, materials in your field; read for practical purposes, for learning, and for pleasure at home
Note taking	. . . take notes in class, in study groups, during studying, and during research	. . . Take notes in work and community meetings and during important phone calls
Test taking	. . . take quizzes, tests, and final exams	. . . take tests for certification in particular work skills and for continuing education courses
Writing	. . . Write essays, reports, letters to the school newspaper, and communicate clearly with others	. . . Write work-related documents, including emails, reports, proposals, instructional materials, and presentations; write personal letters and journal entries
Building successful relationships	. . . get along with instructors, students, and student groups	. . . get along with supervisors, co-workers, team members, friends, and family members
Staying healthy	. . . Stay physically and mentally healthy so you can make the most of school	. . . Stay physically and mentally healthy so you can be at your best at work and at home
Managing money	. . . stay on top of school costs and make decisions that earn and save you the money you need	. . . Budget the money you earn so you can pay your bills and save for the future
Establishing and maintaining a personal mission	. . . develop a big picture idea of what you want from your education, and make choices that guide you toward those goals	. . . Develop a big picture idea of what you want to accomplish in life, and make choices that guide you toward your goals

Delve into other cultures. Invite a friend over who has grown up in a culture different from your own. Eat food from a country you've never visited. Initiate conversations with people of different races, religions, values, and ethnic backgrounds. Travel internationally and locally. Take a course that deals with cultural diversity. Try a term or year abroad. Learn a new language.

Nurture a spiritual life. Wherever you find spirituality—in organized religion, family, friendship, nature, music, or anywhere else—it will help you find balance and meaning.

student PROFILE

Andrew Hillman
QUEENS COLLEGE, FLUSHING, NEW YORK

About me:

I transferred to Queens College from Georgia State University because I wanted to be part of a small school environment. While at Queens College I developed a love for research and how it allows one to offer new information to the world by collecting and analyzing data in innovative ways. I am currently applying to MD-Ph.D. schools so that I may earn a dual degree in medicine and physiology.

What I focus on:

I deliberately investigated career paths at an early stage in my undergraduate career to build my knowledge base as well as gain invaluable experience. I seek out mentors in my field of interest so that I have strong allies. I have also built experience in my areas of interest. No matter what field you choose, there is a plethora of summer enrichment or yearlong programs and fellowships geared toward providing students with real-life experience—something graduate schools and companies value enormously. My pre-professional advisor at Queens College has been influential in informing me about potential fellowships. The research fellowships that I have done for the past two years have given me the experience mandated by MD-Ph.D. schools all across the country. In addition, they allow me to network with people who may offer recommendations for medical school.

What will help me in the workplace:

Doing undergraduate programs geared toward your chosen field offers you the crucial head start of knowing what's going on in that field. Just as importantly, it shows prospective graduate schools and businesses that you take initiative in learning your future profession.

Experience the arts. In a general sense, art is a tool for both knowing yourself and understanding the world. Seek what moves you—music, visual arts, theater, photography, dance, film, television, poetry, prose, and more—and see how it changes your perspective.

Be creative. Take a class in drawing, writing, or quilting. Learn to play an instrument. Write poems for your friends or stories to read to your children. Concoct a new recipe. Design and build something for your home. Express yourself, and learn more about yourself, through art.

Lifelong learning is the master key that unlocks so many of the doors you encounter on your journey. If you keep it firmly in your hand, you will discover worlds of knowledge—and a place for yourself to continue growing within them.

Learned Optimism Will Help You Cope with Change and Challenge

As a citizen of the 21st century, you will experience exciting changes as well as troubling ones. Sometimes you will need to make a change happen, as Stephen did when he chose a post-graduation path. Your ability to respond to change with risk-taking aimed at a positive reward, especially if the change is unexpected and difficult, is crucial to your future success. The ability to "make lemonade from lemons" is the hallmark of people who know how to hang on to hope.

Use your optimistic explanatory style to analyze situations, brainstorm solutions, and take practical action. With this skill you can:

- *See adversity as temporary.* Consider losing a job, for example, as a step along the way to a better one.
- *See the limited scope of your problems.* One issue does not make your entire life a disaster.
- *Avoid the personal.* If you look for explanation in the details of a situation instead of seeing yourself as incompetent, you can keep your self-esteem and creative energy alive.

With successful intelligence, a growth mindset, and learned optimism, you will always have a new direction in which to grow. Your willingness to take calculated, productive risks will allow you to put these valuable tools to work and reward you with the achievement of your most valued goals. Risk being true to yourself, a respectful friend and family member, a focused student who believes in the power of learning, a productive employee, and a contributing member of society to earn the ultimate reward of a meaningful life—a life that can change the world.

revisit RISK AND REWARD

What happened to Stephen? Stephen chose the risk of entering the job market. After graduation, he accepted a job at Chubb as an insurance underwriter, where he found the work to be fulfilling, challenging, and even fun. Setting law school aside, Stephen later transitioned into a marketing role. Twenty-two years later, he's now vice president and branch manager of the Chubb Cleveland office, which generates more than $115 million in annual revenue. "Keep options open. You don't know where those options are going to take you," Stephen says. Work ethic and passion have brought him success in a career path he never envisioned. "Don't let the world define who you are," he says. "You show the world what you are capable of."

Stephen hosts career-building events for Korean American high school students and serves on the board of Achievement Centers for Children, an organization that serves children with disabilities and their families. In 2012, he received an Outstanding 50 Asian-Americans in Business Award. Stephen and his wife have a teenage son. In his spare time, Stephen enjoys Formula One racing, golf, and reading, especially biographies and history.

What does this mean for you? Stephen's success is a lesson in perseverance. "There were a lot of obstacles. But I persevered, because I believed in myself and I had those who believed in me and really pushed me," Stephen says. Identify a challenge you have faced in your life. Then describe what risks you took to emerge from that trying time, including who helped you move ahead and the rewards that have come from that challenge. As Stephen emphasizes, "Our life experiences, regardless of how hard they are, are going to make us better."

What risk may bring reward beyond your world? Like Stephen's work helping Korean Americans think about career paths, you can get involved in programs that use the knowledge you have built from personal experience. Think about the challenge you identified in the previous section. Then research, online or in person, opportunities at your school or in your community for you to use the rewards that challenge brought you. For example, if you have been through a health crisis, find ways to help others going through it. If you have had a particular experience with your family, look to support others having similar experiences.

Complete the following on paper or in digital format.

KNOW IT *Think Critically*

Become a Better Interviewee

Build basic skills. Make a list of questions that a job applicant would typically hear in an entry-level interview. Recall questions from job interviews you've had, look up questions using online sources such as Quintcareers, or consult books on job interviews. List 15 to 20 questions.

Take it to the next level. Imagine yourself as the interviewer. Thinking about learning preferences, life experiences, learning from failure, role models, and more as you ponder, write five additional questions.

Move toward mastery. Pair up with a student in your class and interview each other. Person A interviews Person B for 5 to 10 minutes and takes notes. Then switch roles: Person B interviews Person A and takes notes. Each person uses the set of questions developed in the first and second parts of the exercise.

When you are done, share with each other what interesting ideas stand out from the interviews. If you have suggestions, offer constructive criticism to each other about interview skills.

Finally, to sum up, write a brief analysis and summary of your experience, including what you learned and would keep in mind for a real interview—both the good and the bad.

WRITE IT *Communicate*

Emotional intelligence journal: Revisit your personal mission. If you drafted a personal mission and/or established career priorities earlier this term, look back at what you wrote. Think about how you feel now at the end of the term. Consider what has changed about the outcomes you originally wanted to make happen in your life and write an updated version of your mission. Incorporate one or more of your career priorities into your mission statement.

Real-life writing: Create a résumé. On one electronic page or sheet of paper, list information about your education (where and when you've studied, degrees or certificates you've earned) and your skills (what you know how to do, such as use a computer program or operate a type of equipment). On another, list job experience. For each job, record job title (if you had one), dates of employment, and tasks performed. Include tasks that demonstrate skills. Be as detailed as possible. When you compile your résumé, you will make this material more concise. Keep this list and update it periodically as you complete educational goals, gain work experience, and add skills.

Using the information you have gathered and Key 12.7 as your guide, draft a résumé. There are many ways to construct a résumé; consult resources for different styles (your library or bookstore will have multiple resources, or look online at sources such as Resume-Help or Monster. com). You may want to format your résumé according to a style that your career counselor or instructor recommends. Also, certain career areas may favor a particular style of résumé (check with your career counselor or an instructor in that area).

Keep this résumé draft in hard copy and on a computer hard drive or disk. When you need to submit a résumé with a job application, update the draft and print it out on high-quality paper. For electronic submission, convert your résumé file to PDF format.

Careers and More

WORK IT *Build Your Brand*

Revisit the Wheel of Successful Intelligence

21st Century Learning Building Blocks

- Initiative and self-direction
- Critical thinking and problem solving

Without looking at any previously completed versions of these assessments or the wheel, analyze where you are after completing this course by taking the three assessments.

Assess Your Analytical Thinking Skills

For each statement, circle the number that feels right to you, from 1 for "not at all true for me" to 5 for "very true for me."

1. I recognize and define problems effectively.   1 2 3 4 5
2. I see myself as a thinker and as analytical and studious.   1 2 3 4 5
3. When working on a problem in a group setting, I like to break down the problem into its components and evaluate them.   1 2 3 4 5
4. I need to see convincing evidence before accepting information as fact.   1 2 3 4 5
5. I weigh the pros and cons of plans and ideas before taking action.   1 2 3 4 5
6. I tend to make connections among pieces of information by categorizing them.   1 2 3 4 5
7. Impulsive, spontaneous decision-making worries me.   1 2 3 4 5
8. I like to analyze causes and effects when making a decision.   1 2 3 4 5
9. I monitor my progress toward goals.   1 2 3 4 5
10. Once I reach a goal, I evaluate the process to see how effective it was.   1 2 3 4 5

Total your answers here: _____

Assess Your Creative Thinking Skills

For each statement, circle the number that feels right to you, from 1 for "not at all true for me" to 5 for "very true for me."

1. I tend to question rules and regulations.   1 2 3 4 5
2. I see myself as unique, full of ideas, and innovative.   1 2 3 4 5
3. When working on a problem in a group setting, I generate a lot of ideas.   1 2 3 4 5
4. I am energized when I have a brand-new experience.   1 2 3 4 5
5. If you say something is too risky, I'm ready to give it a shot.   1 2 3 4 5
6. I often wonder if there is a different way to do or see something.   1 2 3 4 5
7. Too much routine in my work or schedule drains my energy.   1 2 3 4 5
8. I tend to see connections among ideas that others do not.   1 2 3 4 5
9. I feel comfortable allowing myself to make mistakes as I test out ideas.   1 2 3 4 5
10. I'm willing to champion an idea even when others disagree with me.   1 2 3 4 5

Total your answers here: _____

Assess Your Practical Thinking Skills

For each statement, circle the number that feels right to you, from 1 for "not at all true for me" to 5 for "very true for me."

1. I can find a way around any obstacle.   1 2 3 4 5
2. I see myself as a doer and the go-to person; I make things happen.   1 2 3 4 5
3. When working on a problem in a group setting, I like to figure out who will do what and when it should be done.   1 2 3 4 5
4. I apply what I learn from experience to improve my response to similar situations.   1 2 3 4 5

5. I finish what I start and don't leave loose ends hanging.   1 2 3 4 5

6. I note my emotions about academic and social situations and use what
   they tell me to move toward a goal.   1 2 3 4 5

7. I can sense how people feel and use that knowledge to interact with
   others effectively.   1 2 3 4 5

8. I manage my time effectively.   1 2 3 4 5

9. I adjust to the teaching styles of my instructors and the communication
   styles of my peers.   1 2 3 4 5

10. When involved in a problem-solving process, I can shift gears
    as needed.   1 2 3 4 5

Total your answers here: _____

After you finish, fill in your new scores in the blank Wheel of Successful Intelligence in Key 12.9. If you completed a wheel at the beginning of the term, compare it to this wheel and look at the changes. Complete the following on a sheet of paper or digital file:

- Note the areas where you see the most change. Where have you grown, and how has your self-perception evolved?
- Note three *creative ideas* you came up with over the term that aided your exploration or development.
- Note three *practical actions* that you took that moved you toward your goals.

Let what you learn from this new wheel inform you about what you have accomplished and what you plan to accomplish. Continue to grow your thinking skills and use them to manage the changes that await you in the future.

KEY 12.9 Use this new Wheel of Successful Intelligence to evaluate your progress.

With your new scores in hand, create the most updated representation of your thinking skills. In each of the three areas of the wheel, draw a curved line approximately at the level of your number score and fill in the wedge below that line. Compare this wheel to your previous wheel and note any change and development.

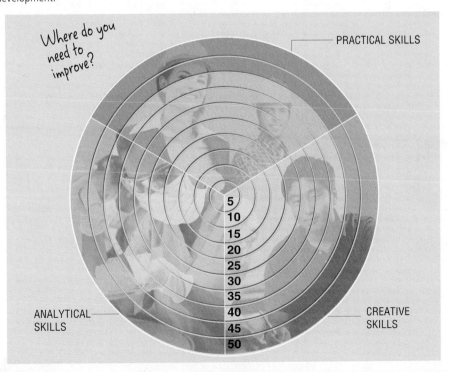

Source: Based on "The Wheel of Life" model developed by the Coaches Training Institute. © Co-Active Space 2000.

The Writing Process

Writing a research paper or essay involves planning, drafting, revising, and editing.

Planning

The planning process involves six steps that help you think about the assignment:

Pay Attention to Logistics

These practical questions will help you decide on a topic and depth of coverage:

1. *How much depth does my instructor expect and how long should the paper be?*
2. *How much time do I have?* Consider your other courses and responsibilities.
3. *What kind of research is needed?* Your topic and purpose may determine this.
4. *Is it a team project?* If you are working with others, determine what each person will do.

Generate Topic Ideas

Start the process of choosing a paper topic by creatively generating ideas within the boundaries that your instructor has set (see Chapter 5).

- Begin by writing down anything on the assigned subject that comes to mind, in no particular order. Tap your multiple intelligences for creative ideas. To jump-start your thoughts, scan your text and notes, check library or Internet references, or meet with your instructor to discuss ideas.
- Next, organize that list into an outline or think link so you can see different possibilities.

Use Prewriting Strategies to Narrow Your Topic

Prewriting strategies, including freewriting and asking journalists' questions,[1] help you decide which possible topic you would most like to pursue. Use them to narrow your topic, focusing on the specific sub-ideas and examples from your brainstorming session.

- *Generating ideas.* The same creative process you used to come up with ideas will help you narrow your topic. Write down your thoughts about the possibilities you have chosen, do some more research, and then organize your thoughts into categories, noticing patterns that appear.
- *Freewriting.* When you *freewrite,* you jot down whatever comes to mind without censoring ideas or worrying about grammar, spelling, punctuation, or organization.
- *Asking journalists' questions.* When journalists start working on a story, they ask: Who, what, where, when, why, and how? Asking these questions will help you choose a specific topic.

Prewriting helps you develop a topic that is broad enough for investigation but narrow enough to handle. Prewriting also helps you identify what you know and what you don't know. If an assignment involves more than you already know, you need to do research.

Conduct Research and Take Notes

Research develops in stages as you narrow and refine your ideas. In the first idea generation stage, look for an overview that can lead to a working thesis statement. In the second stage, track down information that fills in gaps. Ultimately, you will have a "body" of information that you can evaluate to develop and implement your final thesis.

As you research, create source notes and content notes to organize your work, keep track of your sources, and avoid plagiarism.

Source notes, written on index cards, are preliminary notes that should include the author's name; the title of the work; the edition (if any); the publisher, year, and city of publication; issue and/or volume number when applicable (such as for a magazine); and page numbers consulted. Notes on Internet sources should reference the website's complete name and address, including the universal resource locator (URL), which is the string of text and numbers that identifies an Internet site. Include a short summary and critical evaluation for each source.

Content notes, written on large index cards, in a notebook, or on your computer are taken during a thorough reading and provide an in-depth look at sources. Use them to record needed information. To supplement your content notes, make notations—marginal notes, highlighting, and underlining—directly on photocopies of sources.

Write a Working Thesis Statement

Next, organize your research and write a *thesis statement*—the organizing principle of your paper. Your thesis declares your specific subject and point of view and reflects your writing purpose (to inform or persuade) and audience (your intended readers).

Consider this to be your *working thesis*, since it may change as you continue your research and develop your draft. Be ready and willing to rework your writing—and your thesis—one or more times before you hand in your paper.

Write a Working Outline or Think Link

The final planning step is to create a working outline or think link to guide your writing.

Drafting

You may write many versions of the assignment until you are satisfied. Each version moves you closer to saying exactly what you want in the way you want to say it. The main challenges you face at the first-draft stage are:

- Finalizing your thesis
- Defining an organizational structure
- Integrating source material into the body of your paper to fit your structure
- Finding additional sources to strengthen your presentation
- Choosing the right words, phrases, and tone
- Connecting ideas with logical transitions

- Creating an effective introduction and conclusion
- Checking for plagiarism
- Creating a list of works cited

Don't aim for perfection in a first draft. Trying to get every detail right too early may shut the door on ideas before you even know they are there.

Freewriting Your Draft

Use everything that you developed in the planning stage as the raw material for freewriting a draft. For now, don't think about your introduction, conclusion, or organizational structure. Simply focus on what you want to say. Only after you have thoughts down should you begin to shape your work.

Writing an Introduction

The introduction tells readers what the paper contains and includes your thesis statement, which is often found at the end of the introduction.

Creating the Body of a Paper

The body of the paper contains your central ideas and supporting *evidence*, which underpins your thesis with facts, statistics, examples, and expert opinions. Try to find a structure that helps you organize your ideas and evidence into a clear pattern. Several organizational options are presented in Key A.1.

KEY A.1 Find the Best Way to Organize the Body of the Paper

ORGANIZATIONAL STRUCTURE	WHAT TO DO
Arrange ideas by time.	Describe events in order or in reverse order.
Arrange ideas according to importance.	Start with the idea that carries the most weight and move to less important ideas. Or move from the least to the most important ideas.
Arrange ideas by problem and solution.	Start with a problem and then discuss solutions.
Arrange ideas to present an argument.	Present one or both sides of an issue.
Arrange ideas in list form.	Group a series of items.
Arrange ideas according to cause and effect.	Show how events, situations, or ideas cause subsequent events, situations, or ideas.
Arrange ideas through the use of comparisons.	Compare and contrast the characteristics of events, people, situations, or ideas.
Arrange by process.	Go through the steps in a process: a "how-to" approach.
Arrange by category.	Divide topics into categories and analyze each in order.

Writing the Conclusion

A conclusion brings your paper to a natural ending by summarizing your main points, showing the significance of your thesis and how it relates to larger issues, calling the reader to action, or looking to the future. Let the ideas in the body of the paper speak for themselves as you wrap up.

Avoiding Plagiarism: Crediting Authors and Sources

Using another writer's words, content, unique approach, or illustrations without crediting the author is called *plagiarism* and is illegal and unethical. The following techniques will help you properly credit sources and avoid plagiarism:

Make source notes as you go. Plagiarism often begins accidentally during research. You may forget to include quotation marks around a quotation, or you may intend to cite or paraphrase a source but never do. To avoid forgetting, write detailed source and content notes as you research.

Learn the difference between a quotation and a paraphrase. A *quotation* repeats a source's exact words and uses quotation marks to set them off from the rest of the text. A *paraphrase* is a restatement of the quotation in your own words, and it requires that you completely rewrite the idea, not just remove or replace a few words.

Use a citation even for an acceptable paraphrase. Credit every source that you quote, paraphrase, or use as evidence (except when the material is considered common knowledge). To credit a source, write a footnote or endnote that describes it, using the format preferred by your instructor.

Understand that lifting material off the Internet is plagiarism. Words in electronic form belong to the writer just as words in print form do. If you cut and paste sections from a source document onto your draft, you are probably committing plagiarism. Key A.2 will help you identify what instructors regard as plagiarized work.

Students who plagiarize place their academic careers at risk, in part because cheating is easy to discover. Increasingly, instructors are using anti-plagiarism software to investigate whether strings of words in student papers match those in a database. Make a commitment to hand in your own work and to uphold the highest standards of academic integrity.

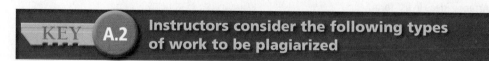

KEY A.2 **Instructors consider the following types of work to be plagiarized**

- Submitting a paper from a website that sells or gives away research papers
- Handing in a paper written by a fellow student or family member
- Copying material in a paper directly from a source without proper quotation marks or source citation
- Paraphrasing material in a paper from a source without proper source citation
- Submitting the same paper in more than one class, even if the classes are in different terms or even different years

Citing Sources

You may be asked to submit different kinds of source lists when you hand in your paper:

- A references list, also called a list of works cited, includes only the sources you actually cited in your paper.
- A bibliography includes all the sources you consulted, whether or not they were cited in the paper.
- An Annotated bibliography includes all the sources you consulted as well as an explanation or critique of each source.

Your instructor will tell you which documentation style to use. Among the most common are:

- The Modern Language Association (MLA) format, generally used in the humanities, including history, literature, the arts, and philosophy
- The American Psychological Association (APA) style, the appropriate format in psychology, sociology, business, economics, nursing, criminology, and social work

Consult a college-level writers' handbook for an overview of these documentation styles, or read about them online at www.mla.org and www.apa.org.

Get Feedback

Talk with your instructor about your draft, or ask a study partner to read it and answer specific questions. Be open minded about the comments you receive. Consider each carefully, and then make a decision about what to change.

Revising

When you *revise*, you critically evaluate the content, organization, word choice, paragraph structure, and style of your first draft. You evaluate the strength of your thesis and whether your evidence proves it, and look for logical holes. You can do anything you want at this point to change your work. You can turn things around, presenting information from the end of your paper up front, tweak your thesis to reflect the evidence you presented, or choose a different organizational structure.

Engage your critical thinking skills to evaluate the content and form of your paper. Ask yourself these questions as you revise:

- Does the paper fulfill the requirements of the assignment?
- Do I prove my thesis?
- Is each idea and argument developed, explained, and supported by examples?
- Does the introduction prepare the reader and capture attention?
- Is the body of the paper organized effectively?
- Does each paragraph have a topic sentence that is supported by the rest of the paragraph?
- Are my ideas connected to one another through logical transitions?
- Do I have a clear, concise writing style?
- Does the conclusion provide a natural ending without introducing new ideas?

Check for Clarity

Now check for sense, continuity, and clarity. Focus also on tightening your prose and eliminating wordy phrases. Examine once again how paragraphs flow into one another by evaluating the effectiveness of your *transitions*—the words, phrases or sentences that connect ideas.

Editing

Editing involves correcting technical mistakes in spelling, grammar, and punctuation, as well as checking for consistency in such elements as abbreviations and capitalization. If you use a computer, start with the grammar check and spell check to find mistakes, realizing that you still need to check your work manually (keep in mind that spell check will not catch misspelled words that are still actual words—for example, if you meant to use the word "hear" but typed "here" by mistake). Look also for sexist language, which characterizes people according to gender stereotypes and often involves the male pronouns *he* or *his* or *him*.

Proofreading, the last editing stage, involves reading every word for accuracy. Look for technical mistakes, run-on sentences, spelling errors, and sentence fragments. Look for incorrect word usage and unclear references. A great way to check your work is to read it out loud.

Your final paper reflects all the hard work you put in during the writing process. Ideally, when you are finished, you have a piece of work that shows your researching, writing, and thinking abilities.

Social Networking and Media

Social networking refers to interacting with a community of people through an online network or tool such as Facebook, Instagram, forums (message boards), or chat rooms. *Social media* are the types of media people use to share information online (examples include web logs or blogs, podcasts, websites, videos, and news feeds). Social media allows participation through comments and ratings. The people who provide social media content range from experts to amateurs, which means the content will not always be accurate or trustworthy.

In general, social networking and media make three things possible:

1. Communicating information about yourself to others
2. Connecting with people who have similar interests
3. Networking with others to accomplish goals

Social networking has grown rapidly worldwide through sites like the following:

- **Facebook** (enables users to set up personal profiles and communicate with other users through profile updates, public or private messages, games, and photos)
- **Twitter** (enables users to send or receive short text updates, or "tweets," to other users signed up on their accounts)
- **Skype** (enables users to make telephone calls over the Internet)

HOW SOCIAL NETWORKING CAN HELP *you in college*

Use social networking and media to:

- *Connect with peers to achieve academic goals.* Students might create groups that correspond to courses, study together on an Internet call, or post course-related questions and comments on a message board or chat room used by the class (try: Facebook, Skype).
- *Manage coursework and projects.* Particular sites can help you search for information, study, and ask questions. When doing a group project, social networking can help you collaborate in an online format (try: Evernote, Google Docs, EtherPad, Wikidot).
- *Network with students who have shared interests.* A student might start a blog on an academic topic and hope to attract interested readers, or look for groups or Internet forums (try: Facebook, Tumblr, Pinterest).
- *Adjust to college.* Ask other students at your school about local issues (bus schedules, library hours), or ask students anywhere in the world about more general concerns (test anxiety). You can even use social media to stay organized (try: Twitter, Facebook, GradeMate, Backpack).
- *Focus on career development.* Put your qualifications and career goals out there for others to peruse, and build a network that may lead you to job opportunities (try: LinkedIn, Zumeo).

- *Stay connected to loved ones.* Students might tweet or blog happenings to family and old friends, post updates and photos, or make free phone calls. A budgeting bonus: Most social networking tools cost nothing to use as long as you have Internet access (try: Twitter, Facebook, Instagram, Skype).
- *Share your opinion.* Blogs allow you to communicate to an audience on a regular basis, and creating a blog is usually free. Another tool, the forum or message board, encourages individuals to come together and discuss a common knowledge or experience (try: Blogger, MySpace).

TEN STRATEGIES
for success

Follow these guidelines to get the most from your time and energy on social networks and with social media.

1. *Control your personal information.* Read the privacy policy of any network you join. Adjust security settings, indicating what information, photos, and so on you want to be visible or invisible. Know what will always be visible to users.

2. *Control your time.* One quick check of your email can lead to hours spent online that you should have spent getting something else done. To stay focused and in control:
   - Create a separate email for alerts from your social networking sites.
   - Set your status to "offline" or "do not disturb" when you are studying.
   - Set up goals and rewards. Try doing a defined portion of your homework and then rewarding yourself with 10 minutes on your favorite social networking site.

3. *Be an information literate critical thinker.* Evaluate what you read on social networking sites or social media with a critical eye. Use the CARS test (page 133) to check Credibility, Accuracy, Reasonableness, and Support of any source or statement.

4. *Keep career goals in mind.* With anything you write, think: How will this look to others who may evaluate me in the future? Also, choose and post photographs carefully, since some employers use social networking sites for background checks.

5. *Use caution with forums and chat rooms.* There is no way to know who is posting on a forum or in a chat room. Consider using a name that differs from your legal name or regular email address. Remember, too, that everything you write can be copied and saved.

6. *Watch your temper.* Wait, and think, before you post on emotional topics. Forums can turn into hostile environments. Snarky tweets and updates can come back to haunt you if they are viewed by potential employers, instructors, or others who may judge you by them.

7. *Separate the personal and the academic/professional.* You probably don't want an employer seeing that crass video your cousin posted on your page. Consider having two profiles on a network if you want to use one to communicate with students or advance your career.

8. *Show restraint.* Although it's easy to get carried away, keep your purpose in mind. For example, if one goal is to keep up with friends using Facebook, you are defeating your purpose if you have so many friends that you can't possibly stay up-to-date with them.

9. *Understand what a blog or website requires.* Blogs need updating at least weekly if not more often, and require time and motivation. Websites can be even more labor intensive.

10. *Network with integrity.* Treat others with respect. Search for, and use, information legitimately. Cite sources honestly.

QUICK START

1. Astin, Alexander W. *Preventing Students From Dropping Out.* San Francisco: Jossey-Bass, 1976.

2. Sternberg, Robert J. *Successful Intelligence: How Practical and Creative Intelligence Determine Success in Life.* New York: Plume, 1997, p. 24.

CHAPTER 1

1. Friedman, Thomas. *The World Is Flat.* New York: Farrar, Straus & Giroux, 2006, p. 8.

2. Pink, Daniel. "Revenge of the Right Brain." *Wired Magazine,* February 2005. From http://www .wired.com/wired/archive/13.02/brain.html?pg=1 &topic=brain&topic_set=

3. Sternberg, pp. 85–90; Dweck, Carol S. *Mindset: The New Psychology of Success.* New York: Random House, 2006, p. 5; Jaeggi, Susanne, Martin Buschkuehl, John Jonides, and Walter J. Perrig. "Improving Fluid Intelligence with Training on Working Memory." 2008, Proceedings of the National Acadamy of Sciences USA 105, pp. 6829–6833.

4. Sternberg, p. 11.

5. Dweck, pp. 3–4.

6. The Society for Neuroscience. *Brain Facts: A Primer on the Brain and Neurosystem,* Washington, DC: The Society for Neuroscience, 2008, pp. 34–35.

7. Sternberg, p. 12.

8. Ibid., p. 127.

9. Ibid., p. 11.

10. Ibid., pp. 127–128.

11. Dweck, Carol. "The Mindsets." 2006. From http:// www.mindsetonline.com/whatisit/themindsets/ index.html

12. Dweck, *Mindset,* p. 16.

13. Ibid.

14. Pitino, Rick. *Success Is a Choice.* New York: Broadway Books, 1997, p. 40.

15. Dweck, *Mindset,* p. 51.

16. *The Fundamental Values of Academic Integrity,* The Center for Academic Integrity, Rutland Institute for Ethics, Clemson University, October 1999. Used by Permission of the Center for Academic Integrity, Duke University. From http:// www.academicintegrity.org/fundamental_values_ project/index.php

17. Taylor, William M. "Academic Integrity: A Letter to My Students." Oakton Community College, Des Plaines, IL. From http://www .academicintegrity.org/educational_resources/ pdf/LetterToMyStudentsRev2010.pdf

18. Gabriel, Trip. "Plagiarism Lines Blur for Students in Digital Age." *New York Times,* August 1, 2010. From http://www.nytimes.com/2010/08/02 /education/02cheat.html?pagewanted=all

19. Taylor, "Academic Integrity."

20. Material in this section from Seligman, Martin E. P. *Learned Optimism: How to Change Your Mind and Your Life.* New York: Vintage Books, 2006, pp. 45–53, 207–222.

21. Mayer, John D., Peter Salovey, and David R. Caruso. "Emotional Intelligence: New Ability or Eclectic Traits?" *American Psychologist,* vol. 63, no. 6, September 2008, p. 503.

22. Lehrer, Johah. "Hearts & Minds." *The Boston Globe,* April 29, 2007. From http://www.boston .com/news/globe/ideas/articles/2007/04/29/ hearts__minds/?page=full

23. Caruso, David R. "Zero In on Knowledge: A Practical Guide to the MSCEIT." Multi-Health Systems Inc., 2008, p. 3.

24. Blakeslee, Sandra. "Cells That Read Minds." *The New York Times,* January 10, 2006. From http:// www.nytimes.com/2006/01/10/science/10mirr.html

25. Mayer, Salovey, and Caruso, pp. 510–512.

26. List and descriptions based on Sternberg, *Successful Intelligence,* pp. 251–268.

CHAPTER 2

1. Covey, Stephen. *The Seven Habits of Highly Effective People.* New York: Simon & Schuster, 1989, pp. 70–144, 309–318.

2. Timm, Paul. *Successful Self-Management: A Psychologically Sound Approach to Personal Effectiveness.* Los Altos, CA: Crisp Publications, 1987, pp. 22–41.

3. Brody, Jane E. "At Every Age, Feeling the Effects of Too Little Sleep." *New York Times,* October 23, 2007. From http://www.nytimes.com/2007/10/23/ health/23brod.html

4. mtvU and Associated Press College Stress and Mental Health Poll Executive Summary, Spring

2008. From http://www.halfofus.com/_media/_pr/mtvU_AP_College_Stress_and_Mental_Health_Poll_Executive_Summary.pdf

5. Burka, Jane B., and Lenora M. Yuen. *Procrastination: Why You Do It, What to Do About It.* Reading, MA: Perseus Books, 1983, pp. 21–22.

6. Sheridan, Richard, and Lisamarie Babik. "Breaking Down Walls, Building Bridges, and Taking Out the Trash." InfoQ, December 22, 2010. From http://www.infoq.com/articles/agile-team-spaces

7. Schwarz, Tony. "Four Destructive Myths Most Companies Still Live By." *Harvard Business Review,* November 1, 2011. From http://blogs.hbr.org/schwartz/2011/11/four-destructive-myths-most-co.html

8. "Takeaways and Quotes from Dr. John Medina's Brain Rules." Slideshare presentation, Slide 79. From http://www.presentationzen.com/presentationzen/2008/05/brain-rules-for.html

9. Schwartz.

CHAPTER 3

1. Gardner, Howard. *Multiple Intelligences: New Horizons.* New York: Basic Books, 2006, p. 180.

2. Gardner, Howard. *Multiple Intelligences: The Theory in Practice.* New York: HarperCollins, 1993, pp. 5–49.

3. Gardner, *Multiple Intelligences: New Horizons,* p. 8.

4. Gardner, *Multiple Intelligences: The Theory in Practice,* p. 7.

5. Boeree, C. George. "Carl Jung." George Boeree personal website, 2006. From http://webspace.ship.edu/cgboer/jung/html

6. Waters, John K. "Broadband, Social Networks, and Mobility Have Spawned a New Kind of Learner." *The Journal,* December 13, 2011. From http://thejournal.com/Articles/2011/12/13/Broadband-Social-Networks-and-Mobility.aspx?Page=1

7. National Center for Learning Disabilities. "LD at a Glance." May 2003. From www.ncld.org/LDInfoZone/InfoZone_FactSheet_LD.cfm

8. National Center for Learning Disabilities. "Adult Learning Disabilities: A Learning Disability Isn't Something You Outgrow. It's Something You Learn to Master" (pamphlet). New York: National Center for Learning Disabilities.

9. "LD Advocates Guide" (no date). National Center for Learning Disabilities. From www.ncld.org/index.php?option=content&task=view&id=291

10. Office of Disability Employment Policy, Department of Labor, "The Why, When, What, and How of Disclosure in a Postsecondary Academic Setting." 2007, United States Department of Labor. From http://www.dol.gov/odep/pubs/fact/wwwh.htm

CHAPTER 4

1. Ruggiero, Vincent. *Beyond Feelings: A Guide to Critical Thinking,* 9th ed. New York: McGraw-Hill, 2012, p. 19.

2. Paul, Richard. "The Role of Questions in Thinking, Teaching, and Learning." 1995. Accessed April 2004 from http://www.criticalthinking.org/resources/articles/the-role-of-questions.shtml

3. "The Best Innovations Are Those That Come from Smart Questions." *Wall Street Journal,* April 12, 2004, p. B1.

4. Begley, Sharon. "Critical Thinking: Part Skill, Part Mindset and Totally Up to You." *Wall Street Journal,* October 20, 2006, p. B1.

5. Dobbs, David. "Beautiful Brains." *National Geographic,* October 2011. From http://ngm.nationalgeographic.com/print/2011/10/teenage-brains/dobbs-text

6. Ibid.

7. Ibid.

8. Thomas, Matt. "What Is Higher-Order Thinking and Critical/Creative/Constructive Thinking?" (no date). Center for Studies in Higher-Order Literacy. From http://a-s.clayton.edu/tparks/What%20is%20Higher%20Order%20Thinking.doc

9. Cave, Charles. "Definitions of Creativity." August 1999. From http://members.optusnet.com.au/~charles57/Creative/Basics/definitions.htm

10. Gibson, Jennifer. "The Art of Medicine." *Brain Blogger,* October 31, 2010. From http://brainblogger.com/2010/10/31/the-art-of-medicine

11. Adapted from Tardif, T. Z., and R. J. Sternberg. "What Do We Know About Creativity?" *The Nature of Creativity,* R. J. Sternberg, ed. London: Cambridge University Press, 1988.

12. Sternberg, p. 212.

13. Cain, Susan. "The Rise of the New Groupthink." *New York Times,* January 13, 2012. From http://www.nytimes.com/2012/01/15/opinion/sunday/the-rise-of-the-new-groupthink.html?pagewanted=1&_r=1&smid=fb-nytimes

14. Ibid.

15. Michalko, Michael. "Twelve Things You Were Not Taught in School About Creative Thinking." *Psychology Today,* December 2, 2011. From http://www.psychologytoday.com/blog/creative-thinkering/201112/twelve-things-you-were-not-taught-in-school-about-creative-thinking

16. Ibid.

17. Ibid.

18. Lehrer, Jonah. "Groupthink." *The New Yorker,* January 30, 2012. From http://www.newyorker.com/reporting/2012/01/30/120130fa_fact_lehrer?currentPage=3

19. Ibid.

20. Sarah Lyman Kravits, 2012.

21. Lehrer, Jonah. *Imagine: How Creativity Works.* New York: Houghton Mifflin Harcourt, 2012, pp. 163–164.

22. Coon, Dennis. *Introduction to Psychology: Exploration and Application,* 6th ed. St. Paul: West, 1992, p. 295.

23. Cain, "The Rise of the New Groupthink."

24. Sternberg, p. 236.

25. Hayes, J. R. *Cognitive Psychology: Thinking and Creating.* Homewood, IL: Dorsey, 1978.

26. Sternberg, Robert J., and Elena L. Grigorenko. "Practical Intelligence and the Principal." Yale University: Publication Series No. 2, 2001, p. 5.

27. Rosenthal, Normal. "10 Ways to Enhance Your Emotional Intelligence." *Psychology Today,* January 5, 2012. From http://www.psychologytoday.com/blog/your-mind-your-body/201201/10-ways-enhance-your-emotional-intelligence

28. Sternberg, pp. 251–269.

29. Schwartz, Barry. TED talk. From http://www.ted.com/talks/barry_schwartz_on_our_loss_of_wisdom.html

30. Sternberg, p. 241.

31. Ibid., p. 128.

CHAPTER 5

1. Robinson, Francis P. *Effective Behavior.* New York: Harper & Row, 1941.

2. Faragher, John Mack, Mari Jo Buhle, Daniel Czitrom, and Susan H. Armitage. *Out of Many: A History of the American People,* 5th ed. Upper Saddle River, NJ: Prentice Hall, 2005, p. xxxvii.

3. Bloom, Benjamin S. *Taxonomy of Educational Objectives, Handbook I: The Cognitive Domain.* New York: McKay, 1956.

4. "10 Points" from The National Council for the Social Studies. Used by permission of The National Council for the Social Studies.

5. Kessler, Sarah. "38% of College Students Can't Go 10 Minutes Without Tech." Mashable.com, May 31, 2011. From http://mashable.com/2011/05/31/college-tech-device-stats

6. Bauerlein, Mark. "Online Literacy is a Lesser Kind." The Chronicle of Higher Education, September 19, 2008. From http://chronicle.com/article/Online-Literacy-Is-a-Lesser/28307

7. Ibid.

8. Hertz, Mary Beth. "The Right Technology May Be a Pencil." Edutopia.com, November 29, 2011. From http://www.edutopia.org/blog/technology-integration-classroom-mary-beth-hertz?utm_source=facebook&utm_medium=post&utm_content=blog&utm_campaign=techisapencil

9. Leibovich, Lori. "Choosing Quick Hits over the Card Catalog." *New York Times,* August 10, 2001, p. 1.

10. Robinson, Adam. *What Smart Students Know.* New York: Three Rivers Press, 1993, p. 82.

CHAPTER 6

1. Tugend, Alina. "Multitasking Can Make You Lose . . . Um . . . Focus," *The New York Times,* October 25, 2008.

2. System developed by Cornell professor Walter Pauk. See Pauk, Walter. *How to Study in College,* 10th ed. Boston: Houghton Mifflin, 2011, pp. 236–241.

3. Klein, Ezra. "Better Note-Taking Through Technology." *The Washington Post,* May 16, 2011. From http://www.washingtonpost.com/blogs/ezra-klein/post/better-note-taking-through-technology/2011/05/09/AFMs8z4G_blog.html

CHAPTER 7

1. Miller, Greg. "How Our Brains Make Memories." *Smithsonian Magazine,* May 2010. From http://www.smithsonianmag.com/science-nature/How-Our-Brains-Make-Memories.html?c=y&page=2

2. Mohs, Richard C. "How Human Memory Works." howstuffworks.com, 2012. From http://science.howstuffworks.com/environmental/life/human-biology/human-memory1.htm

3. University of California–Irvine. "Short-term Stress Can Affect Learning And Memory." *ScienceDaily,* March 13, 2008. From http://www.sciencedaily.com/releases/2008/03/080311182434.htm

4. Ebbinghaus, Herman. *Memory: A Contribution to Experimental Psychology,* trans. H. A. Ruger and C. E. Bussenius. New York: Teachers College, Columbia University, 1885.

5. Miller.

6. Bulletpoints from Petress, Kenneth C. "The Benefits of Group Study," *Education,* vol. 124. 2004.

From http://www.questia.com/googleScholar.
qst;jsessionid=L4TDXZJvQmb4whQFL7v1mjGfB
gp4YGzjJyg0mL3g1SJKyjvXK4hN!-747430471!
743789914?docId=5006987606

7. Academic Skills Center. "How to Avoid Cramming
for Tests." Dartmouth College, 2001. From http://
www.dartmouth.edu/~acskills/handouts.html

8. "Study Shows How Sleep Improves Memory." *Science
Daily,* June 29, 2005. From http://www.ciencedaily
.com/releases/2005/06/050629070337.htm

9. Reynolds, Gretchen. "How Exercise Fuels the
Brain." *New York Times,* February 12, 2012.
From http://well.blogs.nytimes.com/2012/02/22/
how-exercise-fuels-the-brain

10. Robinson, *What Smart Students Know,* p. 118.

11. These strategies from Student Counseling Service,
Division of Student Affairs. "Self-Help: Math
Study Skills." Texas A & M University, 2012.
Adapted from Resnick, William C., and David H.
Heller. *On Your Own in College.* From http://scs
.tamu.edu/?q=node/92

CHAPTER 8

1. "The Role of Sleep in Memory." Mempowered,
January, 2012. From http://www.memory-key
.com/improving/lifestyle/activity/sleep

2. Gose, Ben. "Notes from Academe: Living It Up on
the Dead Days." *The Chronicle of Higher
Education,* June 78, 2002. From http://chronicle
.com/article/Living-It-Up-on-the-Dead-Days/8983

3. Speidel, Barbara J. "Overcoming Test Anxiety."
Academic Success Center of Southwestern College.
From http://www.swccd.edu/~asc/lrnglinks/test_
anxiety.html

4. "Anxiety Management." Michigan Technological
University. From http://www.counseling.mtu.edu/
anxiety_management.html

5. Gwynne, Peter. "The Write Way to Reduce Test
Anxiety." Inside Science News Service, January 14,
2011. From http://www.usnews.com/science/articles/
2011/01/14/the-write-way-to-reduce-test-anxiety

6. From Nolting, Paul D. *Math Study Skills Workbook,
Your Guide to Reducing Test Anxiety and Improv-
ing Study Strategies.* Boston, MA: Houghton Mifflin
Company, 2000. Cited in "Test Anxiety." West
Virginia University at Parkersburg. From http://www
.wvup.edu/Academics/more_test_anxiety_tips.htm

7. Duffy, Jill. "How Students Use Technology to
Cheat and How Their Teachers Catch Them."
PCMag.com, March 25, 2011. From http://www
.pcmag.com/slideshow/story/262232/how-
students-use-technology-to-cheat

8. Vogeler, Ingolf. "How to Prepare for an Essay
Exam." Center for Teaching Excellence at the
University of Wisconsin at Eau Claire, 2008.
From http://www.uwec.edu/geography/ivogeler/
essay.htm

CHAPTER 9

1. "For 7 Million, One Census Race Category
Wasn't Enough." *New York Times,* March 13,
2001, pp. A1, A14.

2. "Conceptual Frameworks/Models, Guiding Values
and Principles." National Center for Cultural
Competence, 2002. From http://gucchd
.georgetown.edu/nccc/framework.html

3. Information in the sections on the five stages of
building competency is based on King, Mark A.,
Anthony Sims, and David Osher, "How Is Cultural
Competence Integrated in Education?" Cultural
Competence. From www.air.org/cecp/cultural/
Q_integrated.htm#def

4. King, Martin Luther, Jr., from his sermon "A
Tough Mind and a Tender Heart." *Strength in
Love.* Philadelphia: Fortress Press, 1986, p. 14.

5. This section and chapter opener story from
Highline College Honors Scholar Program Success
Stories (adapted with permission from original
story, online at http://flightline.highline.edu/
honors/success/gaile.htm).

CHAPTER 10

1. Kolata, Gina. "A Surprising Secret to a Long Life:
Stay In School." *New York Times,* January 3,
2007, pp. A1 and A16.

2. Information based in this section based on
materials from Dr. Marlene Schwartz of the
Rudd Center for Food Policy and Obesity at
Yale University.

3. Strauss, Valerie. "'Freshman 15' Weight Gain a
Myth, Study Says." *The Washington Post,*
November 1, 2011. From http://www
.washingtonpost.com/blogs/answer-sheet/post/
freshman-15-weight-gain-a-myth-study-says/
2011/11/01/gIQATa4RdM_blog.html?
wpisrc=nl_cuzheads

4. Fontenot, Beth. "College Students Get a Failing
Grade on Their Eating Habits." *The Atlantic,*
September 24, 2011. From http://www.theatlantic
.com/health/archive/2011/09/college-students-get-
a-failing-grade-on-their-eating-habits/245296

5. Centers for Disease Control. "Prevalence of Overweight, Obesity, and Extreme Obesity Among
Adults: United States, Trends 1960–1962 Through

2007–2008." June 6, 2011. From http://www.cdc.gov/nchs/data/hestat/obesity_adult_07_08/obesity_adult_07_08.htm

6. Rudd Center for Food Policy and Obesity. "Employment." 2005. From http://www.yaleruddcenter.org/what_we_do.aspx?id=203

7. Mayo Clinic. "Aerobic Exercise: Top 10 Reasons to Get Physical." Mayoclinic.com, 2012. From http://www.mayoclinic.com/health/aerobic-exercise/EP00002/NSECTIONGROUP=2

8. Centers for Disease Control and Prevention. "How Much Physical Activity Do Adults Need?" CDC website, March 30, 2011. From http://www.cdc.gov/physicalactivity/everyone/guidelines/adults.html

9. Evans, Mike. "23½ hours." *YouTube,* December 2, 2011. From http://www.youtube.com/watch?v=aUaInS6HIGo

10. CBS News. "Help for Sleep-Deprived Students." April 19, 2004. From www.cbsnews.com/stories/2004/04/19/health/main612476.shtml

11. "College Students Sleep Habits Harmful to Health, Study Finds." *The Daily Orange—Feature Issue,* September 25, 2002. From http://www.dailyorange.com/2.8656/college-students-sleep-habits-harmful-to-health-study-finds-1.1251402#.TsSALHLNRww

12. Benson, Herbert, and Eileen M. Stuart, et al. *The Wellness Book.* New York: Simon & Schuster, 1992, p. 292; Jacobs, Gregg. "Life Style Practices That Can Improve Sleep (Parts 1 and 2)." *Talk About Sleep,* 2004. From http://www.talkaboutsleep.com/sleep-disorders/archives/insomnia_drjacobs_lifestyle_part1.htm and http://www.talkaboutsleep.com/sleep-disorders/archives/insomnia_drjacobs_lifestyle_practices_part2.htm

13. Briddon, Mike. "Struggling with Sadness: Depression among College Students Is on the Rise." April 22, 2008. From http://www.stressedoutnurses.com/2008/04/struggling-with-sadness-depression-among-college-students-is-on-the-rise

14. SAVE (Suicide Awareness Voices of Education). "Symptoms of Major Depression." 2010. From http://www.save.org/index.cfm?fuseaction=home.viewPage&page_id=A806E240-95E6-44BB-C2D6C47399E9EFDB)

15. National Eating Disorders Association. "Learning Basic Terms and Information on a Variety of Eating Disorder Topics." 2010. From http://www.nationaleatingdisorders.org/information-resources/general-information.php#facts-statistics

16. Knox, Richard. "The Teen Brain: It's Just Not Grown Up Yet." NPR.org, March 1, 2010. From http://www.npr.org/templates/story/story.php?storyId=124119468

17. Foster, Linda. "Teen Alcoholism and Drug Addiction." EverydayHealth.com, April 20, 2009. From http://www.everydayhealth.com/addiction/addiction-in-adolescence.aspx

18. "Alcohol Linked to 75,000 U.S. Deaths a Year." MSNBC, June 25, 2005. From http://www.msnbc.msn.com/id/6089353

19. Centers for Disease Control and Prevention. "Alcohol and Public Health: Frequently Asked Questions—How Does Alcohol Affect a Person?" October 28, 2011. From http://www.cdc.gov/alcohol/faqs.htm#howAlcoholAffect

20. Substance Abuse and Mental Health Services Administration. *Results from the 2010 National Survey on Drug Use and Health: Summary of National Findings.* NSDUH Series H-41, HHS Publication No. (SMA) 11-4658. Rockville, MD: Substance Abuse and Mental Health Services Administration, 2011. From http://www.samhsa.gov/data/NSDUH/2k10NSDUH/2k10Results.htm#Fig3-3

21. Seguine, Joel. "Students Report Negative Consequences of Binge Drinking in New Survey." The University Record, University of Michigan, October 25, 1999. From http://www.umich.edu/~urecord/9900/Oct25_99/7.htm

22. Martin, Terry. "Understanding Nicotine Addiction." About.com, September 19, 2011. From http://quitsmoking.about.com/od/nicotine/a/nicotineeffects.htm

23. Encyclopedia of Drugs and Addictive Substances. "Nicotine – What Kind of a Drug is it?" Gale Cengage, 2006. From http://www.enotes.com/drugs-substances-encyclopedia/nicotine

24. American Cancer Society. "Secondhand Smoke." October 1, 2009. From http://www.cancer.org/docroot/PED/content/PED_10_2X_Secondhand_Smoke-Clean_Indoor_Air.asp

25. Smith, Hilary. "Excerpts from: The High Cost of Smoking." Ash.org, November 11, 2005. From http://ash.org/no-smoking/nov05/11-21-05-2.html

26. National Cancer Institute at the National Institutes of Health. "Cigarette Smoking: Health Risks and How to Quit." From http://www.cancer.gov/cancertopics/pdq/prevention/control-of-tobacco-use/Patient.

27. Substance Abuse and Mental Health Services Administration. From http://www.samhsa.gov/data/NSDUH/2k10NSDUH/2k10Results.htm#2.9

28. Rape Abuse and Incest National Network. "Statistics." From http://www.rainn.org/statistics

29. Rape, Abuse, and Incest National Network. "Campus Safety." From http://www.rainn.org/public-policy/campus-safety

30. "The Sexual Assault Continuum." Sexual Assault Victim Advocate (SAVA) Center: Fort Collins, CO, 2011

CHAPTER 11

1. Adapted from "Hope in a Box." *The Oprah Winfrey Show,* October 1, 2009. From http://www.oprah.com/world/Tererai-Trents-Inspiring-Education

2. Hanson, Jim. "Your Money Personality: It's All In Your Head." University Credit Union, December 25, 2006. From http://hffo.cuna.org/012433/article/1440/html

3. Ibid.

4. Whitehouse, Mark. "Number of the Week: Class of 2011, Most Indebted Ever." *Wall Street Journal,* May 7, 2011. From http://blogs.wsj.com/economics/2011/05/07/number-of-the-week-class-of-2011-most-indebted-ever

5. Ibid.

6. "Attitudes and Characteristics of Freshmen at 4-Year Colleges, Fall 2007." Chronicle of Higher Education.

7. "Fast Facts." National Center for Education Statistics, 2009. From http://nces.ed.gov/FastFacts/display.asp?id=31

8. Supiano, Beckie. "Many Community College Students Miss Out on Aid—Because They Don't Apply." *The Chronicle of Higher Education,* October 7, 2008. Fromhttp://chronicle.com/daily/2008/10/4905n.htm

9. College Board Advocacy and Policy Center. *Trends in Student Aid 2011.* New York: The College Board, 2011, p. 3.

10. Ibid.

11. Tomsho, Robert. "The BestWays to Get Loans for College Now." *The Wall Street Journal,* August 13, 2008, p. D1.

12. Supiano.

13. College Board Advocacy and Policy Center, p. 4.

14. Ryman, Anne. "Defaults on Student Loans Rising." *The Arizona Republic,* March 7, 2010. From http://www.azcentral.com/12news/news/articles/2010/03/07/20100307student-loan-defaults-CP.html

15. Woolsey, Ben, and Matt Schulz. "Credit Card Statistics, Industry Facts, Debt Statistics." CreditCards.com, January 15, 2010. From http://www.creditcards.com/credit-card-news/credit-card-industry-facts-personal-debt-statistics-1276.php#youngadults

16. "Sallie Mae's National Study of Usage Rates and Trends of Undergraduate Student Credit Card Use." April 2009. From https://www1.salliemae.com/about/news_info/newsreleases/041309.htm

17. Most items in bullet list based on Bowler, Michael. "Watch Out for Credit Card Traps." The Lucrative Investor, 2009. From http://www.thelucrativeinvestor.com/watch-credit-card-traps, and Arnold, Chris. "Credit Card Companies Abuse the Unwitting." NPR, November 6, 2007. From http://www.npr.org/templates/story/story.php?storyId=16035323

18. Arthur, Dani. "15 Must-Know Tips for Protecting Your Identity." Bankrate.com, August 5, 2004. From http://www.bankrate.com/brm/news/cc/20020612a.asp

19. Curry, Pat. "How Credit Scores Work, How a Score is Calculated." November 8, 2006. From http://www.bankrate.com/brm/news/credit-scoring/20031104a1.asp

20. The University of Arizona. "Young Adults Financial Capability: APLUS Arizona Pathways to Life Success for University Students Wave 2." September 2011, p. 29. From http://aplus.arizona.edu/Wave-2-Report.pdf

21. Pythagoras Solar, http://www.pythagoras-solar.com

CHAPTER 12

1. Self-Directed Search, http://www.self-directed-search.com

2. Occupational Outlook Quarterly. "High-Paying Occupations with Many Job Openings, Projected 2004–14." Bureau of Labor Statistics, Spring 2006. From http://www.bls.gov/opub/ooq/2006/spring/oochart.pdf

3. May, Kevin. "Humanities and Liberal Arts Majors Are Going into Business." *The BYU Daily Universe,* December 14, 2011. From http://universe.byu.edu/index.php/2011/12/14/humanities-and-liberal-arts-majors-are-going-into-business

4. National Service Learning Clearinghouse. "Service Learning Is . . ." May 2004. From http://www.servicelearning.org/article/archive/35

5. U.S. Department of Labor, Bureau of Labor Statistics. "Number of Jobs Held, Labor Market Activity, and Earnings Growth Among the Youngest Baby Boomers: Results from a

Longitudinal Survey." News release, September 10, 2010. From http://www.bls.gov/news.release/pdf/nlsoy.pdf

6. Dickler, Jessica. CNN Money, June 10, 2009. Accessed on October 1, 2011, from http://money.cnn.com/2009/06/09/news/economy/hidden_jobs

7. Adams, Susan. "Get a Job Using the Hidden Job Market." *Forbes*, July 5, 2011. Accessed on October 1, 2011, from http://www.forbes.com/sites/susanadams/2011/07/05/get-a-job-using-the-hidden-job-market

8. Job Interview and Career Guide. "Resume: Keywords for Resumes—Keywords List." December 8, 2009. From http://www.job-interview-site.com/resume-keywords-for-resumes-keywords-list.html

9. List and descriptions based Sternberg, pp. 251–269.

10. Quoted in Weeks, Linton. "The No-Book Report: Skim It and Weep." *The Washington Post*, May 14, 2001, p. C8.

APPENDIX

1. Analysis based on Troyka, Lynn Quitman. *Simon & Schuster Handbook for Writers.* Upper Saddle River, NJ: Prentice Hall, 1996, pp. 22–23.

INDEX

identifying, 83
supporting ideas with, 84
Examples, in argument, 83–84
Executive function, **81**
Exercise, 172, 250–252
Expenses
adjusting, 278–279
in budgeting process, 277–278
Experian, 291
Explanatory style, 13–15
Exploration, in creativity, 89
External distractions, 142

Facebook, 266, 308
Facts
opinions versus, 84
statement of, 84
in taking tests, 202
Faculty. *See* Instructors
Failure, learned optimism and, 13–15, 216
Fairness, 10
Family obligations, 110, 169, 170
Fastweb.com, 286
Fatigue, 42
Feelings. *See* Emotions
FICO (Fair Isaac Company) scores, 290–291
Fill-in-the-blank questions, 209
Final exams, 197
Financial aid, 283–287
applying for, 286–287
award letters, 286
looking for, 285–286
types, 283, 284–286
Financial literacy, 273–297
benefits of college education, 4, 5
budgeting, 276–279
credit and debit cards, 287–292
financial aid, 283–287
meaning of money, 274–276
money management skills in, 274–276
multiple intelligences, 279, 280
perceiving and using money, 275
planning for the future, 293–295
savings, 276, 293–295
time management, 276
working at school, 282–283, 305
Flash cards, 175
Flexibility, 41, 42, 43
Flowcharts, 154–155
Focus, 44–46, 110, 142, 143
Formal outlines, 150
Formulas
defined, **123**
in reading process, 123
F-pattern reading, 126
Framework for 21st Century Learning, 5, 6
Free Application for Federal Student Aid (FAFSA), 285–286
Friedman, Thomas, 4
Front matter, surveying, 114
Fry, Ron, 195n
futurestep.com, 310

GaleGroup, 129
Gamma hydroxyl butyrate, 260
Gardner, Howard, 55, 56–60
General education requirements, **123**
Generalized anxiety disorder (GAD), 255
Gibson, Jennifer, 89
Giver personality dimension, 61, 63, 64, 67, 229, 303
Glue, 260
Goal management, 30–35
in building schedules, 37–39
in career success, 4–6
goals, defined, **30**
linking tasks to goals, 39
long-term, 31–32, 39
personal mission, 30–31
risk-taking for, 2–3
short-term, 32
SMART goals, 32–35, 194–195
for study, 170
study group, 169
study material, 170–171
successful intelligence and, 6–9
teamwork, 234
test preparation, 194–195
thinking skills in, 7–9
values in, 28–30
working toward goals, 33–35
Golden Personality Assessment, 63
Google, 126, 129
GoogleDocs, 68, 155
Government aid, 285–286
Grants, 283, 284, 285
Griffin, Ricky W., 119n
Growth mindset, 9–15, 19
academic integrity and, 10–13
assessments in, 55
explanatory style, 13–15
lifelong learning, 317–319
optimism in, 13–15, 319–320
self-esteem and, 10
Guided notes, 150
Gurevich, M., 256n

Hallucinogenic mushrooms, 260
Hammil, Greg, 230n
Harris, Robert, 132, 133n
Hashish, 260
Hate crimes, 226, 228
Health. *See* Mental and emotional health; Physical health; Wellness
Hearing loss, 144
Hearing stage of listening, 140, 141
Help
asking for, 43, 64–65, 110, 144, 193
offering, 227–228
Henson, Jim, 90–91
Heroin, 260
Hertz, Mary Beth, 126
Hidden job market, 308–309
Highlighting, 118–121, 126
Hippocrates, 59
Hits, 127, 129

HIV/AIDS, 263–266
Holland, John, 301
Holland Theory, 301
Honesty, 10, 234
HPV (*human papillomavirus*), 266
Humanities, reading strategies for, 124
Hunter, William, 80–81

I-can-do-it attitude, 143
Ideas. *See also* Creative thinking skills
going against established, 91
recording, 90
Identity theft, 289–290
Imagination, 180
"I" messages, 238
Immunizations, 266
Impulse control, 257, 314
Income. *See also* Budgeting; Financial aid
adjusting, 278–279
in budgeting process, 277–278
increasing, 279–287
as reward of college, 4, 5
Independence, 315
Independent learning, 3
Individualized education program (IEP), 72
Individual Retirement Accounts (IRAs), 294, 295
INFOMINE, 129
Informal outlines, 150, 151
Information
determining useful, 86
using in study process, 176
Informational interviews, 308–309
Information gathering, 82–83, 193
Information literacy, 126–130
critical response to reading, 130–133
information gathering in test preparation, 193
library research, 110, 126–127
mapping out possibilities, 126–127
online research, 126–130, 309–310
Information processing model of memory, 164–166
InfoTrac, 129
Instructors
academic integrity and, 11, 12
asking for help, 43, 64–65, 110, 144, 193
connections with, 4
teaching styles, 63–65, 145–148, 150
test taking and, 193, 215
Integrity. *See* Academic integrity
Intelligences. *See also* Emotional intelligence (EI); Multiple intelligences (MI); Successful intelligence
defined, **56**
intelligence quotient (IQ), 6–7
Intention, of study, 171–172
Interests, 304
Intergenerational awareness, 230–232, 317
Internal distractions, 110, 142
International Center for Academic Integrity (ICAI), 10
Internet searches, 127–130, 309–310
Internships, 68–71, **305**
Interpersonal intelligence, 57, 60, 66, 69, 113, 147, 177, 207, 231, 248, 280, 302
Interpreting stage of listening, 141
Interruptions, 234

Photo credits, continued from p. ii: p. 101: Jacob Rudolph; p. 109: LifeBound, LLC; p. 114: Gary Montrose; p. 114: Intellistudies/Shutterstock; p. 115: Gary Montrose; p. 121: Rachel Youdelman/Pearson Education, Inc.; p. 124: LifeBound, LLC; p. 126: Sarah Lyman Kravits; p. 132: Aneela Gonzales; p. 138: Karl Weatherly/Digital Vision/Getty Images; p. 139: Chandra McQueen; p. 142: Gary Montrose; p. 142: LifeBound, LLC; p. 146: WavebreakmediaMicro/Fotolia; p. 152: Tomohito Kondo; p. 154: Bloomua/Fotolia; p. 154: Bloomua/Fotolia; p. 158: Konstantin Chagin/Shutterstock; p. 159: Chandra McQueen; p. 162: Cindy Estrada; p. 163: Cindy Estrada; p. 168: Blend Images/Shutterstock; p. 173: Hemera Technologies/Thinkstock; p. 176: LifeBound, LLC; p. 178: Tanyok/Shutterstock; p. 183: BuFka/Fotolia; p. 187: Cindy Estrada; p. 190: Jay Dobyns; p. 191: Jay Dobyns; p. 193: Pressmaster/Fotolia; p. 197: Alexis Zendejas; p. 198: Sarah Lyman Kravits; p. 208: Marekuliasz/Shutterstock; p. 210: Kevin Ix; p. 216: Jay Dobyns; p. 220: Gaile Edrozo; p. 221: Gaile Edrozo; p. 223: LifeBound, LLC; p. 225: JustinRossWard/Shutterstock; p. 227: Mangostock/Fotolia; p. 228: Sarah Lyman Kravits; p. 230: Riccardo Piccinini/Fotolia; p. 235: Endostock/Fotolia; p. 239: Jad El-Adaimi; p. 241: Gaile Edrozo; p. 244: Addington and Tieder; p. 245: Addington and Tieder; p. 249: Choosemyplate.gov; p. 252: Konstantin Sutyagin/Fotolia; p. 253: LifeBound, LLC; p. 263: iQoncept/Fotolia; p. 266: Joe Martin; p. 267: Andrew Willard; p. 267: Joe Martin; p. 267: OneStudent; p. 268: Addington and Tieder; p. 272: Heifer International; p. 273: Heifer International; p. 277: Fotolia; p. 283: Paul Vasarhelyi/Shutterstock; p. 288: Joe Martin; p. 293: Shutterstock; p. 294: Charlotte Buckley; p. 295: Heifer International; p. 298: Stephen Oh; p. 299: Stephen Oh; p. 305: LifeBound, LLC; p. 308: Bart Ah You/Modesto Bee/ZUMA Press/Alamy; p. 312: Sarah Lyman Kravits; p. 317: Gabriel Blaj/Fotolia; p. 319: Andrew Hillman; p. 320: Leungchopan/Shutterstock; p. 320: Stephen Oh; p. 325: Sarah Lyman Kravits.